CO-ANZ-739

■ AUXINS AND PLANT GROWTH

AUXINS

AND PLANT GROWTH

A. Carl Leopold

UNIVERSITY OF CALIFORNIA PRESS
BERKELEY AND LOS ANGELES 1960

UNIVERSITY OF CALIFORNIA PRESS
BERKELEY AND LOS ANGELES
CAMBRIDGE UNIVERSITY PRESS, LONDON, ENGLAND

SECOND PRINTING, 1960
LIBRARY OF CONGRESS CATALOG CARD NO. 55-5386
PRINTED IN THE UNITED STATES OF AMERICA

Dedicated to Kenneth V. Thimann

PREFACE

It is my strong conviction that the technology or the applied science in a field of knowledge can make efficient progress only when pursued with sound understanding of the fundamental science upon which that technology is based. Progress in technology without a foundation of fundamental science can take only two forms, I believe. First, minor improvements of applications or treatments which are already essentially known can be made by technology alone; and second, occasional (though rare) accidental discoveries of new applications or treatments may be made. Practically every *major* advance in agricultural technology in the past half century has stemmed from fundamental scientific information.

In view of this strong conviction, it is with considerable alarm that I have become more and more aware that a large proportion of research work, dealing with auxins and growth regulators, is being done without cognizance of what auxins do in plants, how they are formed or destroyed there, or even how one tests for them. This book is written in the hope of providing the agricultural research worker with a brief review of the physiological basis, so far as it is known, upon which the applied technologies rest.

Although several books are currently available in the area of auxin physiology it is my feeling that none of them provide the research man with as complete a general integration of the field as is needed. Especially lacking has been an organized description of the various techniques for obtaining, measuring and identifying auxins, as well as an integration of the fundamental and technological aspects of auxin physiology.

It is my intention to present the general status of knowledge of auxins in plant physiology, and to integrate this fundamental information with each of the applied phases of auxin technology. I have written for the graduate student and the professional research man.

This book does not attempt to review in detail the development of knowledge of auxin physiology, for that is a function of the annual and quarterly reviews. On the other hand, it is not intended that the book should become a manual for the practical applications of auxins.

It is hoped that the book will help to reverse the present tendency to design and carry out research programs involving auxin applications without taking advantage of the great progress that has been made in fundamental physiology. By utilizing the footholds which fundamental discoveries have established, agricultural technology will not be restricted to small consolidations of already known phenomena. Nor will it be restricted only to occasional and accidental discoveries of really new applications. Instead technology may advance in a rapid and orderly manner toward greater and greater efficiency in agriculture at a time, now, when greater agricultural productivity is vital to the peaceful progress of our overpopulated world.

Grateful acknowledgment is made to Drs. J. van Overbeek and F. Skoog for reading all of the manuscript critically, as well as to Drs. J. Bonner, J. C. Crane, E. L. Rice, L. M. Rohrbaugh and G. F. Warren and Professors C. L. Burkholder and R. Klackle for assistance and suggestions concerning individual chapters. Special thanks are due to Dr. S. P. Sen for much of the preparative work on the section dealing with paper chromatography, to Mrs. Frances Scott Guernsey for her abundant and enthusiastic help with the first draft, to Dr. N. K. Ellis for encouragement, and to my wife, Keena, for being so patient.

The literature review for this book was concluded in June, 1954.

A. Carl Leopold

Department of Horticulture
Purdue University
Lafayette, Indiana
July 14, 1954

CONTENTS

PART ONE
FUNDAMENTALS OF AUXIN ACTION

PART ONE

FUNDAMENTALS OF AUXIN ACTION

CHAPTER I

Development of Knowledge of Auxins

The development of the knowledge of auxins, as in the case of nearly all major scientific advances, originated in experimental inquiries by scientists seeking answers to fundamental questions. If any one worker could be identified as first in the field, perhaps it would be Charles Darwin, who in 1881 published his book *The Power of Movement in Plants.* His investigations of fundamental questions about plant tropisms opened a minute gate in the dike of the unknown which ultimately led to the flood of information concerning not only tropisms, but the whole general field of plant growth and the growth hormone as well. In the seventy years following this modest beginning, the role of the growth hormone in plants has been clarified to an almost startling degree. The revealed capacity of many chemical compounds to exploit the same mechanisms in plants has led to a situation nearly approaching an agricultural revolution. Auxins and growth regulators promise to have an impact on agriculture as great as the advent of the windmill or perhaps even of the mechanical harvester. At the same time the impact on the science of plant physiology is as great as that of any other single development since the turn of the century.

DEFINITIONS

There has been a considerable confusion among physiologists and agriculturists concerning the terminology of auxins and growth hormones. Before entering into an extensive discussion of these compounds, it will be well to define our terms.

A *hormone* has been accepted for many years as being "a substance which, produced in any one part of an organism, is transferred to another part and there influences a specific physiological process" (Went and Thimann, 1937, p. 3). It may be advisable to emphasize that hormones are *produced in the organism,* and have the property of serving as chemical messengers, i.e., they are *transported* from a site of formation to a site of action. In contrast to some compounds which act as substrates for general physiological processes, hormones influence "a specific physiological process," and in each case minute amounts produce a large physiological effect. It is evident that, by this definition, the word hormone cannot apply to chemicals produced exclusively in a laboratory, nor to such indigenous compounds as sugars, amino acids or other substrates for growth. Although these latter types of compounds may be transported, none of them are specific in their control of physiological process, as far as is known. The status of vitamins in this nomenclature is not clear. They are considered to be phytohormones by some (Bonner and Bonner, 1948) in cases where they are transported in the plant.

A *phytohormone,* or plant hormone, by simple projection of the preceding definition, is a hormone produced specifically in plants. Within this category lie the growth hormone, the still-theoretical flowering hormone, and possibly some vitamins. A few other phytohormones have been proposed from time to time, but these first two are the only ones generally recognized at present. Thimann (1948) has defined a phytohormone as "an organic substance produced naturally in higher plants, controlling growth or other physiological function at a site remote from its place of production, and active in minute amounts."

The *growth hormone* is the phytohormone which is involved in growth. It is normally essential to growth by cellular enlargement, both in length and in width, and is essential to growth of organs—buds, stems, roots, fruits, and so on.

The term *auxin* was originally suggested to refer to substances which were capable of promoting growth in the manner of the growth hormone (Kögl & Haagen-Smit, 1931). The search for the actual growth hormone in plants led to the isolation of the first pure active compound, not as the indigenous active hormone, but instead as an ingredient of such miscellaneous biological materials as urine, corn oil, and malt extract. The first such compound was named auxin *a,* the second auxin *b.* In keeping with the original intent of the term, auxin will be used to refer to "an organic substance which promotes growth (i.e. irreversible increase in volume) along the longitudinal axis when applied in low concentrations to shoots of plants freed as far as practicable from their own inherent growth-promoting substances" (Thimann, 1948). This growth promotion may be conveniently measured by any of the standard auxin assay methods described in chapter II. The growth hormone itself is an auxin, and so are any other chemical compounds which can bring about the same growth effect.

The term *growth regulator* refers to organic compounds other than nutrients, small amounts of which are capable of modifying growth. Included in this category are substances which either stimulate, inhibit, or otherwise alter growth. It is presumed that growth regulators act upon growth by altering the net effect of the growth hormone, though this is speculative in many cases. Included as growth regulators are such substances as auxins, anti-auxins, epinastic agents and other types of materials as discussed in chapter VII.

In the early literature, the term *heteroauxin* was used to refer to indoleacetic acid (Kögl *et al,* 1934). Since the time when this term was suggested, a great quantity of evidence has accumulated indicating that indoleacetic acid is indeed the commonest growth hormone, and hence to classify it as an "outsider" or heteroauxin seems entirely misleading. In accord with the suggestion by Thimann (1948), we will not use the term in the present discussion.

Unfortunately there has been a considerable usage of the term *hormone* in referring to synthetic auxins or other growth regulators. This has been done largely to strike an appeal to potential buyers of commercial products containing auxins. Such a misuse of terms is definitely confusing and has no place in scientific writing. The term hormone will be used in the present discussion to refer only to substances identical with those known to be indigenous to the plant, and known to act as hormones in the plant.

TROPISMS AND THE EARLY WORKERS

When Charles Darwin turned his brilliant mind to the study of plant movement and tropisms, the first glimmering of the existence of the growth hormone was revealed. Darwin's simple and logical experiments, using canary-grass seedlings, a light source and a razor blade, told him that the tip of the shoot is involved in the overall tropic response. Removal of the tip was followed by loss of sensitivity to light in the coleoptile below. He concluded (1881) that "when seedlings are freely exposed to a lateral light, some influence is transmitted from the upper to the lower part, causing the latter to bend."

Darwin's work aroused much interest and discussion, and led eventually to the work of Boysen-Jensen (1913) in Germany, who found that although severing the oat coleoptile tip removed phototropic sensitivity, simply replacing the tip restored the sensitivity again. He concluded that "the transmission of the irritation is of a material nature produced by concentration changes in the coleoptile tip."

Careful repetition of Boysen-Jensen's work in turn by Paál (1919), a physiologist at Budapest, amply confirmed the earlier work and added one simple but crucial point. Paál found that replacement of the severed tip on one side of the coleoptile stump would produce curvatures away from the treated side. This in fact was a *replacement* of the effect of lateral light by the asymmetrical distribution of some stimulus being produced by the tip. Paál then came to the conclusion that "the tip is the seat of a growth regulating center. In it a substance (or mixture) is formed and internally secreted, and this substance, equally distributed on all sides moves downwards through the living tissue. If the movement of this correlation carrier is disturbed on one side, a growth decrease on that side results, giving rise to curvature of the organ."

By his careful research, Paál had come essentially to the explanation of phototropism, but more important still, he had demonstrated the existence of a "substance" or "correlation carrier," which could control growth processes.

The wider concept of Paál's "correlation carrier" as a growth hormone intimately involved in all plant growth was left for two other minds to grasp almost simultaneously.

EMERGENCE OF THE HORMONE CONCEPT

At the time that Darwin was studying the nature of the phototropic stimulus, Sachs (1880) launched the first theory of substances (which we would now call hormones) controlling plant growth. He envisaged the existence of organ-forming substances moving in various polar patterns, and controlling form and development. Fitting (1909) actually extracted substances from orchid pollen which could cause swelling of the ovary in a manner suggestive of fruit-set. He suggested that these substances were hormones. After Paál's (1919) deduction that specific substances produced in the coleoptile tip were responsible for phototropism, Söding (1923) established that these same substances were capable of stimulating straight growth as well.

The demonstrations of a correlation carrier in oat tips attracted many new workers to the field. Among these were Cholodny (1927) in Russia and F. W. Went (1928) at Utrecht, who independently extended the correlation carrier theory to both phototropism and geotropism. Each of them then came to the conclusion that all tropisms were mediated by a growth hormone system which was essential to all plant growth. "Ohne Wuchsstoff, kein Wachstum"; without auxin there is no growth.

In carrying out his exploration of the role of auxin in growth, Went did two things which opened the field of growth hormones to really systematic study. He discovered that the hormone could be collected in an agar block by diffusion. This was not only the first separation of the hormone from a plant, but it also presented a technique for obtaining the hormone from a great variety of plant materials. Then, utilizing this technique, he worked out a quantitative test for auxin. Using the oat coleoptile, about which so much information had now been accumulated, he established a test so accurate and reproducible that it still stands today as the best auxin assay technique, the *Avena* test. Thus there arose simultaneously a general theory of the growth hormone, a technique for obtaining the hormone from plants, and a technique for its quantitative assay.

With such a sound basis on which to proceed, it is hardly surprising that a great deal of very productive work followed. In a short eight-year period, from 1928 to 1936, three auxins were isolated, characterized and identified, the quantitative relationships of auxin to tropisms of roots and shoots were established, and at the end of this period half of the major functions of auxin in growth and development as we now know them had been already discovered.

In series of remarkable inquiries, Kögl (1933) and co-workers in Holland found two materials, strongly active in the *Avena* test, which they named auxin *a* and auxin *b*. When isolated and characterized these materials were found to have the molecular formulas given below. Auxin *a* was first isolated from human urine, and auxin *b* from corn germ oil. These compounds are principally of historic interest, for they have never been positively isolated from growing plant tissue. For this reason they are not considered to be growth hormones by most physiologists today. There were two lines of evidence which led to the early assumption that auxins *a* and *b* were growth hormones. First, their molecular weights are similar to that of the diffusible auxin obtained from oat coleoptiles and some other plant materials (e.g. Went, 1928). Auxin *a* has a molecular weight of 328, which is quite close to Went's figure for diffused auxin from *Avena*, 372. Second, tests for stability show that both auxin *a* and auxin diffused from coleoptiles are stable to warm acid and break down in warm alkali. The poor reliability of these criteria in the positive identification of growth hormones is discussed in chapter III.

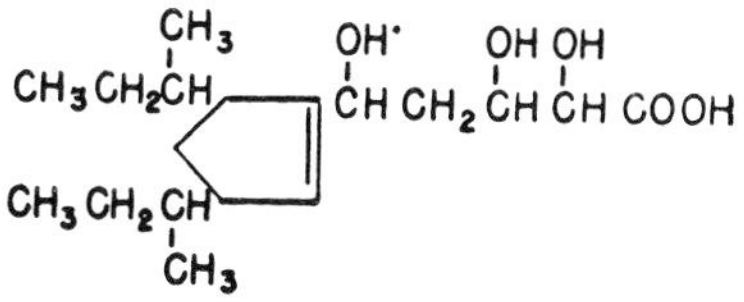

CH_3 | CH_3CH_2CH (ring) — $CH(OH)\,CH_2\,CH(OH)\,CH(OH)\,COOH$; CH_3CH_2CH | CH_3

auxin *a*

CH_3 | CH_3CH_2CH (ring) — $CH(OH)\,CH_2\,C(=O)\,CH_2\,COOH$; CH_3CH_2CH | CH_3

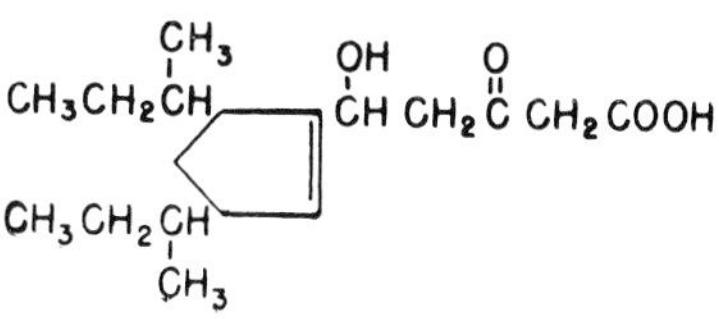

auxin *b*

After some time it was found that not only could auxins *a* and *b* not be found in plant materials, but also synthetic analogues of these acids have failed to show auxin activity in conventional growth tests (Kögl and de Bruin, 1950). Consequently it seems reasonable to discard these early substances from the list of known auxins.

Further research by Kögl's group (1934) identified another auxin compound. Some of the urine samples they worked with exhibited considerably greater auxin activity than could be accounted for as the supposed auxins *a* and *b*. They set about isolating this compound and found it to be identical with indole-3-acetic acid. The presence of this auxin was demonstrated in *Rhizopus* cultures by Thimann (1935), and he showed that it can be differentiated from auxins *a* and *b* by its instability in warm acid and stability in warm alkali. This is the opposite reaction to that of auxin *a*. Auxin *b* is unstable in either acid or alkali. In the subsequent twenty years indoleacetic acid has been conclusively demonstrated to be the principal growth hormone in seven different species of higher plants, and it is generally accepted now as being the commonest growth hormone in higher plants.

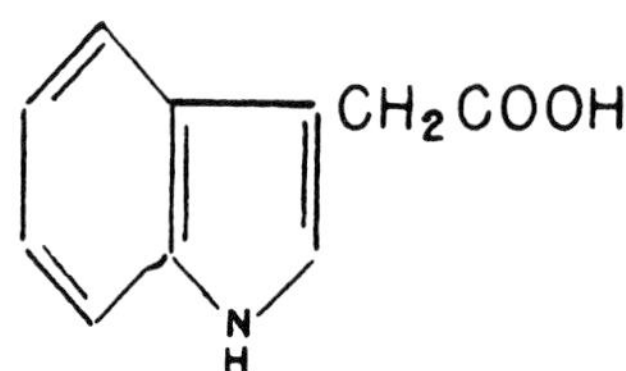

Indoleacetic acid

The quantitative relationship of the growth hormone to tropisms was essentially clarified soon after the *Avena* test was made available. Blaauw (1918) had shown that phototropic movement in *Avena* was owing to a retardation of growth on the lighted side. Went (1928) now associated this retardation with a decrease in the relative hormone content of the lighted as compared to the unlighted side. Dolk (1929) showed that geotropic movement in *Avena* was caused by a simple redistribution of the hormone present. His measurements of diffusible auxin from geotropically stimulated coleoptiles showed that 62.5 per cent was in the lower half. Geotropism in roots was found to be brought about by very similar changes in relative hormone contents of the upper and lower root halves (Hawker, 1932).

With the advent of Went's *Avena* test, it was quickly found that different concentrations of auxins may have opposite effects on growth. Where low concentrations of auxin promote growth, higher concentrations inhibit it. Knowledge of the inhibitory capacity soon led to the discovery by Thimann and Skoog (1933) that auxins which are formed at a plant apex inhibit the growth of lateral buds. This explanation of the phenomenon of apical dominance clarified one of the major correlative effects which had puzzled many earlier physiologists.

Further dramatic demonstrations of the physiological roles of auxins came from the experimental treatment of plants with chemical compounds which had been found to possess auxin activity. Went (1934) discovered that auxins can stimulate the formation of adventitious roots (another correlative effect clarified). The full realization of the developmental importance of auxin in morphological differentiation was brought forth much later by Skoog and Tsui (1948), who found that relative auxin levels in plant tissues play a crucial role in determining what sort of growth will take place. Thus auxin content in relation to other plant constituents determines whether growth will be simple cell proliferation, or bud formation, or root formation.

Another role of auxin was discovered by LaRue in 1936. He found that auxins applied to leaves could retard leaf abscission. Later workers have found that abscission of all plant organs (leaves, flowers, fruits, etc.) is correlated with low natural auxin content.

The discovery that auxin plays a key role in parthenocarpy and in fruit-set in general stems from the work of Gustafson (1936).

In a very short time indeed, after the perfection of the *Avena* test, we see that the essential framework of auxin functions in plants had been brought to light. Auxin was found to be essential for growth, and to be able either to stimulate or to inhibit growth, depending upon the concentration. It was found to be the controlling agent of tropic responses, the major control of apical dominance, and a primary factor in organ formation, in the abscission or non-abscission of plant parts, and in the commencement of fruit development.

Looking at the framework of auxin functions as an assembled structure, the physiologist may see the higher plant as an organism controlled and regulated in its growth and development by generally continuous streams of growth hormones. These hormones, formed in each of the plant extremities, course through the organism from the extremities inward, where they not only control growth itself but mediate the differentiation of new organs and tissues, the shedding of old organs, and the stepwise progression of many of the stages in the life cycle of the organism. In this view, then, the higher plant is not a simple colony of cells but is an entity sychronized in its growth, movement and development principally by streams of the growth hormone flowing through the various plant parts in extremely minute quantities (figure 1).

We should remember that this picture of plant growth is limited in completeness principally by our limitations of knowledge. We are forced to interpret growth phenomena principally on the basis of auxin functions largely because the auxin effects are the ones with which we can experiment most effectively and hence which we know best. This may result in concepts somewhat biased toward auxin, as

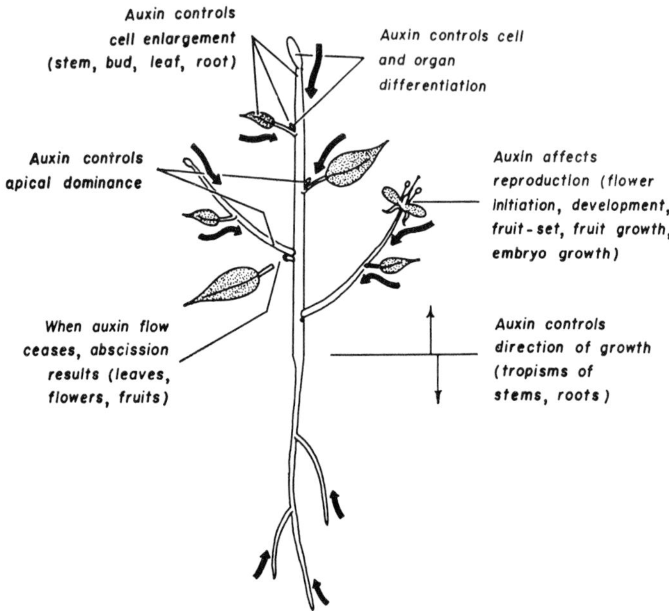

Fig. 1. Diagrammatic representation of the auxin regime in plants. Auxin is formed in the plant extremities and moves inward, as indicated by heavy arrows, controlling an array of growth functions through the plant.

Burström (1953) has pointed out, but until we know of more subtle controlling influences, these concepts will stand as the most complete descriptions of plant growth and development known.

As time goes on, new research appears to be attributing more and more physiological functions to the growth hormones in plants. The magnitude of their influences on the physiology and anatomy of the plant is undoubtedly still not fully recognized.

THE AGRICULTURAL IMPACT

The development of knowledge of the auxins has had a remarkable effect on the agricultural sciences. Not only has it made possible a much better understanding of many physiological phenomena in plants, but also it has given the agriculturist a set of new tools for use in plant culture. The technological applications of auxins have been expanded extremely rapidly. Unfortunately a very great number of workers have launched into research on the uses of auxins without first obtaining a background in the fundamentals of auxin action in plants. This has led to much confusion, a large amount of misinterpretation of results, and a lack of understanding of what intelligent steps can be taken to obtain desired effects. This confusion, caused in considerable degree by lack of background on the part of research workers, has brought some disrepute to the agricultural uses of growth regulators. Now that the early flare of expansion of agricultural uses is apparently past, it is hoped that further research concerning the uses of these physiologically active compounds will be carried out with a more comprehensive background in physiology.

The use of auxins in agriculture started very modestly. The first application to be discovered was in the rooting of cuttings. In 1934, Went published the results of his experiments which showed that auxins could be used to stimulate root formation. This discovery led to a great many studies of the uses of auxins in plant propagation. At present there are several commercial preparations on the market for this use, and when they are used wisely they are very effective indeed.

In 1935, Zimmerman and Wilcoxon discovered that alpha-naphthaleneacetic acid and some chlorinated phenoxyacetic acids are very strong auxins. The activity of these and particularly of 2,4-dichlorophenoxyacetic acid (Zimmerman and Hitchcock, 1942) was so much greater than the compounds which had been used previously, that the way was opened for some of the greatest practical uses of auxins.

Discoveries of further practical uses followed in quick succession. In 1936, Gustafson demonstrated that some fruits could be set parthenocarpically with auxins. Trials of this technique on commercial fruit crops have led to profitable uses in two crops: tomatoes and figs. In the same year, 1936, the discovery by LaRue that abscission of leaves could be delayed led ultimately to the application of auxins to prevent premature abscission of tree fruits. In 1942, Clark and Kerns found that flowering could be induced in pineapple by auxins. The pineapple industry in Hawaii and in Puerto Rico quickly took up the use of auxin sprays to bring about uniform flowering in each field. During World War II, the herbicidal properties of the phenoxyacetic acid derivatives were carefully studied under cover of military secrecy both in England and in the United States. These studies were first legitimately published in 1945 and 1947 by four research teams: Slade *et al* (1945), Blackman (1945), Nutman *et al* (1945) and Kraus and Mitchell (1947). The herbicidal uses of growth regulators are by far the most widespread. It is estimated that 60,000,000 pounds of 2,4-D are manufactured annually in the United States and perhaps 50,000,000 acres of land are treated with this herbicide alone. The dramatic rise in the production of 2,4-D since its first release from secrecy in 1945 can be seen in figure 2.

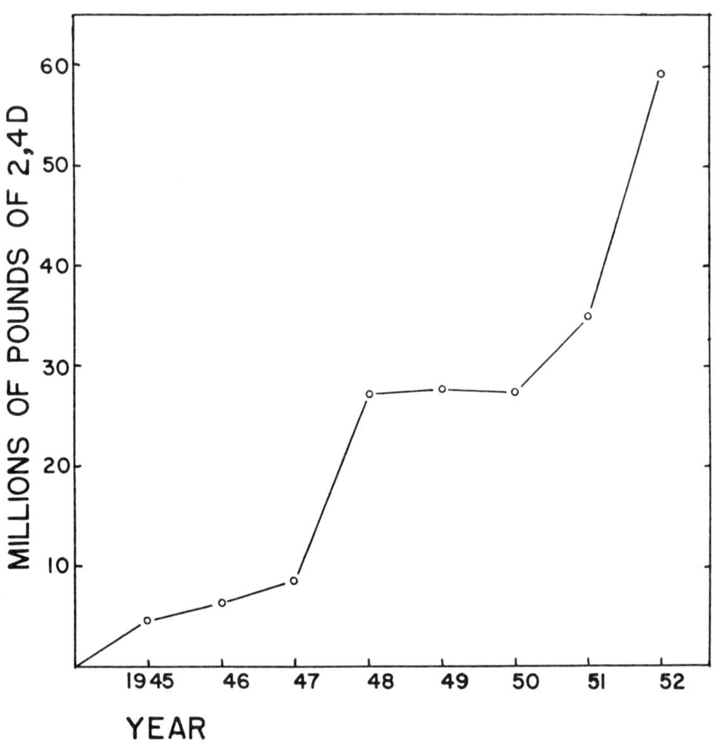

Fig. 2. The rise in the annual manufacture of 2,4-D in the United States since the open publication of its herbicidal effects in 1945. Data of U. S. Tariff Commission.

The development of an understanding of auxins in plant growth has effected startling advances in physiological and technological knowledge. Although the understanding of theoretical physiology has in many respects been outstripped by the technology of the application of auxins, still that is where the foundations of the entire field were laid, and the only sound basis for efficient progress lies in the advances of fundamental physiological understanding.

■ CHAPTER II

Auxin Extraction and Measurement Techniques

The majority of studies involving auxins either requires measurements of auxin activity or would be greatly benefited by the inclusion of such measurements. By the carefully worked out techniques of Went and other more recent workers, such measurements are quite easy to make. Techniques are available for which practically no elaborate equipment is needed and the time involved is quite small indeed.

It should be clearly understood that all procedures for the determination of auxin content of plant materials do not measure the same constituents. There are many forms of auxin in the plant. The diffusion technique yields a readily available auxin. Extraction of plant material with cold solvents for a short period of time is thought to yield the same auxin, and in some cases the diffusible auxin has been shown to be quantitatively similar to that obtained by short time extraction. This supply of auxin is commonly termed "free auxin." When extraction is continued over a long period of time there is clearly a production of additional auxin by the plant tissue during extraction and this production can continue over a period of several months of extraction (Thimann and Skoog, 1940). It is assumed that forms of the hormone which are not extractable in a short time are largely unavailable immediately for plant growth, and these forms are spoken of as "bound auxin."

The concepts of free and bound auxin, however, are not entirely simple. For instance, Thimann and Skoog (1940) have shown that pure indoleacetic acid added to plant material is not entirely recoverable by short time extraction. Some of it is retained by the plant material and appears in the solvent only after several hours of extraction, in a manner more characteristic of bound auxin than of free auxin. More recently Siegel and Galston (1953) have been able to follow the binding of free auxin onto a protein *in vitro*. There are many examples of bound auxin being released in the free form during extraction, as mentioned before. Consequently it appears that the free and bound forms are in a dynamic state, and the measurement of one strictly separated from the other is often difficult.

METHODS OF OBTAINING AUXIN

Diffusion

The simplest method of obtaining the growth hormone from plant material is by diffusion into agar. The usual procedure followed is simply to sever the growing tip or other organ to be tested under conditions which discourage transpiration, and place the cut surface for a period of an hour or so on a block of agar, usually 1.5%. This technique yields auxin immediately available for growth and, in etiolated seedlings, it can be shown in many different ways that growth is proportional to the auxin obtained by diffusion.

Three main difficulties can arise in the use of diffusion techniques:

1. The excessive loss of water, or a negative tension in the vascular system—as for example in leaves which have been recently exposed to sunlight—can prevent the accumulation of diffusate in the agar block. This difficulty can sometimes be alleviated by carrying out the diffusion in a high relative humidity, or even with the diffusion source under water. However, many types of leaves and stems will not yield diffusible auxin quantitatively under such conditions.

2. The destruction of auxin at the cut surface frequently interferes with the quantitative yield. Such destruction is apparently enzymatic, in some cases attributed to polyphenol oxidase and in others to peroxidase. Browning of the cut surface may indicate danger of destruction by polyphenol oxidase. Several methods of reducing this destruction have been used. The cut surface may be pressed onto wet filter paper to reduce the amount of enzyme (van Overbeek, 1938). Another method is the incorporation of 10^{-3} M ascorbic acid into the agar as an alternative substrate for the enzyme (Wetmore and Morel, 1949). A promising method appears to be the use of 0.005 M potassium cyanide in the wet filter paper first used to blot the cut surface, and as a droplet on the surface of the agar block as well. Then before the blocks are used for the *Avena* test, a drop of 0.005 M ferrous sulfate is placed upon the block to precipitate the cyanide ions present. Use of the poison causes no interference with the bioassay (Steeves *et al*, 1954).

3. The existence of growth inhibitors common in many green tissues will prevent the effective use of diffusion techniques. No means of separating auxins from inhibitors have been worked out for quanti-

ties obtained by diffusion, and extraction procedures must be used to this end. Methods of detecting the presence of inhibitors are discussed in the section dealing with the *Avena* test.

Solvent Extraction

A second method of obtaining the growth hormone from plant tissues is by means of solvent extraction. Early studies using this technique employed chloroform as the solvent (Thimann, 1934). It was found that if the plant material were acidified before extraction, larger quantities of auxin were obtained. A serious drawback to the use of chloroform, however, is the slow accumulation of a toxic substance, perhaps an auxin inactivator, thought to be chlorine (Thimann and Skoog, 1940). The most satisfactory solvent has been found to be diethyl ether (Boysen-Jensen, 1936). The presence of spontaneously-

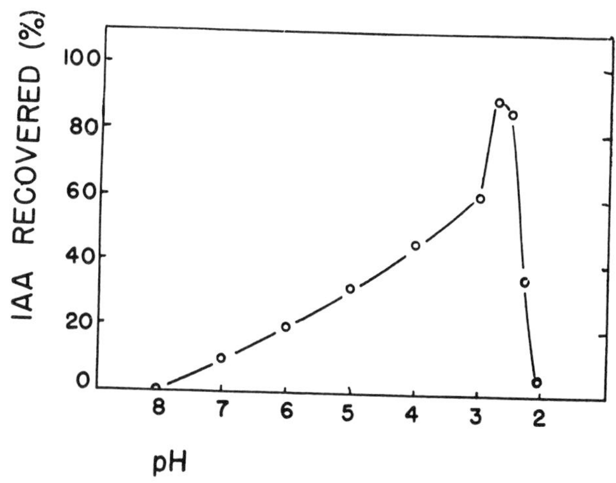

Fig. 3. The effect of pH on the partition of indoleacetic acid from water into ether (Gordon and Nieva, 1949).

formed peroxide in the ether will destroy easily oxidizable auxin, so before use the ether should be redistilled over ferrous sulfate and calcium oxide in a small amount of water. The redistilled peroxide-free ether is made much more effective as a hormone solvent if a small amount of water (5%) is added.

Many other solvents have been used for auxin extraction. Ethyl alcohol has been used, but yields smaller amounts than does ether. Water has been used (Gorter, 1932), but inactivation of much of the auxin may take place during the procedure. Terpstra (1953) has nearly eliminated such inactivation during water extraction by adding sodium diethyl dithiocarbamate (100 p.p.m.). Combination of several solvents for complete auxin extraction has been effectively employed by Avery *et al* (1941).

The relative solubility in ether of indoleacetic acid, with changing pH, has been worked out by Gordon and Nieva (1949). It is evident from figure 3 that most efficient extraction of this auxin from wet plant material into ether can be carried out at pH 2.8. It can also be seen that in slightly alkaline solutions the auxin will move out of the ether and into the water partition, a feature which can be utilized when one wants to take the auxin back into water. A saturated solution of sodium bicarbonate is very effective for this alkaline separation into water.

If the extraction procedure is preliminary to measurement of the free auxin in the plant tissues, the formation of auxin during extraction may be a large source of error. The formation of auxin during extraction has been shown by Skoog and Thimann (1940) to be enzymatic in nature.

To avoid the excessive formation of new auxin during extraction, Gustafson (1941) has established a technique for boiling the plant material a short time prior to solvent extraction. His technique is:

1. Freeze the tissue rapidly on carbon dioxide ice.
2. Grind the tissue with mortar and pestle, or dice.
3. Drop into boiling water and allow one minute of active boiling.
4. Collect plant material on a filter and extract with ether for 16 hours, using 3 changes of ether.

This technique has been used successfully with pineapple, tobacco, and tomato. The main limitation of Gustafson's technique lies in the fact that a certain amount of the free auxin must be destroyed by the heating (Thimann, Skoog and Byer, 1942). And in some green tissues heating causes the release of inhibitors which interfere with auxin assay (van Overbeek *et al,* 1945).

Another means of preventing formation of new auxin during extraction is by the use of a freezing and lyophilization technique first described by Wildman and Muir in 1949. These workers demonstrated that the formation of auxin during extraction could be effectively limited by carrying out the operation at 0° C. Their observations of the effect of temperatures upon auxin yields are shown in figure 4. The apparatus required for the lyophilization may be of several types. A simple apparatus has been described by Campbell and Pressman (1944) and another by Thomas and Prier (1952). By use of such a mechanism the frozen plant material is dried *in vacuo* without ever experiencing temperatures above freezing. The dry material can then be powdered and extracted with wet ether.

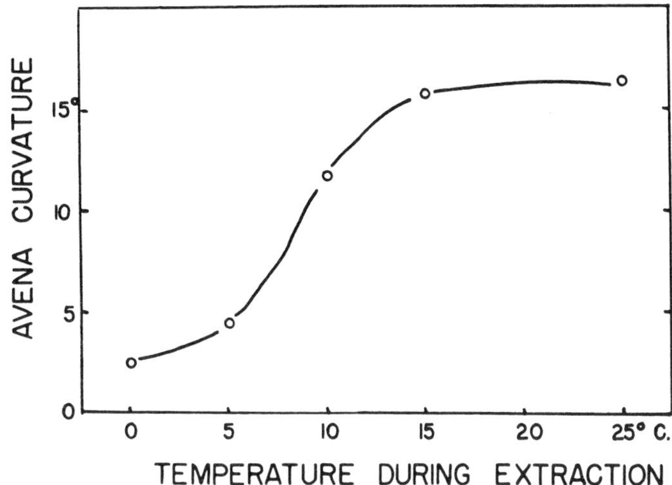

Fig. 4. The effects of temperature upon auxin yield during extraction of tobacco ovaries with wet ether (Wildman and Muir, 1949).

Wildman and Muir have shown that half-hour extractions carried on successively for two hours can effectively extract free indoleacetic acid from lyophilized tobacco ovary tissue. The technique may be summarized as follows:

1. Plunge plant material into liquid air or dry ice and acetone for rapid freezing.
2. Dry by lyophilization.
3. Grind to 40 mesh in Wiley mill.
4. Store *in vacuo* over P_2O_5, in darkness, until use.
5. Extract with peroxide-free ether (95%) at 0° C for four half-hour intervals.
6. Combine ether extracts and reduce in volume to a few ml.
7. Transfer quantitatively to agar for *Avena* assay.

Some plant materials require neither boiling nor lyophilization for solvent extraction of free auxin. Van Overbeek *et al* (1945) have established a technique for obtaining free auxin using short term extraction. Free auxin will be obtainable in higher concentrations in the first few ether extractions, whereas enzymatically released auxin will continue to appear over a period of time. These workers have taken advantage of this fact in framing a very simple technique for obtaining free auxin:

1. Freeze plant material on CO_2 ice.
2. Slice bulky tissues into 2–5 mm. slices.
3. Extract with peroxide-free ether at 0° C for two half-hour intervals.
4. Combine the ether extracts and reduce volume by evaporation to a few ml.
5. Transfer quantitatively to agar for *Avena* assay.

This technique has the advantages of being extremely simple, avoiding interference by inhibitors which would appear upon boiling, and by-passing the requirement for a lyophilization apparatus.

The techniques described above have all been designed for the extraction of free auxin. Extraction of bound auxin can be carried on using either of the latter two methods by carrying on the extraction over a period of time. Van Overbeek *et al* (1947) have determined free auxin by short time extraction and bound auxin by long term extraction (20 to 281 hours) in various pineapple tissues. They have demonstrated that their short term extraction of free auxin yields results practically identical with Gustafson's boiling method. Their comparisons of free and bound auxins in various plant tissues demonstrate the extreme usefulness of this technique.

BIOASSAYS FOR AUXINS

The Avena Test

The original assay for auxin as described by Went (1928) is given in great detail and thoroughness in the book, "Phytohormones" (Went and Thimann, 1937, p. 24–51). The following description of the test is essentially a summary of their presentation.

The physiological basis for the *Avena* or oat test lies in the strict polar transport of auxins in the *Avena* coleoptile. The strict polarity and rapidity of auxin transport result in a difference in growth rate between the side of the coleoptile to which auxin is applied and the side to which none is applied. The differential growth causes curvature of the coleoptile, which is proportional to the amount of auxin applied. It should be remembered that chemicals which are not swept along by the active transport system will not have any effect in the test. Thus salts, metallic ions and sugars have little effect upon the curvature. The same is true of auxins which are poorly transported, even though they may show growth activity in other tests.

The *Avena* coleoptile is a cylinder of relatively uniform, elongating cells. Cell division takes place only until the etiolated coleoptile reaches approximately 1 cm. in length. After that the growth is accomplished almost exclusively by cell elongation and it continues for approximately 4 days at a maximum rate of roughly 1 mm. per hour.

The seedlings are grown in darkness to prevent occurrence of the reduction in sensitivity caused by blue light. However, oat plants grown in total darkness undergo elongation of the first internode to a very inconvenient length. Such elongation can be prevented by exposure to red light for a period of 2 to 4 hours during the second day after germination.

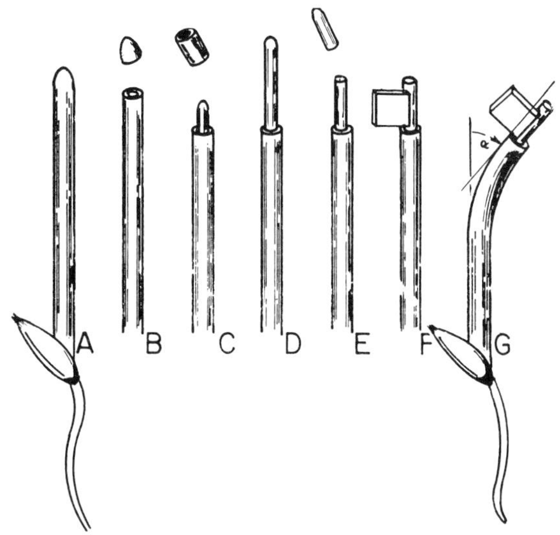

Fig. 5. Diagrammatic representation of the steps involved in the *Avena* test.

The steps involved in carrying out the *Avena* test are shown diagrammatically in figure 5. When the coleoptile is 15 to 30 mm. high (above the glass holder or sand level) the apical 1 mm. is removed in order to cut off the natural source of auxin within the coleoptile. In this decapitated condition the natural auxin content of the stump decreases for a period of two hours after which a regeneration of auxin-forming capacity occurs at the new physiological tip. In order to prevent the renewed formation of auxin during the test period, a second decapitation is carried on three hours after the first. Removal of from 2 to 4 mm. in this second decapitation reduces the curvature responses very little. However, if the second decapitation removes 6 mm. or more the curvature obtainable is seriously reduced. The data of Went and

Thimann (1937, p. 40) showing the effect of different lengths of second decapitation on curvature obtained are given in figure 6. On the basis of these data it is generally assumed that, if a 2 mm. section is removed and the first attempt at this decapitation should fail (the primary leaf may break off while being pulled out), another attempt may be made without seriously interfering with the plant's sensitivity. After the second decapitation, the primary leaf which has been thus exposed is gently pulled up in order to break its connection with the

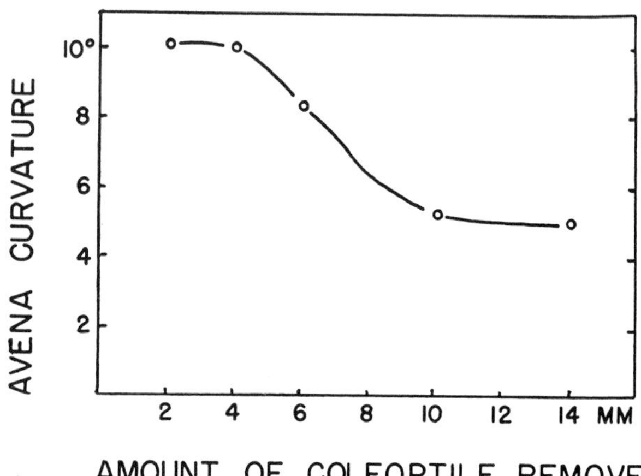

Fig. 6. The effect of removal of various amounts of coleoptile tip upon the subsequent sensitivity (in the *Avena* test) to a standard auxin concentration (Went and Thimann, 1937, p. 40).

growing point of the plant (figure 5 *D*). Now the primary leaf will provide a stable brace upon which an agar block can rest. An agar block is then placed on one side of the cut end of the coleoptile, and auxin from the agar block, transported in a polar direction downward, stimulates growth on the side to which the agar block has been applied and curvature of the coleoptile is obtained.

Three main environmental conditions must be maintained for the *Avena* test. First, only red light should be used because the shorter wave lengths both destroy auxin and reduce sensitivity of the coleoptile to a given supply of auxin. Ruby glass which prevents the transmission of wave lengths shorter than 5200 Ångstrom units is generally used. Many types of vaporproof light fixtures and photographic safelights are commercially available with acceptable ruby glass bowls. Second, temperatures must be controlled in order to maintain constant high sensitivity in the plant material. 30° C is optimal for growth of the coleoptile, but temperatures below 25° C are optimal for greatest auxin sensitivity. Consequently, a temperature of 25° C is generally recognized as a good compromise. Third, humidity must be controlled in order to maintain good conditions for the quantitative diffusion of auxin from the agar block into the severed coleoptile. If humidities below 85 per cent are used, the agar block will tend to dry out. If humidities above 90 per cent are used, the seedlings tend to guttate. In either case, the quantitative diffusion of the auxin out of the agar into the coleoptile is seriously restricted. A relative humidity of 85 to 90 per cent must be strictly maintained. In some laboratories the oat seedlings are cultured in sand instead of in the usual glass holders and in these cases, the optimal relative humidity is found to be 80 per cent (van Overbeek *et al,* 1945).

Fig. 7. Device for holding seedlings for *Avena* test.

The materials required for the *Avena* test are fairly simple and, again, have been described in detail by Went and Thimann (1937). In brief, these may be listed as follows:

1. Seeds of Victory oats. Because the details of the test have been worked out almost exclusively using this variety, it is best to use it in the *Avena* test. However, van Overbeek *et al* (1945), have found that Kanota oats give essentially the same results.

2. Glass holders into which the seedlings fit, brass clips and wooden racks for support of the glass holders, and metal or plastic water troughs into which the seedling roots are suspended. These items are illustrated in figure 7. They are very convenient in that individual plants may be sorted for uniformity and grouped together in

racks of 10 or 12 for each treatment. If these items are not available, the seeds may be planted in small wooden troughs filled with sand.

3. Decapitating scissors (A) and cork-lined tweezers (B) (figure 8) are very useful in setting up the test.

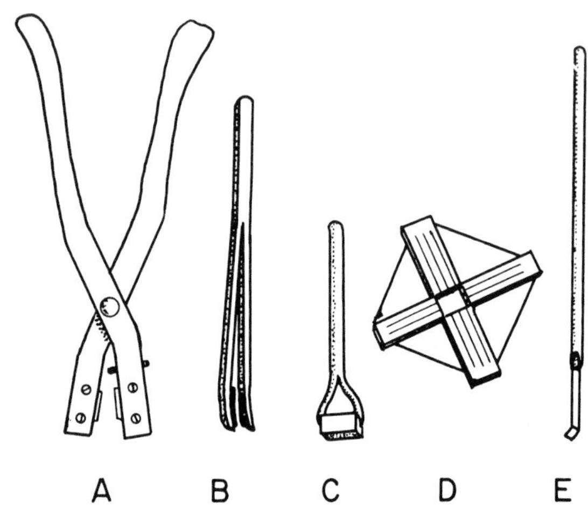

Fig. 8: Tools for the *Avena* test. *A,* decapitating scissors; *B,* tweezers with cork lining; *C,* mold for cutting agar; *D,* guide for cutting 12 agar blocks; *E,* spatula for placing agar blocks.

4. A special cutting mold (C), a guide for dividing the agar into uniform blocks (D) and a small spatula (E) are convenient for the steps involving the agar (figure 8).

5. Shadowgraph apparatus as shown in figure 9. If this apparatus

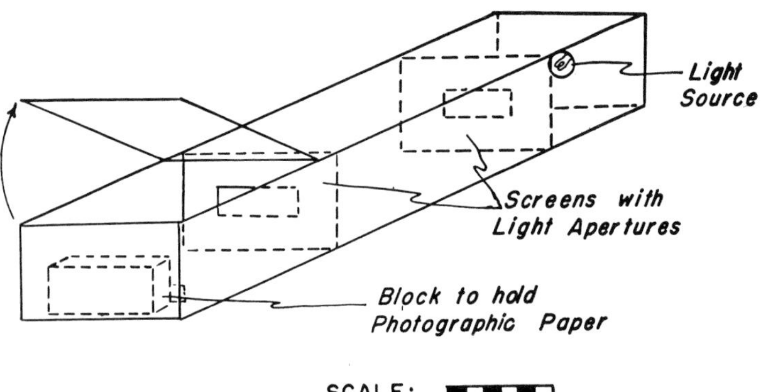

Fig. 9. A box for taking shadowgraphs of the *Avena* test.

is not available, simply placing the plants in front of photosensitive projection paper and exposing to a 40-watt bulb approximately 10 feet away for 3 seconds will be effective. The apparatus shown in the figure, however, is desirable for best photographic detail.

6. A protractor, as in figure 10, with which to read the curvatures as recorded on the shadowgraph.

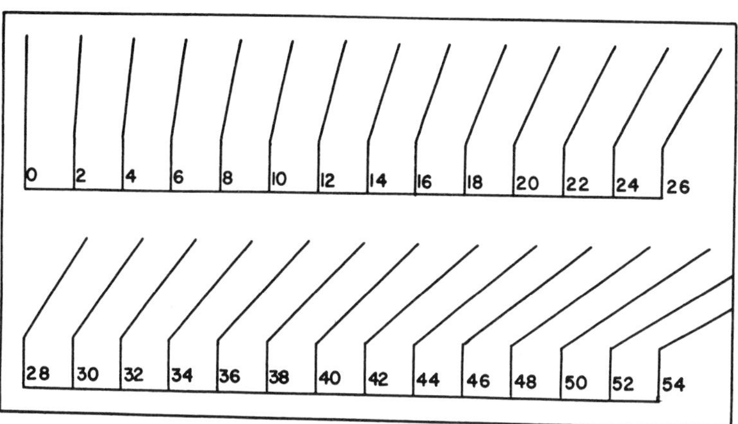

Fig. 10. Simple protractor made of clear plastic for measuring curvature in *Avena* test.

Pure agar is used at a concentration in water of 1.5 per cent. It is very important that the percentage be held constant within any test. Lower concentrations of agar produce more curvature per unit of auxin, thus the lower the concentration of agar used the greater the sensitivity to small quantities of auxin. However, the linear relationship between the quantity of auxin and curvature obtained is best at approximately 2 per cent agar. Consequently, in order to obtain highest sensitivity and yet to approximate linearity in response, a 1.5 per cent agar is accepted as being best. To prepare the agar the weighed, dry material is added to water and carefully heated in a water bath until a uniform translucence is obtained.

PROCEDURE FOR THE AVENA TEST

Planting

Place husked seeds of Victory oats in water in a suction flask and evacuate three times on the water tap. If the husks are left on, poor or no germination will result. Let them soak for about two hours, then discard the soak water, as it contains auxin released by the germinating seeds. On glass plates covered with wet paper toweling, place the seeds groove-side down, and embryo end projecting slightly over the edge of the plate. Put glass in germinating dish in darkroom (25° C), add water to keep seeds moist but not wet; cover. On the day after planting, the germinating seeds should be exposed to 2 hours of red light to inhibit elongation of the first internode.

Loading

Two days after planting, when the roots are 0.5 to 2 cm. long, put each germinated seed in a glass holder, and place in a rack with at least one root in water. Be sure coleoptiles are oriented vertically, and that the water meniscus does not touch the seed itself. The plants will be ready one day after loading.

Preparation of agar

Place mold on microscope slide over ice or ice-filled refrigerator tray. The hot agar is then pipetted into the mold to make an agar plate 1 mm. thick. After gelation, place the cutting form over the molded agar and cut into 12 uniform squares (2 × 2 × 1 mm.) with razor blade.

Setting up

73–75 hours after planting, the test is started:

1. First decapitation. Cut off terminal 1 mm. with conventional scissors.
2. Wait 3 hours; this is a convenient time to prepare the agar blocks.
3. Remove terminal 2–4 mm. of coleoptile without breaking the leaf inside (figure 5 *C*). Use special decapitating scissors, or alternatively, break the coleoptile section off with fine pointed tweezers.
4. Pull primary leaf approximately halfway out. Use cork-lined tweezers or other wide-nosed tweezers.
5. Cut off leaf about one quarter inch above the coleoptile tip.
6. Apply agar block containing auxin on one side of coleoptile tip by placing it against the protruding primary leaf and drawing it down to rest firmly on the coleoptile tip (figure 5 *F*). Use small spatula for this step. Apply one treatment to a rack of 12 plants.
7. Record the time at which the rack was treated. Wait 90 minutes.
8. Place rack in shadowgraph box, with plants pressed close to a strip of photographic projection paper. Expose to unilateral light for 3 seconds for shadowgraph. Record rack number and date on back of paper.
9. Place paper in developer solution until good contrast develops (about 1 minute), rinse in water, and then soak in fixing solution for 5 to 15 minutes. Wash in running water for an hour or more and then lay out to dry.

Reading

Read with a protractor the curvatures recorded on the shadowgraph for each coleoptile. Measure the maximum curvature from the straight lower region to the very tip of the coleoptile. (Angle α in figure 5 *G*.)

Errors introduced in the procedure for carrying out the test all tend to reduce the curvature obtained. (Exception: agar block smaller than standard.) Consequently, variability because of error will cause a skew in distribution of the readings toward low values. For this reason it is accepted as permissible to discard readings of individual coleoptiles with curvatures which are much lower than the bulk of the values obtained in any given treatment. Of course, all readings

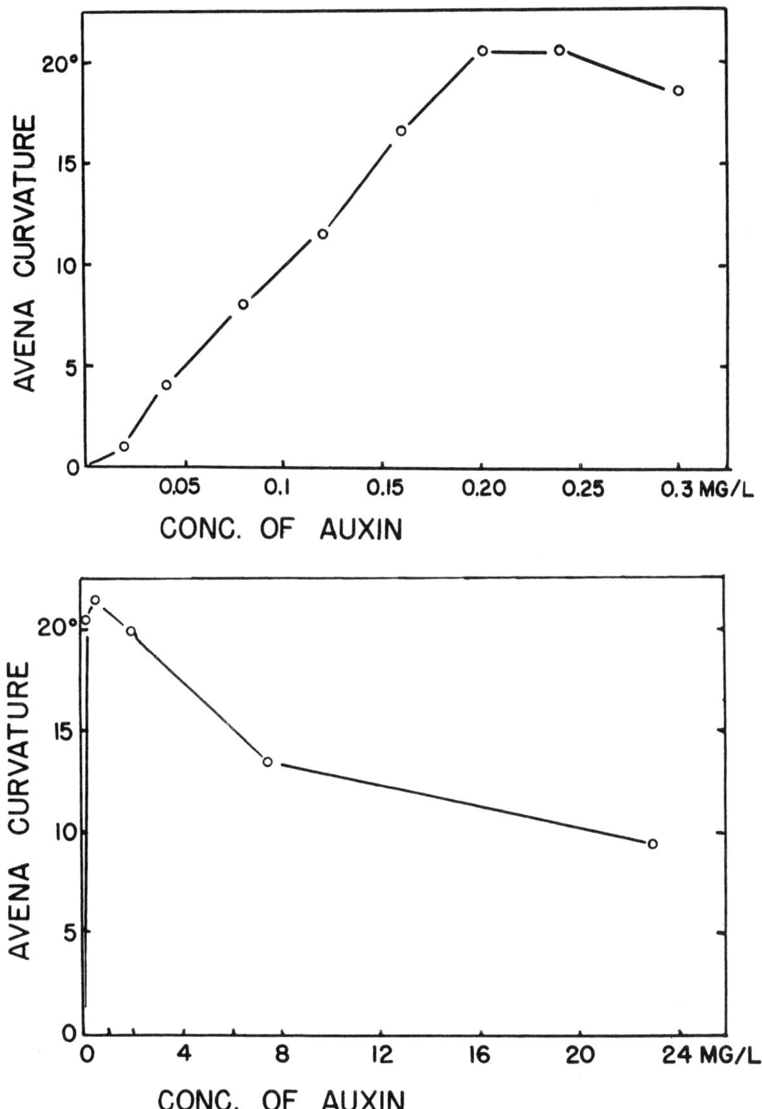

Fig. 11. *A*. Results of an *Avena* test showing the linear response to varying concentrations of auxin, indoleacetic acid (Went and Thimann, 1937, p. 41). *B*. Results of an *Avena* test showing the lack of a quantitative response for concentrations of auxin (indoleacetic acid) higher than optimum (Went and Thimann, 1937, p. 41).

which obviously have been altered by poor placing of the block or by subsequent lifting of the block from the tip by extension of the primary leaf may also be discarded. Usually 12 readings are taken for each treatment and these are expressed as the mean. The variability of the data is usually expressed as the standard deviation of the mean, or standard error: $SE = \sqrt{\frac{\Sigma(\Delta^2)}{N(N-1)}}$ where Δ is the difference of each reading from the mean, and N is the number of readings. A variability or standard error of 10% of the maximum curvature is generally considered to be approximately the greatest permissible in a good test.

Early workers using the *Avena* test have showed that the curvature obtained was in linear proportion to the auxin concentration. This is true generally for concentrations ranging from about 0.02 mg./liter to 0.2 mg./liter of indoleacetic acid. Lower concentrations generally show a skewness and concentrations above about 0.2 mg./liter give curvatures which are not proportionally greater. The linear range and the non-linear range are shown in figure 11.

It should be understood that the straight linear curve is not always obtained even in the most careful tests. Linearity is altered by agar concentration, by the time interval between application of the agar and reading, by range of auxin concentrations being tested, and by the presence of inhibiting substances in the agar with the auxin. By using a high concentration of agar (4%) Pilet (1951) has been able to convert the curvature response from a linear one to a semi-log response.

Although the degree of dissociation of the acid auxin has a very large effect on its activity in other tests, in the *Avena* test the degree of dissociation and pH apparently have no bearing on the curvature obtained. Nielson (1930) found that unbuffered auxin solutions ranging from pH 2.4 to 9.6 produced no differences in curvature.

A certain inherent variability is generally found in the amount of curvature obtained by a given auxin concentration from day to day and from season to season. This variability has been noted by most research workers using the *Avena* test. A notable exception to this was the work of van Overbeek (1943–1947) under tropical conditions in Puerto Rico. In most assay work a known indoleacetic acid control needs to be run with each *Avena* test in order to eliminate the source of error due to the inherent variance from one test to the next.

The presence of some inhibitors along with auxin in the agar block may have a strong effect on curvature obtained. Not only is the curvature from any one concentration of auxin greatly reduced, but the shape of the concentration curve is very greatly altered (Larsen, 1939). Serial dilutions of auxin solutions containing inhibitors characteristically show a reduced slope, a rounded curve instead of linearity, and a lower maximum curvature. A graphic comparison of a pure auxin dilution series with an auxin-plus-inhibitor dilution series is shown in figure 12. If the presence of an inhibitor is suspected

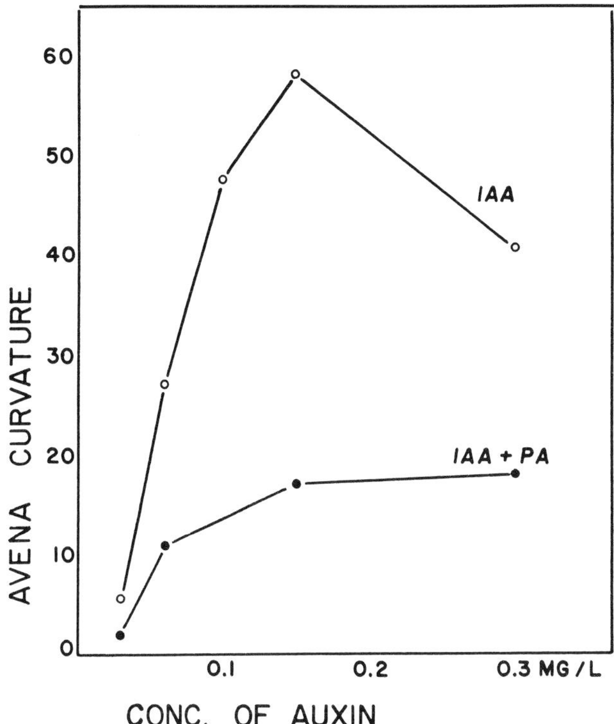

Fig. 12. Dilution curves of indoleacetic acid alone and in the presence of an inhibitor—parascorbic acid (Larsen, 1947).

in a plant extract or diffusate, the establishment of a dilution curve may be extremely helpful in verifying whether an inhibitor is present or not. Another technique for establishing the presence of an inhibitor is to test a constant concentration of indoleacetic acid with a dilution series of the extract containing the suspected inhibitor (van Overbeek *et al*, 1945).

The presence of moderate amounts of most salts, metals, sugars, or amino acids in the agar block will have no perceptible effect on the *Avena* test. However, it should be pointed out that the presence of salts in the agar can strongly affect the diffusion of auxin from plant material into the agar. Potassium ions are particularly active in promoting auxin diffusion into the agar. A concentration of 10^{-3} molar KCl has been found to be optimal in this regard (Thimann and Schneider, 1938).

Occasional positive curvatures are obtained in the *Avena* test. In such cases the coleoptile bends toward the agar block instead of away from it, as one would expect when a growth promoting substance has been applied. Small positive curvatures may be caused by: (1) excessively low auxin concentrations, (2) the presence of growth inhibitors in the agar, or (3) too long or too short an interval between the time of applying the agar block and taking the shadowgraph reading.

Before the recognition of indoleacetic acid as an auxin, a method of expressing auxin concentration was very much needed. Almost simultaneously three different methods were worked out and one occasionally finds them in the literature today. These units of auxin activity expressed as the amount of curvature per unit of agar are: (1) AE (*Avena Einheit*) = 10° curvature from each 2 $mm.^3$ block, (2) p. u. (plant unit) = 1° curvature from a 10 $mm.^3$ block, (3) WAE (*Wuchsstoff Avena Einheit*) = 50° total curvature from a 100 $mm.^3$ block. A detailed comparison is given by Boysen-Jensen (1936, p. 33). The use of these auxin units has been generally discarded now and, instead, with each test the curvature from a known quantity of indoleacetic acid is measured and the auxin is expressed as indoleacetic acid equivalents.

As we have stated before, the sensitivity of any given test is subject to considerable variability both in relation to time of day and season of the year. The maximum angle of curvature obtainable will generally vary from 15° to 35°, but under any given set of conditions, the concentration of auxin required to give the maximum angle will remain the same. Concentrations greater than that required to produce the maximum angle cannot be measured quantitatively by the *Avena* test.

The Slit Pea Test

The slit pea test, originated by Went (1934), is described in "Phytohormones" (Went and Thimann, 1937, p. 54) and in further detail by van Overbeek and Went (1937) and Went (1939). This test has had extensive use in the subsequent years and few changes have been made.

The physiological basis for the slit pea test lies in the differential growth of the epidermal cells of etiolated pea stems in response to auxin. A piece of actively growing stem is slit longitudinally and placed in a solution containing the auxin material. The auxin enters along the entire length of the stem and all enlarging cells which receive such a stimulus respond by increased growth. Epidermal cells respond to auxin by a proportionately greater growth in length than in width, whereas inner cortical cells respond by growth proportionally greater in width than in length (Borgström, 1939, p. 29). Consequently the growth stimulated by an auxin causes a curvature of the stem halves away from the epidermal side. Such a curvature has been shown to be a function of the relative length increases of the outer to inner cells (Thimann and Schneider, 1938). This differential growth is apparently not entirely responsible for the curvature phenomenon for, curiously enough, earlier infiltration of auxin solutions into the pea stem sections before splitting produces almost no curvature at all (van Overbeek and Went, 1937).

It is obvious that the auxin materials are able to enter the pea stem at any point and consequently the transport of such materials within the tissues has no evident bearing on curvature. This is in contrast to the dependence upon transport in the *Avena* test. Some compounds which yield no curvature in the *Avena* test because of poor transportability will yield good curvature in the slit pea test (e.g. phenylacetic acid).

In the absence of the selective effect of an active auxin transport system it is to be expected that agents other than auxins may have a pronounced effect on the growth obtained. The presence of some organic or inorganic substances which alter growth will alter the results of the slit pea test. For this reason the slit pea test can be used to study the effects of some compounds which modify the action of auxin in growth, whereas the *Avena* test is not well adapted for such studies.

It should be mentioned that upon placing the slit stem in water a negative curvature occurs—that is a curvature outward, toward the epidermal layer. This curvature is a function of water uptake by the inner cortical cells and is greatly altered by the acidity of the solution (van Overbeek and Went, 1937). Minute amounts of acid cause very large negative curvatures. For this reason the slit pea test is not well adapted for studies in which pH differences will exist between dishes.

The pea plant produces small scale-leaves at the first two nodes and a trifoliate leaf at the third node. The actively growing section of stem between the second scale node and the leaf node is the material used in the slit pea test. The plants are grown in the darkroom in order to retain maximum sensitivity to auxins. However, plants grown in complete darkness become much more etiolated and the epidermal cells grow excessively long and poorly differentiated, resembling great long cortical cells. Because the slit pea test depends on differential growth in length between epidermal and cortical cells, the ability of the completely etiolated and relatively undifferentiated stem to produce slit-stem curvatures is seriously limited or even reduced to zero. In order to avoid this difficulty, a small amount of red light of the same sort as is used in the *Avena* test should be applied to the growing seedlings. The quantitative requirement for red light to produce

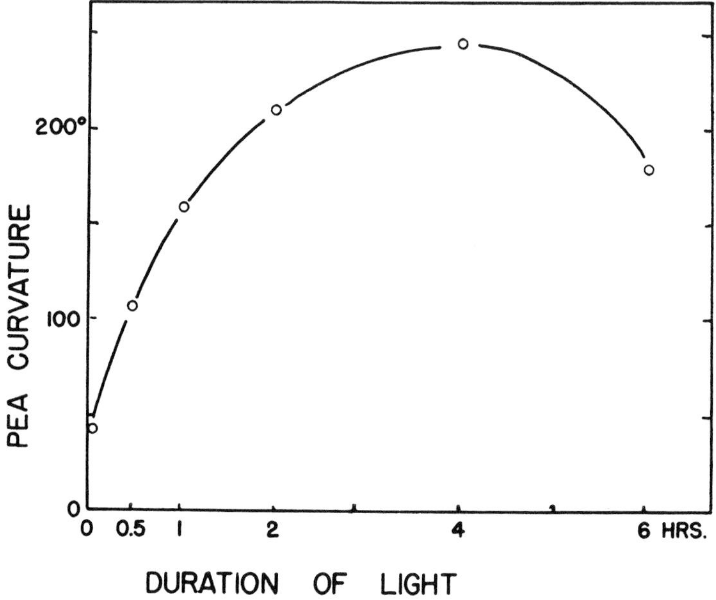

Fig. 13. The effect of red light upon the subsequent sensitivity of pea stems in the slit pea test. Red light of approximately 10 f.c. was applied one day before carrying out the test. Each point represents the average curvature obtained with 10 mg./l. of indoleacetic acid (Kent and Gortner, 1951).

optimal response in the pea test has been established by Kent and Gortner (1951). They found that 4 hours of light applied the day before running the test were best. The quantitative relationship of this light treatment to auxin sensitivity of the slit pea stems is shown graphically in figure 13. A convenient method for growing peas of uniformly high sensitivity is to expose the plants to 3 hours of red light daily by placing a time clock in the red light electrical circuit.

When severed from the plant and decapitated, the pea stem is deprived of its natural source of auxin and of the capacity to regenerate the physiological tip. Slitting the stems and soaking them in water for an hour or more removes for all practical purposes the auxin supply naturally present in the stems. By this means a specimen highly sensitive to added auxin is obtained.

The environmental controls required for the slit pea test are simpler than those for the *Avena* test. Since the material is tested in solution, there is no need for humidity control. Temperature sensitivity is very much lower than in the *Avena* test. Small amounts of diffuse white light do not alter the results.

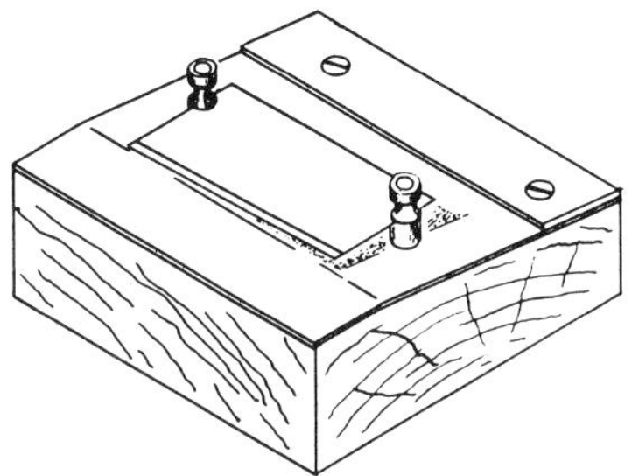

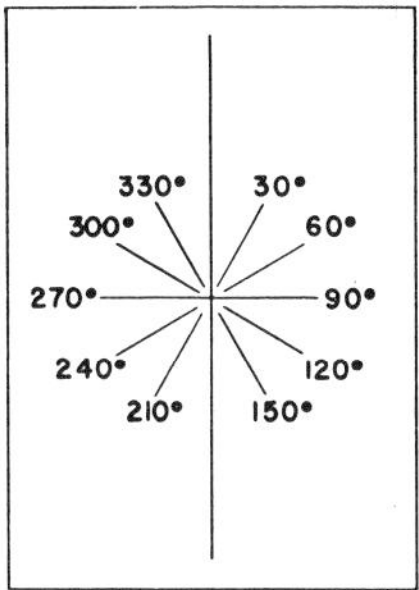

Fig. 14. Tools for the slit pea test. Left: Cutting block for convenience in slitting stems, holds razor in slanted position and provides guide for uniform length of cut. Right: Simple protractor for reading curvatures. (Adapted from van Overbeek and Went, 1937.)

The materials required are as follows:

1. Alaska peas or other pure strain of pea seed.
2. Porcelain trays or sterile wood flats for culturing seedlings. Because of the great sensitivity of this test to metallic ions, the plants should not contact any bare metal. Hard maple sawdust (steam sterilized) or washed sand is frequently used as a medium for the plant's culture. Vermiculite makes a very convenient medium and can be discarded after use.
3. A cutting block such as that illustrated in figure 14. This item is not essential, and instead an ordinary razor blade may be used, though with somewhat less convenience.
4. A 360° protractor, easily fashioned from a piece of glass, as shown in figure 14.

PROCEDURE FOR THE SLIT PEA TEST

Planting

Into a porcelain-ware tray, place about one-half inch of dry vermiculite or sand. Saturate with water. Scatter seeds of Alaska pea evenly over the vermiculite, and cover with dry vermiculite or sand to a depth of about two inches. Place in the darkroom (25° C). Planting should be eight days before the test. The seedlings must receive some red light. Three hours of red light per day is very satisfactory.

Cutting

Select seedlings in which the stem above the first leaf node (the 3rd node) is ¼ to ½ inch long. Uniformity of plants used is important. Cut off the seedlings about 2 inches from the top, decapitate ¼ inch below the leaf node, and slit the stem from the tip to standard distance (3 cm.). For uniform results it is essential to have stems slit exactly down the middle.

Wash

Place the slit sections in a dish of distilled water for one hour.

Place in solutions

Make up the solutions to be tested at a volume of 25 ml. in 100 × 20 mm. Petri dishes. Place 5 or 6 slit peas in each dish, choosing carefully for symmetry and uniformity of negative (outward) curvature. Do not use stems with less than 60° negative curvature on each arm.

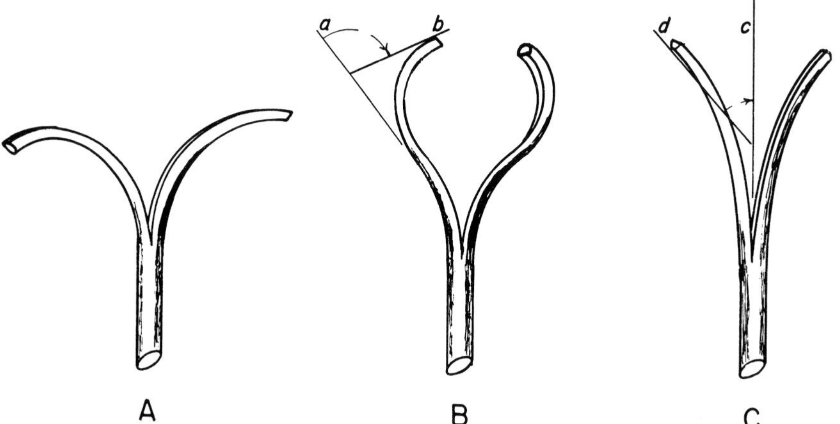

Fig. 15. The slit pea test. *A,* a stem section before exposure to auxin. *B,* after exposure to auxin, showing positive curvature. *C,* after exposure to weak auxin, showing stem-reference method of reading curvature.

Reading

After the peas have been in the test solutions for 6–24 hours, read the curvatures obtained. Inward curvature is due to growth. Read curvature as the angle formed between (a) the tangent at the point where inward curvature commences, and (b) the tangent at the point where inward curvature ceases (i.e. the apical tip) as shown in figure 15 *B.* Read the curvature on both halves of each stem. This will give you 10 to 12 readings for each solution tested.

Stem-reference reading

If it is desired to extend the readings to the lowest ranges of auxin concentrations, the negative curvatures may be read in addition to the conventional positive curvature readings (Thimann and Schneider, 1938). To do this, place the cut stem so that the intact base is vertical on the protractor and measure the negative curvature of each arm, viz., the angle formed between (c) the vertical axis of the intact base, and (d) the tangent at the point where curvature ceases (i.e. the apical tip) as shown in figure 15 *C*. The results are expressed as the mean plus or minus the standard error.

Although in the *Avena* test the curvature obtained is proportional to the concentration of auxin, in the slit pea test curvature is more nearly proportional to the log of the concentration. Although the sensitivity to low concentrations of auxin is much less in the slit pea than in the *Avena* test the range of auxin activity which can be tested

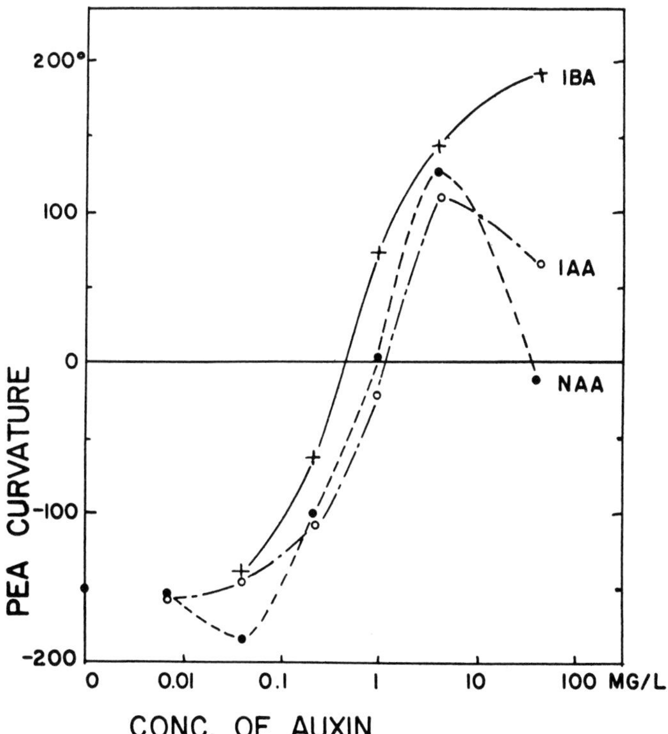

Fig. 16. Sample results of slit pea tests showing the relationship between curvature obtained and the concentration of three auxins; IAA: indoleacetic acid; NAA: naphthaleneacetic acid; and IBA: indolebutyric acid (Thimann and Schneider, 1939).

is much greater. Some sample data for dilution curves of several auxins are shown in figure 16. By use of the stem-reference technique for reading, the slit pea test can be used to measure quantitatively as little as 0.01 mg./liter of indoleacetic acid. The maximum curvature is usually obtained at approximately 10 mg./liter of indoleacetic acid, or fifty times as great an auxin concentration as that producing the maximum curvature in the *Avena* test.

Very dilute or very weak auxins can sometimes produce negative curvatures (Thimann and Schneider, 1938).

The advantages of the slit pea test over the *Avena* test are: (1) less exacting requirements for environmental controls, (2) the test does not depend upon the ability of the plant to transport the auxin, (3) the manipulations are very easy and there is no exacting time schedule, and (4) the measurable concentration range is much greater. Along with these advantages, however, there are certain disadvantages: (1) the slit pea test is quantitatively much less sensitive in low auxin concentration ranges, (2) it requires relatively large quantities of the auxin solution, and (3) it is sensitive to metallic impurities. These characteristics make the slit pea test highly desirable for the determination of growth regulator activity of synthetic substances but unusable for the quantitative measurement of the small amounts of auxins in plant extracts.

The Straight-Growth Tests

The physiological basis for straight-growth tests is the simple stimulation of straight growth by auxins. There is no transport limitation and no dependence upon differential growth to produce curvature. The presence of salts, sugars, and many other substances will alter the results obtained.

The straight-growth test, using short oat coleoptile cylinders, was first described by Bonner (1933), and that using pea stem sections was described by Thimann and Schneider (1939).

The environmental requirements are the same as in the slit pea test. Usually the temperature is maintained at 25° C and only red light is used.

The materials needed for straight-growth tests are as follows:

1. Seedlings of Alaska pea or Victory oats or other pure strain.

2. Materials for culture of the seedlings. For peas there may be porcelain trays and vermiculite or sterile wooden flats and hard maple sawdust. For oats, large germinating dishes containing glass plates wrapped with paper toweling are effective.

3. A device for cutting sections of a standard length. Two razor

blades clamped to a block are perfectly satisfactory. For *Avena* straight growth tests, guillotines such as those described by van der Weij (1932), Yamaki (1948) or by Galston and Hand (1949) are very helpful.

4. When guillotines are used, it is convenient to mount the coleoptile cylinders on the teeth of fine hair combs (Schneider, 1938). See figure 17.

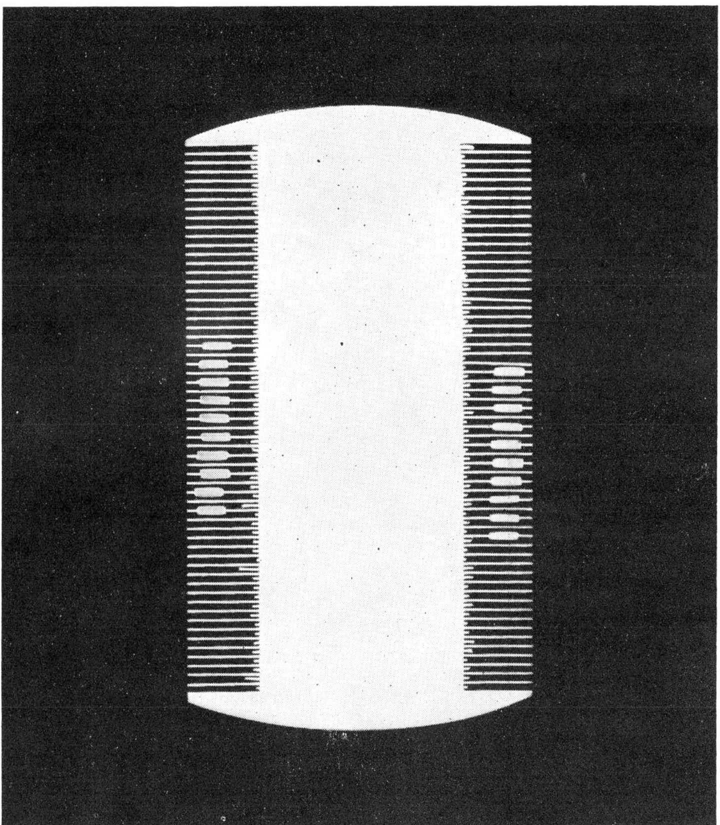

Fig. 17. An *Avena* straight-growth test carried out on comb teeth by the method of Schneider (1938).

5. A fine ruler or a dissecting microscope with an ocular eyepiece for measuring length of the sections.

PROCEDURE FOR THE AVENA STRAIGHT-GROWTH TEST

Planting

Place husked seeds of Victory oats in water in a suction flask and evacuate. Soak for two hours, then discard the soak water. On glass plates covered with paper toweling place the seeds, grooved side down, with the embryo end projecting slightly over the edge. Place the glass in a germinating dish in the darkroom; add water to keep seeds moist but not wet; cover. One day after planting, germinating seeds should be exposed to two hours of red light to inhibit elongation of the first internode.

Cutting

Three days after planting, when coleoptiles are 20 to 30 mm. long, cut uniform sections 3 to 5 mm. in length. Discard the apical 4 mm. of the coleoptile. For greatest sensitivity, the coleoptiles should be prepared with the primary leaf removed. Leaving the primary leaf within the cylinder is permissible when a supply of growth substances from the primary leaf is not objectionable. Two sections may be taken from each coleoptile provided that the distribution of first and second sections is constant from treatment to treatment.

Place the sections on comb teeth as shown in figure 17. This step is optional, but is particularly convenient when a guillotine or van der Weij cutter is used. Two out of every three comb teeth are removed, and the remaining teeth are filed down to fit inside the coleoptile cylinders.

Place the sections directly into the solutions to be tested, or for more exact studies to determine auxin activity, the sections should be placed in water for an hour before testing. If combs are used, 40 ml. of test solution per Petri dish will be necessary. If the sections are floating individually, 10 ml. of solutions are sufficient. The sections must break surface.

Reading

Measure growth after 24 hours, when 80 to 90 per cent of growth has been completed, or at 48 hours when growth is essentially complete. If the growth rate is the function to be determined, growth is measured after 12 hours (McRae and Bonner, 1952). The growth rate is approximately constant for the first 18-hour period.

PROCEDURE FOR THE PEA STRAIGHT-GROWTH TEST

Planting

In a porcelain-ware tray place about one-half inch of dry vermiculite or sand. Saturate with water. Scatter seeds of Alaska pea evenly over the vermiculite; cover with dry vermiculite to a depth of about 2 inches. Place in the darkroom (25° C). Planting should be 8 days before the test. The seedlings may be given some red light.

Cutting

Select seedlings in which the stem internode above the first leaf node is 1/4 to 1/2 inch long. (If completely etiolated peas are used, select seedlings in which the internode above the second scale leaf node is 1/2 to 1 inch long.) Uniformity of plants used is important. Cut off the seedling near the base and then cut a section of uniform length (a size between 3 and 5 mm. is satisfactory) beginning at a uniform place such as 1/4 inch below the leaf node. Place directly in Petri dishes containing solutions. The use of 10 ml. of solution keeps all sections at the surface. Submerged sections grow crooked.

Reading

Measure after 24 hours when approximately 90 per cent of growth has usually occurred, or at 48 hours when growth is essentially finished. Again, if growth rate is to be studied, readings will have to be made 6 hours after the test is started, for the rate begins to decline after that length of time (Christiansen and Thimann, 1950).

As in the previous tests, results are expressed as the mean per treatment plus or minus the standard error. In general where serial dilutions are used and a smooth curve is obtained repeatedly, the standard error may be considered to be unnecessary.

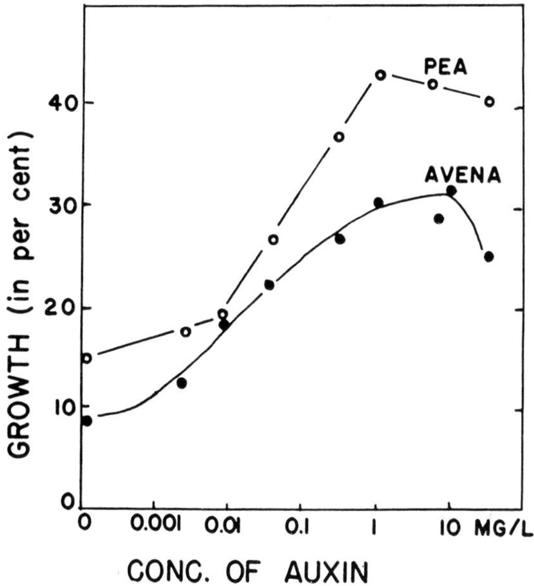

Fig. 18. Results of an *Avena* straight-growth test and a pea straight-growth test showing the approximate semi-logarithmic proportionality of growth to the concentration of the auxin, indoleacetic acid (Thimann and Schneider, 1939).

The growth obtained is approximately proportional to the logarithm of the concentration of auxin applied. In both the *Avena* and the pea straight-growth tests the minimum amount of growth regulator detectable is approximately 0.01 mg./liter of indoleacetic acid. Maximum growth is obtained at approximately 10 mg./liter of indoleacetic acid. Sample curves for each test are shown in figure 18.

Since straight-growth tests are not dependent as is the *Avena* test upon polar transport of auxins, they can be used to test the growth regulator activity of compounds without interference from transport characteristics.

Buffers and salts can be used as variables in the straight-growth tests. The same cannot be said for the slit pea test. It will be recalled that very small changes in pH can considerably alter the initial negative curvature of the slit pea test. Consequently, for tests in which the pH is to be varied the straight-growth test is more desirable. Studies requiring the addition of accessory substances affecting growth, such as inhibitors or organic nutrients, are most often carried out with straight-growth tests.

The addition of sugar generally inhibits growth in the pea straight-growth test. Apparently a sufficient supply of sugars and fats is contained within the pea stem so that increases in growth are not obtained by adding more sugars. This is not true of *Avena* coleoptile sections, nor apparently is it true of pea sections taken from completely etiolated plants. Galston and Hand (1949) have shown quantitative growth increases of almost completely etiolated pea sections upon the addition of sugar. Christiansen and Thimann (1950), using peas which were exposed to occasional red light, found no promotion of growth by the addition of sugar. Such differences in response to the addition of sugar can be brought about either by differences in light treatment or in temperature experience (Leopold, unpublished).

It should be pointed out that completely etiolated peas cannot be used in the slit pea test, but they are perfectly acceptable material for the pea straight-growth test. Large differences in growth patterns over the length of the pea stems result from the presence or absence of small quantities of red light during the growth of the seedlings. The growth pattern for various parts of a completely etiolated pea shows a faster growth rate in the younger sections and continued growth in the older sections of the stem. The growth pattern of peas exposed to red light, however, shows a rapid decline in growth as the distance from the leaf node increases, indicating clearly the importance of uniformity of the place from which the sections are taken. Such growth patterns are shown in figure 19.

A modification of the *Avena* straight-growth test has been employed by Hancock and Barlow (1952) in assaying auxins which have been separated by paper chromatography. The technique is very effective. The concentration by paper chromatography of the auxins in plant extracts makes the straight-growth test sensitivity adequate for measuring the auxin present.

The advantages of these straight-growth tests are essentially the same as those of the slit pea test. An additional advantage is the fact that accessory substances can be used without extreme sensitivity to small pH changes. The disadvantages of the straight-growth tests are likewise the same as those listed for the slit pea test, except that the *Avena* straight-growth test is not as sensitive to metallic ions as is the pea test.

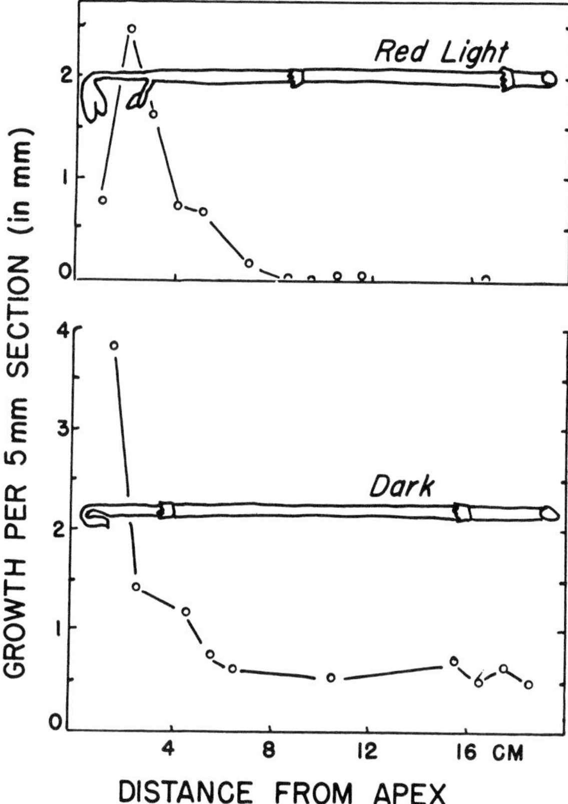

Fig. 19. The comparative growth of pea stem sections from various parts of pea plants grown in the presence of intermittent red light and in complete darkness (Leopold and Guernsey, unpublished).

Pea Root Test

The physiological basis for the pea root test is essentially the same as for the other straight-growth tests. It is a measure of simple growth and does not depend upon the polar transport of auxins. The meristematic tip of the root is included in the test material and consequently the growth obtained is a result of cellular elongation and cell division. That the root is an organ of extreme sensitivity to auxins has been recognized for many years (Fiedler, 1936). Most roots respond to applied auxins by inhibitions of linear growth only; however, the use of pea roots under the conditions specified for this test yields good quantitative promotions of growth with very low auxin concentrations (Leopold and Guernsey, 1953).

It should be pointed out that the promotion of growth by auxin does not necessarily involve the same growth characteristics as does the inhibition of growth. Therefore, measurements of auxin activity using root inhibition tests such as those described in the next section are all subject to some criticism in that they do not necessarily measure the same characteristic of auxins as do tests involving growth promotion.

A small amount of calcium is essential for normal root growth (Mevius, 1927), and this ion plus sugar and a buffer are included in the test solution. The capacity of roots to respond positively to auxin disappears 12 hours after cutting and consequently it is important to begin the test promptly after cutting.

PROCEDURE FOR THE PEA ROOT TEST

Planting

Place seeds of Alaska pea or other pea strain between wet towels in the darkroom (25° C).

Cutting

Three to 4 days after planting cut uniform lengths of root tip (5 to 10 mm. long). Roots should be carefully selected for straight, thin, uniform appearance. Place directly into solutions. Add 10 to 20 sections per dish.

Solutions

The use of 10 ml. of solution per Petri dish keeps all sections at the surface. All solutions contain 0.0025 M $CaSO_4$ and 1% sucrose, and, if desired, McIlvaine's buffer diluted 1:10 at pH 5.0.

Measure

Measure after 24 hours.

As in the previous tests, results are expressed as the mean per treatment plus or minus the Standard Error. A Standard Error of less than 3 per cent of maximal growth should be obtained where 10 sections per dish are used. This is a considerably smaller Standard Error than is usually found in the other straight-growth tests.

The growth obtained is approximately proportional to the logarithm of the concentration of auxin. The minimum concentration of indoleacetic acid detectable is 10^{-11} M or about 0.000,001 mg./l. This is a sensitivity 10,000 times greater than the other straight-growth tests. Optimum growth is usually obtained at about 10^{-7} M indoleacetic acid. At higher concentrations, the roots are inhibited. A sample concentration curve is shown in figure 20.

The ability of the roots to respond positively to auxin varies considerably between different lots of seed, even of the same strain. The effective use of the pea root test is dependent upon finding seeds of appropriate sensitivity to auxin.

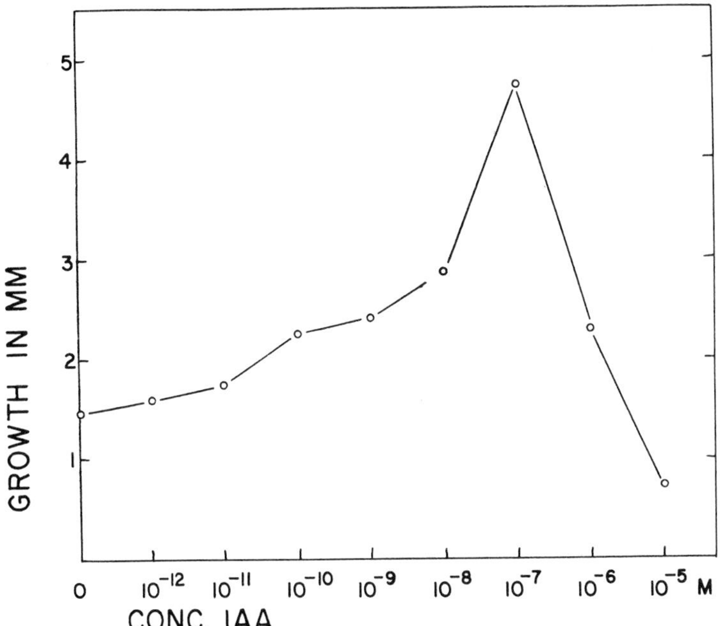

Fig. 20. Sample results of a pea root test showing the semi-logarithmic proportionality of growth to the concentration of auxin, indoleacetic acid (Leopold and Guernsey, 1953).

The pea root test has the same advantages and disadvantages as those enumerated for the other straight-growth tests, but because of the much greater sensitivity this test is usable as an assay of plant extracts (Leopold and Guernsey, 1953). It has also been used for detection of auxins separated by paper chromatography (Audus and Thresh, 1953).

Root Inhibition Tests

A great many tests have been established for auxin using inhibitions of root growth as the assay method. The first quantitative test of this sort was established by Swanson (1946) and most of the tests described subsequently are near adaptations of his technique, generally using other species of plants. Among these could be mentioned Ready and Grant (1947), Moewus (1949), Åberg (1950), Leaper and Bishop (1950) and Audus (1951). An elegant technique has been used by Burström (1950) in which the primary modification has been the use of a constantly flowing test solution. For simplicity Swanson's technique will be described here.

The physiological basis of the root inhibition tests is the inhibition of growth of most roots by very low auxin concentrations. Most roots have an extremely low auxin requirement for optimal growth (Fiedler, 1936), and consequently most roots will respond to added auxins by growth inhibition.

PROCEDURE FOR THE ROOT INHIBITION TEST

1. Sterilize seeds of Silver King corn in hypochlorite.
2. Germinate on moist filter paper, embryo side down.
3. After 48 hours select seedlings with roots 15 to 25 mm. long; measure, and place in Petri dish containing 15 ml. of test solution.
4. Measure growth after 48 hours.

This test has been used successfully to assay for auxins in soil leachings, and filtrates from various biological materials. It is sensitive to

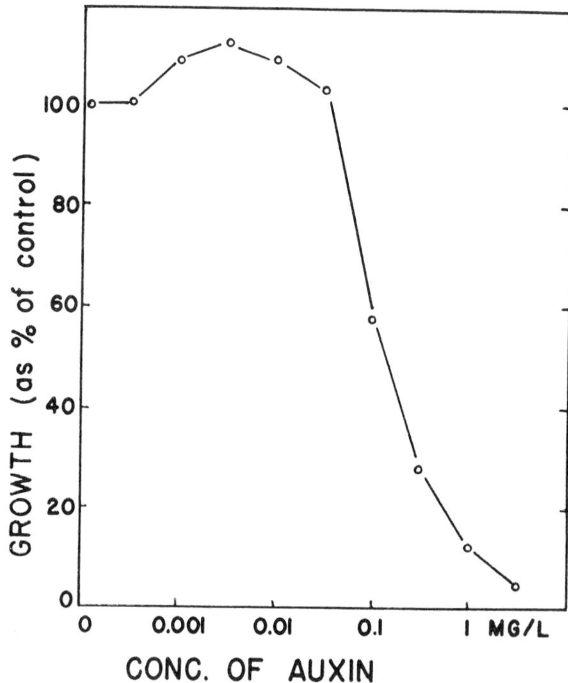

Fig. 21. Results of a cress root inhibition test (Moewus *et al*, 1952).

2,4-D concentrations ranging from 10^{-8} to 10^{-6} M. This is approximately 0.002 to 0.2 mg./liter. The procedure of Moewus for cress roots is much more sensitive, having an effective range from 10^{-10} to 10^{-7} M of indoleacetic acid.

It should be pointed out that this test is not specific for auxins, and other compounds in a test solution which may inhibit root growth can influence the results obtained. However, if the experiment is carried out with sufficient controls, this defect should not be serious. It is a very valuable technique for field herbicide studies and it is so accurate quantitatively that it has provided an excellent technique for studying inhibition effects on root growth.

A particularly effective modification of the test has been developed by Audus (1951). This involves placing cress seedlings on the rim of a cylinder of filter paper in a glass tube containing the solution for testing. Consistently straight roots can be obtained, and measurements can be made at intervals through the glass without disturbing the test plants.

A concentration curve for a root inhibition test is given in figure 21.

Leaf Repression Test

A method of comparing growth regulator activity by using a leaf repression technique was described by Thompson *et al* (1946), but it remained for Rice (1948) and Brown and Weintraub (1950) to establish this method as a quantitative assay. The test has generally been used as a means of comparing activity of chemicals such as potential herbicides, but it has also been used as an assay for 2,4-D penetration into plants (Rice, 1948).

The basis for such a test lies in the capacity of auxins to inhibit leaf enlargement. It should be pointed out, of course, that inhibition of leaf enlargement is a characteristic not confined to auxins alone and consequently it should be remembered in describing results of such a test that auxin activity in the strict sense is not necessarily being measured.

The technique of Brown and Weintraub will be described here because of its slightly greater simplicity and quantitative accuracy.

PROCEDURE FOR THE LEAF REPRESSION TEST

Plant material

Seedlings of garden bean are grown in the greenhouse until the first trifoliate leaf is beginning to enlarge and the internode below it is 3 to 7 mm. long. Black

Valentine beans are recommended as the most sensitive variety and red kidney beans as a somewhat less sensitive alternative.

Application

Solutions to be tested are made up in 95% ethyl alcohol containing 1% Tween 20 or other detergent. Pipette 0.005 ml. of each solution on each of 10 to 20 expanding trifoliate leaves.

Reading

After 5 to 13 days remove the expanded trifoliate leaves and compare on either a weight or leaf area basis.

This leaf repression method is an effective test for solutions of 2,4-D ranging from 1 to 100 mg./liter. Each plant receives from 0.005 to 0.5 micrograms of auxin. Comparisons of leaf area give results with slightly greater sensitivity than comparisons of weight differences;

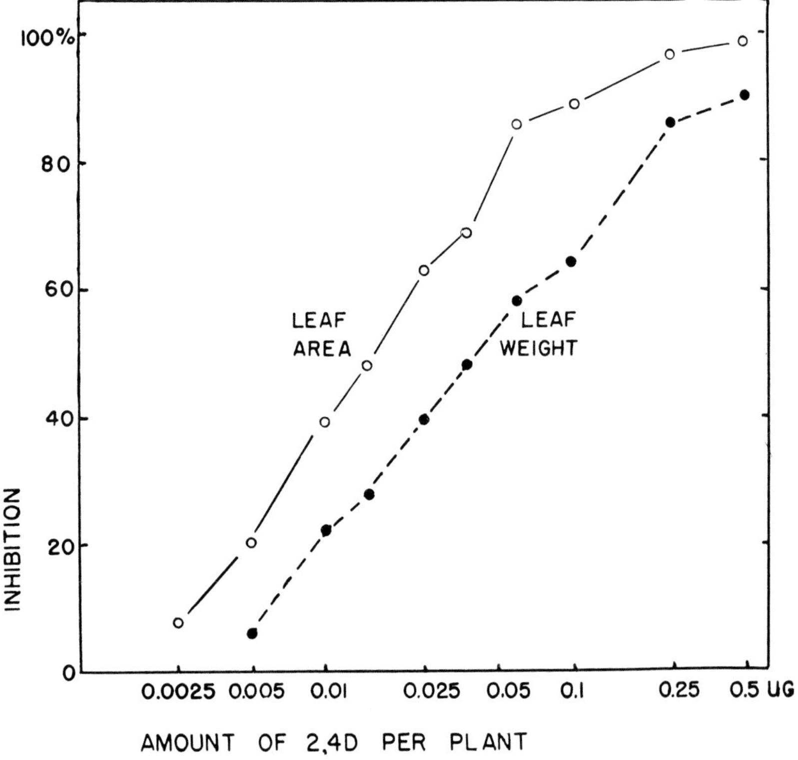

Fig. 22. Results of a leaf repression test showing the semi-logarithmic inhibition of leaf area and leaf weight at varying concentrations of auxin, 2,4-dichlorophenoxyacetic acid (Brown and Weintraub, 1950).

however, the simplicity of weight determinations would appear to make this a generally more feasible method.

A concentration curve obtained from a leaf repression test is shown in figure 22. Both leaf area and weight responses are included for comparison.

The leaf repression test is valuable as an easy test for which no environmental controls are necessary. Its limitations are a low sensitivity and a lack of specificity for auxins. These limitations, however, are negligible when it is used for herbicide studies. The technique is so simple and convenient that it affords a valuable means of comparing such substances as potential herbicidal materials.

The Tomato Ovary Test

A well-known property of auxins is the capacity to set parthenocarpic fruit, particularly in the tomato. The utilization of this property as an assay method has been worked out by Luckwill (1948). The method has not been standardized for auxins other than β-naphthoxyacetic acid (BNOA) but shows considerable promise as an assay technique.

PROCEDURE FOR THE TOMATO OVARY TEST

Plant material

Tomato plants are grown to the stage where the first two clusters each have two nearly opened flowers. Flowers are emasculated 1 to 2 days before opening and the corolla and style are removed. All other flowers are removed from the flower cluster. The use of male-sterile strains of tomato relieves the necessity for emasculation.

Application

Solutions to be tested are applied with a 1 ml. hypodermic syringe, using 0.0225 ml. per flower.

Reading

Ovary diameters are measured after 6 days.

The growth of the ovary is proportional to the logarithm of the concentration of the growth regulator within the limits of 0.1 to 10 micrograms per flower. This range represents a concentration in the stock solutions of 1 to 100 mg./liter of BNOA. A sample dilution curve is shown in figure 23.

It is well known that the capacity to set fruit is not limited to auxins alone. For example, substances such as colchicine and fluoreneacetic acid which apparently show no auxin activity in growth tests are effective fruit-setting agents (Avery and Johnson, 1947, p. 175). Therefore, this test is not specific for auxins but may be very useful in comparing potential fruit-setting agents. It has been used as a growth hormone assay (Luckwill, 1948).

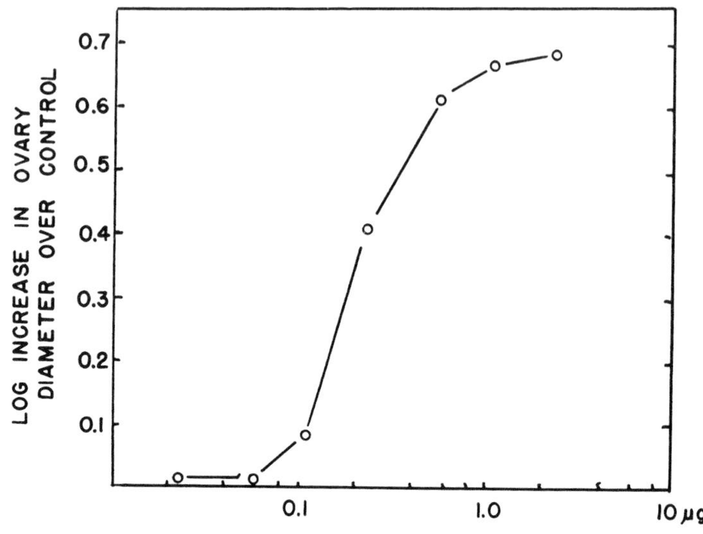

Fig. 23. Results of a tomato ovary test showing a quantitative increase in ovary size as a function of concentration of beta-naphthoxyacetic acid (Luckwill, 1948).

Other Tests

A simple method for measuring auxins by means of lanolin paste preparations smeared onto one side of a seedling was first described by Laibach (1934). A simple version of the test has been used by Wittwer (1943). An auxin preparation or plant extract is prepared in pure lanolin, and a small dab applied to one side of the hypocotyls of young bean seedlings. Three hours after the paste has been applied the negative curvature of the stem is read with a simple protractor. The test is sensitive to a range of concentrations from 0.1 to 1000 mg./liter of indoleacetic acid. This test is extremely convenient and sufficiently accurate for many studies.

Another method of measuring the growth-promoting properties of auxins has been established using the hypocotyls of decapitated bean seedlings (Weintraub *et al,* 1951). To each hypocotyl is applied about 0.001 ml. of an auxin solution in alcohol. The curvature obtained is proportional to the logarithm of the concentration of 2,4-D between the limits of about 10 to 60 mg./liter.

An assay for the capacity of substances to produce epinastic responses has been described by Hitchcock (1935). This test is carried out using plants such as the tomato high in epinastic sensitivity. Lanolin pastes containing the substances to be tested are applied to one side of the petiole or sometimes to the whole plant, and arbitrary ratings of the responses are used to estimate the quantitative differences.

Auxins are involved in the movements of leaves, and this property has been used as the basis for an assay technique by Ferri and Camargo (1950).

The capacity of auxins to stimulate root formation has been utilized as an auxin assay (Raalte, 1950). Placing petioles of *Ageratum* in auxin solutions for 24 hours causes the production of roots, the logarithm of the number of which is proportional to the logarithm of the concentration of indoleacetic acid between 10^{-6} and 10^{-4} M or about 0.001 to 0.1 mg./liter.

CHEMICAL AND PHYSICAL ASSAYS

Two color tests for indoleacetic acid were proposed by Mitchell and Brunstetter in 1939, one utilizing a reaction with nitrous acid and the other a reaction with ferric chloride. The nitrite reaction has not found widespread use as a quantitative test, but is a good indicator for use in paper chromatographic separations. The ferric chloride reaction, however, has been developed into a good quantitative assay by Tang and Bonner (1947) and by Gordon and Weber (1951). Each of these workers has described an acid ferric chloride reagent which forms a color complex with indoleacetic acid (IAA). The color is measured quantitatively with a colorimeter. The components of each of the two described reagents are as follows:

Tang and Bonner	*Gordon and Weber*
15 ml. 0.5 M $FeCl_3$	1 ml. 0.5 M $FeCl_3$
300 ml. H_2SO_4 (Sp. gr. 1.84)	50 ml. 35% $HClO_4$
500 ml. H_2O	

These reagents differ only in the selection of mineral acids, and in each case apparently the same color complex with IAA is formed.

The procedures used in each of these techniques are as follows:

Tang and Bonner	*Gordon and Weber*
Take 1 ml. of aqueous IAA sample.	Take 1 ml. of aqueous IAA sample.
Add 4 ml. acid reagent.	Add 2 ml. acid reagent.
Read with colorimeter after 30 min.	Read with colorimeter after 25 min.
(Maximum absorbancy at 525 mμ)	(Maximum absorbancy at 530 mμ)

The range of sensitivity of these tests is from 0.2 to 100 mg./liter of indoleacetic acid. Sample curves for each of these techniques are found in figure 24. The range of sensitivity is too limited to be of use in assaying most plant extracts, but the method is very useful for *in vitro* studies such as the enzymatic inactivation of indoleacetic acid in solutions. The tests are fairly specific for indoleacetic acid, although some color is obtained with indole, skatole, and indolebutyric acid.

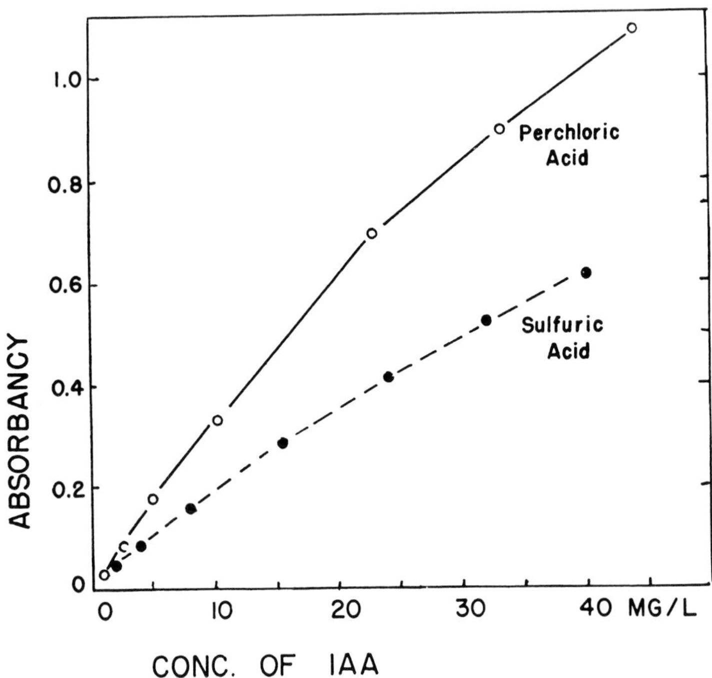

Fig. 24. Results of ferric chloride color tests for indoleacetic acid showing the relative effectiveness of perchloric acid and sulfuric acid as reaction solvents (Gordon and Weber, 1951).

The perchloric acid technique of Gordon and Weber is more specific for indoleacetic acid, is slightly more sensitive, and the color developed is more stable than in the Tang and Bonner technique.

A color test for 2,4-D using chromotropic acid has been suggested by Freed (1948), and this test has been used as a quantitative assay by Marquardt and Luce (1951) and by Stewart *et al* (1952). The method involves taking the 2,4-D up in carbon tetrachloride, evaporating to dryness, and then adding chromotropic acid which develops a purple color with 2,4-D. The test is sensitive to concentrations of

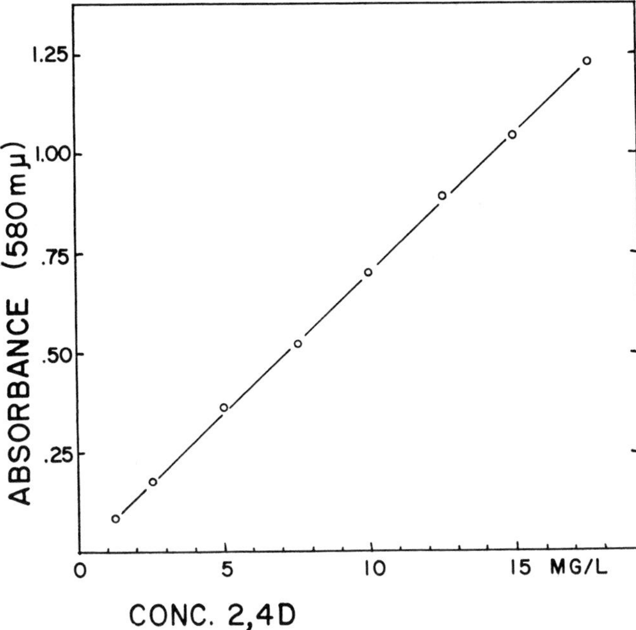

Fig. 25. The chromotropic acid color test for 2,4-D (LeTourneau and Krog, 1952).

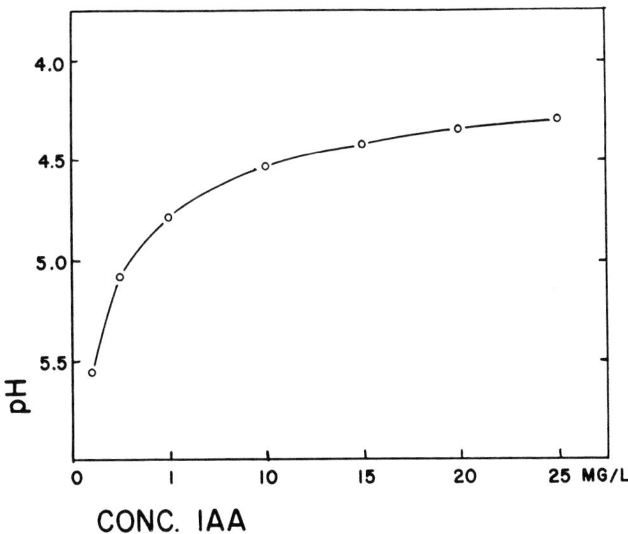

Fig. 26. The relationship between concentration of indoleacetic acid and pH (Brauner, 1953).

2,4-D ranging from 1 to 20 mg./liter, as shown in figure 25. Similar color reactions are obtained with each of the several phenoxyacetic acid derivatives tested (Le Tourneau and Krog, 1952).

A spectrographic technique for measuring phenoxyacetic acid compounds has been worked out by Bandurski (1946). By measuring changes in the absorption characteristics at 325 mμ, changes in 2,4-D content can be followed in clear solutions.

A very simple method of following changes of auxin concentrations in quite pure solutions is by measurement of pH changes (Brauner, 1952). The changes in acidity in relation to concentration of indoleacetic acid (IAA) are shown in figure 26. This method has proved to be effective for following the photo-destruction of auxin *in vitro,* especially when used in conjunction with other tests such as the ferric chloride test for the entire IAA molecule and the Hopkins-Cole test for the indole ring (Brauner 1953).

CHROMATOGRAPHIC SEPARATION OF AUXINS

The recent development of chromatographic techniques for separation and identification of compounds has provided a new and valuable means for separation and identification of growth hormones, their precursors and breakdown products in plants.

The technique of paper chromatography, first introduced by Consden *et al* (1944), has only recently been extensively applied to the investigations of plant growth regulators. This technique utilizes the principle of separation of substances by partition between two liquid phases, one stationary and the other mobile, cellulose acting as an inert support. Different substances move at different rates, depending on their distribution ratios between the solvents, and by this means separation is effected. Though the phenomenon is primarily a case of partition, adsorption has also an important role—a role which becomes a major one in certain cases (Burma, 1953).

Detailed descriptions of the procedures involved in paper chromatography are available in the book by Block *et al* (1952). Comprehensive surveys of the R_f values and color detection methods for indole derivatives and auxins have been carried out by Sen and Leopold (1954), Weller *et al* (1954) and Stowe and Thimann (1954).

Jerchel and Müller (1951) were possibly the first to chromatograph indoleacetic acid on paper. The R_f values (the ratios of the distance moved by a substance to that moved by the solvent front) of indole, indoleacetic acid, isatin and tryptamine were also reported by Berry *et al* (1951). Since then indoleacetic acid and allied substances have been sought for in extracts of plant tissues by Pacheco (1951), von Denffer *et al* (1952) and many others.

When a growth substance extracted from plants is chromatographed for detection and isolation, the R_f values of substances which might appear in the extract must be determined by previous chromatography of the synthetic materials for comparison. In table 1 R_f values of a number of indole compounds and growth regulators are given.

Yamaki and Nakamura (1952) tried a large number of solvents for chromatographic separation of indoleacetic acid—of which 70% eth-

TABLE 1

R_f VALUES OF SOME PLANT GROWTH REGULATORS AND ALLIED COMPOUNDS
(Sen and Leopold, 1954)

Substance	Phenol-water	70% Ethanol	Isopropanol-ammonia-water (10:1:1)	Water
Indole	.92	.86	.99	
Skatole	.98	.88	.98	
Indolealdehyde		.86	.86	.47
Indolecarboxylic acid		.81	.22	.92
Indoleacetic acid	.80	.77	.37	.89
Indoleacetic acid—ethyl ester	.96	.80	.97	.59
Indoleacetaldehyde		.45		
Indolepropionic acid	.82	.91	.44	.85
Indolebutyric acid	.87	.84	.56	.89
Tryptophan		.40	.19	.63
Tryptamine		.71	.75	.28
Indoxylacetate	.96	.89	.88 + 96*	.57
Indoleacetonitrile	.95	.86	.99	.41
Indolebutyronitrile	.80	.88	.95	.54
2,3,5-triiodobenzoic acid	.92		.78	
Phenoxyacetic acid			.67	
o-chlorophenoxyacetic acid			.60	
p-chlorophenoxyacetic acid			.56	
2,4-dichlorophenoxyacetic acid	.83		.67	
2,4,5-trichlorophenoxyacetic acid	.76		.80	
Phenylacetic acid	.83		.51	
α-naphthaleneacetic acid	.93		.58	
β-naphthoxyacetic acid	.90		.61	

* Two spots are obtained.

anol, butanol-acetic acid-water (12:3:2), 70% methanol, phenol saturated with water, and ligroin saturated with water gave clearly defined spots of indoleacetic acid. For separation of indoleacetic acid from indole, indolepropionic acid, indolebutyric acid, indoleacetaldehyde, indoleethylamine or tryptophan the first two were the best. In 70% ethanol, however, most of the compounds have R_fs between .80–.92

TABLE 2

Color Reactions Useful in the Detection of Indole Compounds
(Sen and Leopold, 1954)

Substance	Ultraviolet fluorescence	Color with $FeCl_3$ and $HClO_4$	Color with *p*-dimethyl-aminobenzaldehyde*
Indole	Pale green	Orange red	Light red
Skatole	Light blue	Pinkish dull brown	Blue
Indolealdehyde	Pale yellow	——	Light brown
Indolecarboxylic acid	Blue	Orange	Pink
Indoleacetic acid—ethyl ester	Light blue-green	Pink	Blue
Indoleacetic acid	Faint blue	Pink	Greenish blue
Indolepropionic acid	Light blue	Light brown	Bluish-green
Indolebutyric acid	Light blue	Brown	Bluish-green
Indoleacetonitrile	Green-blue	Green	Yellow
Indolebutyronitrile	Violet	Orange-brown	Light brown with blue halo
Tryptophan	Yellowish-green †	Light brown	Yellow
Tryptamine	——	Dull brown	Green
Isatin	Brown	——	Yellow
N-acetyl indoxyl	Blue	Light brown	Orange

* Color on standing for 24 hours.
† After treatment with $HClO_4$ (Tauber, 1948).

and it is therefore not the ideal solvent. The separation is much better with isopropanol-ammonia-water. This solvent has been used in different proportions by many workers, e.g., 16:3:1 (von Denffer *et al,* 1952) or 10:1:1 (Bennet-Clark *et al,* 1952). Isopropanol may be replaced by butanol (Luckwill, 1952; Bennet-Clark *et al,* 1952) or the ammonia may be placed at the base of the tank without being a component of the developing solvent.

Although the indole-aliphatic acids are separable with comparative ease, most of the neutral compounds have R_fs between .80–1.00

in most of the organic solvents. Of a large number of solvents tried pure water was found to be the most suitable for such neutral compounds. In water the R_f values of most of the compounds which travel fast with the organic solvents are reduced while the aliphatic acids of indole travel faster. Thus water paired with any of the suitable solvents mentioned above may be utilized with good success in two dimensional chromatography of these indole compounds.

After chromatographic separation of growth substances of the indole group, perhaps the simplest means of detecting and identifying the spots is by their fluorescence characteristics in ultra-violet light. This method was first used by Pacheco (1951) and by Jerchel and Müller (1951) for detecting and identifying indoleacetic acid. The method has subsequently been extended for use with many indole derivatives, as shown in table 2.

The indole derivatives can also be detected on the paper by spraying with a solution of 50 parts of 5% $HClO_4$ and 1 part of 0.5 M $FeCl_3$ (Pacheco, 1951; Bennet-Clark *et al,* 1952). Most of the indole compounds give pink, orange, brown or blue colorations with this reagent on heating (table 2).

A 2 per cent solution of *p*-dimethylaminobenzaldehyde in 1.2 N HCl (Berry *et al,* 1951; Pacheco, 1951) is also a very good indicator, and the indole compounds show diverse colors after 24 hours. The paper, however, becomes brittle after spraying with the HCl.

Another color test for detecting indole compounds on paper is the nitrous acid test. The paper is sprayed with a solution of KNO_2 (1 g.), HNO_3 (20 ml.) and 95% ethanol (80 ml.), which gives a red color with indoleacetic acid and a yellow color with indolealdehyde (von Denffer and Fischer, 1952).

Instead of using color tests, bioassays for growth-promoting and for growth-inhibiting substances can be used. A variety of growth tests have been used for this purpose, including the cress root test (Bennet-Clark *et al,* 1952), the *Avena* straight-growth test (Hancock and Barlow, 1953) and the pea root test (Audus and Thresh, 1953). The plant material may be placed directly on the moistened chromatogram or the spots may be eluted into a small volume of water and the growth test carried out in the solution.

Indoleacetic acid may be estimated by eluting the appropriate part of the chromatogram with water and measuring the absorption spectrum of the eluate at 280 mμ. (Jerchel and Müller, 1951) or at other suitable wavelengths depending on the color produced by the reagent sprayed. A rough quantitative estimation of a substance can be made from a measurement of the area of the spot, the logarithms of which are proportional to the concentrations within limits (Bennet-Clark *et al,* 1952).

Several other types of techniques have been used for the separation and identification of plant growth hormones and growth inhibitors. Column chromatography has been successfully used in some instances (Bein *et al,* 1947; Linser, 1951). Countercurrent distribution apparatus has been employed for the separation of the auxins in cabbage (Holley *et al,* 1951). Von Denffer *et al* (1952) have used paper electrophoresis for separation of the end products of auxin destruction as well as for identification of the native auxins in cabbage and Brussels sprouts in conjunction with column chromatography and ordinary paper chromatographic methods. Ion-exchange resins, which have been used successfully in the separation and quantitative estimation of amino acids and other compounds, may also be employed for plant growth regulators though they have not been applied as yet for the purpose.

MOLECULAR WEIGHT DETERMINATIONS

Determination of the molecular weight of an auxin can sometimes be very helpful either in identifying the auxin or in establishing changes in molecular size resulting from biological reactions. The method has been described in detail by Larsen (1944) and a clear presentation of its utilization is given by Kramer and Went (1949).

The method generally used in determining molecular weights of auxins is based on the determination of the rate of diffusion of the substance in agar (as the diffusion coefficient), which value is inversely proportional to the molecular weight under certain specific conditions.

PROCEDURE FOR MOLECULAR WEIGHT DETERMINATIONS

1. Blocks or discs of 1.5% agar containing the auxin are made up so that the final thickness is uniform. A convenient method is to pipette 0.5 ml. of agar into a circular mold 10.6 mm. in diameter, making the final thickness 1.42 mm.
2. One block containing auxin is placed upon a pile of 3 plain agar blocks of identical shape.
3. Diffusion is permitted to continue for 1.5 hours at 26° C in a moist atmosphere.
4. The blocks are then separated and the content of auxin in each block is assayed by the *Avena* test, the ferric chloride test, or other assay.

The distribution of the auxin in each of the four blocks is then converted into a percentage of the total auxin. For each block, an "*x*" value is obtained from the tables of Kawalki, reproduced graphically

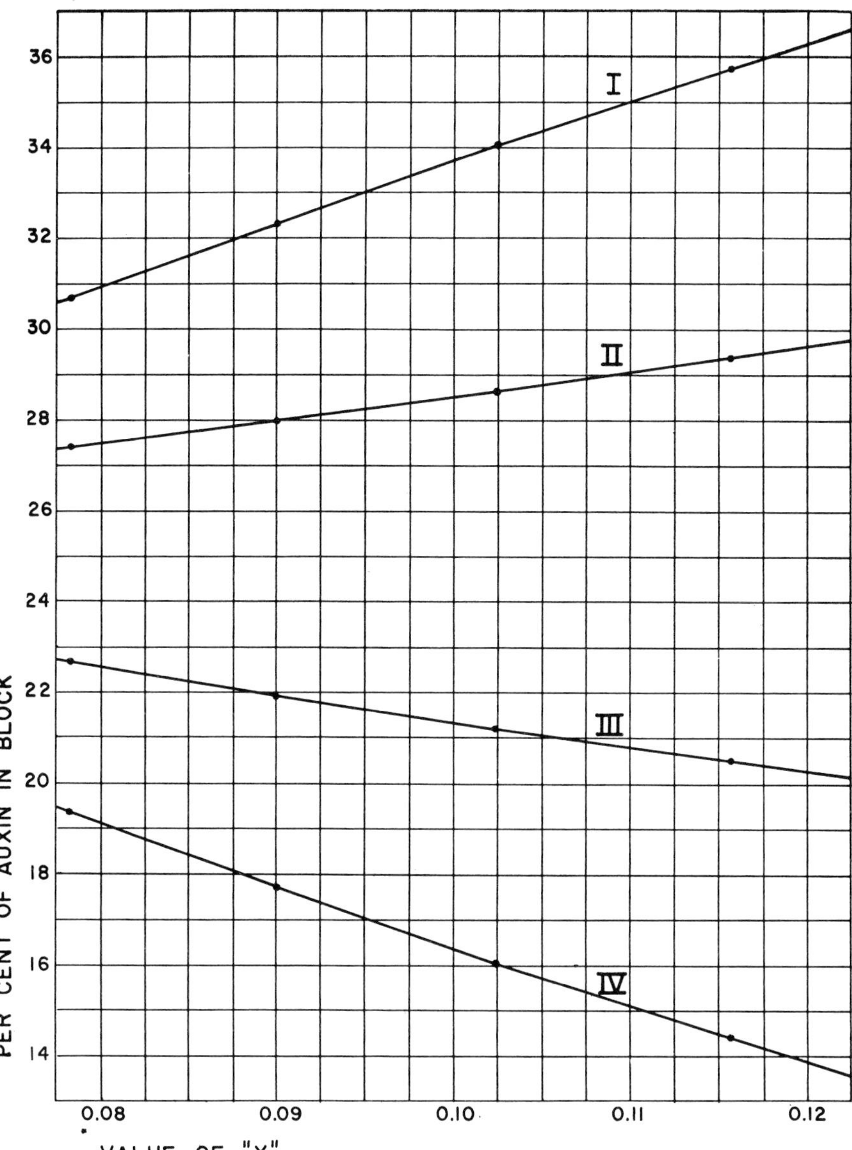

Fig. 27. A graphic plot of the probability integral for use in determining the coefficient of diffusion (Kawalki, 1894).

in figure 27. For example, if in the top block (the donor block) one found 32 per cent of the auxin after the diffusion period, the x value for that block would be 0.088, as derived in figure 27. The x values obtained in this way for each of the four blocks are then averaged together, and the mean x value is used to solve for the coefficient of diffusion (D) in the following formula:

$$D = \frac{h^2}{4xt} \qquad (1)$$

where h is the thickness of the block in cm. (0.142 cm.), and t is the time of diffusion in days (1.5/24 or 0.0625 days). The value of D varies with temperature, so the temperature should be kept constant during the diffusion time. Knowing D at a given temperature, the molecular weight (M) can be approximated by the formula:

$$M = \left(\frac{k}{D}\right)^2 \qquad (2)$$

where k is a constant for the temperature. When diffusion is carried on at 26° C, $k = 8.8$ (Kramer and Went, 1949). It is best to calculate k under the actual experimental conditions by determining D for an auxin of known molecular weight, and then solving the second formula for k. Using the experimentally determined k, the formula (2) can be solved for the molecular weight of the unknown auxin.

A sample determination of molecular weight may serve to illustrate the method. Using agar blocks of 0.127 cm. thickness, an auxin

TABLE 3

SAMPLE DATA FOR DETERMINATION OF MOLECULAR WEIGHT BY THE DIFFUSION METHOD
(Curvature data from Kramer and Went, 1949)

Block No.	Avena test curvature	Distribution	"x" value
	°	%	
1	5.64	33.4	.097
2	4.75	28.1	.091
3	3.58	21.2	.104
4	2.92	17.3	.094
Total	16.89	100.0	.386

Conditions:

Block thickness	.127 cm.
Time of diffusion	1.5 hours
Temperature	26° C

preparation was diffused for 1.5 hours and then assayed for the activity in each block as shown in table 3. Block #1, which originally contained all of the auxin, contained 33.4 per cent of it after the diffusion time. An x value for 33.4 per cent can be taken from the graphic form of Kawalki's table given in figure 27. The x value is found to be 0.097. Block #2, which contained 28.1 per cent of the auxin, has an x value of 0.091. Similar values are established for each of the other blocks, and their sum is taken to be $4x$, one of the values needed for solution of formula (1). Solving the formula for D, one obtains:

$$D = \frac{h^2}{4xt} = \frac{(.127)^2}{(.386)\left(\frac{1.5}{24}\right)} = 0.667$$

For the purpose of this example, we will take the value of k in formula (2) to be 8.8. We can now solve for the molecular weight as follows:

$$M = \left(\frac{k}{D}\right)^2 = \left(\frac{8.8}{.667}\right)^2 = 174.$$

It would appear that the auxin being tested was indoleacetic acid, which has a molecular weight of 175.

This technique can be very useful in obtaining evidence of the identity of an auxin or for determining whether chemical reactions altering auxins have occurred. However one should be always aware that the coefficient of diffusion obtained in this way will be greatly altered by the acidity of the agar, the concentration of the auxin, and the presence of electrolytes. Also the assay of the agar blocks may be misleading because of the presence of mixtures of different auxins and of auxins and inhibitors. Some of these variables may account for the conflicting results obtained by physiologists in the past. For more precise determinations of molecular weight, a description of methods in *The Enzymes* (Sumner and Myrbäck, 1952, vol. 1, p. 29) may be useful.

SUMMARY

The extraction method and the auxin assay method used for any given study should be selected to yield sufficient accuracy to solve the problem involved with the greatest convenience. To assist in selecting the test to be used, table 4 presents a comparison of several auxin assay methods in their approximate order of sensitivity. It should be pointed out that the *Avena* test permits the best quantitative accuracy for establishing small differences in auxin content. The pea root test is sensitive to the smallest quantities of auxin. All of these tests except the *Avena* test and the ferric chloride test respond to differences in auxin concentration in a semi-logarithmic function. Thus the *Avena* test and the ferric chloride test are most effective in measuring small differences, while the other tests permit measurements over a greater range of auxin concentrations.

TABLE 4

RELATIVE SENSITIVITIES OF SOME AUXIN TESTS

Test	Sensitivity range (micrograms of IAA required for 10 readings)	Sensitivity range	Environmental controls needed
		(mg./l. of IAA)	
Pea Root	.00001–.1	.000001–.01	Light, temp.
Root Inhibition	.0001–1.0	.00001–.1	Light, temp.
Avena	.00026–.0026	.02–.2	Light, temp., humidity
Slit Pea	.25–250	.01–10.0	Light, temp.
Pea and Avena Straight-Growth	.1–100	.01–10	Light, temp.
Green Bean Stem	.001–10	.1–1000	——
Leaf Repression	.005–.5 *	1–100 *	——
Tomato Ovary	1–100 †	1–100 †	——
Ferric Chloride	20–500	2–50	——

* 2,4-D.
† Beta-naphthoxyacetic acid.

In selecting a test, care must be taken to choose one which will yield the type of information desired. For example, if one is seeking to measure auxin activity, in the strictest sense, a test which is specific for auxin activity must be selected, such as the various straight-growth and curvature tests. If a measure of epinastic activity is being sought, such tests as the leaf repression test are best. If the capacity of a given substance to set fruit is being measured, the tomato ovary test is very desirable and the *Avena* test might be quite misleading.

In many cases a test is needed to determine whether a given compound exhibits auxin activity. In order to establish the existence of such activity, it is important that *auxin-free* material be used, because non-auxins having competitive effects with auxin will promote growth if added to plant material in the presence of a true auxin. For such determinations, it is desirable to use a slit pea test or one of the straight-growth tests with a 4 hour wash period before the test has begun. Unfortunately there are a good many papers in the literature which demonstrate apparent auxin activity for compounds which are not auxins at all, the tests having been carried out in the presence of some indigenous auxin. This type of error has led to some highly erroneous conclusions.

Lack of activity in the *Avena* test does not conclusively demonstrate the absence of auxin activity. Substances, such as phenylacetic acid, which are not effectively transported in the coleoptile and hence fail to produce curvature may show auxin activity in the straight-growth tests.

In conclusion it should be reiterated that there is such a wide variety of tests for auxins, some of them so extremely easy and others so extremely sensitive, that one should not have to omit auxin assays from any study where such data are needed.

CHAPTER III

The Occurrence and Role of Growth Hormones in Plants

From the experiments on phototropism by Darwin and later workers it is evident that, at least in the seedlings with which they were working, the apex was the primary source of auxin. Removal of the coleoptile apex deprived the coleoptile of its auxin source until regeneration of the physiological tip. Among plants in general, apices are perhaps the greatest source of free auxin in the plant. The apices are usually associated with meristems, of course, and the apical meristems of shoots, roots, and buds are rich sources of auxin when growth is taking place. Other meristems besides apical ones are also sources of auxin, as for example the meristems in cambium, seeds, and intercalary meristems at the nodes of grasses. Besides meristems, enlarging organs are another auxin source. Enlarging leaves, flowers, fruits, nodules and tumors all have been shown to produce large amounts of auxin. In addition to meristems and enlarging tissues, at least one mature type of organ provides an auxin source to the plant, and that is the mature leaf.

In general it appears that where there is active growth there is auxin production. Growing meristems and enlarging organs of vascular plants have invariably been found to produce auxins. The formation of auxins by a mature organ such as a leaf, however, suggests that growth may not be a prerequisite to auxin production, for leaves produce sizeable quantities of auxin over a considerable length of time during which there is very little growth in size.

DISTRIBUTION OF AUXINS

The distribution of auxins over entire plants has been studied in several instances and suggests a general pattern of quantitative auxin relationships within plants. An example of such a distribution study is that of the etiolated *Avena* seedling carried out by Thimann (1934). Using a solvent extraction technique, he demonstrated an auxin gradient through the plant with by far the highest concentration occurring at the coleoptile tip and a lesser concentration at the root tip. A sagging gradient was found to lie between these two peaks (figure 28). It is evident that the coleoptile apex and the root apex are the two primary loci of auxin formation in the etiolated oat seedling and that the root apex is much less active in this respect than the coleoptile.

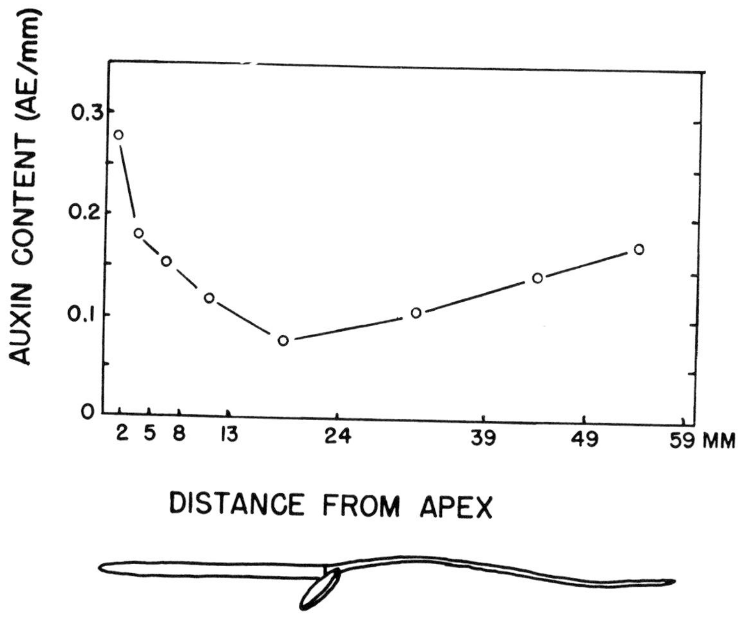

Fig. 28. Distribution of auxin in an etiolated *Avena* seedling (Thimann, 1934).

Another survey of auxin distribution through a plant was an examination of *Vicia faba* seedlings grown in normal lighted conditions (Thimann and Skoog, 1934). In this instance, the lateral buds and leaves and the apical bud were analyzed. Small amounts of auxin were found in all lateral buds and leaves, with the young expanding leaves containing most of the substance. The apical bud, however, yielded almost six times as much auxin as the most productive leaves (figure 29). These data provide a revealing instance of the relative productivity of the growing apex as an auxin source.

As pointed out in the preceding chapter, auxins exist in plants in more than one form. We speak of "free" auxin as being that readily available by diffusion or rapid extraction and "bound" auxin as that obtained only after enzymatic activity, gentle hydrolysis or prolonged extraction. Van Overbeek *et al* (1947) surveyed the distribution of these two types of auxin in the pineapple plant. Using their ether extraction technique, they plotted the flush of auxin obtained in the first hour of extraction as free auxin and that obtained after a passage of time as bound auxin. This distinction appears to be entirely justi-

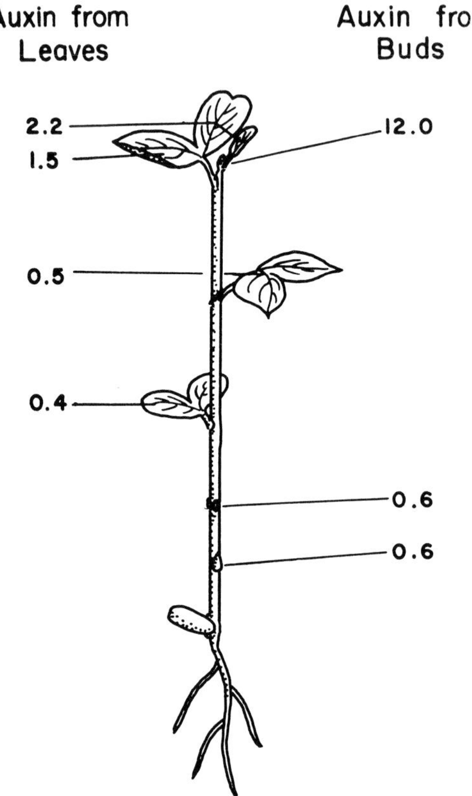

Fig. 29. The auxin content of leaves and buds of a seedling of *Vicia fava*. The figures represent *Avena* Einheits of diffusible auxin per hour (Thimann and Skoog, 1934).

fied in view of evidence presented in their paper. In general it appeared that free auxin occurred most abundantly at the stem apex. Leaves, whether expanding or mature, yielded only small amounts. In contrast, bound auxin was most abundant in the young expanding leaves, and relatively scarce in the stem apex (figure 30). If the stem apex is unable to produce the large amounts of free auxin which apparently exist there (that is, they do not have the bound form from which to produce free auxin), then it would seem likely that the adjoining young leaves, rich in bound auxin, may be the primary source of the free auxin which appears at the stem apex.

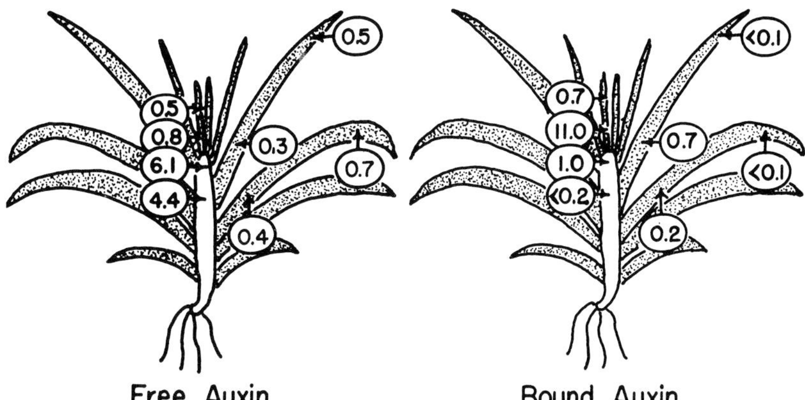

Fig. 30. Diagram of the distribution of free and bound auxin in the vegetative pineapple plant. Figures represent microgram equivalents of indoleacetic acid per kg. fresh weight (van Overbeek *et al,* 1947).

Surveys of auxin distributions in other plants have been made and the highest auxin concentrations found in some of these are listed in table 5. It seems evident that the greatest quantities of auxin charac-

TABLE 5

Some Examples of Auxin Concentrations Found in Plants

Species	Greatest conc. found (μg IAA equivalents/kg. fr. wt.)	Organ or tissue	Reference
Corn	105,000	endosperm	Berger & Avery, 1944
	14,800	whole kernel	Haagen-Smit *et al*, 1946
Lily (white trumpet)	83,900	stem tip	Stewart & Stuart, 1942
Wheat	22,000	endosperm	Haagen-Smit *et al*, 1942
	170	endosperm	Avery *et al*, 1941
Oat	1,000	grain	Avery *et al*, 1941
Rice	250	endosperm	Avery *et al*, 1941
Turnip	250	seed	Avery *et al*, 1941
Sunflower	74	stem	Henderson & Bonner, 1952
Beet	50	seed	Avery *et al*, 1941
Pineapple	11	young leaf	van Overbeek *et al*, 1947
Bean	8	young leaf	Shoji *et al*, 1951
Macrocystis pyrifera	0.5	terminal blade	van Overbeek, 1940

teristically exist in seeds or structures which are part of seeds, in stem tips, and in young expanding leaves.

CORRELATION WITH GROWTH

Many examples of a strong correlation between auxin content and growth have been demonstrated. A particularly graphic correlation of this sort was shown by Went and Thimann (1937, p. 59). They found that a similar rise in diffusible auxin available from the coleoptile tip was associated with the rise in growth rate of *Avena* coleoptiles (figure 31). As the cells of the coleoptile approach maturation and

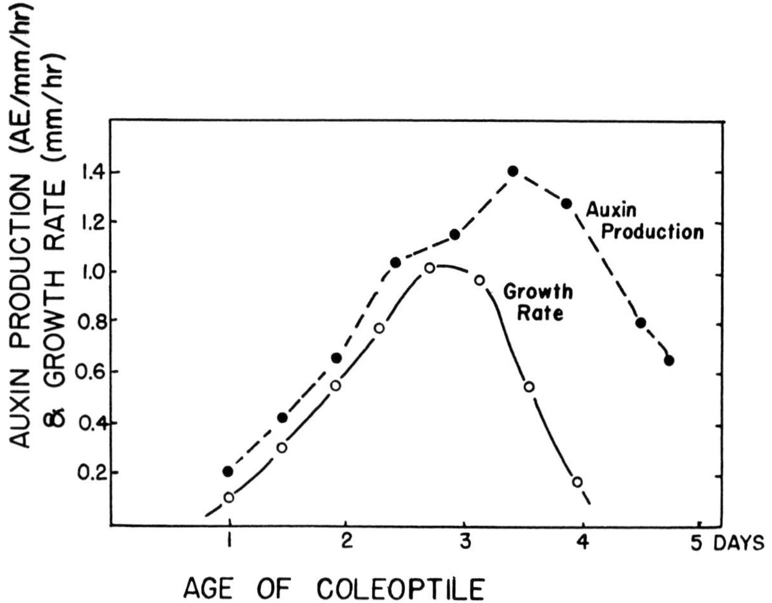

Fig. 31. The proportionality between auxin production and growth rate in *Avena* coleoptiles of various ages (Went and Thimann, 1937, p. 59).

are no longer capable of responding to growth stimuli, the growth rate of the coleoptile falls off rapidly to zero. At the same time the auxin production does not decrease, but an additional supply is produced over a short subsequent period. The close correlation between growth rate and auxin production is thus obtained as long as the capacity for growth persists, and after that time the correlation is not to be expected.

In several instances the commencement of growth has been correlated with the appearance of free auxin. Almost universally there appears to be very little free auxin in dormant meristematic tissues. Until shortly before growth commences dormant tree buds, seeds, and tubers contain little or no identifiable free auxin. Then, as tree buds begin to grow in the spring, a flush of auxin is produced (e.g. Avery *et al,* 1937). When seeds are soaked for germination, the auxin produced is so abundant that large amounts actually appear in the soak solution. It will be remembered that in the procedure for the *Avena*

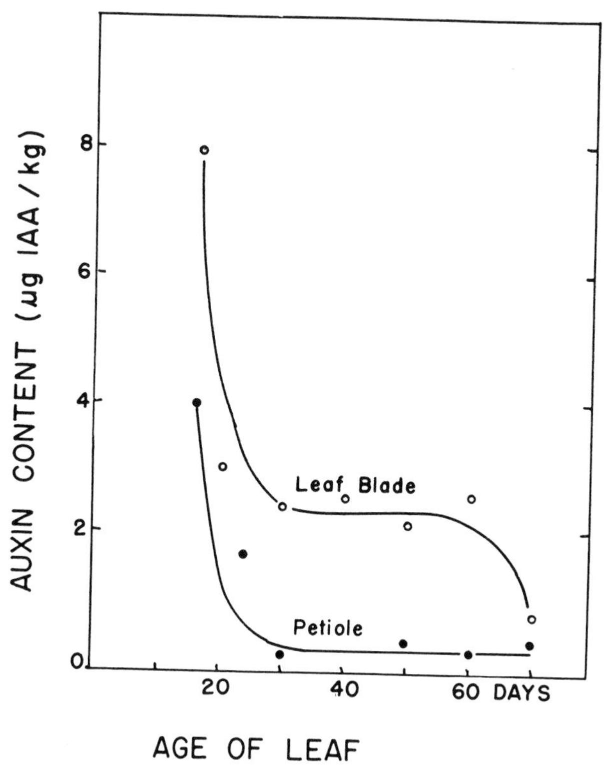

Fig. 32. Changes in ether-extractable auxin content of bean leaves and petioles with age (Shoji *et al,* 1951).

test (chapter II) it is imperative to discard the solution in which the *Avena* seeds were soaked. If the seed is left in the solution rich in auxin from the germinating seed, growth—particularly of the roots—will be inhibited. Again, when potato tubers emerge from dormancy, free auxin becomes detectable in the buds shortly before growth commences (Hemberg, 1947).

The production of auxin by leaves correlates with growth up to the time that maturity is reached. For example, in figure 32 the diffusible auxin of young bean leaves is very high indeed until they reach the age of twenty days, when growth is essentially complete. The production of fairly constant amounts of auxin over the following two months' period demonstrates a possible exception to the correlation of auxin production with growth rate.

All leaves do not show the same picture of auxin production as seen in bean leaves. While coleus, aster, bean and goldenrod seem to follow such a pattern, auxins have not been found in expanding leaves of the ginkgo (Gunckel and Thimann, 1949). It is not clear if the failure to find the usual pattern of auxin production is due to the presence of growth inhibitors in the leaf which interfere with auxin assays.

There is evidence that the apex of the woody plant loses its role as the primary auxin source shortly after twig elongation begins. A typical succession of events in the auxin production of a twig might be as follows: a) in the dormant bud there is essentially no diffusible auxin; b) at the time that swelling of the buds commences, a relatively large amount of auxin appears in the bud; c) as elongation of the internodes begins, auxin production by the tip reaches a peak. In cases where twigs do not elongate, as in the short shoots of ginkgo or spurs of fruit trees, this peak is not very pronounced; d) as elongation proceeds, the apex becomes poor in auxin and each internode is apparently supplied with auxin primarily by the region of the node above it; e) as growth ceases, with maturity of the entire twig or an individual internode, auxin content apparently remains high for a brief additional period. These stages of auxin production in woody shoots can be seen in the data of Zimmerman (1936), Avery *et al* (1937), Gunckel and Thimann (1949), and Hemberg (1949).

One would expect that the growth rate should correlate with the growth hormone content, and that the growth response to applied auxins should likewise correlate with the amount of auxin applied. The response to applied auxins is in fact proportional to the amount of auxins applied (see chapter IV). The degree of responsiveness varies greatly with the type of tissue, and the type of response also varies with a variety of physiological factors, but the correlation between growth and auxin holds under a wide diversity of situations, both natural and artificial.

FREE AND BOUND AUXINS

From the time that physiologists first began studying the results of long term diffusion experiments and long term extraction experiments it has been evident that auxins in the plant do not all exist in the same form or state. Although some auxin becomes available immediately either through diffusion or extraction, an additional amount of auxin can be usually obtained if the treatment is extended over a longer period of time. These are called "free" auxin and "bound" auxin respectively.

Free auxin is capable of moving freely in the polar transport system and is apparently immediately effective in growth. Bound auxin on the other hand is sometimes active in growth and sometimes not. It is not so unrestricted in movement as free auxin. Larsen (1951) recognizes four different types of bound auxin: an auxin-protein complex, neutral precursors of auxin, precursor complexes, and structural protein sources of auxin.

The existence of the first of Larsen's categories, auxin-protein complexes, was first specifically demonstrated by Wildman and Gordon (1942). It appears that auxin molecules, presumably indoleacetic acid, are loosely adsorbed on the surface of various protein fractions. These auxin molecules are active in growth but, as already mentioned above, they are incapable of moving about freely. Generally they may be removed from the adsorbed condition by treatment with mildly alkaline solutions or by gentle proteolysis (Gordon, 1946). A more stable complex has been found in pea roots, however (Siegel and Galston, 1953). The formation of this auxin-protein complex utilizes high-energy phosphate bonds and is inhibited by several metabolic poisons such as iodoacetate. The auxin is not removed by either boiling or strong acid or alkaline conditions.

A neutral precursor of auxin was first separated from plants by Larsen (1944). This can be considered as bound auxin, since it is not immediately available for growth but can be converted into auxin very easily. These precursors may be aldehydes which become actual auxins upon conversion to free acids. Tests of the growth activity of indoleacetaldehyde have indicated that it promotes growth by reason of its conversion to indoleacetic acid in the test plant (Larsen, 1949). Indoleacetonitrile may be another neutral precursor.

Precursor complexes have been demonstrated by Berger and Avery (1944) and re-examined by Funke and Söding (1948). These complexes appear to be close associations between auxin precursors and certain growth inhibitors. When the complex is broken two fractions generally appear, one a neutral precursor (or sometimes an auxin) and the other a growth inhibitor. These precursor complexes have been found mainly in storage tissues such as seeds and tubers.

Structural proteins containing tryptophan were first recognized as potential sources of auxin by Skoog and Thimann (1940). They observed that protein-hydrolyzing enzymes were capable of producing auxins from various protein materials. It seems evident that any protein containing tryptophan, a recognized precursor of auxin, could produce auxin upon hydrolysis and oxidation. Certain reservations must be made, however, about the importance of this source in the production of auxins for growth. Although structural protein materials may conceivably serve as an auxin source, auxin production has not been generally associated with protein breakdown in the plant. In fact, auxin production in growing tissues may instead be more logically associated with protein synthesis. Therefore, it seems unlikely that structural proteins serve to any appreciable extent as bound auxin or precursor of auxin in the normal growing plant. It is curious to observe that some proteins which do not contain perceptible amounts of tryptophan have been reported to produce auxin with enzymatic hydrolysis (Kulescha, 1948).

IDENTITY OF GROWTH HORMONES

Before discussing the actual identity of known auxins it might be well to speak of the methods generally used for identifying these plant materials. All of the methods must be usable with minute amounts of auxin, for the growth hormone occurs in most plant parts in fantastically small amounts. A striking illustration of this is the fact that one *Avena* coleoptile tip will generally contain only 1/50,-000,000 of a milligram of auxin (Haagen-Smit, 1951).

Because of the minute amounts of auxins in plant parts, the actual purification of the growth hormone and preparation of a derivative for identification is seldom carried out.

When it is separated and purified, indoleacetic acid can be identified by the picrate salts (Kögl and Kostermans, 1935), by its addition product obtained with 1,3,5-trinitrobenzene (Redemann *et al,* 1951), or more simply by its melting point and infrared spectrum (Berger and Avery, 1944).

A more common means of identifying growth hormones is by determining the molecular weight, using the diffusion experiments described in chapter II. Molecular weight determinations have undoubtedly given some confusing information, however, because auxins diffused from plant parts will sometimes show apparent gross reductions in molecular weight when purified by separation into ether (Wildman and Bonner, 1948). Molecular weight determinations by the agar diffusion technique are valid only for pure preparations, and the presence of other compounds, which may be expected to diffuse out of plant parts at the same time, can greatly alter the results obtained. Because of this a certain amount of reserve should be exercised in interpreting such molecular weight determinations. Before conclusions about the identity of the auxins being measured are drawn, steps should be taken to purify the auxin and re-determine its molecular weight, using the method of Wildman and Bonner (1948) and Kramer and Went (1949).

A method often used for distinguishing between the hypothetical auxins *a* and *b* and indoleacetic acid is by observing the stability to hot acid or alkali. The indole ring is destroyed by hot acid, auxin *a* is destroyed by hot alkali, and auxin *b* is destroyed by either the acid or the alkali. This means of identifying auxins is confused, however, by the fact that one would expect the immediate precursor to indoleacetic acid, viz., indoleacetaldehyde, to be destroyed by either the hot acid or the alkali. Refluxing with acid should destroy the indole ring just as happens with indoleacetic acid, and refluxing with alkali would probably produce a variety of destructive combinations of the aldehyde by reactions similar to the well-known aldol condensation reaction. Indoleacetonitrile, another naturally occurring compound which shows auxin activity in some tests, is destroyed by alkali and is somewhat resistant to acids (Bentley and Housley, 1952). It is easily conceivable, then, that indoleacetaldehyde could be confused with auxin *b* and the nitrile could be confused with auxin *a* if instability to acid and alkali were used as the criteria for establishing auxin identity.

A comparison of dilution curves, as measured by any of the standard assay procedures, is a helpful means of distinguishing between auxins. The dilution curve for indoleacetic acid shows a less rapid decline in activity upon dilution than for indolepyruvic or indolebutyric acid, for example, but a much more rapid dilution effect than for indole sulfonic acid (Went and Thimann, 1937, p. 135).

The dissociation characteristics of acid auxins have been used at times as evidence for the identity of the material. Indoleacetic acid, for example, has a pK of 4.75 and the known parallelism of the effects of pH changes upon dissociation and growth promotion has been used as evidence in identifying indoleacetic acid as a growth hormone (Bonner, 1934).

Aside from the actual crystallization of a pure derivative of an auxin, the best means of identification is certainly by chromatography. Precise separation of compounds can be achieved, and the identity can be established in a variety of ways, including the R_f values, fluorescence and color reactions as described in chapter II.

Indoleacetic acid was first definitely shown to be an auxin in plant material by Kögl and Kostermans (1934) who identified it in yeast. It has also been positively identified in corn seedlings (Haagen-Smit *et al,* 1946), and indirect evidence has indicated that it is the major growth hormone in the organs of seven other growing plants: bean stems (Verkaaik, 1942), sugar cane stems (van Overbeek *et al,* 1945), potato tubers (Hemberg, 1947), *Avena* coleoptiles (Wildman and Bonner, 1948), pineapple leaves (Gordon and Nieva, 1949), and tomato stems (Kramer and Went, 1949). In each of these plant materials several different criteria have been used to establish that indoleacetic acid is the principal growth hormone. By the use of chromatography, auxins have been separated from plants and shown to have R_f values identical with indoleacetic acid in many additional species of plants, including cabbage (Holley *et al,* 1951), Brussels sprouts (Linser, 1951), and cauliflower (von Denffer *et al,* 1952).

There is evidence for the existence of the ethyl ester of indoleacetic acid in corn kernels (Redemann *et al,* 1951) and in apple endosperm (Teubner, 1953). The ester form is less effective in promoting growth than the free acid, but more effective than the acid in causing fruit set. This reported difference may be attributed to greater penetration or persistence of the ester rather than to better auxin properties *per se.*

The discovery of auxins *a* and *b,* originally isolated from human urine, has been described in an earlier section. There is some indirect evidence, principally in terms of molecular weight determinations, enzymatic inactivation and stability to acid and to alkali, for the presence of these compounds in plants. However, repeated attempts to find them in growing plants have failed.

Indolepyruvic acid has been identified in plants by chromatographic techniques (Stowe and Thimann, 1953). This compound is known to have auxin activity. It is also readily broken down into indoleacetic acid, so the extent of its role as a growth hormone is difficult to determine.

Investigations of callus tissues resulting from the wounding of various plants have led to the identification of traumatic acid as a growth promoting substance associated with tissue proliferation around wounds. Traumatic acid is a straight chain dicarboxylic acid: $HOOCCH = CH\,(CH_2)_8COOH$. It lacks the unsaturated ring characteristic of all known auxins. As far as is known, traumatic acid is not active as an auxin, but seems to act in conjunction with auxins to produce the wound growth response (see review by Thimann, 1948, p. 84).

Three other compounds which show auxin activity have been

identified in plants, but the possibility of their actually acting as growth hormones is obscure. The first of these is *cis*-cinnamic acid, which occurs in plants both as the free acid and as its esters. It is found in notably high concentrations in the oil of balsam. Another substance, phenylacetic acid, which is weakly active as an auxin (Thimann and Schneider, 1939), is a constituent of peppermint oil and oil of Neroli. Phenylacetic acid is unable to move in the active transport system and so it seems very unlikely that it serves as a growth hormone. Another compound, indoleacetonitrile, has been identified in several plants and shows auxin activity in the *Avena* test (Jones *et al,* 1952). The lack of activity in the pea test and the ready conversion to indoleacetic acid suggest that this compound may be more important as a precursor of auxin than as an auxin itself.

It should be emphasized that there must surely be growth hormones other than indoleacetic acid in plants. To cite only a few cases, of the auxins obtained from *Avena* coleoptiles (von Guttenberg and Lehle-Joerges, 1947), from wheat seeds (Gordon, 1946) and from cabbage (Holley *et al,* 1951), sizeable portions could not be identified as indoleacetic acid. Also, a crude auxin material has been extracted from bean seeds, a material which has the remarkable property of inducing prolonged growth increases in bean seedlings when applied to the stems or foliage, a property quite foreign to indoleacetic acid (Mitchell *et al,* 1951). With the advent of the new and more effective chromatographic methods of identifying auxins, it is probable that the identity of other growth hormones will be soon established.

From this discussion it can be seen that the identity of the growth hormones in plants has not yet been clarified. From the evidence at hand it would appear that indoleacetic acid is the most common growth hormone, but it seems clear that it is not the only growth hormone. Also, auxin may exist in several different types of complexes such as complexes with protein, complexes with precursors, and complexes with inhibitors.

FORMATION OF AUXIN

Factors in Formation

The apparent role of the apex in auxin formation and the apparent frequent correlation of auxin formation with growth have been pointed out. Several factors, both internal and environmental, are known to play a part in auxin formation.

In the first place, the amount of auxin produced per apex has been found to be closely correlated with the age of the plant in

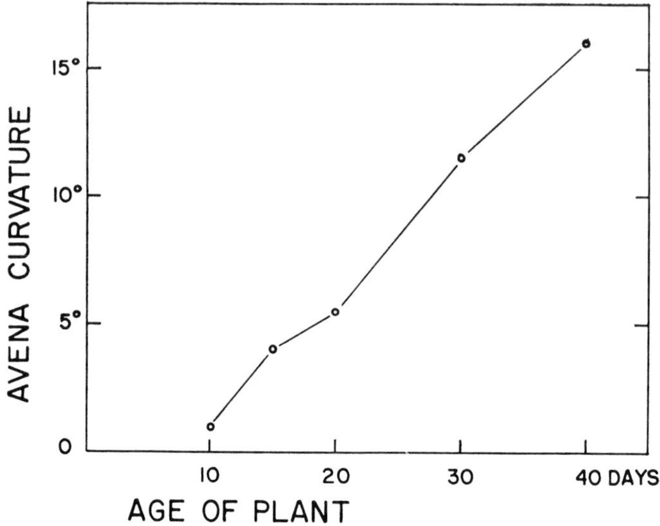

Fig. 33. The amount of auxin diffusible from the apices of tomato plants as related to the age of the plant (Kramer and Went, 1949).

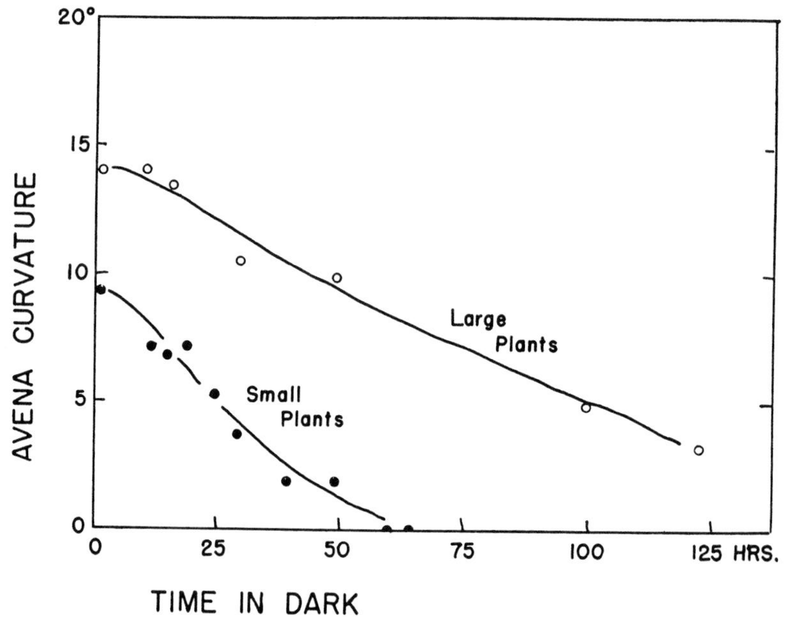

Fig. 34. The disappearance of auxin from tobacco plants held in darkness for various intervals of time. Auxin obtained by diffusion (Avery *et al,* 1937).

tomato (Kramer and Went, 1949). Small, young apices yielded little diffusible auxin and older apices yielded proportionally more, as shown in figure 33. The diffusible auxin more than doubled with each ten day period in the development of the plant.

Light is an important factor in auxin formation, although not a simple one. There is some confusion concerning the necessity of light for auxin formation, but in general it would appear that green plants do require light for this function, whereas excised plant parts grown on an organic medium or seedlings with a stored food supply can produce auxin in the absence of light.

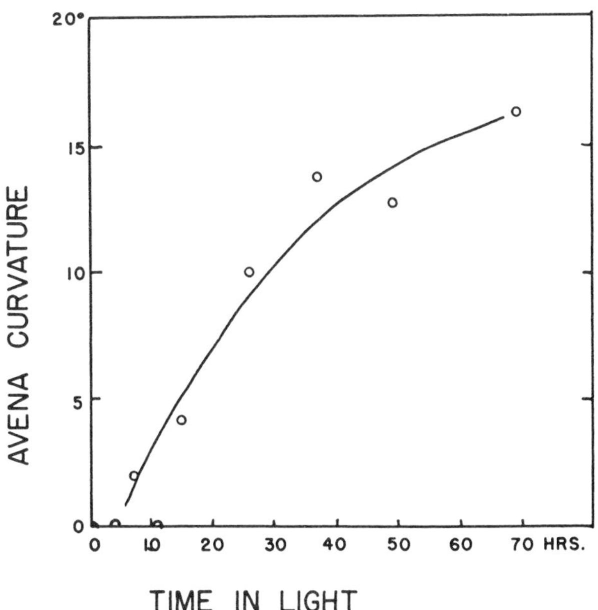

Fig. 35. The reappearance of auxin in tobacco apices when the plants were placed in light (8000 ergs/cm²/sec.) (Avery *et al,* 1937).

An excellent quantitative study of the relationship of light to auxin formation was carried out by Avery *et al* (1937) using tobacco plants. They observed that the auxin diffusible from the apices of tobacco plants diminished rapidly when the green plants were held in darkness (figure 34). Using this information, they then developed a technique for following the resurgence of auxin formation after starvation in the dark. Exposure of the plants to ten hours of light was sufficient to allow the reappearance of auxin, and a quantitative increase with greater duration of light was observed (figure 35). This reappearance was roughly proportional to the light intensity applied (figure 36). Some evidence was brought forth to suggest that conditions favoring auxin formation were the same as those favoring photosynthesis.

The role of light in the formation of auxin presents something of a paradox, for not only does light cause the formation of auxin, but simultaneously it causes the destruction of auxin as was deduced from some of the early experiments on phototropism. The destruction of auxin by light is more striking, however, in etiolated plant mate-

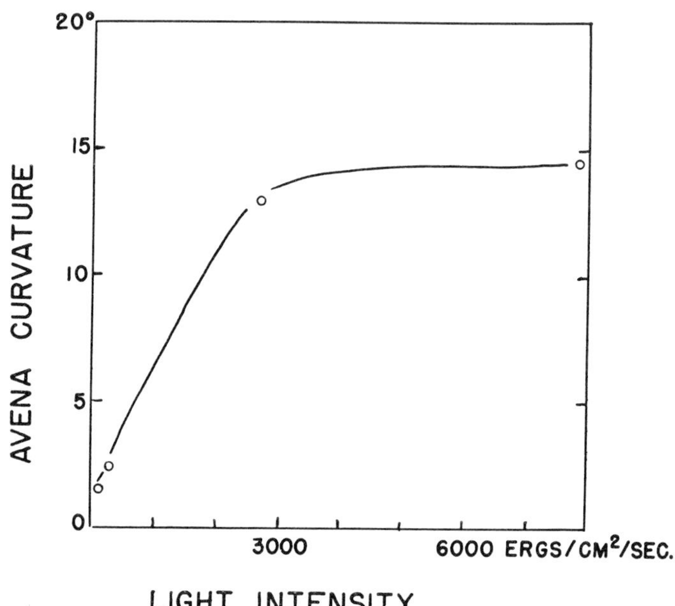

Fig. 36. The effectiveness of light of various intensities upon auxin formation in tobacco plants (Avery *et al,* 1937).

rial than in green plants. Moderate amounts of light can cause destruction of a large proportion of the auxin in etiolated seedlings, contributing to the tropic responses, whereas green plants can maintain high auxin levels even under rather high light intensities.

Evidence that auxins gradually disappear in darkened plants has been accumulated by several workers. A good example of this was the demonstration by Zimmerman and Hitchcock (1937) that darkened tomatoes lose their sensitivity to geotropism and that the sensitivity can be restored by the application of auxins to the plants.

The formation of auxins in the light and their disappearance in the dark would suggest that a diurnal periodicity of auxin content may be present in a normal growth situation. Evidence for such periodicity in tomatoes has been produced by Went (1944). He found a generally higher auxin concentration during the day followed by a generally lower level at night, though secondary rises and drops occurred too.

Quite a different role of light has been suggested by Liverman and Bonner (1953). They observed small increases in growth rate of *Avena* coleoptiles in response to red light (600–800 mμ), which could be reversed by far-red light (700–800 mμ). Kinetic considerations in the manner described in chapter VIII led them to suggest that red light increases the effectiveness of auxin by increasing the availability of the hypothetical substance with which auxin reacts to cause growth. It was further suggested that far-red light reduces growth by decreasing the availability of the receptor substance.

Differences in day length or photoperiods will cause differences in auxin levels. Russian workers (Cajlachjan and Zdanova, 1938) have found consistently higher auxin levels under long-day conditions than under short-day conditions, no matter what the photoperiod classification of the plants tested. Their observations were made on diffusible auxin from stems, and similar results for diffusible auxin from leaves have been obtained (Leopold, 1949).

The formation of auxin in response to light appears to be a function of leaves. Defoliation of expanding ginkgo twigs reduced the diffusible auxin in the apex 80 per cent in two days. This is particularly striking since Gunckel and Thimann (1949) obtained no diffusible auxin from the leaves themselves. It is suggestive, at least, that the leaves may be supplying a precursor from which auxin is produced in the tip.

The capacity of excised tissues growing on organic media to produce auxin in the dark has been demonstrated in tobacco callus (Skoog, 1944) and in excised roots (van Overbeek and Bonner, 1938). In both of these studies the auxin was obtained with ether extraction techniques.

Zinc appears to be essential for auxin formation. The usual symptoms of zinc deficiency are primarily a general failure of elongation. Skoog (1940) considered this lack of growth to be associated with a low auxin content. Supplying deficient plants with zinc restored the auxin supply. Likewise the addition of auxin or tryptophan relieved the deficiency symptoms (Tsui, 1948). It would appear then that the absence of zinc prevents the normal production of tryptophan, a precursor of indoleacetic acid. Other evidence (Elliott, 1952) indicates that zinc deficiency may limit tryptophan formation in turn by limiting serine formation. Serine is considered to be condensed with indole to form tryptophan, and either tryptophan or serine were found to relieve the symptoms of zinc deficiency, while indole did not.

Several developmental steps are believed to be associated with the production of large amounts of auxin. Synapsis, the stage at which reduction division occurs in the floral parts, is coincident with a surge of growth in grown plants and an apparent increase in auxin content (Wittwer, 1943). Pollination, too, is associated with a large production of auxin (cf. figure 91, p. 216). It is recognized that the pollen brings a certain amount of auxin to the ovary, but Muir (1951) has demonstrated that shortly after pollination thirty times as much auxin is produced in the tobacco ovary as could be accounted for from the pollen itself. He suggests that pollination stimulates the release of an auxin-forming enzyme system in the ovary.

While auxin is produced in the ovary shortly after pollination, this source dwindles after the commencement of embryo growth in the apple (Luckwill, 1948). The embryo itself becomes the primary source of auxin in the developing fruit. An elegant demonstration of the embryo as an auxin-producing center has been carried out with the strawberry (Nitsch, 1950). It was demonstrated that the removal of the achenes containing developing embryos prevented normal fruit enlargement, and the role of the achene could be replaced by auxin pastes (see figure 50, p. 110). Fruit shape was controlled by removal of the achenes from some sections of the fruit, resulting in decreased growth in the parts so deprived of the auxin supply.

Biochemistry of Formation

From the early observations of Skoog and Thimann (1940) it is evident that the production of auxin during long term extraction procedures is primarily an enzymatic process. The addition of certain enzymes to various plant materials has greatly stimulated auxin production. Again it will be recalled that the effect of temperature during extraction on the yields of auxin clearly indicate an enzymatic auxin production (cf. figure 4, p. 17). It has been observed that the appearance of large amounts of auxin associated with pollination of tobacco ovaries is due to an enzymatic production (Muir, 1951).

An enzyme actually capable of producing auxin has been separated from spinach leaves (Wildman *et al,* 1947). This enzyme preparation is capable of converting tryptophan into indoleacetic acid. More detailed studies (Wildman and Bonner, 1948) have shown that such an enzyme is distributed through the *Avena* coleoptile in a manner strikingly parallel to the distribution of auxin itself. By far the greatest concentration of enzymatic activity, as measured by the production of auxin from tryptophan, was found at the tip of the coleoptile. The relative activity of the enzyme in successively lower sections of the coleoptile falls off in a pattern essentially like the pattern of auxin concentrations. This enzyme from the *Avena* coleoptile is destroyed by boiling. Its activity increases at the tip of the decapitated coleoptile at the same time that regeneration of the physiological tip takes place. Another clear demonstration of an enzyme system which produces auxin has been carried out by Gordon and Nieva (1949) in the pineapple.

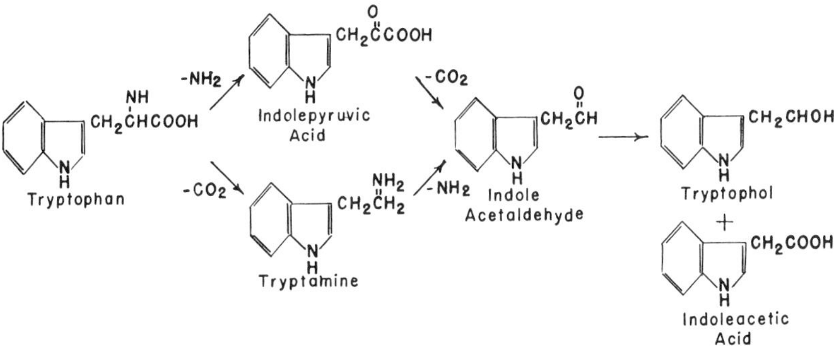

Fig. 37. The pathways of formation of indoleacetic acid from tryptophan.

The actual steps by which tryptophan is converted into indoleacetic acid have been followed in considerable detail by Gordon and Nieva. They found that leaf discs or crude enzyme preparations from pineapple leaves were quite active in producing auxin when the leaf discs were incubated with tryptophan, indolepyruvic acid, or tryptamine. In these same experiments they also found that large amounts of a neutral precursor of auxin were formed from these substrates, and they identified the neutral precursor as being indoleacetaldehyde. They proposed then that the formation of auxin might occur through two alternative routes, as shown in figure 37. The tryptophan may be deaminated to indolepyruvic acid, and thence decarboxylated to indoleacetaldehyde, or alternatively, the tryptophan may be first decarboxylated to tryptamine and then deaminated to indoleacetaldehyde. The aldehyde, then, is the immediate precursor of indoleacetic acid by either route of formation.

Larsen first suggested in 1949 that indoleacetaldehyde was a precursor of auxin. He recognized it as a neutral substance which was capable of being converted into auxin. Larsen's concept was graphically confirmed by Gordon and Nieva in their pineapple studies. They observed that the rate of auxin production in leaf breis rose with time as extraction proceeded until the supply of the neutral precursor (indoleacetaldehyde) was essentially exhausted, at which time the auxin production rate fell off. These changes, graphically shown in figure 38, provide evidence that the formation of indoleacetic acid takes place at the expense of the neutral aldehyde precursor. One is struck, however, by the fact that the amount of auxin formed was considerably

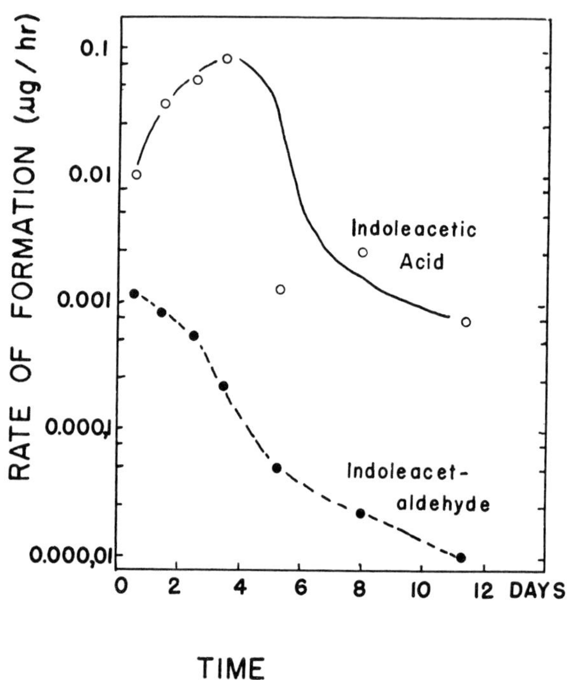

Fig. 38. The rates of formation of indoleacetic acid and of indoleacetaldehyde from tryptophan in leaf discs of pineapple (Gordon and Nieva, 1949).

greater than the amount of indoleacetaldehyde disappearing. This discrepancy is particularly notable in view of the findings discussed below, that two mols of aldehyde are required for the production of one mol of the acid.

Several lines of evidence indicate that the neutral precursor is indeed indoleacetaldehyde. In the first place, it is readily oxidized by Schardinger's enzyme which is approximately aldehyde-specific. The neutral precursor in pineapple has been shown to form a bisulfite addition product from which it can be regenerated by neutralization.

Furthermore the neutral precursor forms an addition product with dimedon which, like the bisulfite addition product, is specific for aldehydes (Gordon and Nieva, 1949).

The conversion of indoleacetaldehyde to indoleacetic acid can be carried out by using crude enzyme preparations from various plant materials (Larsen, 1949, 1951; Gordon and Nieva, 1949; Ashby, 1951). As already noted, Larsen has observed that the yield of the free acid is lower than one might expect on a mol for mol basis. Using naphthaleneacetaldehyde as a substrate, he has demonstrated that the enzyme preparation produces only one-half mol of acid for each mol of aldehyde consumed, and he proposes that the oxidation must be a dismutation which produces one-half mol of the acid and one-half mol of the alcohol, as shown in figure 37.

It should be pointed out here that the indoleacetaldehyde is apparently not an auxin itself, but is probably active in growth only upon conversion to the acid (Larsen, 1949). The two major pieces of evidence for this conclusion are the observation that the aldehyde produces a growth response only after a delay in time (presumably because it must first be converted to the acid), and the observation that the concentration curve obtained by the *Avena* test is quantitative only over a very narrow range of concentrations. Perhaps the latter occurs because the enzyme system for the conversion of the aldehyde to the acid becomes saturated at higher concentrations of the aldehyde.

Some interesting data supporting the contention that indoleacetaldehyde affects growth after conversion into the free acid have been obtained by Bentley and Housley (1952). They grew *Avena* coleoptile sections in solutions of various strengths of indoleacetaldehyde, obtaining the growth data shown in figure 39 *A*. After the coleoptile sections had been removed from the solutions, the neutral substances remaining in the solution were separated from the acidic substances, and a fresh set of coleoptiles was then grown in each of these fractions. The growth responses shown in figure 39 *B* indicate that sufficient acidic growth substances were present in the solution to account for the entire amount of growth obtained in the first dilution series. It may be deduced, then, that the apparent stimulation of growth by the aldehyde was in fact due to the formation of the free acid in the solution during the test.

Another pathway by which indoleacetic acid may be formed in plants is through the oxidation of indoleacetonitrile, a compound found to occur naturally in plants by Jones *et al* (1952). The nitrile shows apparent auxin activity in the *Avena* straight-growth test (Bentley and Housley, 1952), but its lack of activity in the pea straight-growth test led to the eventual finding that it probably has its effects on growth partly through its conversion to the free acid and partly through its synergistic action in the presence of acid auxins (Osborne,

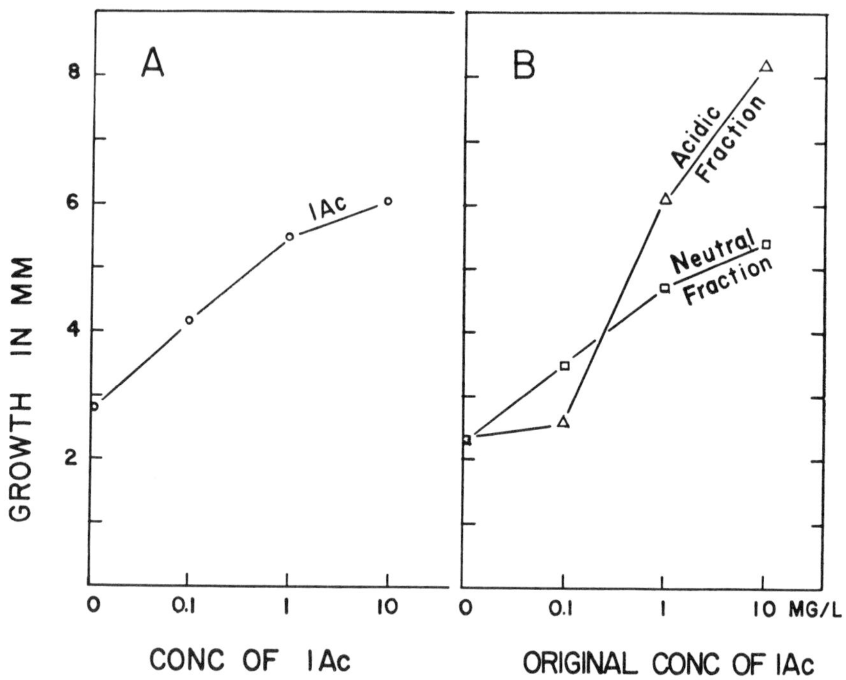

Fig. 39. The effect of indoleacetaldehyde on growth in the *Avena* straight-growth test. *A,* growth responses to indoleacetaldehyde; *B,* the growth responses to the acidic and to the neutral fractions taken from the solutions after completion of *A* (Bentley and Housley, 1952).

1952). The most likely pathway for the conversion of the nitrile to indoleacetic acid would be through the oxidation to the acetamide as an intermediate compound:

$$\text{indoleacetonitrile }(\text{-}CH_2CN) \xrightarrow{H_2O} \text{indoleacetamide }(\text{-}CH_2C(=O)NH_2) \xrightarrow{H_2O} \text{indoleacetic acid }(\text{-}CH_2COOH) + NH_3^+$$

indoleacetonitrile

indoleacetamide

indoleacetic acid

MOVEMENT

Early work on the movement of auxins in the *Avena* coleoptile demonstrated that no particular type of tissue was exclusively involved in auxin transport. Exhaustive studies of transport through the non-vascular parts of the coleoptile, as compared with the vascular elements, demonstrated little or no difference provided only that physiological concentrations of auxin were used. In stem and pedicel tissues the phloem appears to be the most active in auxin transport (Cooper, 1936), but apparently any live metabolizing tissues are able to transport auxin.

The most striking characteristic of auxin movement is its generally strict basipetal polarity. This can be studied most readily in short sections of stems or coleoptile tissue, to which a supply of auxin is provided in an agar block at the physiological apex of the piece and from which the transported auxin is collected in an agar block at the physiological base. Such an experiment will give one a measure of basipetal or downward transport. Repetition of the same procedure with the stem or coleoptile section inverted will give one a measure of acropetal or upward transport. By such experiments as these, van der Weij (1932) found that auxin is transported exclusively basipetally in the *Avena* coleoptile. This is true regardless of the position in which the tissue is held during the experiment; the transport is always toward the physiological base of the tissue. The same strict polarity of auxin transport is true of many stems (van der Weij, 1933; van Overbeek, 1933; Thimann and Skoog, 1934; Cooper, 1936) and leaves (Avery, 1935).

A striking demonstration of the inflexibility of the polar transport mechanism can be seen in the polarity of stem cuttings of *Tagetes* which were rooted in soil in an inverted position. Even though they were rooted and grown in the inverted position, they would transport auxin only to their old physiological base for 36 days, at which time new conductive tissues seem to have been established with the new polar orientation (Went, 1941).

The strict downward transport of the growth hormone in plants is a classic instance of polarity in a biological system and affords an excellent opportunity for a study of polarity in general.

A strict polarity of auxin movement apparently does not always exist, for Leopold and Guernsey (1953) have shown that in the coleus plant the basipetal polarity becomes weaker and weaker as the distance from the vegetative stem apex increases (figure 40). Furthermore, in flowering stems there is some acropetal movement even at the stem tip. They have produced some evidence that a substance is formed in the flowering stem apex which permits acropetal transport of auxin.

The movement of auxin in roots can take place either acropetally or basipetally (Heidt, 1931) although in at least some cases a strict polar-

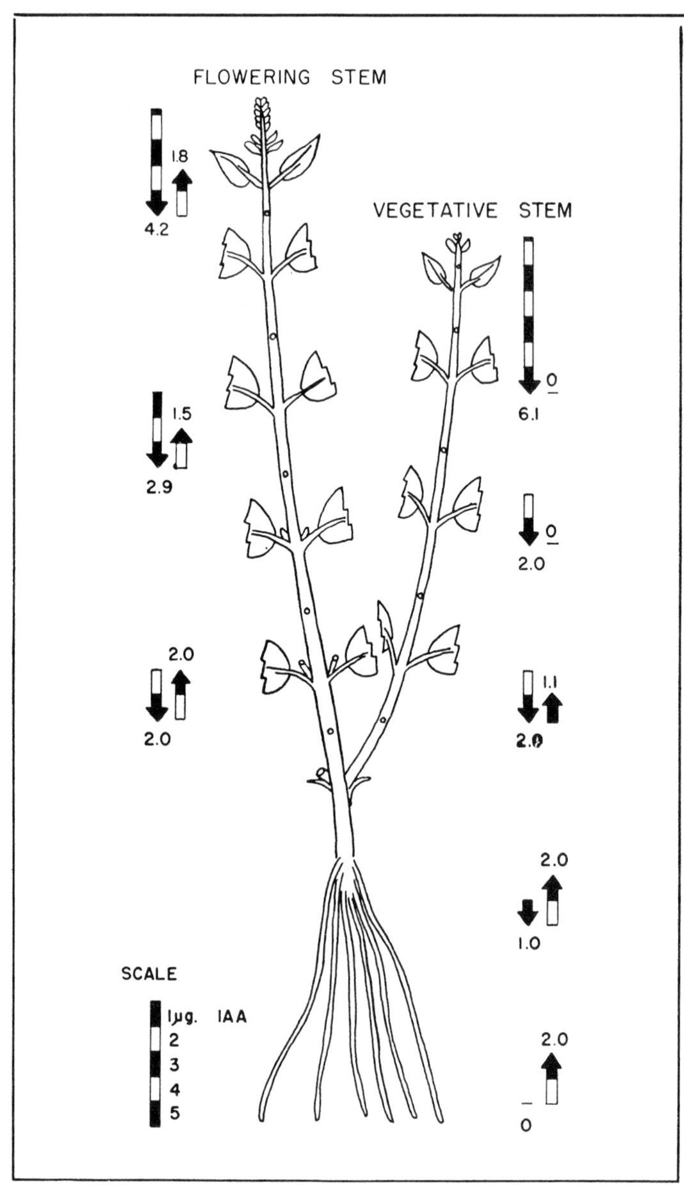

Fig. 40. The difference in polarity of auxin transport in the stems and roots of coleus, showing a polar gradient from apex to base and the difference in polar gradients between flowering and vegetative stems. The arrows represent the amount of auxin transported in each direction through 7 mm. sections of stems or roots taken from different regions of the plant (Leopold and Guernsey, 1953).

ity away from the root tip does exist (Cholodny, 1934). These differences in polarity have been shown to fit together in an overall polarity gradient in the coleus, from a complete basipetal polarity in the vegetative apex to a complete acropetal polarity in the root apex, with a gradual gradient between (figure 40).

Another exception to the strictly polar transport of auxins is to be found in the case of high auxin concentrations. Although polarity of auxin transport is entirely independent of auxin concentrations over the physiological range, higher auxin concentrations will cause a loss of polarity (Snow, 1936). A non-polar movement of auxins will also occur when auxins are applied in such a manner as to enter the transpiration stream (Snow, *op. cit.).*

The speed of auxin movement has been measured in several experiments and where in general the polar transport mechanism is active, such as in *Avena* coleoptiles, the rate is very rapid: 10 to 12 mm. per hour. Where the polar mechanism is less active, such as in roots, the rate is considerably less: 4 mm. per hour (Faber, 1936). These rates are definitely higher than movement by diffusion, which would be approximately 2 mm. per hour. The velocity of auxin transport is unaffected by temperature; however, the amount transported is strictly proportional to temperature. For each 10° C rise in temperature, approximately 3 times as much auxin is transported (van der Weij, 1932). The characteristics of auxin transport may be described as follows:

> The best simile for the transport is that of objects along a moving band; the band goes at constant speed, so that the number of objects arriving at the end per unit time is independent of the length (capacity independent of length of section); the time required for the first object to reach the end is proportional to the length of the band (velocity constant); if not removed from the end the objects continue to pile up (transport against the gradient). (Went and Thimann, 1937, p. 96.)

The characteristic polarity of auxin transport is the mechanism by which some of the most striking activities of the growth hormone in plants occur. The amount of auxins formed in any of the aerial portions of the plant will influence the more proximal parts. Thus the auxin produced in leaves moves downward in a polar manner, contributing to the inhibition of lateral buds and the growth patterns of the stem. The auxin produced in any organ serves to prevent abscission of that organ. If the polar transport of the auxin is hindered by wounding, for example, the inhibition of lateral buds may be overcome, and if the hindrance is great enough there may be a formation of roots just above the barrier due to the accumulated auxins, or the organ may abscise. The vertical orientation effects of this sort are called "correlation effects." The term is especially common in the early literature. Auxin has been found to be the primary agent responsible for the correlation effects, and the polarity of its movement is the basis for its correlative action.

Lateral movement of auxins can be induced by the lateral application of such stimuli as light, gravity or physical contact. The physiological significance of lateral transport in the tropic movements of plants is discussed in the section on tropisms (chapter IV).

The physiological basis for the polar movement of auxins is not understood. One promising theory has been advanced to explain it, and that is that movement is controlled by bioelectric potentials in the plant. The concept was first suggested by Brauner (1927), and has since found much support in the work of Lund (1947) and Schrank (1951). Some of the best evidence in support of the theory has been obtained from studies with the *Avena* coleoptile. A natural bioelectric gradient exists in the coleoptile, the base of which is electropositive to the apex. Upon exposure to light, the shaded side becomes electropositive to the lighted side. Upon lateral exposure to gravity, the lower side becomes electropositive to the upper. In each instance the auxin moves toward the more positive charge. The bioelectric change precedes the curvature response as one would expect if the charge bears a causal relationship to the curvature. Furthermore, the charge fades at the same rate as the curvature action (Webster and Schrank, 1953). There are some unsettled questions, however. One would expect that the artificial application of an electric gradient to a coleoptile would simulate the tropic stimuli. Instead, however, the application of a potential results in a bending of the coleoptile toward the positive pole of the applied current—quite the opposite to the response which is associated with natural tropisms where the bending is toward the negatively charged side (Schrank, 1951). Also the bioelectric gradient down the coleoptile shows a peak in electronegative charge some 5 mm. below the apex, and no comparable reversal of auxin polarity from that point to the apex has been found. However, the theory is still the best one at present.

A further suggestion to explain the movement of auxin has been advanced by Showacre and du Buy (1947), who note that many of the same factors influence both tropisms and protoplasmic streaming. Light retards streaming in the cytoplasm of cells of *Avena* coleoptiles, and this effect would be expected to be most pronounced on the lighted side when unilateral light is used. It is suggested that the retarded streaming may result in retarded auxin transport, and as a consequence auxin flowing from the apex would be shunted to the shaded side, and unilateral growth would ensue. The investigators point out that the tropic stimuli may exercise their effects by altering the bioelectric potential of the plant part, which in turn may alter protoplasmic streaming and hence auxin transport.

Quite a different type of auxin transport which is non-polar is known to exist, and this is discussed in chapter VI.

AUXIN INACTIVATION

It would be logical to expect that there must be some mechanism in the plant by which auxin may be disposed of, inactivated, or destroyed. Early workers in the field of phototropism demonstrated that

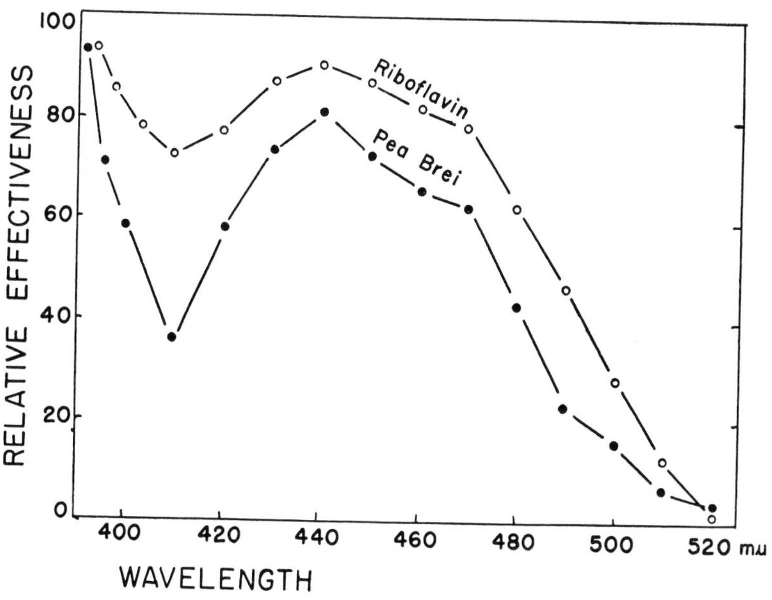

Fig. 41. Action spectra for photo-inactivation of indoleacetic acid by pure riboflavin and by breis of pea plants (Galston and Baker, 1949).

the exposure of the *Avena* coleoptile to light resulted in a reduction in the total amount of auxin present (e.g. Went, 1928). More recent observations have led to the conclusion that light-activated processes—both enzymatic and non-enzymatic—can inactivate auxin in plants (Tang and Bonner, 1947; Galston, 1949).

Photoinactivation of auxin has been studied both *in vitro* and *in vivo*. The inclusion of either pea brei or riboflavin with indoleacetic acid results in a disappearance of auxin when exposed to light. Studies of the wavelengths of light which are effective in causing this destruction have demonstrated that the action spectrum for auxin destruction in both such systems (figure 41) is strikingly parallel to the absorption spectrum of riboflavin shown in figure 42 (Galston and Baker, 1949). The light-inactivation of auxin can also be mediated by pigments other than riboflavin and so it would seem unnecessary to assume that riboflavin is the only pigment in plants which serves this function. β-carotene has an absorption spectrum very similar to riboflavin

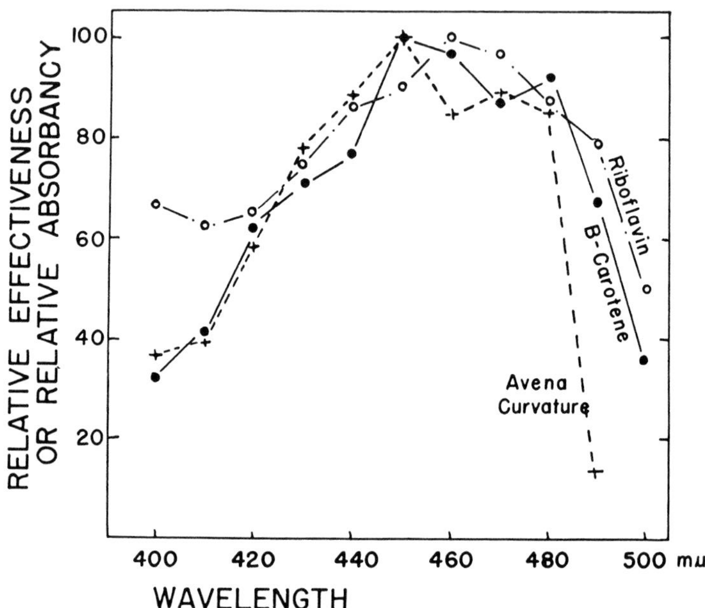

Fig. 42. A comparison of the action spectrum for phototropism in the *Avena* coleoptile with absorption spectra of riboflavin and β-carotene (Galston and Baker, 1949).

(figure 42) and it has been pointed out that it is difficult to distinguish between the two possible pigments on the basis of the action spectrum information (Galston, 1950).

In vivo studies have clearly shown that the effectiveness of a given amount of auxin is strongly reduced by exposure of plant material to light, as in the pea straight-growth test (Galston and Hand, 1949). How much of this reduced growth response is owing to the enzymatic destruction and how much is caused by non-enzymatic destruction is not yet clear. Some preliminary evidence suggests that the enzymatic process may be responsible for destruction in weak light, and the non-enzymatic process may dominate in strong light (Bruson and Leopold, unpublished).

Both the enzymatic and the non-enzymatic auxin-destroying systems have been shown to involve the consumption of oxygen. Evidence concerning the nature of the enzymatic destruction of auxin in peas has indicated that two participants to the enzyme systems are involved: a flavo-protein and a peroxidase (Galston and Baker, 1951).

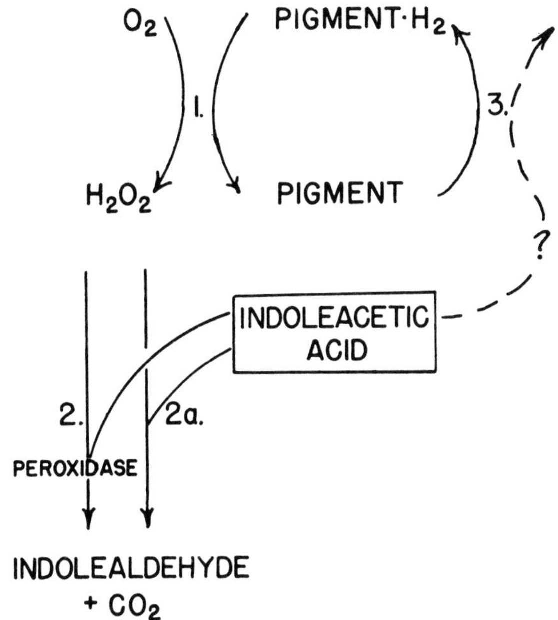

Fig. 43. A scheme for the photo-destruction of indoleacetic acid (adapted from Larsen, 1951).

Figure 43 represents diagrammatically a concept of the auxin-destroying mechanisms in plants. In this scheme, step 1 involves the oxidation of a reduced pigment or flavo-protein complex. This step utilizes oxygen, and presumably forms peroxide. Step 2 is the enzymatic step involved in auxin destruction and the evidence indicates that, in peas at least, the enzyme involved may be a peroxidase. By means of this step indoleacetic acid is oxidized to indolealdehyde plus carbon dioxide. An alternative reaction, 2*a* can occur at this point, a process by which indoleacetic acid is oxidized without the participation of an enzyme. This auto-oxidation is a non-enzymatic destruction of auxin. Still another non-enzymatic destruction of auxin may conceivably occur in step 3, wherein the pigment or flavo-protein is regenerated to its original reduced form.

If auxin destruction takes place in aerobic conditions, oxygen is consumed in amounts comparable to the amount of auxin destroyed (Galston, 1949). The non-enzymatic destruction can occur in the absence of oxygen though more slowly. In this case the pigment is

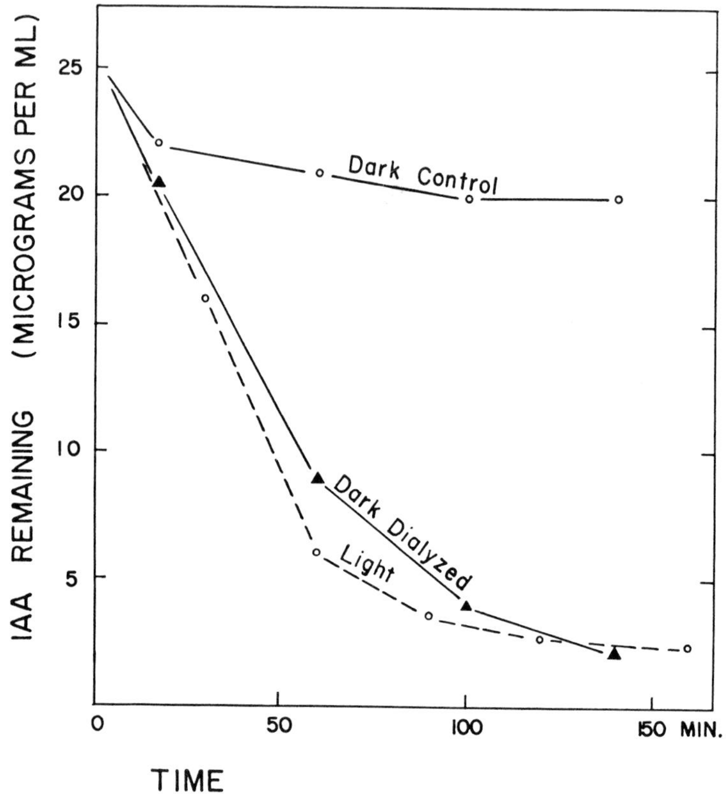

Fig. 44. The destruction of auxin by the pea enzyme in dark, in light, and after dialysis of the enzyme (Galston and Baker, 1951).

bleached, probably because of its being reduced by hydrogen from the auxin (Galston, 1949) as in step 3 (figure 43) or possibly by hydrogen from water (Brauner and Brauner, 1954).

In an investigation of the nature of the light effect in the enzymatic reaction, Galston and Baker (1951) have found that there is a natural inhibitor of the reaction in pea tissues, and that light serves to overcome the effect of this inhibitor. In this way light permits the destruction of auxin to proceed. Some data on this point can be seen in figure 44 where the enzymatic destruction of auxin is being followed in relation to time. It can be seen that the destruction proceeds very slowly in the dark control solutions containing the crude enzyme taken from peas. If the solutions are exposed to light, the destruction occurs very rapidly. Moreover, if the solutions are dialyzed, some water-soluble inhibitor to the reaction is lost, and the destruction proceeds even in the dark. It is deduced that the effect of light is in part a prevention of the effect of the inhibitor of enzymatic destruction of auxin. Both light and the inhibitor are believed to act on step 1 of figure 43.

The nature of the enzyme which destroys auxin is a subject of some disagreement. It was first thought to be an iron enzyme (Tang and Bonner, 1947), and probably identical with peroxidase associated with a flavin material (Galston, Bonner and Baker, 1953). Other workers, using another means of following the reaction, have found evidence that the enzyme may be a copper enzyme instead (Wagenknecht and Burris, 1950). An auxin-destroying enzyme from the parasitic fungus, *Omphalia flavida,* appears to be neither a peroxidase nor a polyphenol oxidase (Sequeira and Steeves, 1954).

The products of the reactions in which auxin is destroyed have been clarified only in part. Tang and Bonner (1947) observed that carbon dioxide was formed at the same rates as oxygen was consumed in the reaction. It was later suggested (Wagenknecht and Burris, 1950) that the reaction might proceed as follows:

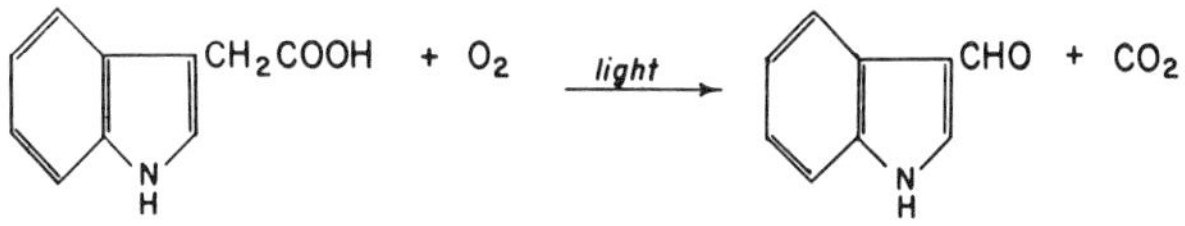

$$\text{(indole)}-CH_2COOH + O_2 \xrightarrow{\text{light}} \text{(indole)}-CHO + CO_2$$

indoleacetic acid   indolealdehyde

Von Denffer and Fischer (1952) have shown that indolealdehyde is in fact a product of the non-enzymatic destruction, and it seems entirely likely that this same product would be produced from the enzymatic destruction as well. There must be further products of the reaction, however, even in the non-enzymatic system, for Brauner (1953) has shown clearly that the indole ring of the auxin is destroyed in light, though at a somewhat slower rate than the destruction of the carboxyl group. He followed the disappearance of the acidic part of indoleacetic acid by measuring pH changes, and simultaneously followed the destruction of the indole ring by use of the Hopkins-Cole reaction. The auxin was added to a dilute solution of riboflavin and exposed to ultraviolet light for different intervals of time, as shown in figure 45. One sees that the acid group was destroyed most rapidly, but that a simultaneous destruction of the indole ring also occurred. A different type of product of auxin destruction has been proposed by Siegel and Weintraub (1952), who found that auxins combine with peroxides to form some complex which can then be restored to indoleacetic acid upon removal of the peroxides by catalase or other reagents. Some evidence has been advanced to indicate that peroxides may be formed as a product of

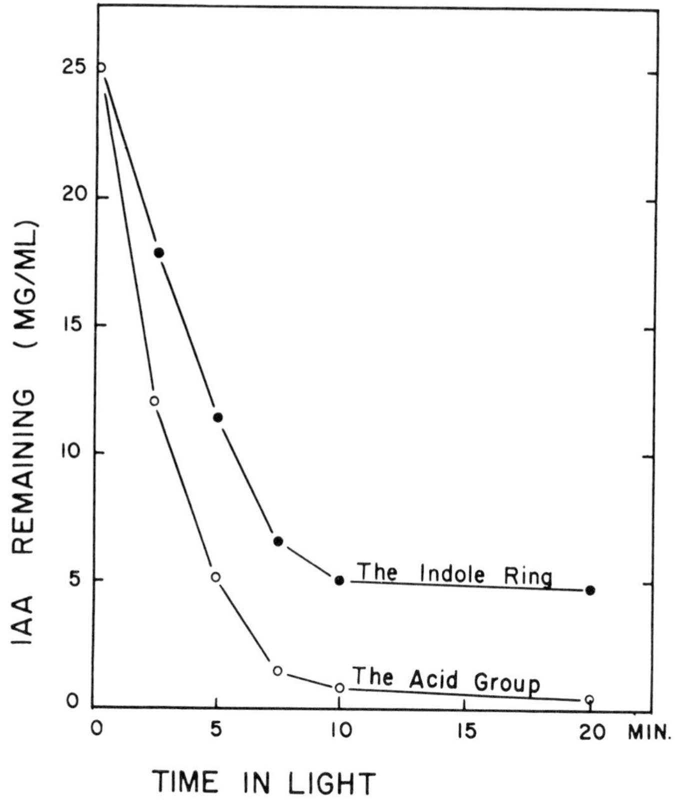

Fig. 45. Relative rates of disappearance of the indole ring (as determined by the Hopkins-Cole Test) and the acid group (as determined by pH) of indoleacetic acid during photo-destruction with riboflavin (Brauner, 1953).

the enzymatic destruction of auxin (Andreae and Andreae, 1953). Thus it appears that indolealdehyde is one product of auxin destruction, though it may be further degraded, and perhaps even different pathways of destruction may be followed.

Several materials can alter the enzymatic destruction of auxin. For example, scopoletin, a naturally occurring lactone, is a competitive inhibitor of the reaction (Andreae, 1952). Many compounds which can readily be oxidized may inhibit auxin destruction by competing for the oxygen in the reaction given above. A good example of this type of inhibitor is ascorbic acid (Brauner and Brauner, 1954). Also, 2,4-dichlorophenol (a common contaminant of 2,4-D) stimulates the enzymatic destruction of indoleacetic acid (Goldacre *et al,* 1953), and it has been found that this compound, like light, increases the formation of peroxides *in vivo* (Siegel and Galston, 1954). Hence they each apparently facilitate auxin destruction by bringing about peroxide formation.

It has been found that indoleacetic oxidase, as the auxin destroying enzyme is called, is an adaptive enzyme. That is, tissues which are not active in destroying auxin can become highly active in a matter of 5 to 120 minutes after exposure to auxin (Galston and Dahlberg, 1953). This remarkable property is more evident in old, non-growing tissues than in young growing ones, and so it may play a role in aging phenomena as well as in the control of apical dominance.

Another interesting point concerning the effects of light on auxin has been brought out by Galston and Baker (1951) who demonstrated that, while light inhibits auxin action in etiolated plant parts, it actively promotes auxin-induced growth in green tissues. These workers observed, however, that much higher light intensities were effective in this stimulation of growth than were involved in the auxin-destroying system. Furthermore, the stimulatory effect of light could be at least partly substituted for by sugars. They suggested, therefore, that the light-stimulation of growth in green tissues is a function of the photosynthetic production of sugars.

The action of light upon growth appears to be very complicated indeed, involving its role in auxin formation, enzymatic and non-enzymatic auxin destruction, and the production of substrates for growth. As will be pointed out later, light also reduces the sensitivity of tissues to auxin and through its effect on polarity alters the type of growth obtained.

The auxin-destroying enzyme has been found to be most abundant in roots (Tang and Bonner, 1947; Wagenknecht and Burris, 1950). This is rather interesting since the polar transport of auxin would otherwise be expected to accumulate large quantities of auxin in the roots. Inasmuch as the roots are the most sensitive to auxin of any plant organ, such an accumulation would be certainly detrimental to the plant.

It should be pointed out here that auxin destruction does not specifically require any given pigment. While riboflavin is very effective in the destruction of auxin, a similar effect can be obtained *in vitro* with eosin, lumichrome, and even chlorophyll (Skoog, 1935; Galston, 1949; Brauner, 1953). It is interesting to note that *in vitro* suspensions of auxin with β-carotene do not destroy indoleacetic acid in light (Reinert, 1952).

Long ago, eosin was observed to have no appreciable effect on plant growth if applied in the dark, but upon exposure of eosin-treated plants to light all growth was blocked and the responses of the plants to phototropism were lost (Boas and Merkenschlager, 1925). The studies of Skoog (1935) indicate that this growth inhibition by light was attributable to the destruction of auxin.

Ferri (1951) pointed out that the various dyes which are capable of oxidizing auxin are all fluorescing substances. He has suggested that the destruction of auxin may be more nearly a function of the fluorescing characteristics that a simple light-absorbing quality of the dye. He has produced rather dramatic support for this suggestion by demonstrating that quinine, a colorless substance which fluoresces under illumination, is capable of destroying indoleacetic acid *in vitro* in the light.

Another means by which auxins can be destroyed is by x-irradiation. Early workers observed that x-rays could cause large increases in branching (Johnson, 1936). As we know, apical dominance or the natural control of branching is a function of the growth hormone. With this idea in mind Skoog (1935) found that x-rays could indeed destroy auxin. Working with simple solutions of indoleacetic acid, Skoog was able to determine that 25 roentgens could destroy as much as 30 per cent of the auxin activity. The x-rays apparently cause a rupture of the indole ring (Gordon, 1953). While the great bulk of experimentation on x-ray inactivation of auxin has been carried on *in vitro,* evidence of auxin destruction by this agent in intact plants has also been obtained (Skoog, 1934, 1935). A further effect of x-rays is an apparent interference with the enzyme system which converts indoleacetaldehyde into the acid auxin (Gordon, 1953).

Another means by which auxin can be inactivated in the plant, or perhaps more accurately by which the auxin supply can be lowered in the plant, is heat treatment. Working with sugar cane, Brandes and van Overbeek (1949) found that placing stem sections in hot water (52° C) for 20 minutes caused breaking of essentially all lateral buds and a loss of geotropic sensitivity of the stem. Both apical dominance and geotropic sensitivity could be restored after the treatment by supplying auxins artificially. Analysis of the auxin content of the stem sections indicated that the heat treatment resulted in a 50 per cent decrease in free auxin content 24 to 48 hours after treatment. The delay in expression of the auxin reduction would suggest that the auxin-producing system had been suppressed by the heat treatment.

It is known that high temperatures can reverse both the vernalizing effects of low temperatures and also the reproductive stimulus following the auxin treatment of seeds (Purvis and Gregory, 1945; Leopold and Guernsey, 1953). It is possible that these high temperature effects may act in part through auxin destruction or suppression of auxin formation. Exposure of rice seedlings to warm temperatures (26° C) is known to produce striking reductions of auxin content when they are compared to seedlings in cool temperatures (10° C) (Sircar and Das, 1951).

CHAPTER IV

Developmental Effects of Auxins

The mechanisms in the plant which are controlled or at least influenced by auxins are sometimes difficult to distinguish one from another and any classification of such effects will necessarily be rather arbitrary. For convenience, the effects of endogenous auxins may be grouped into six general classes: (1) the effects of auxins on growth itself, (2) the effects on tropisms and movement, (3) the effects on the inhibitions of development of various plant parts, (4) the participation in morphological differentiation, (5) the effects on flower and fruit development, and (6) the control of abscission.

GROWTH

It is obvious that all of the six general effects of auxins given involve the effects of auxin on growth itself. Certain generalizations about growth phenomena can be recognized as applying in common to all the auxin effects.

The concept established by Went (1928), that without auxin there is no growth, has been consistently borne out in the great body of more recent studies. Strong differences in the specific auxin levels required to stimulate growth in different plant organs were observed by many early workers. In many cases a mistaken point of view was adopted that, whereas auxins promote growth of stems, they inhibit the growth of roots. The situation was corrected by Boysen-Jensen (1936) who showed that roots simply have a higher sensitivity to auxin, and thus are stimulated to grow by much lower concentrations than those required to stimulate growth of stems. A generalized scheme for the effects of auxins upon growth of roots, buds, and stems was made by Thimann (1937) in which he graphically represented the relative ranges of auxin responses in various organs as shown in figure 46. From this schema it can be seen that concentrations of auxin which promote growth of stems inhibit the growth of buds and roots. Lower concentrations can promote the growth of buds and still lower concentrations can promote the growth of roots. Other growth phenomena could similarly be entered in this graph of relative sensitivity.

The promotion and inhibition of flowering by auxins have been plotted in this way (Leopold and Thimann, 1949), and similar curves could be drawn for fruit growth and leaf growth.

A remarkable dualism exists in the actions of auxin. Auxin can either stimulate or inhibit the various growth functions. Auxins can promote or inhibit the differentiation of buds, promote or inhibit the production of flowers, promote or inhibit abscission, promote or

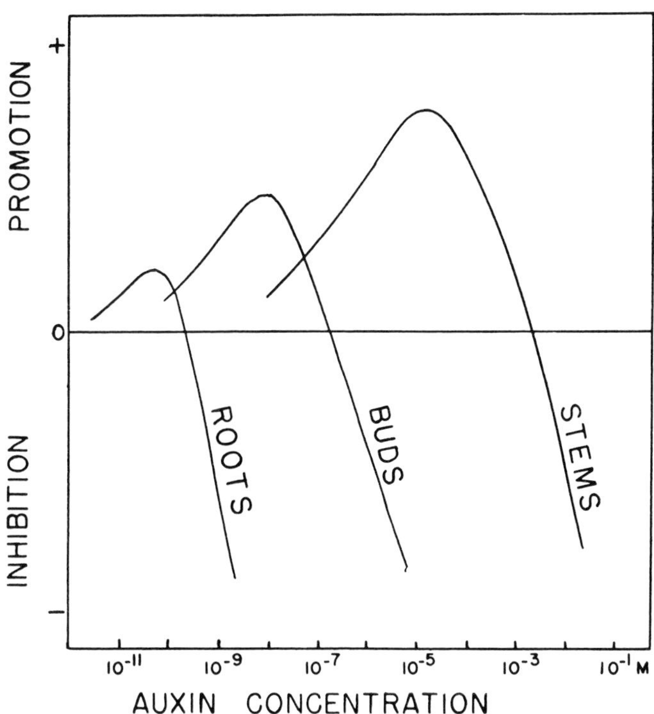

Fig. 46. Ranges of growth responses to auxin (indoleacetic acid) for various plant organs (modified from Thimann, 1937).

inhibit respiration or activity of some enzymes, promote or inhibit protoplasmic streaming, promote or inhibit the accumulation of certain biochemical plant constituents, and promote either differentiation or dedifferentiation of living cells. In each case, the effect obtained is primarily a function of the effective auxin concentration in the tissue. A logical explanation on a biochemical basis of the dualism of auxin effects upon growth is discussed in chapter VIII.

TROPISMS

The first recognized developmental effect of auxin was its participation in tropisms and plant movements. Indeed, the very discovery of auxins resulted from studies of the tropisms and it is through the effects of auxins on the curvature of *Avena* coleoptiles that the principal bioassay for auxin is carried out.

Phototropism

If we consider first phototropism, it will be recalled that Cholodny (1927), and Went (1928) each concluded independently that unequal distribution of growth hormone was responsible for the turning of plants toward light. Perhaps one of the most graphic demonstrations of the differences in auxin distribution following unilateral exposure to light is one in which auxin was diffused simultaneously from the lighted and from the unlighted sides of coleoptile tips. Not only was it found that more auxin was obtained from the unlighted side than from the lighted, but also the unlighted side yielded more than similar halves of non-stimulated control tips. Thus it was clear that a lateral redistribution of auxin was involved (Went, 1928). The unequal distribution of auxin in the coleoptile results, of course, in unequal growth on the lighted versus the unlighted side and a consequent curvature toward the light.

The unequal distribution of auxin is apparently largely a result of light-induced lateral translocation of auxin. The work of van Overbeek (1933) indicates that the total amount of auxin in coleoptiles which have been exposed to weak light is essentially the same as in coleoptiles kept in the dark, but that 85 per cent of this auxin present exists on the shaded side and only 15 per cent on the lighted side. The fact that almost the same lateral distribution resulted if the coleoptile tip were replaced with an auxin block indicated that the irregular distribution is not attributable solely to lateral differences in production of auxin by the tip. The auxin block, of course, furnished auxin uniformly to all sides of the coleoptile and the resultant uneven distribution must necessarily have been a result of lateral transport of the auxin.

A clear demonstration of the lateral redistribution of auxin in response to light can be found in the studies of Boysen-Jensen and Nielsen in 1926. These workers showed that by making a vertical slit through the coleoptile and inserting a tinfoil barrier in such a way that the lighted side was not in contact with the unlighted side, a loss of phototropic sensitivity could be produced. After the tinfoil barrier was removed, phototropic sensitivity was restored.

Differences in electrical potential between the lighted and unlighted side were proposed as early as 1927 by Brauner as a possible explanation of the lateral transport of auxin. There are many types of evidence which suggest that electrical phenomena may be involved in auxin transport, and the evidence for and against such a mechanism has been ably reviewed by Schrank (1951).

A second mechanism which may participate in the phototropic response is the light reaction of growing cells. There is good reason to believe that light causes a desensitization of growing cells to a given amount of auxin (van Overbeek, 1933; Galston and Baker, 1953). Accurate experimental distinction between the reduction in sensitivity to auxin and the capacity of the cells to destroy auxin remains to be drawn. It has been estimated, however, that as much as 50 per cent of the curvature of *Avena* coleoptiles toward light may be a result of the reduced growth associated with the light reaction (van Overbeek, 1933).

A third factor which may participate in phototropism is the formation of auxin in response to light. Van Overbeek noted as early as 1932 that light can bring about auxin formation, and the action is discussed in some detail in chapter III. As a factor in phototropism, auxin formation serves mainly to reduce the tropic bending of green plants and to affect the orientation of green leaves and stems in light (Laibach and Fischnick, 1936).

A fourth factor which may participate in phototropism is auxin destruction by light. The action spectrum for phototropism, which compares the relative effectiveness of different wavelengths of light in stimulating the reaction, has been worked out in detail by Galston and Baker (1949) as shown in figure 41 (p. 85). It can be seen that blue light of wavelengths from 400 to 500 mμ is effective, and peak effectiveness is obtained with 440 mμ. There is a striking similarity between the wavelengths which are effective in causing phototropism and those which are effective in causing auxin destruction (cf. figures 41 and 42). Phototropism as a response to weak light does not apparently involve a reduction in total auxin present in a coleoptile, but it is obvious that under strong light intensities auxin destruction will certainly occur on the lighted side, and will undoubtedly play a part in phototropism.

Early workers (Wald and DuBois, 1936) suggested that β-carotene may be the pigment responsible for the perception of light in phototropism of the *Avena* coleoptile. The action spectrum of phototropism is very similar to the absorption spectrum of β-carotene and they found this pigment to be present in the coleoptile. More recently Galston (1949) has demonstrated that riboflavin can mediate the photodestruction of auxin, that it is present in the coleoptile, and that it too shows approximately the same absorption spectrum. The debate as to whether β-carotene or riboflavin is the phototropic pigment is not yet settled. β-carotene lacks the ability to mediate the photodestruction of auxin *in vitro* (Reinert, 1953), and by masking the riboflavin absorption wavelengths it can reduce the photodestruction in solutions of riboflavin as well as reduce phototropic sensitivity of the mold, *Phycomyces* (Reinert, 1952). The largest factor in phototropic responses to weak light, however, is the induction of lateral transport of auxin, and the relative merits of β-carotene and riboflavin in this function have never been explored. It seems possible that phototropism may not be mediated by a single specific pigment, but more than one pigment may absorb the light which activates the response just as more than one pigment may activate the photodestruction of auxin.

An interesting question related to phototropism has been raised in the literature. What is the identity of the auxin responsible for phototropism? Several workers have found that the exposure of decapitated coleoptile sections to unilateral light will result in curvature if preparations of auxin diffused from plants are added, but if indoleacetic acid is added instead no curvature will be obtained (van Overbeek, 1936). On this basis it has been proposed that auxin *a* may be the auxin responsible for phototropism. Carrying this a step further it has even been proposed that the effect of indoleacetic acid upon growth in general is obtained simply by causing the release of auxin *a* (von Guttenberg, 1942). The evidence on this point with reference to phototropism is carefully reviewed by Galston (1950) who raises the logical question of the purity of auxin *a* preparation in the phototropism studies, and points out that conclusions from these experiments must be tentative until pure auxin *a* preparations can be compared with indoleacetic acid in this respect. There is considerable doubt of course as to whether auxin *a* even occurs naturally in plants and whether it would be an active auxin if it did occur there (see chapter III).

Geotropism

The phenomenon of geotropism was clarified almost simultaneously with phototropism. This tropism appears to be dependent upon only one or possibly two of the four functions known to be responsible for phototropism.

Lateral transport of auxin has been shown to be caused by exposure to lateral gravitational forces (Dolk, 1929). Geotropic stimulation produces no overall change in growth rate, but brings about a lateral redistribution of auxin such that approximately 62 per cent of the auxin appears on the lower side of the coleoptile, root tip, or stem. This asymmetrical distribution results in asymmetrical growth, with coleoptiles and stems bending away from the gravitational force and roots bending toward it. The shift in auxin distribution is not the result of a unilateral production by the apex, since newly decapitated sections exposed to a geotropic stimulus show the same bending and the same auxin redistribution pattern. After the removal of the geotropic stimulus, coleoptiles recover symmetrical growth much more rapidly than after phototropic stimulation. For example, the *Avena* coleoptile recovers normal growth one hour after termination of geotropic stimulation (Dolk, 1929), whereas pea stems recover normal growth 24 hours after exposure to light (Galston and Baker, 1953). Recovery data for *Avena* coleoptiles after light exposure are not available. This may be taken as indirect evidence that sensitivity of the cells to auxin after geotropic stimulus does not change as it does after exposure to light. As in phototropism, changes in electric potentials occur following geotropic stimulation (Bose, 1907). The lower side is positively charged in relation to the upper side by as much as 5 to 10 millivolts. Again, the participation of this electric potential difference in auxin movement has been postulated.

A second factor which sometimes is involved in geotropism is the formation of auxin. In studying the geotropic responses of sugarcane stems, van Overbeek *et al* (1945) found that meristems located just above each node were sites of renewed auxin formation after geotropic stimulation. When the stems were placed in a horizontal position, auxin was synthesized on the lower sides, and growth of the stem meristems were consequently activated. In non-meristematic tissues such as the *Avena* coleoptile, the formation of auxin is unaffected by geotropic stimuli (Dijkman, 1933).

Root Tropisms

Tropisms in roots are apparently controlled by the same mechanisms as are tropisms of coleoptiles and shoots, except that the direction of response is reversed. Roots have an extremely low optimum auxin concentration for growth, as can be seen in figure 46. In fact, the auxin level in most roots is at the optimum or above it. Consequently tropic stimuli which result in lateral movement of auxin and an attendant increase of auxin content on one side inhibit growth on that side. In the case of shoots, on the other hand, growth is stimulated instead. Therefore, while stems turn toward light, roots turn away; and while stems turn away from the force of gravity, roots turn toward it. A clever demonstration of the difference in sensitivity between roots and stems which produces this oppositeness of tropic response has been made by Geiger-Hüber and Hüber (1945). They found that repeated decapitation of roots, which drastically lowers the auxin content, causes these structures to respond as stems, i.e. away from gravitational pull. Likewise the addition of rather large quantities of auxins to stems resulted in root-like responses to gravity, presumably because the lateral redistribution of auxin furnished inhibitory levels of auxin to the side toward the gravitational pull.

Some provocative studies of root tropisms have been made by Pilet (1951), who found that very young roots of lentil bean have a suboptimal auxin concentration, and hence respond tropically in the manner of stems. Roots less than 20 mm. long turn toward light, and as they grow older their auxin content rises and a reversal of the tropic behavior results. This situation is probably not common to plants in general. Moewus and Moewus (1952) found that cress roots contained suboptimal auxin concentrations either when very young or when they had aged beyond the stage of optimal growth. It may be that the lateral spreading of root systems may be due in part to weakened geotropic sensitivity as the roots grow older and their auxin concentration is reduced.

The action of auxins in other types of tropic responses such as thigmotropism and traumatropism is discussed by Went and Thimann (1937, p. 178) and Schrank (1951).

INHIBITION EFFECTS

With the first discovery of auxins, it was found that they could inhibit the growth of coleoptiles, stems, and of course roots. The first inhibition effect of auxin to be described as a positive force in plant development was that of auxins upon lateral bud growth and the resulting phenomenon of apical dominance. Thimann and Skoog (1933) clearly demonstrated this function of auxin by establishing, first, that the apex is the largest source of auxin for the plant; second, that removal of the apex results in the loss of apical dominance and stimulates the development of lateral buds; and finally that the artificial supplying of auxin after decapitation restores apical dominance, effectively preventing lateral bud growth. If the plant apex were the only source of auxin in the plant one would expect that it alone would control bud inhibition. But of course young expanding leaves are also rich sources of auxin, and leaves are known to exert an inhibitory effect on the development of the bud in their axil (Snow, 1929; Goodwin, 1937). The production of relatively large amounts of auxin in the apex has been associated with the development of a relatively unbranched plant form and conversely, plants which contain relatively low auxin levels develop a branching habit (Delisle, 1937). Perhaps the most dramatic demonstration of auxin levels as determining factors in plant form was that made by van Overbeek (1935), in which he showed that a dwarf variety of corn (variety *Nana*) contained a much lower auxin level than non-dwarfed varieties. Associated with this low auxin level was a less rapid rate of elongation, a branching habit, and even a tendency to lose the upright position and to become prostrate. This effect of low auxin levels was demonstrated to be attributable not to a lower auxin production rate, but instead to a high rate of auxin destruction.

Since the auxin level in a plant or a branch of a plant is a primary factor in the inhibition of lateral buds, then treatments which would reduce the auxin level should stimulate branching. Various treatments which might destroy auxin in a plant, such as x-irradiation, the injection of dyes in the light, the addition of auxin antagonists, and changes in photoperiod, have all been found to increase branching of dicots or tillering of grasses (Skoog, 1935; Johnson, 1936; Cajlachjan and Zdanova, 1938; Leopold, 1949).

The control of branching in roots appears to involve an auxin mechanism similar to that operative in shoots, for the decapitation of roots can cause branching. However, an additional feature appears to be involved in the control of root branching, presumably a factor originating elsewhere than in the tip (Torrey, 1950).

The inhibition of the growth of buds by auxins is not an entirely simple phenomenon and it has been shown that bud inhibition may not be strictly a function of absolute auxin level. Le Fanu (1936) reported that auxin applied to the base of pea stem cuttings is considerably more inhibitory than auxins applied to the apex. The evidence that some auxin can move in a non-polar manner would seem to suggest that the direction of auxin movement may have a considerable bearing upon its inhibitory effectiveness.

The development of flowers at the apex of a stem is often associated with the development of lateral branches and a loss of apical dominance, a good case in point being the zinnia. Since it has been demonstrated that, at least in the coleus, the appearance of apical flowers is associated with a strong alteration of the polarity pattern in a stem, it is tempting to speculate that the associated increase in branching may be due to a less active polar transport of auxins from the apex (Leopold and Guernsey, 1953).

A contrast may be drawn between the role of auxin in dormancy and its role in apical dominance. In the former case, there appears to be an insufficient supply of effective auxin for growth because of the presence of antagonists which can interfere with the normal function of whatever auxin is present (Hemberg, 1947). In the latter case lateral buds are prevented from developing by reason of the high, inhibitory levels of auxins moving past the buds or, at least, present in the stems adjacent to them.

The possibility that auxins commonly exist in roots at levels which are inhibitory to root growth has been evident for many years. The early experiments by Cholodny (1929) support this concept admirably. He found that decapitation of roots of many different kinds of plants could result in an increase in subsequent root elongation. Not only that, but the replacement of the root tip would again reduce the rate of growth. This evidence strongly suggests that auxins produced in the root tip are at a super-optimal concentration for root growth. Some exceptions to this inhibitory situation have been mentioned in the previous section. A common exception is found in the pea, reported as early as 1936 by Thimann. He found that pea roots could be stimulated by the addition of auxin and inhibited in growth rate by decapitation. The capacity of pea roots to respond positively to further additions of auxins has been utilized in a highly sensitive bioassay for auxin (see chapter II).

ORGAN DIFFERENTIATION

Soon after the discovery of the growth hormone it was found that the hormone and other auxins affected not only growth by elongation, but also affected the morphological type of growth obtained. Thus an application of auxin to a young stem might result in a callus type of growth. Also, stem cuttings treated with auxin could be induced to form roots. More recently it has been discovered that auxin levels play a determining role in the differentiation of many types of meristems including roots, buds and sometimes even flowers. In time, therefore, it has become apparent that auxins participate in a general control of organ differentiation. By some means as yet unknown, auxins are a factor in determining whether a cluster of cells will be differentiated into callus, roots, vegetative buds (stems and leaves), or flower buds.

As in the auxin control of growth, a dualism is exerted in the auxin control of organ differentiation. A relatively high concentration of auxin, physiologically speaking, can bring about dedifferentiation instead of differentiation of cells. Auxin applications to plants will sometimes cause large areas of differentiated parenchyma, pericycle, or endodermis tissues to dedifferentiate into callus. Again, under certain circumstances auxin levels can exert a control over the redifferentiation of these callus tissues and meristems, giving rise to roots, buds, or flowers. Carrying the feature of dualism still further, we know of course that the appearance of a given organ may be promoted by one range of auxin concentrations and inhibited by higher concentrations.

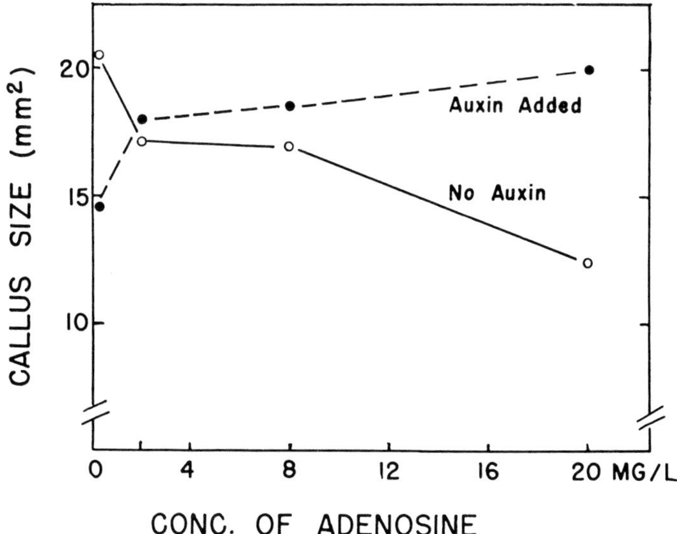

Fig. 47. The effect of adenosine on the growth of tobacco stem callus in the presence and absence of auxin, 0.25 mg./l. naphthaleneacetic acid (Skoog and Tsui, 1948).

Before discussing the interaction of auxins with other plant constituents in the control of organ differentiation, it might be well to mention a graphic case to emphasize how sharply auxin action may be altered by other plant constituents present. Skoog and Tsui (1948) have shown that applications of auxin alone to cultures of excised tobacco stems will inhibit growth of the stem sections. When applied in conjunction with adenosine the same auxin applications will stimulate growth (figure 47). This interaction lays a cornerstone for the understanding of the interactions of other compounds with auxin. It is a clear demonstration that the effect of a given auxin application will be determined not by the auxin alone, but by the other materials present as well. It is also suggestive that the differences in auxin sensitivity of various tissues shown in figure 46 may be essentially attributable to differences in chemical composition of the tissues.

Carrying this concept of interaction of materials with auxin directly to the study of organ differentiation, Skoog and Tsui demonstrated that auxin applications to tobacco stem sections could bring

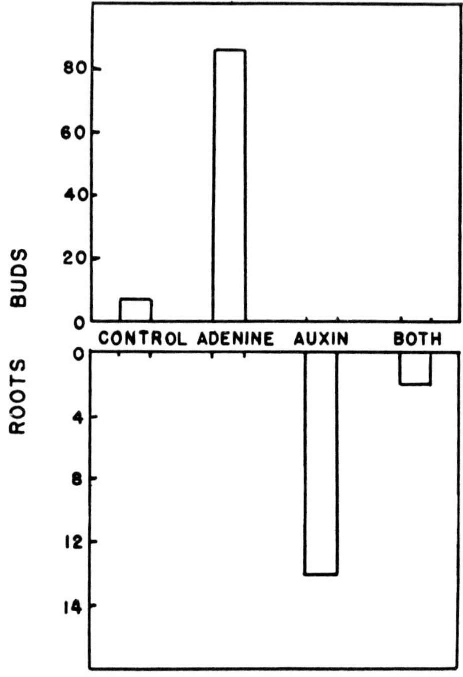

Fig. 48. The separate effects of adenine (40 mg./1.), auxin (0.02 mg./1. naphthaleneacetic acid) and both upon bud and root formation in tobacco stem segments (from Skoog and Tsui, 1948).

about the development of roots, callus, or buds, depending upon the materials which were added with the auxin. From their work they concluded that the type of growth obtained is controlled at least in part by the ratio of auxin to organic nitrogenous compounds, particularly purines. Figure 48 exemplifies such an interaction in morphological differentiation, where bud and root formation on tobacco stem sections are compared. The addition of adenine to the culture medium results in a large increase in number of buds differentiated. The addition of auxin (naphthaleneacetic acid) favors root formation. When the two are added together more growth is obtained, but neither type of differentiation dominates.

The concentration of adenine required to obtain a given number of buds was found to be higher if more auxin was added and lower with less auxin. This type of interaction holds not only for buds but for callus and root formation as well.

A simplified way of looking at Skoog and Tsui's concept might be to assume that the concentration ratio of auxin to adenine will determine to a large extent whether buds, callus, or roots will be formed. At low auxin to adenine ratios, buds will be produced; and at high ratios (i.e. high auxin: low adenine), roots will be produced:

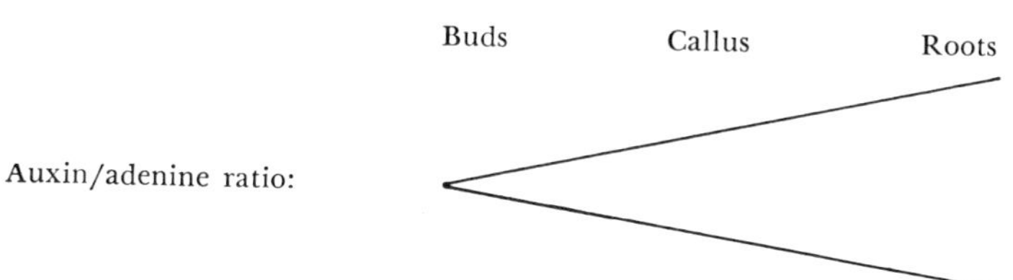

Investigating the specificity of this function, Skoog and Tsui found that adenine, guanine, and adenylic acid were all highly effective in producing buds on excised plant material. Organic nitrogenous compounds other than the purines were found to be much less effective in this control of differentiation. An interaction between these compounds and phosphates was found.

Further evidence of the intimate relationship between adenine and auxin is found in experiments with the purine inhibitor, 2,6-diaminopurine (Miller, 1953). This compound inhibits bud formation in tobacco stem sections, and the inhibition is relieved by further additions of adenine. The auxin stimulation of growth in straight-growth tests is likewise inhibited, and again the inhibition is relieved by addition of adenine.

The impact of these studies upon the understanding of auxin action in morphology is great indeed. They bring together previously heterogeneous observations of the effects of auxin upon callus and root formation and correlation phenomena in general. For years we have recognized that callus formation in whole plants or in cuttings from plants occurs at places where auxin content would be expected to be high due to its basipetal movement. Girdling of woody twigs results in callus formation followed generally by root formation above the girdle where auxins accumulate. Buds are commonly formed below the girdle, where the auxin content would be expected to be low in proportion to the nitrogenous food materials moving up from the roots. Cuttings, particularly of woody plants, commonly grow callus followed by root formation at the physiological base of the cutting. These events can be greatly encouraged by the applications of rather weak auxins, the one in most common use being indolebutyric acid. The fact that auxin treatment is effective in bringing about root formation but not bud formation becomes understandable.

Morphological studies of the development of callus show that whatever the tissue of origin, a successive series of cell divisions occurs which typically ends in a fan-shaped arrangement of cells shaped like packed bubbles without any real differentiation of the usual cell types. This represents a rather complete stage of dedifferentiation of individual cells into masses of dividing cells, each one closely comparable to its neighbors and showing no inclination to differentiate into a mature type of tissue such as xylem, phloem, or even parenchyma.

The first stage in differentiation from this undifferentiated callus is the formation of a meristem. Sterling (1951) has shown in some detail that clusters of cells on the surface or subadjacent to the surface first become differentiated into a tunica-like arrangement of rectangular cells and from this first step in differentiation a compact meristem soon emerges, being either root primordium or a bud apex depending on the biochemical factors mentioned above.

It may not be out of place briefly to consider the phenomenon of abscission at this point. The abscission layer in the petiole of a leaf or the pedicel of a flower or fruit is generally a meristematic zone which develops, as far as we know, when the auxin supply from the plant organ becomes low. Thus we may consider that the abscission of these plant parts is caused by the development of a meristematic tissue when the relative auxin content is low. The prevention of abscission of plant parts by the auxin formed in them then appears to be a natural control of meristematic differentiation by auxin.

Bud formation is another type of organ differentiation which is strongly altered by auxin concentrations as has been discussed already. It is interesting to notice that while buds are relatively easy to induce in stem material, they are quite difficult to induce in most root cuttings. Consequently, plant propagation techniques practically never utilize root cuttings. Although they will form new roots easily, buds will be produced readily in only a few species. In view of the high auxin sensitivity of roots and the demonstration by Skoog and Tsui that the effective ratio of auxin to adenine must be low for the formation of buds, it is perhaps not surprising that such a ratio is seldom attained in roots. Means of bringing that about artificially are described in chapter X.

Root formation has been induced in stem cuttings for many years by the application of auxins. The factors controlling the differentiation of root primordia will be discussed in chapter X, but it may be of interest to mention here the hypothesis of Bouillene and Went (1933) that a special hormone, rhizocaline, was involved in this type of morphological differentiation. They found that some substance which brings about differentiation of roots is formed in leaves and in buds, and moves in a strictly polar manner toward the physiological base. Although the polarity of this compound was similar to auxin and the loci of its formation again similar to those of auxin, the investigators were unable entirely to replace the effects of leaves and buds by simply adding auxin. Consequently they concluded that such a special hormone existed. Since that time, however, Thimann and Poutasse (1941) and more particularly van Overbeek *et al* (1946) have shown that the effects of leaves and buds in bringing about root formation can be entirely supplanted by organic nitrogenous compounds, sugars, and even in part by inorganic nitrogen sources if applied with auxin.

Flower formation as a type of organ differentiation has not been clarified with the same precision as bud and root formation. Clark and Kerns (1942) discovered that the pineapple plant could be forced to differentiate flowers by the application to the plant of small quantities of auxin. It is very suggestive to note that applications of higher auxin concentrations have the opposite effect, that is, they can absolutely prevent flower initiation in the pineapple. While we are unable to fit this phenomenon into agreement with the concept of Skoog and Tsui, it is tempting to believe that the auxin effects on flowering are being obtained through a change in balance or interaction between auxin and some other plant constituents. There are several reasons for believing this. Pineapple plants grown to different ages will require different dosages for initiation of flowers. Plants moderately high in carbohydrates require less auxin for flower initiation than do plants low in carbohydrate. Furthermore a given amount of auxin applied at different times of day, under different conditions of light and temperature, can produce entirely different results in forcing or inhibiting flowering. Most revealing of all is the finding that flower forcing techniques fail to bring about flowering unless at least one leaf remains on the pineapple plant (Traub *et al,* 1939). It appears that the action of auxin is not a simple one in this case either, but that an interaction or balance with other plant constituents is crucial to its function.

More direct evidence of an interaction between auxin and other plant constituents in flowering has been produced recently by Leopold and Guernsey (1953) who have demonstrated that various carbohydrates, amino acids, and organic acids applied to pea seedlings in minute amounts could quantitatively inhibit flower formation, and application of auxins would in the same manner quantitatively inhibit flower formation. The criterion of flowering, or earliness, was taken

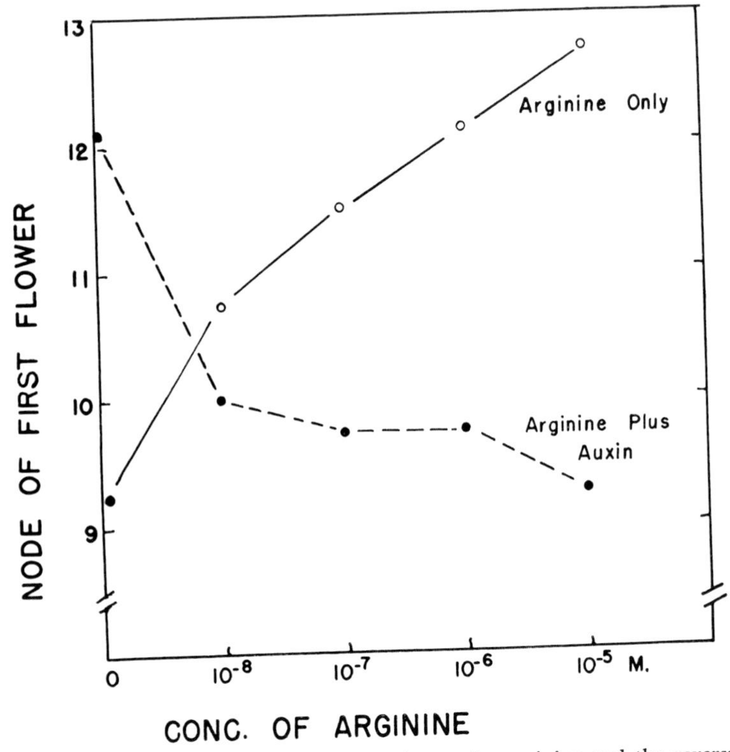

Fig. 49. The inhibition of flowering in the pea by arginine and the reversal of its effect by the addition of auxin, 0.01 mg./l. naphthaleneacetic acid (Leopold and Guernsey, unpublished).

to be the node of first flower. However, as figure 49 indicates, the inhibitory action of the carbohydrates, amino acids, or organic acids, could be erased by the concomitant addition of auxin.

The interesting subject of the influence of auxins on flowering is discussed in more detail in chapter XIV.

FRUIT DEVELOPMENT

The classic researches of Gustafson (1936 *et seq.*) have established that auxins are capable of causing the commencement of fruit development in many species without pollination. Indeed it appears that the normal process of fruit-set with pollination involves a release of large amounts of endogenous auxins. Since Gustafson's discovery, auxins have come to be widely used in commercial practice for bringing about fruit-set in some crops when natural set does not take place readily.

The researches of Muir (1951) have indicated that tobacco fruit, set either by pollination or by auxin sprays, builds up high concentrations of auxins, much too high to be accounted for in terms of the amount of auxin in the spray or in the pollen. This flush of auxin appears to be directly involved with the phenomenon of fruit-set and subsequent commencement of fruit growth. A flush of auxin from an auxin spray leads to a parthenocarpic fruit in some species.

TABLE 6

THE AUXIN CONTENTS OF OVARIES OF SEEDED VARIETIES OF SOME FRUITS AS COMPARED WITH SEEDLESS OR PARTHENOCARPIC VARIETIES.
(Gustafson, 1939)

Variety	Auxin content of ovaries in µg IAA equivalents/kilogram fresh weight		
	Seeded varieties	Seedless varieties	Per cent difference
Orange (Valencia)	0.58	2.39	+312
Lemon (Eureka)	0.43	0.78	+82
Grape (Thompson)		2.74	+705
(Muskat)	0.34		

Since the artificial application of auxins to some kinds of flowers can cause parthenocarpic fruit-set, one might expect that the presence of natural auxins in the ovary might be related to natural parthenocarpy. In fact it has been found that species which produce seedless fruits have a rich supply of auxin in the ovaries (Gustafson, 1939). Some sample data can be seen in table 6, in which the auxin contents of seedless varieties of orange, lemon and grape are compared with seeded varieties. The seedless varieties in each instance contain at least 75 per cent more auxin than the seeded varieties.

The actual means by which auxin brings about fruit-set is not clear, but there appear to be at least two roles for auxin. One of these is the incitement of growth of the young fruit and the other is the prevention of abscission of the flower. The separation of these two functions has been indicated by Leopold and Scott (1952), who found that fruit-set could be obtained after abscission, and conversely that abscission could be prevented without fruit-set in tomato flowers.

The physiological processes involved in fruit-set will be discussed in more detail in chapter XI. In brief, it is evident that auxin is a primary control of fruit-set. In normal pollination, an auxin-producing system is activated which results in fruit-set, whereas in parthenocarpy the unfertilized ovary contains sufficient auxin—either due to natural production or artificial application.

It is difficult to distinguish between the role of auxin in fruit-set and its role in the actual growth of the fruit. Assuming that such a distinction can be made, it can be said that in general there are two phases of auxin production by young fruit. In the earliest stages of growth, auxin production is essentially carried out in the ovary tissue surrounding the young embryo (Gustafson, 1939), whereas in later

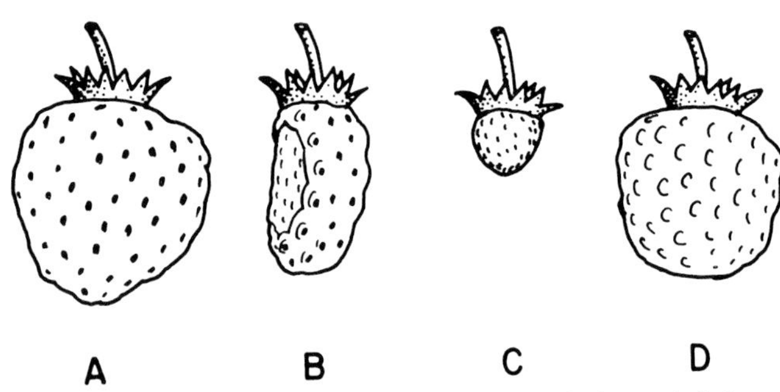

Fig. 50. The role of ovules in growth of strawberry fruits, and their replacement with auxin. (*A*) normal intact fruit; (*B*) removal of achenes from the sides of the fruit results in localized growth; (*C*) removal of all achenes prevents fruit growth; (*D*) removal of all achenes and application of auxin (100 mg./l. β-naphthoxyacetic acid) permits normal growth again (redrawn from Nitsch, 1950).

stages the major source of auxin is the young developing embryo. That developing embryos are a particularly rich source of auxin has been dramatically shown in several instances (Wittwer, 1943; Luckwill, 1948; Mitchell *et al*, 1951) and the great role that these auxin sources play in development of the fruit has been abundantly demonstrated by Nitsch (1950) working with strawberry fruits. His experiments have indicated that the greatest part of growth of the fruit is brought about by the auxin produced in the developing achene. It can be seen in figure 50 that removal of some of the ovules or young achenes caused localized fruit growth around the remaining ones (*B*). Complete removal of the ovules deprived the fruit of the hormone needed for growth (*C*), and supplying auxin replaced the function of the achenes in causing fruit growth (*D*).

ABSCISSION

That auxins can control abscission of various plant parts was first suggested by the work of Laibach (1933) when he demonstrated that orchid pollinia contained a material which prevented leaf abscission. LaRue (1936) was the first to use a synthetic auxin to control leaf abscission, and subsequently auxins have been found to control abscission not only in leaves and petioles but in flowers, fruits, and even stems.

Morphologically, abscission can take place in two ways. A meristematic abscission layer may form across the base of the organ. Enlargement of cells just distal to the meristematic zone may then force the organ to abscise. This meristematic type of abscission is characteristic of most leaves (coleus, pepper, tomato, citrus) and most flowers and young fruits (apple, tomato). The other general type of abscission involves a fracturing of the cell wall independently of meristem activity. This type of abscission is common in some types of leaves (Impatiens) and in the abscission of mature fruits (apple, peach, citrus). In this latter type there appears to be a degeneration of the cellulose materials of the primary cell wall followed in turn by a hydrolysis of the pectic materials (Sampson, 1918). The middle lamella is apparently not always the locus of the breakdown, but layers of the primary wall immediately adjacent to the middle lamella are places where these changes may also occur and the fracture actually take place. The distinction between these two morphological types of abscission is difficult to draw sometimes. Organs which normally abscise by activity of the meristematic abscission layer can be forced to abscise by means of wall fracture upon exposure to ethylene gas (Gawadi and Avery, 1950). Each of the morphological types of abscission can be prevented by auxin applications.

The effects of auxin on abscission, like the effects on so many other physiological functions, are of a dual nature. This has been demonstrated in the remarkable experiments of Addicott and Lynch (1951), showing that auxin can either accelerate or retard abscission depending upon the locus of its application. These two opposite effects are demonstrated in figure 51 from which it can be seen that auxin applied to the distal side of an abscission layer retards abscission, whereas auxin applied to the proximal side has the opposite effect. This observation may have a strong bearing on the use of auxins either to thin fruits or to hold fruits on trees, depending upon the time and place of application.

Several factors are recognized in the auxin control of abscission.

The first of these is the actual auxin content of the organ which may be abscissed, particularly with respect to the gradient of auxin levels between the organ and the stem to which it is attached. The importance of the auxin gradient was established by Shoji *et al* (1951). They found that abscission of leaves occurred when auxin production became low and the gradient of auxin across the abscission layer became small. This gradient is a function of the rate of auxin production in the organ and the auxin level in the stem. Either of these can be altered by the addition of auxins or materials modifying auxin action.

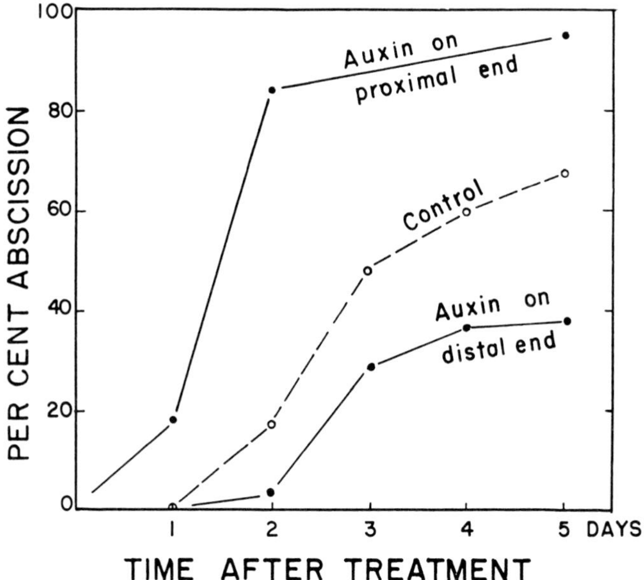

Fig. 51. The dual effects of auxin on abscission of excised bean leaf petioles. The addition of auxin (105 mg./l. of indoleacetic acid) to the distal end of the petiole prevents abscission, whereas addition to the proximal end forces more rapid abscission (Addicott and Lynch, 1951).

A general demonstration of the role of auxin production in the prevention of leaf abscission was made by Myers (1940). His measurements of auxin levels revealed that coleus leaves produced relatively small amounts of auxin in the winter season and much larger amounts in the spring. Applications of auxins to prevent abscission were much more effective in the winter during the period of relatively low auxin production. Many workers have reported that removal of leaf blades caused subsequent petiole abscission. The ability of auxins to substitute for the leaf blade in preventing that abscission has clearly demonstrated the role of auxin (LaRue, 1936). If, instead of removing the leaf, one applies substances which cause the death of the leaf tissue, abscission will also result. Livingston (1950) has shown clearly that commercial products designed to force foliar abscission do not themselves promote abscission, but essentially kill the leaf tissue. The effective auxin level of the leaf can be likewise modified by the addition of anti-auxins or auxin competitors. Hall *et al* (1953) reported that the anti-auxin trans-cinnamic acid can accelerate leaf abscission, and Weintraub *et al* (1952) have shown that TIBA (2,3,5-tri-iodobenzoic acid) is remarkably effective in causing stem abscission. The action of TIBA in this regard may be a result either of its competitive inhibition of auxin action, or more likely of its disruption of the polarity of auxin movement, a property demonstrated by Niedergang and Skoog (1952).

An interesting possible role of auxin in causing abscission is in the dropping of the corolla and stamens of flowers at the time of fruit-set. The abscission of these flower parts normally occurs promptly after fruit-set, and of course fruit-set is associated with a high auxin content of the ovary. With the advent of high auxin levels, abscission of the floral parts distal to the auxin supply would be predicted on the basis of the data in figure 51. It may be worthy to note in this connection that the spraying of floral parts of tomatoes with auxins to force fruit-set sometimes prevents abscission of floral parts after fruit-set. In these cases the spray apparently brings about an auxin level sufficiently high in the corolla and stamens to prevent their abscission for a week or so. Subsequently these persistent floral parts are ruptured and finally forced off by the enlarging young fruit.

The abscission of cotton bolls correlates with the accumulation of some auxin antagonist in the bolls (Carns *et al,* 1954). The antagonist apparently reduces the effectiveness of the auxin supply in the boll, and abscission results.

An actual destruction of auxin has been indicated as a cause of abscission in leaves infected with the fungus, *Omphalia flavida.* This parasite is responsible for large losses in coffee production by causing extensive leaf abscission, and an enzyme produced by the parasite has been found which destroys indoleacetic acid (Sequeira and Steeves, 1954). Abscission resulting from this pathological situation is thus apparently a consequence of auxin phenomena.

The important role that auxins play in the developmental functions of fruit-set, the control of abscission and the control of fruit size, has led to many uses of growth regulators in commercial fruit production. These will be discussed in chapters XI to XVII.

■ CHAPTER V

Physiological and Anatomical Effects of Auxin Applications

In the preceding chapters attention has been given primarily to the physiological functions of auxins as they occur naturally in plants. The introduction of synthetic auxins into plants has furnished much information concerning the physiological powers of auxins. Some of these powers relate to concentrations of auxins which may occur naturally, but more of them relate to unnaturally high auxin levels. A knowledge of the physiological and anatomical effects of auxins not only is valuable physiological information, but also has a strong bearing on the intelligent application of auxins in agricultural research.

GROWTH EFFECTS

After the discovery of the existence of growth hormones and the subsequent finding that many chemical compounds were able to stimulate growth in a similar manner, hope naturally arose that the simple application of these growth regulating materials to growing plants might increase growth and productivity. Unfortunately, it was found that auxins sprayed onto plants had very little beneficial effect on growth in general. Promotions were obtained only in stem elongation for a day or two after the spray was applied. Indeed, instead of beneficial effects, spray applications were generally followed by such undesirable consequences as epinastic bending of leaves, interference with normal leaf development, and the formation of swellings and adventitious roots.

A rather striking exception to the virtual lack of stimulation in growth found in most growth regulator applications to green plants appears in the study of Mitchell *et al* (1951). They observed that the application of hormone extracts from young bean fruits to bean seedlings increased growth of internodes and leaves by more than 200 per cent and this stimulation continued for at least 5 successive internodes. Tests of auxin activity of these extracts were not made with any standard assay procedures. There appears the inviting possibility that the hormones extracted were stabilized against normal auxin-destroying systems in the plant and hence could continue their stimulative effects over a long period of time.

Another overall stimulation of growth by auxin applications to intact plants has been achieved by means of the short-time application of auxins to seeds. Experiments in which seeds are germinated in auxin solutions and permitted to remain in them nearly always re-

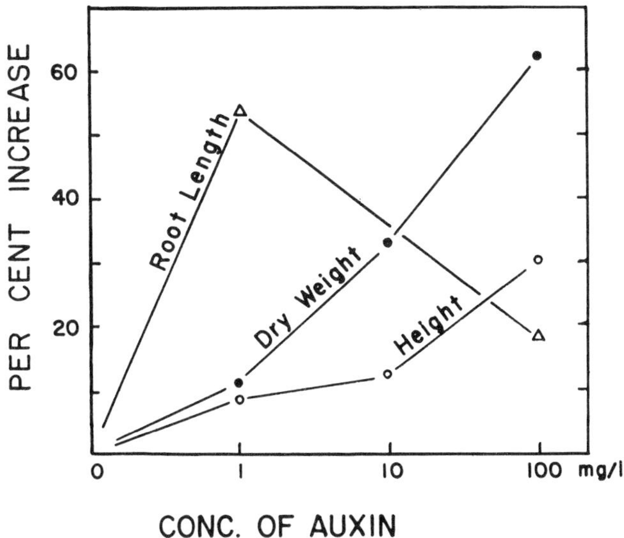

Fig. 52. Effects of the soaking of oat seeds with various concentrations of indoleacetic acid on later growth. The data on root length taken after six days; the dry weight and height after maturity (from Thimann and Lane, 1938).

sult in gross inhibitions of growth and development. However, short-time treatments of seeds in auxin solution have frequently given very considerable gains in subsequent growth rate of both shoots and roots. A graphic case is the report of Thimann and Lane (1938). They soaked oat seeds for 24 hours in indoleacetic acid solutions, and obtained 30 to 60 per cent increases in subsequent root length, plant height and final plant weight (figure 52). The auxin treatments of seeds yielded earlier and more abundant flowering. The possibility of using this type of treatment to obtain greater growth in crop plants has led to many attempts of this sort. However, it seems that gains in growth are secured only occasionally (Stier and du Buy, 1938; Tang and Loo, 1940) and in many instances inhibitions alone follow the treatment (Stewart and Hamner, 1942). A complete review of the many studies of auxin treatments of seeds up to 1952 has been made by Kruyt (1954), who concludes that a more profound understanding of germination and of auxin action is needed before consistent results can be obtained. More precise control of the environment appears to yield more consistent effects (chapter XIV).

Cholodny (1936) pointed out that possibly the stimulation of growth and development obtained by auxin treatments of seeds may be related to the effects obtained by low temperature treatments, or vernalization. The researches of Gregory and Purvis (1940) at London have indicated that vernalization is not a function of the growth hormone. More recent evidence suggests that some subtle relationship between auxin and vernalization may exist (Leopold and Guernsey, 1953).

ANATOMICAL EFFECTS

A voluminous literature has accumulated on the subject of the anatomical responses of various plants to the application of various auxins. Perusal of the observations that have been made brings one to the realization that the responses which will be obtained depend upon many factors both in the environment and in the plant itself.

Tissue Sensitivity

The literature on anatomical and morphological responses to applied auxins brings out three general factors which seem to have a bearing on the responses obtained: 1) the degree of differentiation of tissues in the plant when the application is made, 2) the formative activity of the particular auxin used, and 3) the transport of the auxin and its ultimate distribution through the plant.

In regard to the degree of differentiation of various tissues as a factor in the anatomical effects obtained, it would appear that tissues which are least differentiated have the greatest potential for response to an auxin or a growth regulator. Conversely, tissues which are highly differentiated and matured are least responsive (Beal, 1951). Thus, if one were to list the tissues of a stem in order of increasing degree of differentiation one would find that in general the tissues highest on the list (i.e. least differentiated) would have the greatest potential for response, and with increasing degrees of differentiation, responsiveness declines. A list of this sort might appear as follows:

Cambium	Increasing differentiation ↓	↑ Increasing responsiveness to auxins
Pericycle		
Endodermis		
Ray and phloem parenchyma		
Pith		
Young phloem		
Xylem and mature phloem		

In this connection, it is interesting to observe that the seedling stage is invariably highly sensitive to auxin applications (see chapter XVI), and it is the stage with much the largest proportion of weakly differentiated cells. Herbicide studies have shown many times over that plants go through different stages of susceptibility to auxin herbicides, and that the seedling is one of the most sensitive stages. The young vegetative plant is less sensitive and also less meristematic than the seedling. In the case of more mature plants of grain species, particularly at the stage of bolting when the rachis of flowers is being lifted on a rapidly growing stem, a much higher sensitivity to auxin herbicides is found (Blackman, 1950). It seems likely that the differences in sensitivity to auxins with different stages of plant development may be accounted for to a considerable extent on the basis of the relative abundance of weakly differentiated cells in the plants at the time of treatment.

A striking example of anatomical changes brought about by auxin treatment is shown in the sequence of pictures in figure 53. Stems of decapitated bean plants were treated with lanolin paste containing 5,000 p.p.m. of 2,4-D, and sections taken at various time intervals after application (Beal, 1946). The first picture (*A*) shows the normal anatomical arrangement before treatment. The second picture (*B*) shows the appearance after 24 hours, when meristematic activity has already started in the endodermis and phloem parenchyma, and activity is beginning to appear in the cambium, ray parenchyma and pericycle. The third picture (*C*), at 33 hours, shows widespread meristematic activity in all tissues from the endodermis to the cambium, including the parenchymatous areas between the vascular bundles. The fourth picture (*D*) shows at 72 hours the immense spread of undifferentiated callus-like tissues through the stem, associated with gross swelling of the stem. This stage is followed by the differentiation of root primordia, which become scattered through the mass. It can be seen in this sequence that the weakly differentiated endodermis, cambium and parenchymas were the first tissues to respond. With

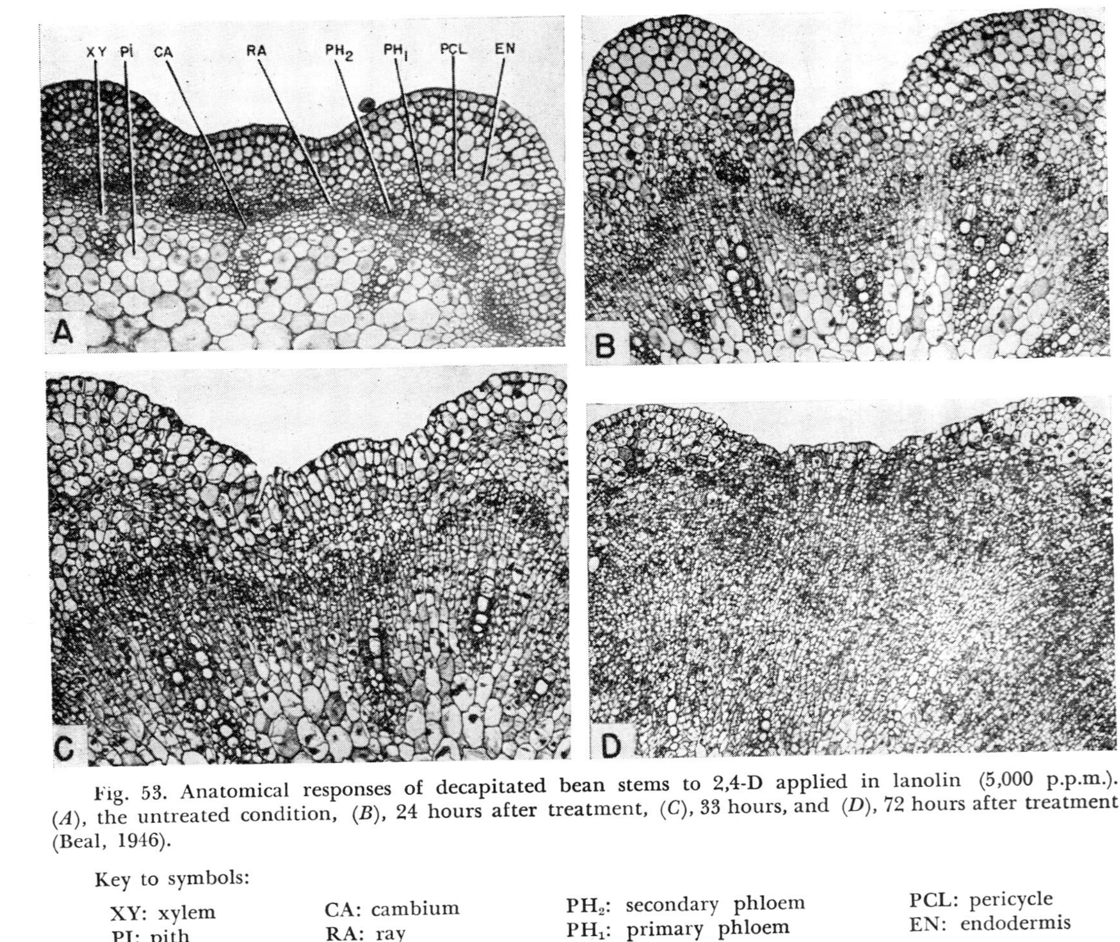

Fig. 53. Anatomical responses of decapitated bean stems to 2,4-D applied in lanolin (5,000 p.p.m.). (*A*), the untreated condition, (*B*), 24 hours after treatment, (*C*), 33 hours, and (*D*), 72 hours after treatment (Beal, 1946).

Key to symbols:

XY: xylem	CA: cambium	PH_2: secondary phloem	PCL: pericycle
PI: pith	RA: ray	PH_1: primary phloem	EN: endodermis

weaker applications these might have been the only ones to show meristematic activity.

The tissues which respond to the greatest degree vary somewhat with the age of the individual plant part. Thus pea stems proliferate most actively and form root primordia mostly from endodermis in younger stems, and mostly from pericycle in older stems (Palser, 1942).

Large differences in response of various tissues to different auxins have been observed. One auxin may characteristically cause the proliferation of the phloem; another one may primarily affect the endodermis. Some examples of the gross differences in response obtained with different auxins are discussed in the section in this chapter on leaf effects.

The mode of transport of the auxin applied and its ultimate distribution in the plant undoubtedly strongly influence the type of anatomical effects obtained. For example, if the auxin is transported primarily in the phloem, as it frequently is, then the phloem is prone to be one of the first tissues to show anatomical response. Much less transport probably occurs in the cambium. Having less auxin there, the cambium may not be the first tissue to undergo proliferation even though its sensitivity to auxin is very great.

Hamner and Kraus (1937) have shown that a uniform ring of auxin paste around a stem produced much greater amounts of callus in zones overlying the vascular bundles than in zones between bundles. A parallel observation has been made on roots (Wilde, 1951), where active proliferation of pericycle tissues in young roots was heavily concentrated over the vascular strands with much less proliferation between the strands.

The ultimate distribution of the growth regulator in the plant will be determined not only by the locus of transport, but by the transportability of the molecule itself and the general rate of translocation of other materials occurring in the plant.

It seems safe to assume that some environmental influences may alter the anatomical effects of auxins, especially since they will change the amount of translocation and otherwise adjust the constituents of the plant.

Stem Effects

Among the many studies of changes in stem anatomy following growth regulator applications, those by Beal (1945–46) might be selected as showing particularly well the differences in anatomical response owing to differences in the translocation of the applied auxin. For example, he found that the application of 2,4-D in lanolin paste to the leaf bases of intact bean plants produced extensive growth abnormalities over the entire plant, particularly in areas directly basipetal to the point of application. If application of the same material was made on decapitated beans, translocation was very much retarded in the absence of the leaves. The usual extensive growth abnormalities over the plant were not observed. Instead, a great local swelling occurred on the stem near the point of application and from this swelling there emerged great numbers of adventitious roots.

Gustafson (1941) reports another instance of the distribution of auxin affecting the morphological response obtained. He applied phenylacetic acid to young bean seedlings. This auxin is transported in plants only with great difficulty (Thimann and Schneider, 1939). Whereas 2,4-D causes distortions all the way to the base of the plant and causes as well the inhibition of lateral buds, phenylacetic acid was found to produce only a local callus-like growth in the vicinity of the application. Bud inhibition was notably absent. It seems fair to assume that such differences between auxins may be accounted for on the basis of the simple susceptibility of the auxin to translocation in the plant.

One rather startling effect of auxins on stem growth is the destruction of the primary phloem, brought about by the active proliferation of the young phloem cells or of parenchyma adjacent to the phloem (Eames, 1950). Since large quantities of auxin are transported in the phloem, it is hardly surprising to find that the phloem responds quite generally to auxin sprays by rapid proliferation, even though phloem cells are generally more differentiated and less sensitive to auxins than some other tissues. In cases where the phloem is actually destroyed by proliferation, Eames points out that the capacity of the plant to survive may be very seriously impaired, and so this phenomenon may account in part for the herbicidal effects of auxin sprays. Struckmeyer (1951) has made the interesting suggestion that the susceptibility of dicotyledonous plants to auxins may be due in part to the presence of cells in and about the phloem which are only weakly differentiated and hence capable of proliferation. In the resistant monocotyledonous plants, on the other hand, the phloem is usually surrounded by highly differentiated fibrous cells which are much less responsive to auxins.

The responses of stems to auxin applications vary somewhat from species to species. Among the lilies, for example, it has been reported that the white trumpet lily (*L. longiflorum,* Thunb.) responds to indoleacetic acid principally by proliferation of parenchyma adjacent to the vascular bundles, whereas the closely related Easter Lily (*L.*

longiflorum var. *eximium* Nichols) responds chiefly by proliferation of the epidermis (Beal, 1938).

Leaf Effects

The most common immediately observable response to auxins applied to foliage of plants is the development of *epinasty;* that is, the downward curling and bending of leaves occasioned by swelling of cells, particularly those on the dorsal sides of veins. In some cases the leaves bend upward, which is known as *hyponasty.* Figure 54

Fig. 54. Epinastic responses of tomato induced by naphthaleneacetic acid; *left,* untreated control, *center,* NAA sprayed upon the foliage, and *right,* NAA solution injected in stem (Zimmerman and Wilcoxon, 1935).

shows some typical epinastic curling and epinastic distortion of leaf outline in tomatoes sprayed with 2,4-D. Epinasty is not strictly an auxin function, for many poisons which inhibit cell enlargement can also cause epinastic responses. These are discussed in more detail in chapter VII.

As in the case of stems, leaves too will differ in their responses from species to species and will also differ with the growth regulator used. For example, 4-chlorophenoxyacetic acid produces extensive epinasty in tobacco and Kalanchoe leaves, whereas 2-chlorophenoxyacetic acid produces relatively little or none. Yet these two auxins produce indistinguishable epinastic responses on the leaves of tomato (Zimmerman, 1951).

It is difficult to say whether the epinastic activity of a growth regulator is proportional to its auxin activity. There are certainly cases where there is no such relationship, for many compounds which are not auxins at all are rather strong epinastic agents. However, strong auxins are almost always rather strong epinastic agents, depending of course on the plant material used for testing. It seems that the phenoxyacetic acids are sometimes stronger epinastic agents than the homologous forms of alpha-proprionic acids or alpha-butyric acids (Zimmerman, 1951). For this reason, the proprionic and butyric acids have been suggested as more appropriate agents for inducing fruit-set in tomatoes than the acetic acid derivatives because fruit-set can be obtained with less epinasty of the leaves (Howlett, 1950).

Besides the epinastic curling of leaves, there is commonly a distortion in the outline of leaves which grow out after auxin applications. Such distortions of subsequently expanded leaves are owing to the inhibition of normal cell division and cell enlargement in the young expanding leaves.

An especially interesting study of the effects of growth regulators on the meristematic growth of bean leaves has been made by Burton (1947). He observed that when 2-chlorophenoxyacetic, 4-chlorophenoxyacetic, and 2,4-dichlorophenoxyacetic acids are compared, the 2-chloro acid inhibits most strongly the meristem which produces the epidermis and consequently causes a pronounced decline in the size of the intercellular spaces. The 4-chloro acid is most toxic to the plate meristem which gives rise to the islets of mesophyll between the veins, and consequently the development of these areas is retarded. 2,4-dichlorophenoxyacetic acid on the other hand, is as toxic to the epidermal meristem as the 2-chlorophenoxyacetic acid, and is as toxic to the plate meristem as the 4-chlorophenoxyacetic acid. Thus the 2,4-D characteristically causes both types of leaf distortion in bean plants.

The greatest effects from auxin sprays appear on organs which are growing rapidly at or shortly after the time of application. In leaves, the type of distortion resulting from the treatment will depend in part upon the stage of development of the leaf at the time of treatment. The various leaf patterns of bean plants developed after 2,4-dichlorophenoxyacetic acid application have been described in detail by Eames (1951). Many other authors have found the same types of distortions in other plants (Watson, 1948; McIlrath and Ergle, 1953; Loustalot and Muzik, 1953).

Figure 55 illustrates the sequence of leaf distortion patterns as successive leaves are developed subsequent to auxin application to peppermint plants. Leaves which are near maturity at the time of treatment with 2,4-D will mature normally as seen in the left leaf in the figure. Leaves which are somewhat less mature at time of treatment characteristically show distortion of the lower half of the leaf, where the mesophyll islets fail to develop normally, so that cladification or expansion fails over the lower part of the leaf. Still younger

Fig. 55. Distortions of leaves of peppermint which develop after application of 2,4-D (1,000 mg./l.). Leaf at left is normal, and successively to the right leaves show inhibition of cladification, excessive enlargement of veins, shortening of leaves, and development of marginal ruffles. The leaf at far right is normal, developed entirely after the auxin effect was dispersed.

leaves at the time of treatment show the failure of cladification over the entire leaf, and the resultant leaf is a narrow structure with nearly parallel veins. The veins are abnormally large, principally because of the formation of opaque heavy-walled cells termed "replacement tissue" by Watson (1948).

Leaves which have been only slightly differentiated at the time of treatment with 2,4-D show extreme distortions such as the middle leaf in the figure exhibits. In these the leaf is reduced to a bundle of enlarged veins surrounded by sheaths of replacement tissue. In many species the marginal meristems of these leaves tend to develop normally, so that a margin or frill of green tissues appears as in the center leaf. In bean leaves this frill extends around the entire leaf (Eames, 1951).

The number of leaves showing extreme distortions apparently depends upon the degree of persistence of the active auxin in the meristems. In beans and peppermint, for example, only two or three leaves will be so distorted, whereas in cotton plants the extreme distortion may affect as many as eight leaves (McIlrath and Ergle, 1953). Leaves which develop after the influence of the auxin has been largely dispersed show beginnings of normal development of islets of mesophyll at the leaf bases but still suffer a persistent distortion of the apices. Finally, leaves which develop entirely after the effect of the auxin has been lost show completely normal form again, as seen in the right leaf in the figure.

Auxin treatments can engender a wide variety of leaf deformities, depending upon the specific tissues influenced by the treatment. For example, epidermal development may be retarded so that the leaf surface puckers (Burton, 1947). Characteristically the spongy mesophyll tissue divides excessively, so that the intercellular spaces of the leaves fill up (Watson, 1948). A great reduction in the photosynthetic capacity of the leaves is brought about in addition by the reduced frequency of chloroplasts as well as by the shrinkage in leaf size. High concentrations of 2,4-D can effectively stop photosynthesis in bean leaves within 24 hours, as a result of the collapse of cells and proliferation of replacement tissue in the spongy mesophyll of the leaf (Loustalot and Muzik, 1953).

Root Effects

The capacity of auxins, both endogenous and applied, to induce root formation has been recognized since the earliest days of auxin research. The initiation of adventitious roots on stems and of lateral roots on roots is one of the main morphological responses commonly observed following treatment. The structure of lateral root primordia led Thimann (1936) to suggest that the origin of nodules on leguminous plant roots may be partly a result of the high auxin production known to occur in *Rhizobium* infections of roots.

In some cases auxin applications may bring about such abundant lateral root formation that a fasciated condition occurs, with whole clusters of root primordia in longitudinal rows down the sides of the young growing roots. A striking example of this type of response in the bean root is shown in figure 56 (Wilde, 1951). These fasciated rows of roots are located over the vascular strands, presumably because of concentration of the auxin in the strands.

Auxins were thought only to inhibit root growth until it was found that the optimum auxin level for root growth is very low indeed (Boysen-Jensen, 1936). Promotions of root growth with auxin have been obtained in two ways: (1) The exposure of roots of some species to very low concentrations of auxins can sometimes promote

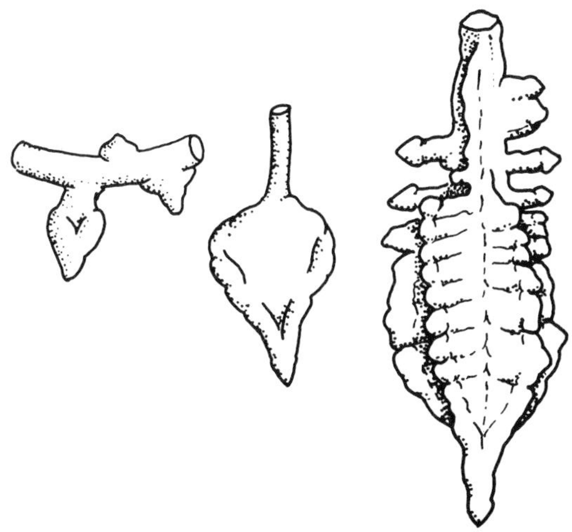

Fig. 56. Root abnormalities after treatment of bean roots with 2,4-D showing proliferation of lateral root primordia (redrawn from Wilde, 1951).

growth (Thimann, 1936; Moewus, 1949; Naylor and Rappaport, 1950). (2) The exposure of roots to auxin solutions for only a brief period can sometimes promote growth (Thimann and Lane, 1938). The basic requirement for stimulation by auxins seems to be that roots be used which do not already have optimal or super-optimal auxin concentrations. This can be done by selecting roots which are either very young or somewhat senescent (Pilet, 1951; Moewus and Moewus, 1952).

Flowers and Fruits

Auxins can exert strong influences on the process of floral initiation, on setting of fruits, and on subsequent fruit growth.

In the preceding chapter it was pointed out that increasing the auxin content of a plant at the time of flower initiation can either promote or inhibit the process. The addition of auxins to pineapple plants can actually cause floral initiation. The application of these influences upon initiation are discussed in chapter XV.

If auxins are applied to flowers, they sometimes cause the flowers to set fruit and in other cases cause the flowers ultimately to abscise. The species which can be made to set fruit are consistently among the types with many-seeded fruits—the tomato, pepper and the cucurbits (Nitsch, 1952). In many species, flowers can be made inviable or young fruits can be aborted by auxin treatments. The physiological means by which these results are obtained are discussed in chapter XII.

Auxins applied to developing fruits may increase the rate of fruit growth, or prolong the period over which fruit growth occurs. If the auxins are applied or are still retained when fruit is nearly mature, they may in some instances cause early ripening or pigmentation of the fruit. The first of these effects, increase in rate of fruit growth, is strikingly illustrated in the report of Crane and Blondeau (1949) using 2,4,5-T on figs (figure 122). In the case of the tomato the greater growth rate may be restricted to only a few days following treatment (Singletary, 1950). The second effect, the prolongation of growth of fruits, is typified by the response of pineapple reported by Krauss *et al* (1948). These workers found that spraying pineapple fruits with β-naphthoxyacetic acid seven weeks before maturation would bring about a continuation of fruit growth for two weeks longer than the controls, resulting in larger fruits. The third effect, the hastening of pigmentation of fruits was originally noted by Gardner *et al* (1940). Subsequent reports indicated that 2,4-D could induce ripening of fruits in storage (Marth and Mitchell, 1949), but this effect is very probably attributable to impurities in the auxin material. Compounds like the phenols which cause metabolic uncoupling (discussed in the next section) may in fact cause ripening, and such phenols are commonly found as impurities in 2,4-D preparations (Hansen, 1951; Goldacre *et al,* 1953). The intensification of pigmentation seems to be a genuine auxin effect and is used commercially in apple production which will be discussed in chapter XIII.

METABOLIC EFFECTS

Soon after the discovery of the profound effects on growth obtained with auxins, Bonner (1933) carried out the first experiments on respiratory responses to auxins. The possibility that an increase in respiration rate might be associated with the increase in growth following auxin treatment was pointed out and good experimental data were presented to show this correlation. Not only did the respiration rate increase with growth-promoting concentrations of auxin but it decreased with growth-inhibiting concentrations. In a subsequent study, Bonner (1936) found that when a preparation presumed to be auxin *b* was substituted for the indoleacetic acid used in the first report, such a stimulation of respiration was not found. The failure to repeat the respiration observation led to a general loss of interest in the possibility of a respiratory function being involved in auxin action. The field was opened again in 1941 by the work of Commoner and Thimann, who reported that a stimulation of respiration was

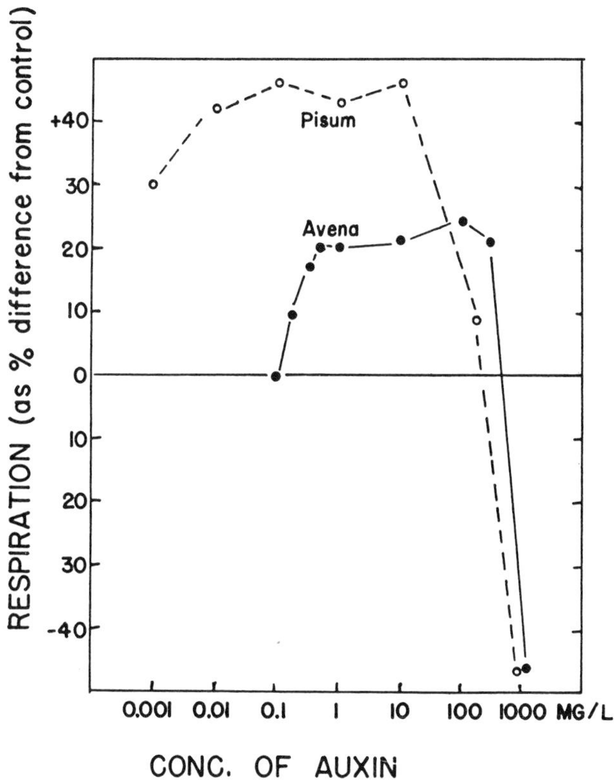

Fig. 57. The relative effects of varying concentrations of auxin (2,4-D) upon respiration (QO_2) of etiolated *Avena* coleoptile and pea stem sections (Kelly and Avery, 1949).

associated with the auxin stimulation of growth if a supply of organic acids was made available, malic acid being particularly effective. Since that time, several laboratories have confirmed the observation that auxins stimulate respiration in the same concentration ranges that stimulate growth. However, the inhibition of growth with auxins is not necessarily associated with similar inhibitions of respiration (Smith, 1951).

An interesting difference in sensitivity of the respiratory systems of monocots and dicots has been demonstrated by Kelly and Avery (1949). They found that respiration of pea stems is stimulated by concentrations of auxin over one hundred times more dilute than those needed to stimulate respiration in the *Avena* coleoptile. The greater respiratory sensitivity of the pea as shown in figure 57 is strongly reminiscent of the greater herbicidal sensitivity of dicots in comparison with monocots.

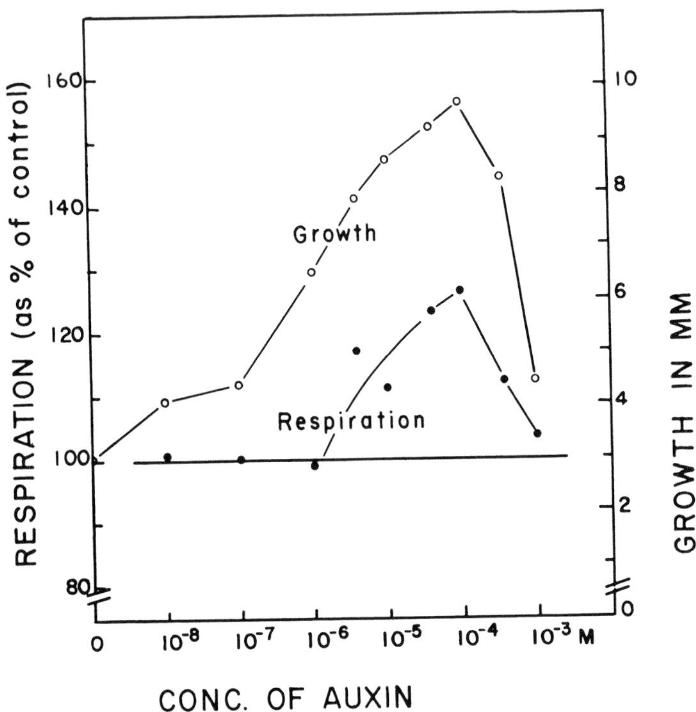

Fig. 58. The influence of auxin (indoleacetic acid) on growth and respiration of corn coleoptile sections. Growth is expressed as mm. of growth per 10 sections 6 mm. long, and respiration as relative oxygen consumption (French and Beevers, 1953).

There are many and diverse observations of increases in respiration subsequent to auxin applications to plants. A few general examples that might be cited from applied studies are increases of respiration rate of fruits following auxin application to prevent abscission (Smock and Gross, 1947), and increases in respiration of plants following sprays for herbicidal effects (Brown, 1946).

The interesting question arises concerning the relationship between the stimulation of respiration and the stimulation of growth. Assuming that the energy of respiration must ultimately be responsible for growth, one would hope to find some sort of proportionality existing between them. Commoner and Thimann (1941) found that concentrations of iodoacetate which completely inhibit growth, inhibit respiration only approximately 10 per cent. This raises the interesting possibility that the respiratory functions which are involved in growth may be only a small part of the overall respiration regime. Responses other than growth very frequently do not correlate with respiratory changes. Several instances of the lack of correlation have been cited by Smith (1951) and include the inhibition by auxins of nitrate uptake by roots and inhibition of germination and root growth. A correlation between respiratory and growth responses to auxin was demonstrated for each of several auxins by French and Beevers (1953). Sample data for responses to indoleacetic acid are given in figure 58, from which it can be seen that the ranges of auxin levels which promote these two functions are roughly similar. Although small growth responses could be obtained without a measurable reflection in respiration, the peaks of both functions appear at the same auxin level.

A particularly interesting suggestion concerning the relation of respiration responses to growth responses has been recently made (French and Beevers, 1953). Simultaneous measurements of respiratory and growth responses showed that respiration was promoted by some substances which could not produce growth promotions. This led to the suggestion that a more indirect connection between respiration and growth may exist. It was proposed that the respiratory promotion by auxins might be a consequence of the growth promotion rather than its cause. In this concept, respiration produces energy which is captured in high-energy phosphate bonds, and this energy may then be utilized for growth. Auxins may stimulate growth resulting in a utilization of the phosphate bonds. Respiration may then proceed faster because of the presence of more phosphate acceptors. Non-auxins like 2,4-dinitrophenol can produce the same respiratory promotions by uncoupling the phosphorylase system from growth. According to this idea, then, auxins increase respiration by utilizing the products of phosphorylation in growth, whereas non-auxins like dinitrophenol increase respiration by stripping off the products of phosphorylation without utilizing them in growth. A similar relation between the effects of auxin on respiration and water uptake has been suggested by Bonner *et al* (1953).

Some possible means by which respiratory energy may be utilized for growth are discussed in chapter VIII.

The effects of auxins on specific enzyme systems have been investigated in many instances. It is very difficult to evaluate the results obtained from most enzyme studies in terms of the actual mechanism of auxin action in the plant. Studies of the effects of auxins on enzymes in a semi-purified state almost invariably demonstrate that the auxins inhibit these enzymes (cf. review of Bonner and Bandurski, 1952). The complexity of the problem is illustrated by the fact that auxin applied to intact *Avena* coleoptiles evokes large increases in dehydrogenase activity, whereas *in vitro* application of auxin to the partly purified dehydrogenases only inhibits their activity (Berger and Avery, 1943). Eyster (1946) suggested that physical phenomena may confuse the results of such studies. He has shown that alpha amylase is inhibited by many auxins but that the inhibition is largely removed when the enzyme is suspended on colloidal particles. He was able to show that, instead of inhibiting amylase activity, auxins in a colloidal suspension could actually stimulate the enzyme, although the effect of the auxins on the acidity of the mixture may have accounted for a large part of the effect. These observations leave us with a certain feeling of uneasiness about the physiological significance of demonstrations of the inhibitions of semi-purified enzymes by auxins *in vitro.*

The applications of auxins to whole plants or plant parts and the subsequent determinations of enzyme activities may be a more reliable source of information concerning the means by which auxins may alter metabolism of the plant. The starch-hydrolyzing activity of bean stem sections has been shown to be enormously increased by the presence of small amounts of 2,4-D (Gall, 1948). A remarkable increase in ascorbic acid oxidase activity of tobacco segments with auxin has been shown by Newcomb (1951). He found that small quantities of auxin would stimulate apparent ascorbic acid oxidase activity as much as 300 per cent in a period of 6 to 10 days. Some of his data are shown in figure 59. Supplying the excised plant pieces with ascorbic acid substrate and then measuring oxygen uptake revealed this large increase in activity. One of the most interesting aspects of this phenomenon is that the enzymatic response appears to precede the growth response. This suggests the real possibility of a causal relationship. A variety of other enzymes have been found to increase in activity after auxin treatment, including pectinase (Neely *et al,* 1950), phosphorylase, β-amylase, catalase (Wort and Cowie, 1953), and possibly proteinase and polypeptidase (Freiburg, 1952). Many enzymes have been found to be inhibited by auxin applications (see review of Bonner and Bandurski, 1952).

Mitochondrial preparations containing all of the enzymes necessary for the complete respiration of pyruvic acid to carbon dioxide have been tested for auxin sensitivity (Price *et al,* unpublished). Interestingly enough, essentially no response to the auxins was obtained. This suggests that the effect of auxin on respiration may not be through an effect on enzymes involved in pyruvate metabolism. This observation has been used as indirect support for the hypothesis that auxin acts principally through a phosphate transfer system (Bonner and Bandurski, 1952).

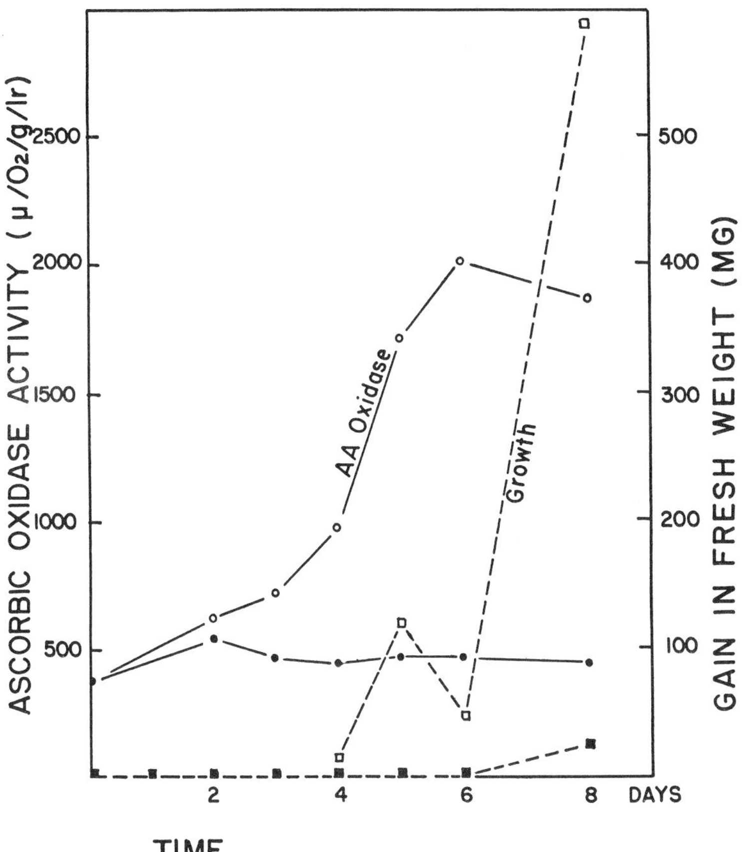

Fig. 59. A comparison of the effects of auxin (3.5 mg./1. indoleacetic acid) upon ascorbic oxidase activity and growth of excised tobacco pith tissue. Solid symbols represent controls, hollow symbols auxin treated; continuous lines represent ascorbic oxidase activity, dashed lines growth (from Newcombe, 1951).

EFFECTS ON PLANT CONSTITUENTS

Auxins may have very different effects on the constituents of plants, depending upon the concentration of auxin applied. For this reason it would seem worthwhile to discuss the effects of low or physiological concentrations of auxins separately, and then turn to the effects of stronger treatments.

Auxins affect the nucleic acids of plants (Silberger and Skoog, 1953). Both the ribose-nucleic acids and the desoxyribose nucleic acids were found to increase following the addition of from 0.01 to 10 mg./liter of indoleacetic acid to tobacco pith tissue in sterile culture.

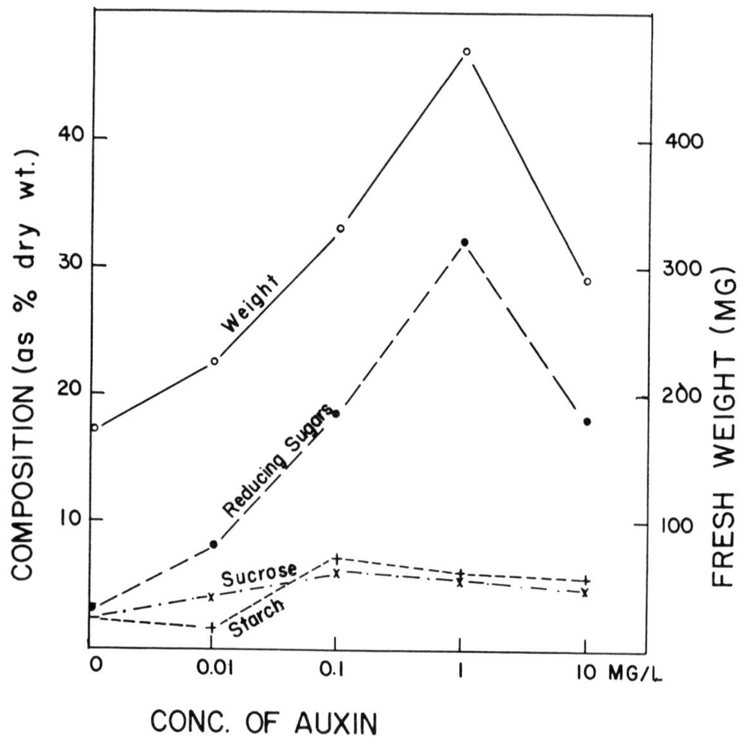

Fig. 60. The relationship between the stimulation of growth by auxin (indoleacetic acid) and some changes in carbohydrate constituents of excised tobacco stem sections (Skoog and Robinson, 1950).

The increases were complete in the first four days, and growth increases which were very comparable to the ribose-nucleic acid increases followed in the next three days.

Changes in reducing sugars after auxin treatment have been noted by several workers, and sometimes these changes show striking similarities to the growth responses. An example of this is shown in figure 60. It appears from these data that the increase in sugars is not due to an hydrolysis of the starches, but is probably a result of the assimilation of carbohydrates from the culture medium.

Studies of the herbicidal activities of stronger treatments with plant growth regulators have clarified some of the changes in plant constituents after auxin applications. Sell *et al.* (1949) demonstrated gross changes in carbohydrate and nitrogenous constituents following the application of large amounts of 2,4-D to bean leaves. Some of the most striking changes were found in the stems. The 2,4-D caused a rapid decrease in carbohydrate content of stems including reducing sugars, non-reducing sugars, and starch dextrins (see table 7). The

TABLE 7

CHANGES IN CONSTITUENTS OF STEMS OF RED KIDNEY BEAN TREATED WITH 2,4-D (ONE DROP OF 1000 P.P.M. APPLIED AT BASE OF BLADE OF PRIMARY LEAF) AS COMPARED WITH AN UNTREATED CONTROL. DATA EXPRESSED ON A LIPID-FREE DRY WEIGHT BASIS.

(Sell *et al*, 1949)

Constituent	Non-treated stems (per cent in the sample)	Treated stems (per cent in the sample)	Difference (per cent)
Reducing sugars	1.66	—	−100
Non-reducing sugars	4.78	—	−100
Starch	7.22	2.08	−71
Ash	11.41	15.98	+40
Protein	16.89	30.54	+81
Leucine	.72	1.44	+100
Valine	.73	1.04	+43
Arginine	.84	1.49	+78
Lysine	.51	1.48	+190

depletion of the carbohydrate fractions was associated with an apparent increase in protein and amino acid fractions. The overall protein content was almost doubled and many of the specific amino acids measured were, in fact, more than double those in the controls. Furthermore, substantial increases in the ash content were observed and increases in several of the pigments. It should be recognized that data such as these may be complicated by the fact that the actual dry weight of the plant material is reduced as a result of the treatment and consequently expressing plant constituents as a percentage of the control per unit dry weight can be somewhat misleading (Klingman and Ahlgren, 1951). However, the general trends of disappearance of carbohydrate fractions and accumulation of nitrogenous materials seem to be common results following applications of large amounts of auxins.

Here again the role of reducing sugars is distinctive. Although treatment of plants with strong auxin applications may lead to an ultimate depletion of carbohydrate reserves, still there is frequently a large rise in the reducing sugar content. This can be readily seen in the data of Rasmussen (1947) concerning the effects of 2,4-D on dandelion root composition given in figure 61.

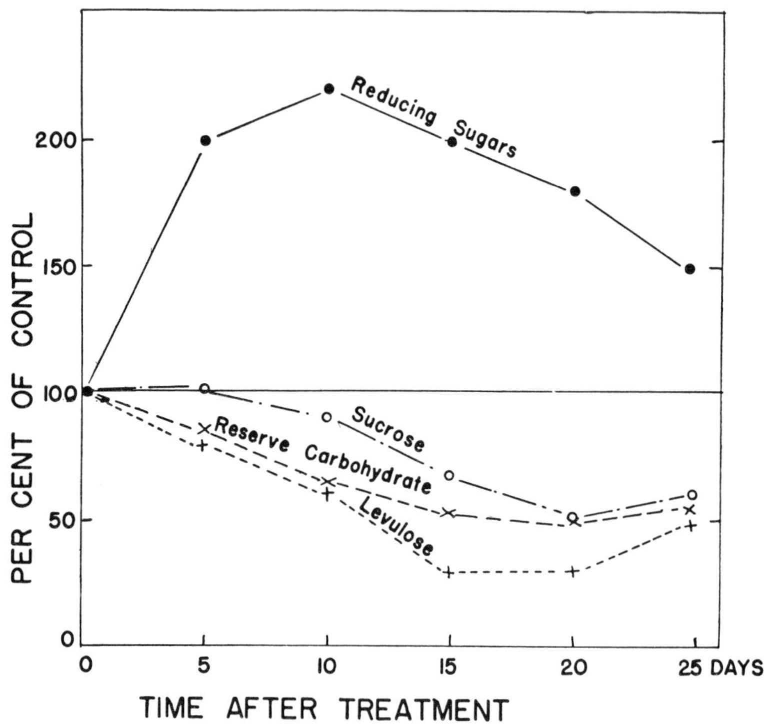

Fig. 61. Changes in chemical composition of dandelion roots after treatment with 480 mg./l. of 2,4-D (from Rasmussen, 1947).

The changes in nitrogenous constituents of plants are not even as well understood as are the carbohydrate changes. Under some circumstances large increases in nitrogen content have been observed after treatment (Wort, 1949) and in other cases pronounced decreases are found instead (Rhodes *et al,* 1950). Using plants supplied with different levels of nitrogen, Wolf *et al* (1950) found that bean plants grown with low concentration of nitrogen showed not only much less injury but also much less mobilization of nitrogenous constituents following 2,4-D treatment.

The interesting suggestion has been made (van Overbeek, 1952) that the accumulation of nitrogen in leaves in the form of amino acids may be responsible in part for the deformities of leaves following auxin applications. Steinberg (1949) has shown that the frenching of tobacco leaves is associated with abnormal accumulation of amino

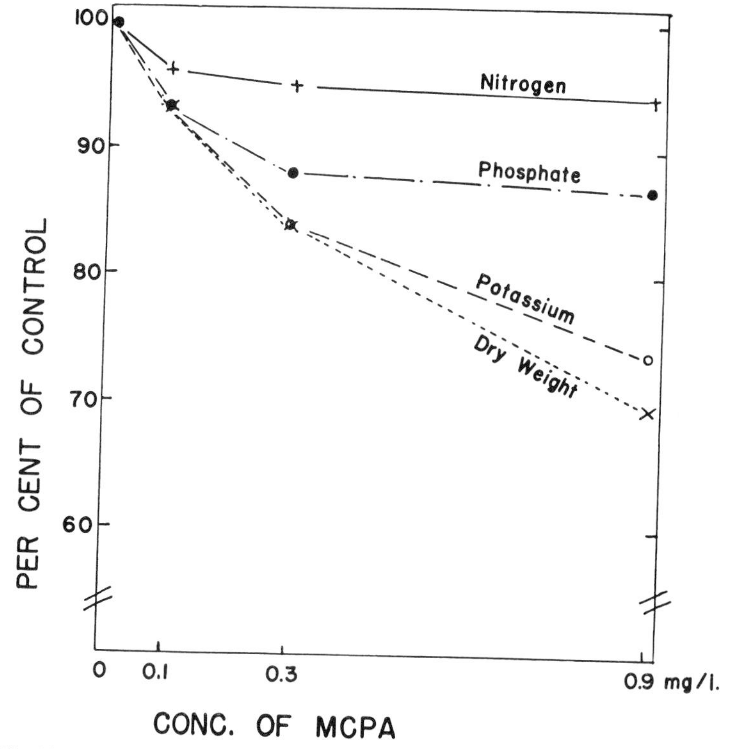

Fig. 62. Changes in mineral content and dry weight of tomato plants after exposure of roots to 2-methyl, 4-chlorophenoxyacetic acid (from Rhodes *et al*, 1950).

acids, and frenching symptoms appear to be much the same as the leaf deformities caused by auxin.

Studies of overall changes in nitrogen, potassium, and phosphorus contents of plants have been made (Rhodes *et al*, 1950). They found that the treatment of plants with MCPA (2-methyl, 4-chlorophenoxyacetic acid) at increasing concentrations gave quantitative reductions of total nitrogen, potassium, and phosphorus in tomato plants. The decreases they observed (figure 62) were greatest for potassium and less for phosphorus and nitrogen. Furthermore, the potassium changes were very much in the same order as the decrease in dry weight. On the basis of their data they suggest that toxic effects of MCPA may be exerted through some effect on potassium availability.

While herbicidal applications of auxins may mobilize nitrogenous materials in some parts of the plant, the uptake of nitrate by the plant may be inhibited. Nance (1949) has found that the uptake of nitrates by wheat roots is drastically inhibited by small concentrations of 2,4-D. It is possible that the reduction in nitrogen content of tomato plants (shown in figure 62) may be caused by the inhibition of this function in the roots. This inhibition of nitrate absorption is not associated with any observable change in oxygen consumption and the inhibition is reversed by supplying small amounts of citrate. These observations led Nance to suggest that 2,4-D may selectively block the anion respiration mechanism described by Lundegårdh (1947).

An interesting effect of lethal doses of 2,4-D on the inorganic phosphate content of bean plants was noted by Loustalot and Morris (1953). They found that treatment with 1,000 mg./liter of 2,4-D notably increased inorganic phosphate as the plants approached death. They suggest that, since the accumulating phosphate must originate in the organic constituents of the plants, the herbicidal result may be effected through interference with normal phosphorylation reactions.

In conclusion, it must be reiterated that the application of auxins to plants can result in a host of complex interactions. It has been pointed out that auxins may have great effects on many developmental growth functions including tropisms, inhibitions, morphological differentiation, and flower and fruit development. Auxins can bring about a great variety of anatomical effects, including cellular proliferation, mitotic irregularities, and epinastic deformities. Auxins can bring about large changes in the metabolism of the plant as reflected in gross changes in respiration, the activity of various enzymes, in the abundance of various common plant constituents, and in the availability of some ions to the roots. Theories as to how this immense diversity of responses may be brought about are discussed in chapter VIII.

CHAPTER VI

Factors Altering Effectiveness of Auxin Applications

The effectiveness of an auxin material applied to a plant is a function of the distribution of the auxin through the plant and the responsiveness of the plant parts into which the auxin moves. The former of these is determined by two separate steps—the absorption of the auxin into the plant and the translocation from one plant part to another. The latter function is determined in turn by the status of the plant and its nutritional condition. Any environmental factor influencing the effectiveness of auxin application may have its influence through one or several of these particular phases of auxin action.

ABSORPTION

The absorption of auxin sprays applied to foliage is strongly affected by the physical structure of the foliage itself. Surfaces to which the spray adheres poorly permit less effective absorption than surfaces which wet more easily. For example, garden pea leaves have a waxy surface which make them rather difficult to wet. As a result foliar sprays of a given concentration may have less effect on this plant than they do on tomato, the leaves of which wet very easily. Not only does the waxiness of the surface influence this function, but the physical form of the leaf may influence absorption as well. For example, an onion leaf presents a small surface per unit volume and its position is such as to encourage run-off of the spray droplets.

Several investigators have studied the possible role of stomata in the absorption of auxin materials applied to the leaf, but in each case evidence brought forth suggests that stomata do not have much bearing on such absorption (Weaver and DeRose, 1946). This is in contrast to volatile spray materials which may enter leaves principally through stomatal openings (van Overbeek, unpublished).

Temperature conditions profoundly influence absorption. Rice

(1948) has shown that the absorption of 2,4-D is considerably more rapid at 90° than at 50° F. In figure 63 it can be seen that, while absorption of simple aqueous solutions was somewhat greater at the higher temperatures, the absorption of a solution including a fatty carrier (Carbowax 1500) showed a much greater temperature differential. With Carbowax in the spray, the final absorption at 90° F was nearly three times that occurring at 50° F. These studies were carried out by applying known quantities of 2,4-D solution on the leaf, washing off the unabsorbed auxin, and measuring it quantitatively by spectrophotometric determination.

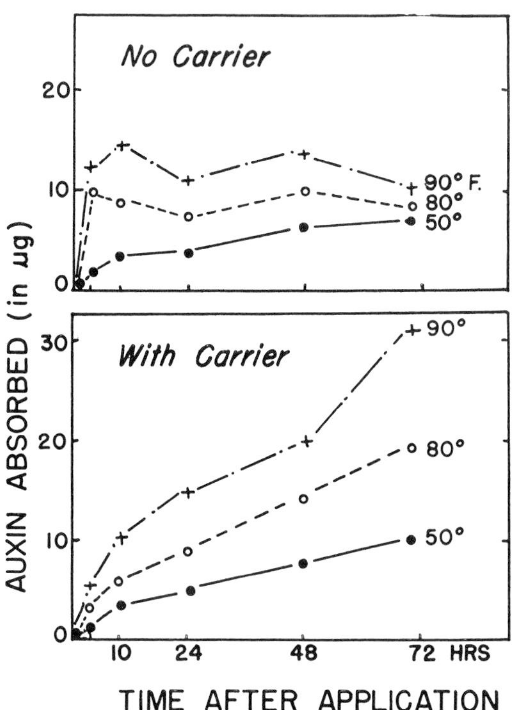

Fig. 63. The time course of absorption of auxin (2,4-D) by bean leaves at three different temperatures with and without a carrier, Carbowax #1500 (Rice, 1948).

Although the total absorption is greater at higher temperatures, the duration of absorption is apparently reduced by warmth in the absence of a carrier; in other words, the rate of absorption is increased by higher temperatures, but the time over which the absorption occurs is somewhat decreased. This may be presumed to be an effect of the more rapid drying of the spray droplets at the higher temperatures.

Another factor in absorption is light. Rice (1948) found that in the dark there is a substantially greater absorption of 2,4-D than in the light (see figure 64). Why absorption is greater in the dark is not clear, but it seems possible that under the conditions of his experiment, Rice may have been getting a longer period of wetting in the dark. That is, the light may have caused more rapid evaporation of

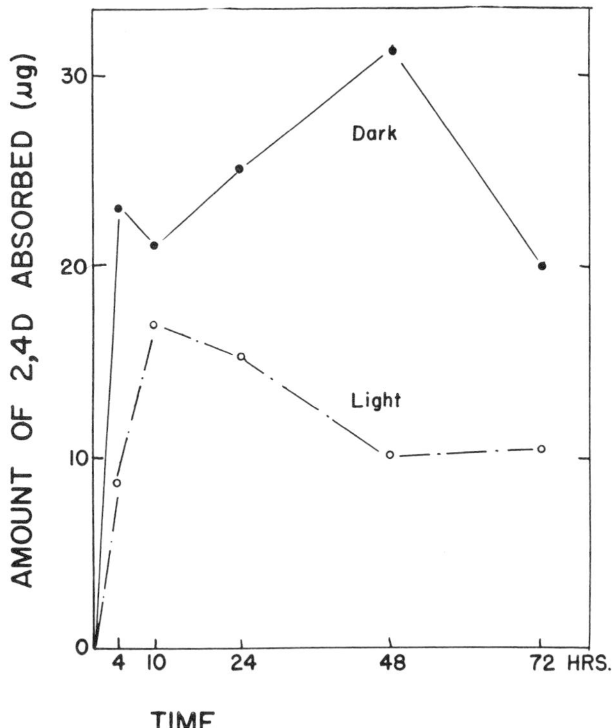

Fig. 64. Absorption of 2,4-D by bean leaves in dark and in light, 900 f.c. (Rice, 1948).

the water droplets from the leaf surface, resulting in a shorter period of absorption. He observed no significant difference in absorption with light intensities from 100 to 900 foot candles. It is also possible that the physical characteristics of the leaf surface are altered by light and dark (Rice, unpublished). Wettability of leaves is discussed in chapter XVI.

It is well-known that carriers such as Carbowax 1500—a mixture of polyalkylene glycols—or detergents or emulsifying agents can notably increase the effectiveness of an auxin spray applied to foliage. From the data of Rice given in figure 63, it seems evident that one of the primary effects of a carrier is to increase the time over which absorption takes place. Whether the rate of absorption is altered is not clear. The data in the figure suggest that the rate of absorption might be somewhat reduced by the carrier, even though the total absorption is increased. The use of more viscous carriers such as lanolin paste permits an even greater duration of absorption.

The rapidity of absorption of auxin sprays can be seen in the inability of rain to vitiate the effect, even when the rain occurs very soon after the spray has been applied. Studies of the effects of rain at various intervals after auxin sprays to prevent preharvest drop of apples (Overholser *et al,* 1943) show that simulated rain applied four hours after auxin application did not perceptibly reduce the auxin effect. A more elaborate study of this sort by Weaver *et al* (1946) established that when auxin is applied as the acid form in water, entry is nearly complete in one hour, and full effectiveness is attained in six hours. Data from two such experiments with simulated rain are given in figure 65. In the same experiments, the auxin was applied in diesel oil to other plants, and rain only fifteen minutes after the spray did not reduce the effectiveness at all (figure 65).

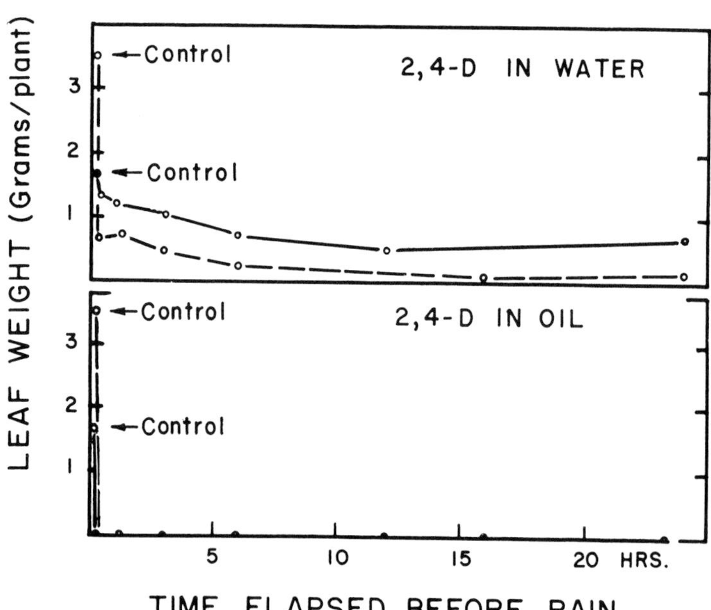

Fig. 65. The effects of rain applied artificially at various intervals of time after 2,4-D spray. Two sample experiments for 2,4-D in water and in oil, at an estimated 0.65 lbs/acre, followed by rain of one inch. Inhibition of leaf weight taken as index of the amount of absorption (from Weaver *et al,* 1946).

The rapidity of absorption of aqueous auxin sprays indicated by the observations of Overholser *et al* (1943) and subsequent workers is not at all unique to auxins. The effectiveness of sprays of inorganic salts such as copper sulphate is practically unaltered by washing off as soon as three hours after application (Blackman *et al,* 1949).

The acidity of the auxin solution may greatly change the rate of absorption (Crafts, 1949), and the level of acidity most effective for rapid absorption will often be closely dependent upon the age and constitution of the foliage. Crafts has pointed out that young foliage is generally more responsive to polar solutions, whereas the surface of the more heavily cuticled, older foliage is itself more lipoidal and consequently more responsive to non-polar solutions such as esters. For this reason free acids or salt formulations are most effective on young foliage, while esters are most effective on old foliage. Similarly the surfaces of roots are generally polar in nature. Hence acids and salts are generally more effective than esters when applied to soil solutions.

The use of carriers such as polyalkylene glycols or detergents apparently permits the entry of polar acids and salts by normally non-polar pathways. This may account for the somewhat slower rate of entry apparent in figure 63. It is pertinent to note that such carriers have no beneficial effect upon absorption of non-polar formulations such as the esters of auxins (Staniforth and Loomis, 1949).

The absorption of auxins by plant tissues in solutions should be mentioned here. Albaum *et al* (1937) followed the entry of indoleacetic acid into *Nitella* cells by means of the ferric chloride color test. They observed that the auxin appeared in the cells most rapidly at pH's below the pK value (4.75). They conclusively demonstrated that auxin entered the cells as the undissociated acid, and that such entry was a simple diffusion process. This problem has been reopened by Reinhold (1954), who followed uptake by the disappearance of auxin from the external solution surrounding pea and carrot sections. She obtained evidence for two uptake mechanisms—a physical diffusion mechanism, and a metabolic mechanism as well. The former appears to be operative upon undissociated auxin molecules as Albaum *et al* had reported, but the metabolic mechanism was independent of dissociation of the auxin. How much of the disappearance of auxin from the medium by the metabolic process is in fact destruction of the auxin was not established.

TRANSLOCATION

Once the auxin is inside the plant, a major factor determining its ultimate effectiveness will be the ease with which it is translocated through the plant. If the auxin is held in the leaves only and is not translocated to the lower parts of the plant a systemic effect will not be obtained. This is especially undesirable in herbicide work. If the auxins are not translocated through the plant the foliage may be killed and the stem and other essential parts left unharmed.

Environmental Factors

The effects of some environmental conditions upon translocation of 2,4-D in bean leaves have been studied by Rice (1948) who concluded that the translocation was unaffected by temperature differences ranging from 50° to 90° F. On the other hand, he confirmed that

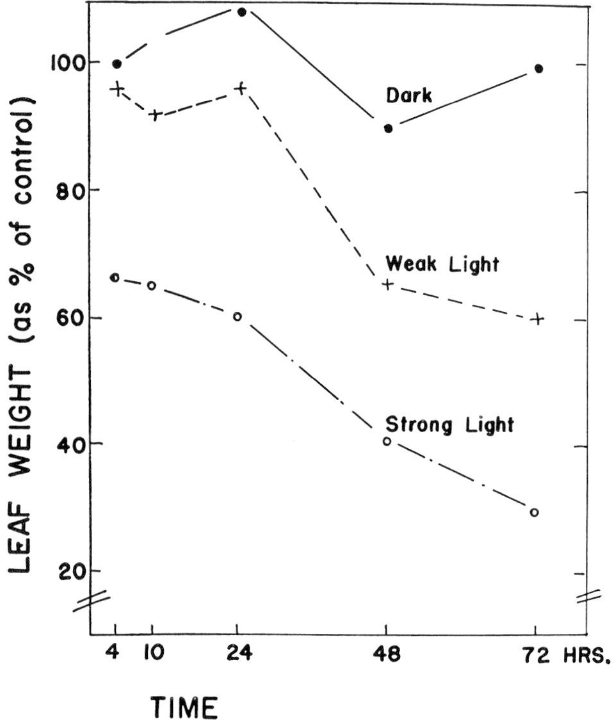

Fig. 66. Translocation of 2,4-D as evidenced by inhibition of leaf weight of young expanding leaves after application, comparing translocation in dark, in weak light (100 f.c.), and in strong light (900 f.c.) (Rice, 1948).

light exerts a profound effect upon translocation and that this effect is proportional to the intensity (figure 66). Rice applied 2,4-D on the primary leaf of bean seedlings and used as a criterion of translocation the effect of the auxin in inhibiting enlargement of the trifoliate leaf above the treated leaf. This is a technique similar to that described for the leaf repression test in chapter II. As the auxin is translocated to the tip, growth is inhibited. The extent of inhibition of leaf size is taken as a measure of the extent of translocation. It can be seen in the figure that the inhibition was much greater in the high light intensity than in the low. This is in spite of the fact that less auxin had been absorbed in the light (cf. figure 64.)

It should be recognized that the acropetal or upward type of translocation which is being measured is not the same as the polar transport system by which normal physiological concentrations of auxins are translocated in stems and leaves.

Role of Carbohydrates

The translocation of 2,4-D has some relationship to carbohydrates, for it takes place more readily from well-lighted leaves than from shaded ones, and also more readily from leaf bases than from leaf tips (Weaver and DeRose, 1946).

Rice has demonstrated that 2,4-D applied in darkness to lower leaves did not alter the subsequent growth of the expanding leaf, even though it was clear that large amounts of 2,4-D had been absorbed at the point of treatment (cf. figure 64). The fact that translocation was achieved only in lighted plants, and with increasing effectiveness as the light intensity was increased, suggests that light may be affecting translocation by production of photosynthetic products. Plants which had been treated in the dark and subsequently moved into the light became capable of translocating the 2,4-D very well (Weintraub and Brown, 1950).

The effect of light in altering translocation through the formation of sugars was tested directly by Rohrbaugh and Rice (1949). They found that the application of sugar to darkened leaves treated with 2,4-D would substitute for light in bringing about translocation of 2,4-D from the treated leaf. This has been confirmed by Weintraub and Brown (1950) who proved that any one of a wide variety of sugars will work equally well in bringing about translocation of 2,4-D.

Because the transport of sugars is prerequisite to 2,4-D translocation, factors altering the former may be expected to alter the latter as well. For example, boron is known to be essential for sugar transport in some circumstances (Gauch and Duggar, 1953), and its importance in 2,4-D translocation has likewise been established (Mitchell *et al,* 1953). A beneficial effect of phosphorus on 2,4-D translocation in deficient plants has also been reported (Rohrbaugh and Rice, 1954), possibly consequent to facilitating sugar synthesis.

Thus, it appears that translocation of auxins applied in large amounts is accomplished by their being swept along by a carbohydrate translocating system. Either light or the addition of sugars can bring about translocation. Light without carbon dioxide is ineffective (Weintraub and Brown, 1950). Translocation is not carried out principally in the xylem, for steam killing of petioles effectively prevents translocation (*loc. cit.*).

Movement in Xylem

Under certain circumstances auxins can be translocated in the xylem. This can be deduced from the experiments of Hitchcock and Zimmerman (1935) who showed that auxins applied to the soil can move acropetally in plants, apparently in the transpiration stream. A particularly graphic demonstration of transport in the xylem was made by killing a section of stem with a flame, and showing that movement of 2,4-D from the soil to the growing point was unimpeded (Weaver and DeRose, 1946). No downward movement could be found through the dead stem section. It seems unlikely that this type of translocation occurs to any appreciable extent when auxins are applied as foliar sprays, but it does occur when the auxin is applied to the soil or to a cut plant part, which gives direct access to the transpiration stream.

Movement in Oil

The movement of auxins applied to plants apparently cannot be explained entirely on the basis of the systems described so far, for a puzzling report by Penfound and Minyard (1947) indicated that treatment of leaves with an ester of 2,4-D applied in kerosene was just as effective in weak light or dark as in strong light. The existence of still another means of auxin movement was established by Rice and Rohrbaugh (1953). They followed the movement of 2,4-D applied to bean plants in kerosene, and discovered that in such an oil base the auxin moved about the plant through the cell walls and intercellular spaces by capillarity. This movement is independent of light and sugars and has no polarity, of course. The form of the auxin had no detectable influence on such movement; the acid, butyl ester and propylene butyl ester of 2,4-D showed the same behavior.

The rate of movement through the plant with kerosene was studied by the use of radioactive 2,4-D. Carbon^{14} was incorporated into the carboxyl position of the auxin, which was applied in kerosene to a small local area on one leaf. The distribution was determined by autoradiography as illustrated in figure 67. One hour after application the plant was cut into several pieces, and the autoradiograph showed that already the auxin had permeated to the stem and to the opposite leaf in part. The rate of movement was estimated at about 4 cm. per hour.

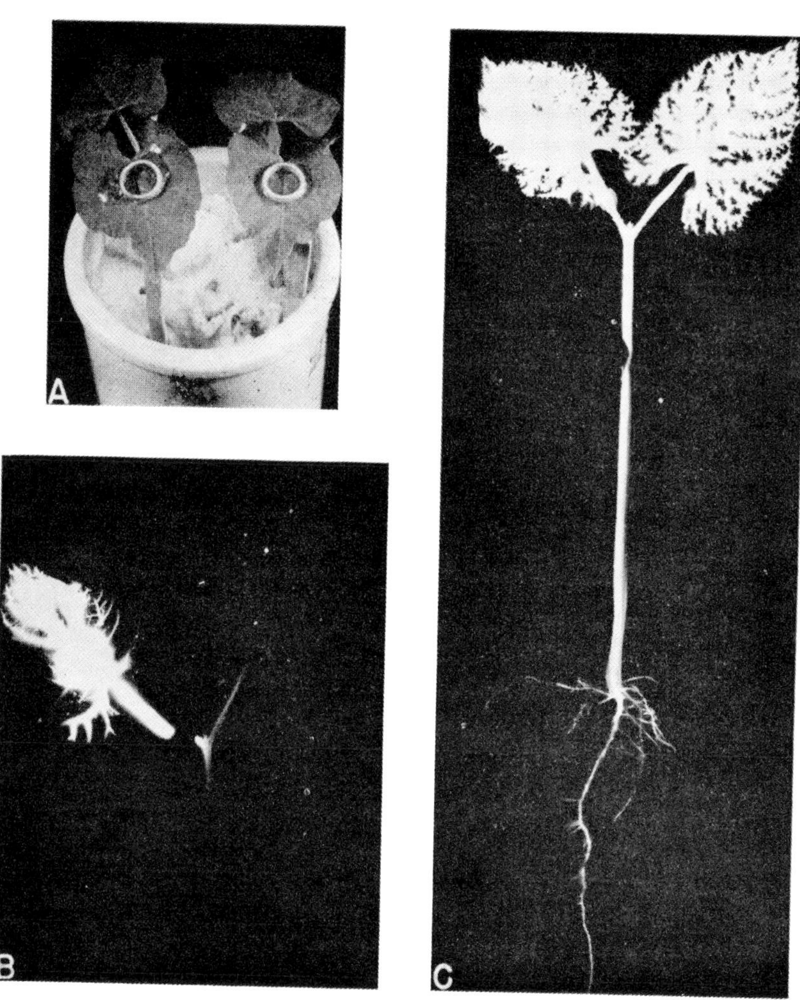

Fig. 67. The movement of radioactive 2,4-D in bean plants when applied in kerosene oil. (*A*) Rings attached to leaves to assure localization of application on leaf surface. (*B*) Autoradiograph of a plant dismembered 1 hr. after 2,4-D application. (*C*) Autoradiograph of a plant not dismembered after 2,4-D application (Rice and Rohrbaugh, 1953).

Molecular Structure and Translocation

An interesting aspect of the translocation of auxins in the carbohydrate transport system is the large effect which molecular structure may have on this function. The studies in which observations of translocation for several auxins have been made are very few, but some general patterns may be perceived in the available data. First, in the phenoxy acid series tested by Osborne and Wain (1950), it appears that chlorination of the phenyl ring may increase translocation. For example, 4-chlorophenoxyacetic acid was translocated less readily than 2,4-D. The extreme mobility of 2,4,5-T in plants is well known (Young and Fisher, 1950). Second, α-propionic acid side-chains may be associated with poor translocation. For example, α-phenoxypropionic acid had a largely local effect, though with some movement to the growing point (Osborne and Wain, 1950). A similar auxin with a 2-chloro substitution was somewhat more mobile, and the 2,4-dichloro derivative was reported to induce responses like 2,4-D. This α-propionic derivative of 2,4-D has been reported as being very poorly transported in the *Avena* test (Collins and Smith, 1952), and the (L) isomer of α-indolepropionic acid is also poorly transported (Kögl and Verkaik, 1944).

The presence of nitrogen in indoleacetic acid appears to be related to its translocation in the plant, for substituting a carbon or an oxygen atom for the nitrogen essentially eliminates translocation, even though auxin activity remains (Thimann, 1951).

Translocation Rates

Rates of entry and translocation of 2,4-D through bean seedlings have been estimated through some ingenious experiments by Day (1952). Movement of the material through the epidermis is estimated at about 30 micra per hour. This might be considered to represent the rapidity of absorption of the auxin through the surface of the leaves. This slow rate does not continue, however, after the auxin has reached the vascular system. Once in the phloem the rate of movement is estimated to be between 10 to 100 cm. per hour. This rate is in the same range as the rate of carbohydrate translocation, estimated to be about 85 cm. per hour (Vernon and Aronoff, 1952). The rate of movement of 2,4-D in kerosene was considerably slower, 4 cm. per hour. It might be recalled that the polar transport of auxin in the *Avena* coleoptile is approximately 1 cm. per hour.

Several clear distinctions can be drawn between auxin transport which occurs in conjunction with carbohydrate translocation and the classical polar transport of auxin. As in the polar system, velocity is independent of auxin concentration in the carbohydrate-linked transport (Day, 1952). It is different from the polar transport in that (a) it is dependent upon the concurrent translocation of carbohydrates, (b) it is at least ten times more rapid than polar transport, and (c) it is not polar in direction. Indigenous growth hormones are translocated principally by the polar system, whereas auxins applied at high concentrations are translocated principally by the carbohydrate system, unless they are applied in an oil carrier.

THE STATUS OF THE PLANT

Stage of Development

A clear demonstration that the age of the plant at the time of treatment has a very strong bearing on the effectiveness of an auxin application has been brought forward by Blackman (1950). In a series of studies using 2,4-D and 2-methyl-4-chlorophenoxyacetic acid, he found that there are strong differences in herbicidal toxicity associated with the stage of development of the plant and the auxin applied. In the discussion of the anatomical effects of auxins in chapter V, we pointed out that cells which are less differentiated in development are the most responsive to auxin applications. On this basis, one would expect that plants which naturally contain a high proportion of cells in a weakly differentiated condition would be most susceptible to auxin applications. This is in fact the case. It seems generally true that germinating seedlings, which are almost entirely made up of weakly differentiated cells, are more sensitive than at later stages of growth. This factor contributes to the selectivity of auxins for germinating weed seedlings in a standing crop.

Experiments on the toxicity of 2,4-D for crop plants established that young plants of cabbages, soybean and tomato could be killed by concentrations that had little or no detrimental effect on older plants of the same species (Weaver *et al,* 1946).

Blackman (1950) has found that other stages in the development of the plant may show renewed sensitivity to auxins. The boot stage of cereal grains is a particularly susceptible stage (Olson *et al,* 1950). The flowering stage of Hoary Pepperwort is a particularly susceptible stage to 2,4-D (Blackman *et al,* 1949). The excess of weakly differentiated cells in the plant is not entirely responsible for the degree of susceptibility, however, for in some instances a slow-growing stage, such as the vegetative rosette of dandelion which occurs in the fall, is a particularly susceptible stage to 2,4-D applications.

It should be pointed out here that the nature of the growth regulator used has a strong bearing on the relative susceptibility at any given stage of development. Blackman (1950) points out, for example, that the Hoary Pepperwort is most susceptible to 2,4-D injury at the flowering stage; whereas the greatest sensitivity to 2-methyl-4-chlorophenoxyacetic acid occurs at the pre-flowering stage (see table 8).

TABLE 8

CHANGES IN SENSITIVITY OF HOARY PEPPERWORT (*Cardaria draba*) TO MCPA AND TO 2,4-D WITH VARIOUS STAGES OF DEVELOPMENT
(Blackman, 1950)

Stage of growth at time of spraying	Percentage kill	
	MCPA	2,4-D
Pre-flowering	77.0	46.9
Flowering	58.2	69.4
Regeneration (autumn)	42.2	11.8

The stage of development of plants as it bears on herbicide susceptibility and selectivity is discussed further in chapter XVI.

Nutritive Condition

The nutritive condition of the plant is a powerful factor in determining the responsiveness to auxin application. This phenomenon has been studied by Wolf *et al* (1950), who grew soybeans at various nitrogen levels and measured the degree of injury caused by 2,4-D applications to the roots. The relative degree of injury obtained at each of the nitrogen levels is shown diagrammatically in figure 68. One can see that at low nitrogen levels the soybeans showed little injury following 2,4-D application, whereas at increased levels of nitrogen the toxicity became much more pronounced. There is evidence for believing that 2,4-D causes a mobilization of nitrogen into the stems and roots of plants, apparently at the expense of the leaf proteins (Freiberg and Clark, 1952). It is possible that the availability of nitrogenous materials for such a mobilization may account for the influence of nitrogen supply on susceptibility to 2,4-D.

Differences in plant constituents which exist at various stages of development may be in large part responsible for the differences in sensitivity with age of the plant. For example, the soluble nitrogen content of rice plants reaches the highest values in the seedling stage and at the time of bolting (Sircar and De, 1948), and these two stages are characteristically the most sensitive to 2,4-D injury (see chapter XVI). In pineapple plants a fairly high carbohydrate level is known to be best for uniform forcing with auxin and it can be assumed that under such conditions the nitrogen level in the plant would not be excessive.

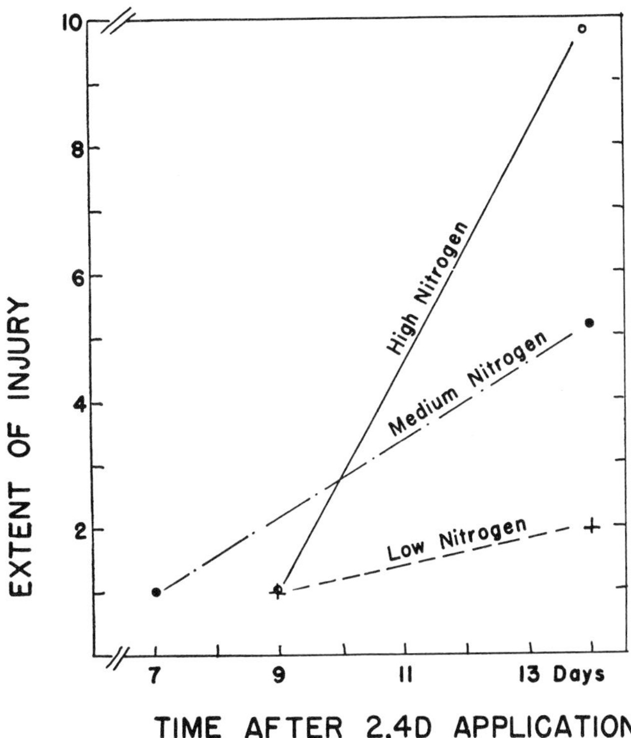

Fig. 68. Injury to soybean plants by exposure to 20 mg./l. of 2,4-D in a nutrient solution, comparing extent of injury at three levels of nitrogen nutrition (14, 56, 335 ppm). Injury was estimated on an arbitrary visual basis (Wolf *et al*, 1950).

ENVIRONMENTAL FACTORS

Environmental factors apparently have a bearing on the responsiveness of the plant through means which cannot be explained solely on the basis of absorption, translocation, plant developmental stage and nutritive conditions as we understand them. Perhaps the most striking of these unexplained factors is that of temperature. It is well known that maximal auxin effectiveness is obtained at high temperatures and this can undoubtedly be explained in part by the greater absorption which one would expect on the basis of Rice's experiments. Kelly (1949) has found, however, that the transfer of crab grass and bean seedlings from low temperatures into higher temperatures after the time of spraying immensely increased the effectiveness of the spray. For example, bean plants sprayed at a temperature of 15° C with 5,000 mg./1. 2,4-D showed no killing for a period of 4 days. Transfer of the plants into 25° temperature then produced a very strong killing effect (85 per cent). However, plants sprayed at 5° and then subsequently moved into temperatures of 15° showed a strong killing effect (60 per cent) even though the initial temperature of 15° had not given any kill. Increase in killing associated with the change of temperature apparently cannot be attributed to renewed absorption of the 2,4-D. Experiments were made in which the leaves were washed before being transferred to a higher temperature, and still the increase in kill was obtained. Greater respiratory stimulations follow auxin applications at high temperatures than at low (Brown, 1946).

Temperature and light conditions bear on the nutritional status of the plant. These two factors strongly influence the carbohydrate level of the plant, and accordingly they not only affect absorption and translocation of the auxin but they simultaneously alter the sensitivity of the plant to the auxin after absorption and translocation have been effected.

In occasional instances it has been found that relative humidities may influence auxin effectiveness (e.g. Hitchcock and Zimmerman, 1935). One can deduce that humidity may have an effect on auxin activity in the unusual situations where translocation of the auxin is taking place in the xylem, as when the auxin has been introduced into the vascular system. In addition, relative humidity may alter the rate of drying of droplets of auxin solution on the leaves. In this way, low humidities may somewhat impair absorption of auxin. There is some evidence that water solutions enter leaves more readily from large droplets than from small (Smith, 1946), presumably because of slower drying action.

The effects of environmental factors on the absorption, translocation, and final effectiveness of the auxin at the cellular level may be rather complex. Thus, for example, light retards absorption of aqueous auxin sprays, light stimulates translocation, and light may alter the final effectiveness of the auxin at the cellular level. Because of the compounded effects of light on the various phases of auxin action, it is evident that differences in light conditions at the time of auxin application may have large effects on the net result, though the direction of the effects may be difficult to predict without prior experimentation. Like light, temperature may alter each of the phases of auxin action, and may produce changes equally complex.

The manner in which environmental factors alter the various uses of auxins will be discussed under each use in turn.

CHAPTER VII

The Chemical Nature of Growth Regulators

Ever since the discovery of auxins, numerous workers have attempted to find other new substances which would modify growth either in the same manner as auxins or in some other manner. Perhaps one of the first to sort through large numbers of compounds and mixtures of compounds was Seubert (1925) who found that application of such things as urine, saliva, and other materials to *Avena* coleoptiles elicit growth responses. Since that time a host of other materials has been found to possess biological activity and much confusion has arisen in interpreting the different types of responses that have been obtained. While it is not possible to establish an absolute classification of types of growth responses that different substances will bring about in plants, certain general categories can be recognized and, furthermore, one can easily test for the characteristics on which the categories are based.

By the definition given in chapter I, auxins are compounds which can stimulate growth in the manner of the growth hormone. Auxins can be distinguished from other substances which influence growth by any growth test which utilizes auxin-free material. A common way of testing for the property of stimulating growth is to utilize the slit pea test or the *Avena* straight-growth test after washing the sections for 2 to 4 hours as described in chapter II. The *Avena* test is an excellent test for substances which are translocated readily. Substances which show this property of growth stimulation are auxins in the true sense of the word; that is, they themselves can substitute for the growth hormone in causing growth.

A variety of compounds other than auxins can stimulate growth, though only in the presence of auxins. Compounds which serve to increase the effectiveness of auxin have been called synergists or in some cases hemi-auxins. Other substances can bring about a swelling of cells which may result in twisting and deformation of leaves or stems instead of orderly elongation. These compounds are the epinastic agents.

It is apparent that accurate distinctions between types of agents which increase growth will not always be easy. Thus the stimulation of growth in a plant or plant part by small amounts of a compound may be due to auxin activity, synergistic activity or epinastic activity of the compound. It should be remembered that one compound will not necessarily show only one type of growth effect. An auxin may have epinastic activity, and compounds which are auxin synergists in one circumstance may be growth inhibitors in another.

MOLECULAR STRUCTURE AND AUXIN ACTIVITY

The exhibition of auxin activity by compounds of diverse molecular structures has led to the fascinating study of the relationship of molecular structure to this activity. The field has been slightly confused by the neglect in some studies of structural requirements to use tests which are specific for auxin activity. Even with the limitations of the data available some remarkable generalizations can be drawn. To date such generalizations have been highly productive in the development of an understanding of the mechanism of auxin action.

The basic molecular requirements for auxin activity recognized by Koepfli *et al* (1938) are as follows:

(a) An unsaturated ring
(b) An acid side-chain
(c) A particular spatial arrangement between the ring and the side-chain.

These workers did not stipulate what spatial arrangement was essential, but they realized that spatial arrangement played an important role in auxin activity.

The Structure of the Ring

Analysis of the structure of the ring as it pertains to the auxin activity of indoleacetic acid (I) shows that the nitrogen in the indole ring is not essential, for substitutions of an oxygen (II) or a carbon (III) for the nitrogen will still permit auxin activity (Thimann, 1935).

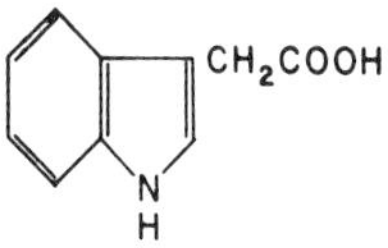

CH_2COOH N H   I

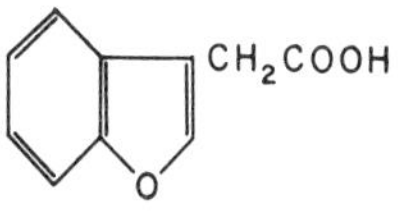

CH_2COOH O   II

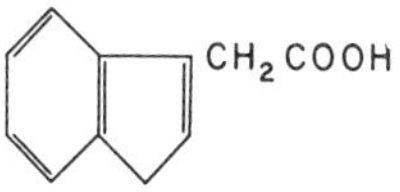

CH_2COOH III

This is not surprising since many other rings can serve as well as the indole ring. The ring may be small, as in the case of a phenyl ring

(IV), or as large as the anthracene ring (V) which contains 14 carbon atoms.

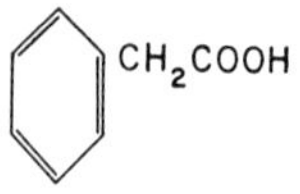

CH_2COOH CH_2COOH

IV 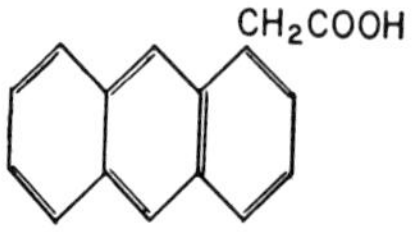 V

The ring must be unsaturated; that is it must have at least one double bond. Went (1949) stated that one double bond must be located adjacent to the side-chain. For example, the saturated cyclohexane acetic acid (VI) is inactive, whereas 1-cyclohexene-1-acetic acid (VII) possesses auxin activity, and 2-cyclohexene-1-acetic acid (VIII) is inactive.

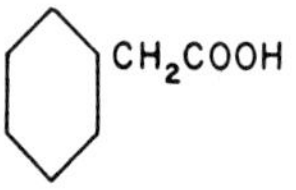

CH_2COOH CH_2COOH CH_2COOH

VI 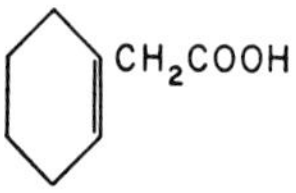 VII 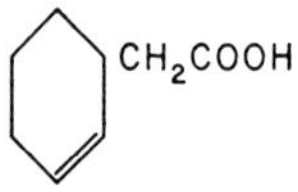 VIII

Substitution of various groups into the unsaturated ring may profoundly affect auxin activity. The nature of the substituent and its location on the ring will both influence activity. A graphic example of this is the substitution of a single chlorine atom on each of the possible positions on the ring of phenoxyacetic acid. The striking differences in activity obtained in the *ortho, meta* and *para* positions using this same single substituent are shown in figure 69. Curiously enough, the *ortho* chlorine increases growth activity but slightly, while the *meta* and *para* chlorines each furnish very large increases in activity. Again, substitutions in more than one position on the ring will have strong effects on activity both in regard to what groups are substituted and the position at which they are substituted. A striking case in point is the substitution of more than one chlorine atom into phenoxyacetic acid as shown in figure 69. It can be seen that chlorines at both the 2 and 4 positions (2,4-D) impart immensely more growth activity than did either one of the chlorines alone. The further addition of a chlorine in the 5 position (2,4,5-T) alters the growth response very little, whereas the addition in the 6 position essentially eliminates activity (figure 69). If other groups such as bromine, iodine, methyl or nitro groups are used for substitutions, somewhat smaller effects are generally obtained (Koepfli *et al*, 1938; Thimann, 1952).

An interesting and productive finding concerning substitutions in the ring of the phenoxyacetic acid series has been made by Muir *et al*

(1949). They established that for this family of auxins at least one position *ortho* to the side-chain must be unfilled for effective auxin activity. Thus while 2,4-D is highly active, 2,4,6-T is essentially inactive. They pointed out that the substitutions in the 2 and 4 positions would activate the 6 or *ortho* position, and concluded that the ring of the auxin must combine with some substance at that position. Subsequently it was discovered that certain benzoic acid derivatives also exhibit auxin activity (Bentley, 1950), and it was startling to find that in these substances the *ortho* positions must be *filled* by chlorine, methyl or other groups for auxin activity to exist. The strongest auxin

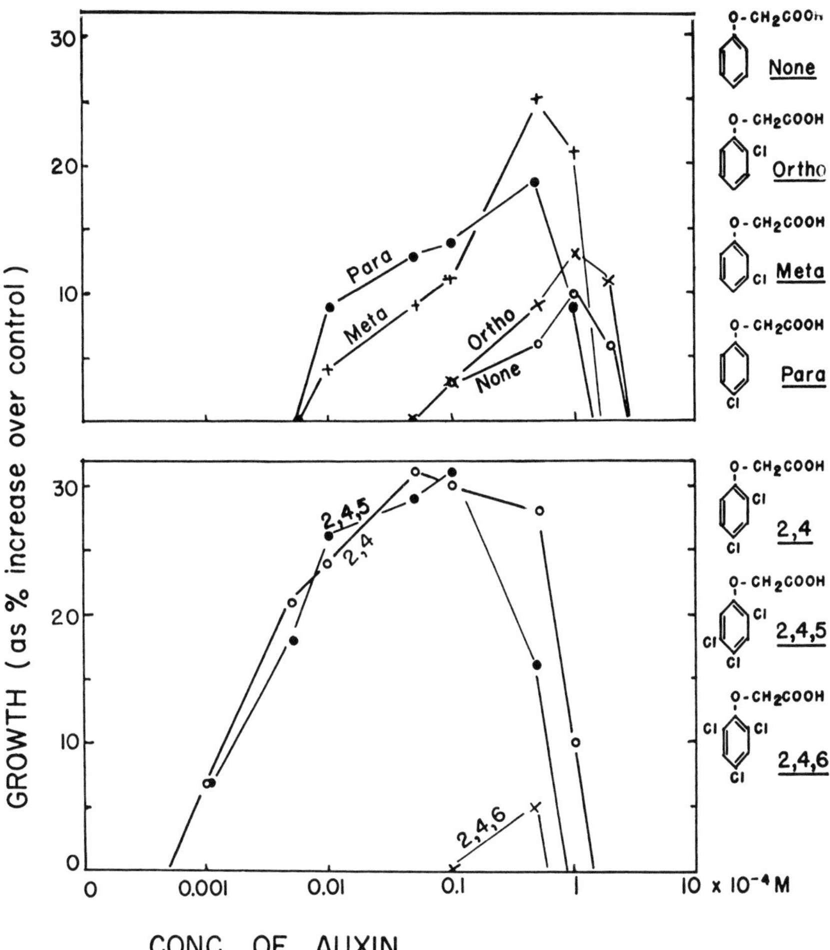

Fig. 69. The effects of various concentrations of some chlorinated phenoxyacetic acids upon growth in the *Avena* straight-growth test (from Muir *et al,* 1949).

activity has been obtained with 2,3,6-trichlorobenzoic acid (IX). In the benzoic acids, the *meta* position appears to be the active site of reaction, and the substitutions in the other positions serve to activate the *meta* position (Thimann, 1952). It is interesting to note that as the acid side-chain shortens, the active site on the ring retreats to a position more remote from the side-chain.

The importance of the *ortho* positions in other auxins such as indoleacetic and naphthaleneacetic is obscure, but nevertheless the important point made by the Muir theory is that the ring of an auxin must have an active position at which a reaction with another material is assumed to take place. This contribution has provided a cornerstone for some of the most provocative theories of auxin action, described in chapter VIII.

Structure of the Side-Chain

Changes in the acid side-chain can have a profound influence on auxin activity. For example, side-chains with two carbons or two carbons plus an oxygen appear to be optimal for auxin activity. Longer side-chains such as the propionic (X) and butyric acid (XI) derivatives are generally less active (Koepfli *et al,* 1937).

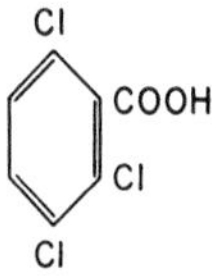

Cl COOH Cl Cl — IX

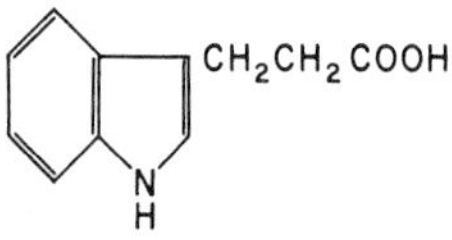

CH_2CH_2COOH N H — X

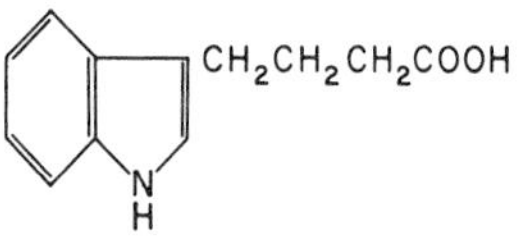

$CH_2CH_2CH_2COOH$ N H — XI

When the side-chain of the phenoxy acid series contains an even number of carbons, auxin activity is obtained, whereas with odd numbers of carbons auxin activity is almost absent (Synerholm and Zimmerman, 1947). This is evidently because these acids, like fatty acids in general, are broken down by removal of 2-carbon fragments. In figure 70 the auxin activities of phenoxy acids with side-chains of various lengths are compared with the rates of destruction of the side-chain, indicated by the appearance of phenol in plant tissues supplied with them. It is evident that odd-numbered carbon side-chains give rise to large amounts of phenol, denoting that they have been metabolized to the one-carbon formic derivative which is unstable and decomposes to phenol (Fawcett *et al,* 1952). Even-numbered carbon side-chains do not break down in this way. Presumably they are metabolized down by 2-carbon fragments to the acetic acid derivative which is stable as well as being the most active auxin.

Whereas in most instances greatest auxin activity is obtained with side-chains two carbons in length, the interesting benzoic acid auxins are exceptions (Bentley, 1950). The entirely different ring substitution requirements of the benzoic acid auxins have been discussed above.

The presence of various substituent groups on the acid side-chain can also have a strong influence on auxin activity. For example, starting with the auxin, phenylacetic acid (IV), the substitution of a

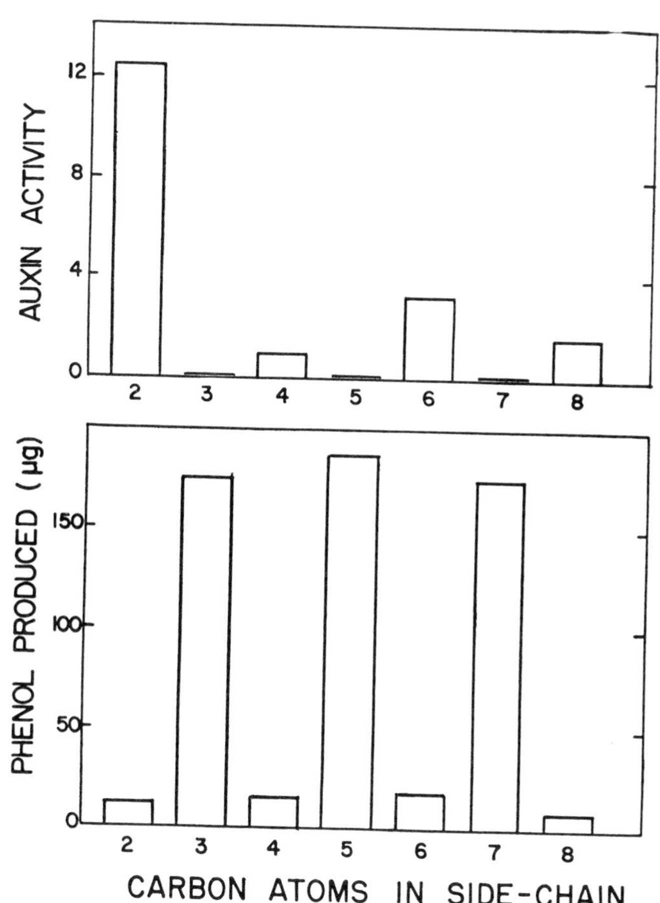

Fig. 70. *A*, the effects of different lengths of side-chains of 2,4-dichlorophenoxy acids upon auxin activity in the tomato test. *B*, the effects of different lengths of side-chains of phenoxy acids upon the breakdown to phenol after exposure to flax seedlings. Auxin activity expressed as the inverse of the minimal dosage required for cell elongation (calculated from Synerholm and Zimmerman, 1947); the phenol produced is expressed as micrograms recovered from 2.5 x 10^{-3} M of the acids after 10 days (Fawcett *et al*, 1952).

methyl group for a hydrogen on the alpha carbon (XII) or a methylene group for both hydrogens (XIII) does not take away activity, but the substitution of two methyl groups, as in the case of the *iso*-butyric acid derivatives (XIV) removes activity entirely (Koepfli *et al,* 1938). Such iso-butyric acids are anti-auxins (Burström, 1950).

C_6H_5–$CH(CH_3)COOH$ XII

C_6H_5–$C(=CH_2)COOH$ XIII

C_6H_5–$C(CH_3)_2COOH$ XIV

This information suggests then that steric hindrance on the acid side-chain can effectively prevent auxin activity. The presence of hydrogens on the alpha carbon is apparently not essential for activity.

The substitution of a hydroxyl group on the side-chain has a remarkable effect (Thimann, 1951). In two such auxin derivatives (XV and XVI) auxin activity is eliminated by the hydroxyl substitution. Other acids with hydroxyl groups on the side-chain have been found to lack auxin activity. These include synthetic analogues of auxins *a* and *b* (Kögl and de Bruin, 1950). This finding has cast considerable doubt upon the existence of auxins *a* and *b* as growth hormones.

C_6H_5–$CH(OH)COOH$ XV

C_6H_5–$CH(CH_2OH)COOH$ XVI

The degree of acidity of the acid side-chain plays a part in auxin activity. Salts of the acid may be less effective in growth than the free acid, and substitution of weak acid groups for the carboxyl reduces auxin activity. For example, the substitution of —SO_3H (XVII) or —NO_2 (XVIII) for the terminal carboxyl will reduce the activity, but such compounds sometimes still show distinct auxin activity or sometimes none (Wain, 1949). Ester and amide derivatives of the carboxyl appear to be less effective than the free acid, although they may have distinct auxin activity (Kögl and Kostermans, 1935; Thimann, 1951). Some evidence has suggested that indoleacetonitrile (XIX) may possess auxin activity (Bentley and Housley, 1952), but such activity may be owing to its conversion to the acid plus synergistic properties of the nitrile described in the next section.

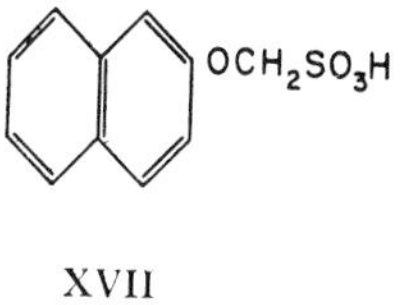

OCH_2SO_3H CH_2NO_2 $CH_3C{\equiv}N$

N
H

XVII 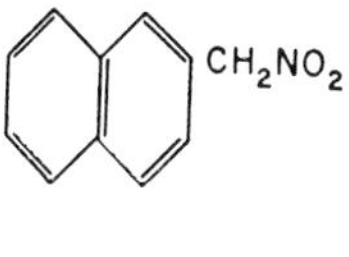 XVIII 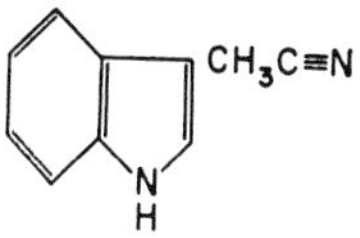 XIX

The degree of acidity of the carboxyl group itself varies from one compound to another, and the auxin activity has been found to vary with the degree of acidity expressed as the dissociation constant. Van Overbeek *et al* (1951) have shown that the relative activity of a given auxin in growth of pea sections can be related to the relative number of undissociated molecules available at a given pH, whereas Lundegårdh (1949) has found quite the opposite for wheat roots: growth was related to the number of dissociated ions. While the issue is not settled as to whether the carboxyl group is more effective in the undissociated or the dissociated state, the fact that strong auxins have low dissociation constants suggests that the degree of acidity of the side-chain has an influence upon activity.

The requirement of an acid group on the side-chain for auxin activity indicates that the carboxyl is probably another site for reaction of auxins.

Spatial Configuration

Since Koepfli *et al* (1938) first suggested that the spatial configuration of the auxin molecule was important to its activity, the requirements in this regard have become much better known, though the reasons for them still remain obscure. Veldstra (1944) examined a large variety of auxin materials, and concluded that the configuration must allow the acid side-chain to be out of the plane of the ring nucleus. He proposed that the ring must have surface activity by which it becomes absorbed on some lipoidal materials in the cell, and the side-chain must project out of that plane. The acidic group on the end of the side-chain would function by attachment to a non-lipoid material. The classical example illustrating Veldstra's theory of configuration conferring activity is cinnamic acid (XX), in which the *cis* form fulfills Veldstra's requirement and is an auxin, whereas in the *trans* form the side-chain cannot exist in any other plane than that of the ring (figure 71) and it is not an auxin. Its anti-auxin characteristics are discussed later in this chapter.

In another instance, tetrahydronaphthylideneacetic acid (XXI) has a *cis* and a *trans* form of which the *cis* form is active and the *trans*

Fig. 71. Hirschfelder models of *cis-* and *trans*-cinnamic acids (left and right respectively). *Cis*-cinnamic acid with the side-chain out of the plane of the ring is an auxin, while *trans*-cinnamic acid with the side-chain in the plane of the ring is an anti-auxin.

form is not. In this case the activity cannot be explained by the Veldstra scheme, for both isomers must exist with the carboxyl in the same plane as the ring (Thimann, 1951).

CH=CH–COOH (*cis*) CH=CH–COOH (*trans*)

XX

HOOC CH (*cis*) CHCOOH (*trans*)

XXI

Optical isomerism can also strongly influence auxin activity. Perhaps the clearest case of such an influence is in 2,4-dichlorophenoxy-α-propionic acid (XXII), which exists in *D* and in *L* forms. The *D* isomer is an active auxin and the *L* is essentially inactive (Thimann, 1951). Comparison of optical isomers of a variety of acids has shown that in all of the cases studied the *D* form was more active than the *L* (Matell, 1953), and in many cases the *L* isomers are anti-auxins (Åberg, 1953).

CH_3–OC*(H)–COOH, Cl, Cl

XXII

I, COOH, I, I

XXIII

Such a strong influence of optical isomerism on auxin activity has suggested that a third site of reaction of auxins is at the α carbon on the side-chain (Wain, 1951). If a hydrogen atom were necessary for substitution on one side of the carboxyl, then the influence of the optical isomerism could be explained. However, several compounds which have no hydrogen in an α position on the side-chain still have auxin activity (α-methylene phenylacetic acid XIII, the benzoic acid auxins IX). No other theory has been proposed which accounts for the optical isomerism effect.

What can be concluded from these findings relating to molecular structure? Certainly the three requisites to auxin activity recognized by Koepfli *et al* (1938) have been confirmed many times: that an unsaturated ring is necessary, that an acid side-chain is necessary, and that some spatial configuration is necessary.

There seems to be a need for the unsaturated ring to be reactive in the 2, 4 or 6 positions in the case of the phenoxyacetic acid series, and in the 3 or 5 positions in the benzoic acid series (Thimann, 1952). Substitution of chlorine into *some* of these active positions seems to activate the others, whereas substitution into *all* of them essentially removes activity. All of this plus the requirement for an unsaturated bond in the ring implies that some rather specific reaction or attachment of the ring must occur as a part of auxin activity. Particularly nice evidence supporting the concept of two points of attachment in auxin action has been reported by Foster *et al* (1952). Their evidence is discussed as a mechanism of action in the next chapter.

The acid side-chain, which is assumed to be the second point of attachment, must apparently be of such size and shape as to fit some spatial pattern in relation to the point of attachment of the ring. If the side-chain is too long, too short, or of the wrong configuration to permit easy fit to this pattern, auxin activity is apparently reduced or lost.

The molecular requirements for auxin activity have evoked some highly provocative theories about the mechanism of auxin action, and these are discussed in the next chapter.

The selection of certain auxins for specific uses in agriculture can be explained in many instances on the basis of knowledge of configuration characteristics. Thus, where high activity and high mobility are desired, as in herbicide work, chlorinated phenoxyacetic acids are unexcelled. Where moderate activity and low mobility are desired as for parthenocarpic fruit-set, weakly substituted phenoxyacetic and phenoxy-α-propionic acids are superior.

SUBSTANCES WHICH MODIFY AUXIN EFFECTS

Auxin Synergists

Many substances which are not auxins, since they cannot stimulate growth in auxin-free tissues, can promote growth through a synergistic action with auxin. Conversely they can inhibit growth when present in relatively high concentrations.

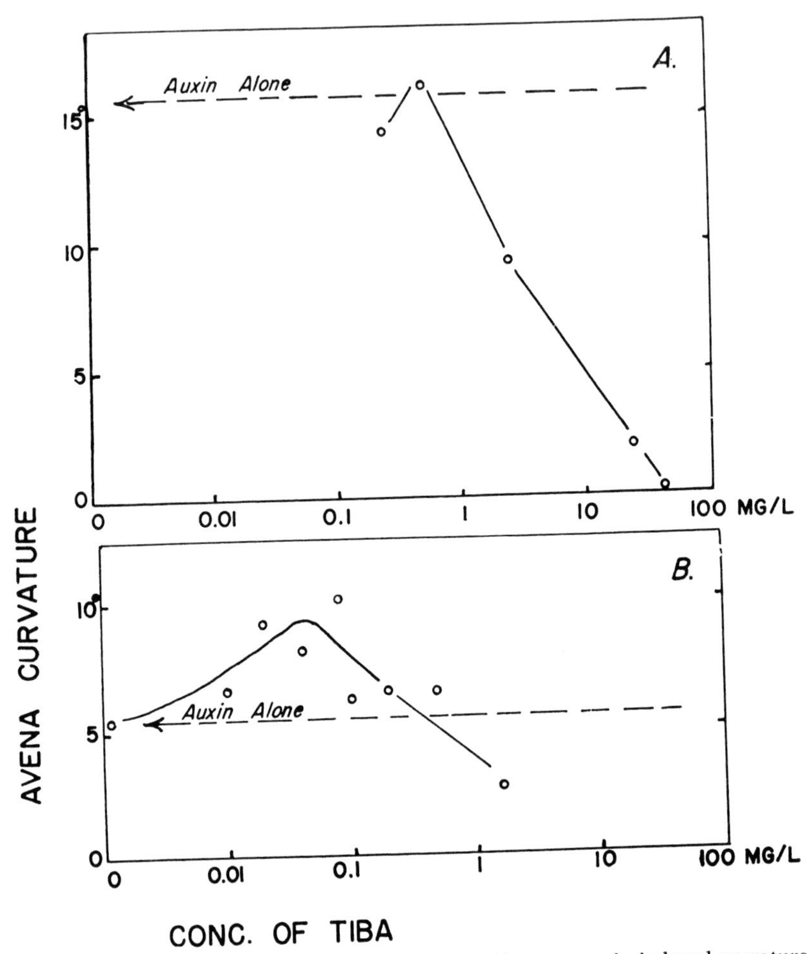

Fig. 72. Effects of TIBA (2,3,5-triiodobenzoic acid) upon auxin-induced curvature in the *Avena* test. *A*: the inhibition of *Avena* curvature by high concentrations of TIBA. The indoleacetic acid concentration was held constant at 0.175 mg./l. (from Galston, 1947); *B*: increases in auxin-induced curvature by applying low concentrations of TIBA. The indoleacetic acid concentration was held constant at 0.15 mg./l. (from Thimann and Bonner, 1948).

Perhaps the best known example of an auxin synergist is 2,3,5-triiodobenzoic acid or TIBA (XXIII). Using an *Avena* test with a small amount of indoleacetic acid incorporated with each application of TIBA, Galston (1947) showed that this substance will inhibit growth. Such inhibitory effects on growth can be seen in figure 72 *A*. The fact that TIBA can also stimulate growth in the presence of auxin was demonstrated by Thimann and Bonner (1948). They found that if very small amounts of TIBA were incorporated with auxin growth was stimulated (figure 72 *B*). By testing various molar ratios of TIBA to indoleacetic acid, they found that this synergistic stimulation of growth was greatest at a molar ratio of approximately 1.0. When TIBA was present in excess it inhibited growth, and this was apparently the type of inhibition which was measured by Galston previously.

A simple means of testing for synergistic action with auxin is to hold the auxin level constant over a rather wide range of concentrations of the suspected synergist. Results of such a test should show a stimulation with low concentrations of the synergist, and probably inhibition at higher concentrations as shown in figure 73. Of course a parallel test of the suspected synergist alone should be run to establish that the growth effect is not due to auxin activity.

Compounds other than TIBA which have been found to be auxin synergists include unsaturated lactones such as coumarin and protoanemonin (Thimann and Bonner, 1949), dicarboxylic acids such as chelidonic acid (Leopold *et al,* 1952) and phthalamic acid derivatives (Leopold, unpublished), indole (van Raalte, 1951), and some vitamins such as ascorbic acid, niacin, pantothenic acid, *p*-aminobenzoic acid and pyridoxine (Scheuermann, 1951; Leopold, unpublished). Also the antibiotic bacitracin has been found to be a synergist with auxin (Leopold and Guernsey, unpublished). Some examples of these are included in figure 73.

From the observations summarized here, it is clear that a large variety of compounds with diverse molecular constitutions may act as auxin synergists in growth. It is not clear through what phase of growth they exert their effects, but some evidence is available to indicate that three of them (protoanemonin, coumarin and chelidonic acid) may act competitively against sulfhydryl compounds (Thimann and Bonner, 1949; Leopold *et al,* 1952).

Using a somewhat different testing method, Went (1949) has described a group of compounds which increase growth in response to auxins. To these compounds he has given the name, "hemi-auxin." Application of these compounds to slit pea sections prior to placing

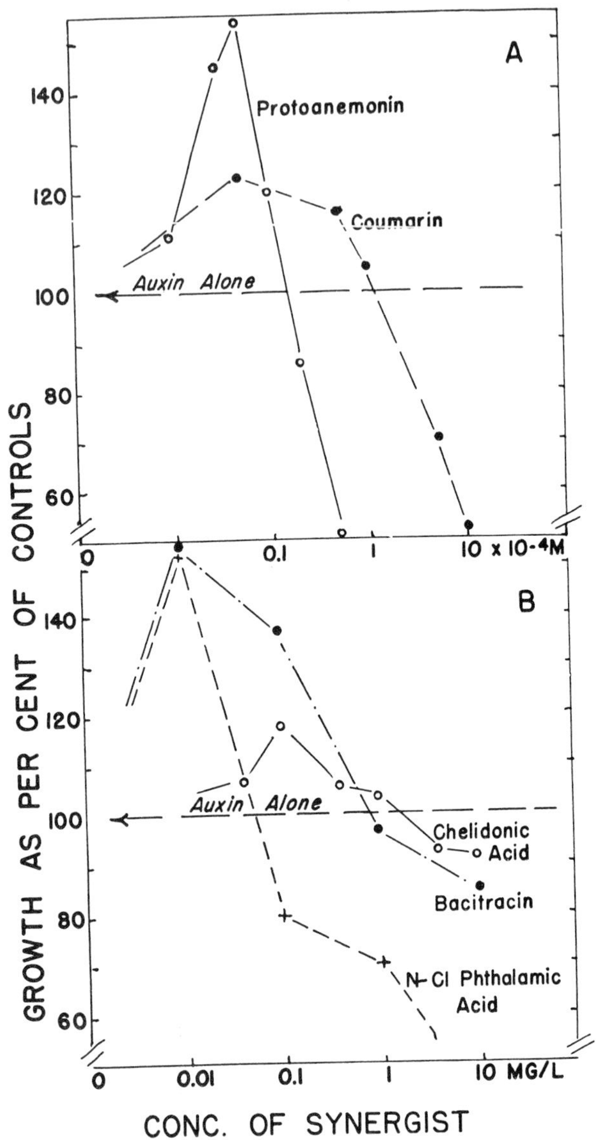

Fig. 73. Synergistic effects of some substances with auxin in growth: *A*: effects of various concentrations of protoanemonin and coumarin on the *Avena* straight growth test; all solutions contained 1 mg./l. indoleacetic acid and 1% sucrose (Thimann and Bonner, 1949). *B*: effects of various concentrations of chelidonic acid, bacitracin, and N-chlorophthalamic acid on the pea straight growth test; all solutions contained 0.1 mg./l. indoleacetic acid (Leopold *et al,* 1952; Leopold and Guernsey, unpublished).

the sections in auxin solutions increases the positive curvatures. While such tests are carried out without mixing the two types of growth regulators in the solutions, still they may be presumed to act together in the tissue. Consequently it seems logical to suppose that hemi-auxins are in fact synergists with auxins. Some interesting compounds in this category are γ-phenylbutyric acid (XXIV), cyclohexaneacetic acid (VI), and 2-cyclohexene-l-acetic acid (VIII). Some of these compounds appear to resemble auxins closely, but some are of an entirely different molecular constitution, e.g. vinylacetate (XXV).

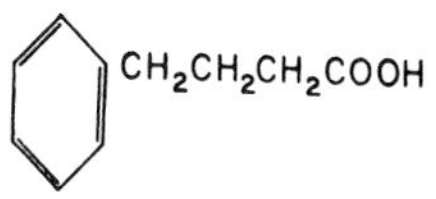

$C_6H_5CH_2CH_2CH_2COOH$ (XXIV) $CH_2COOCH{=}CH_2$ (XXV)

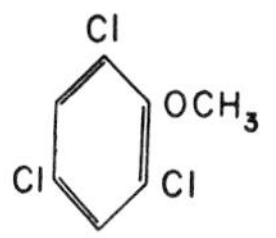

XXIV XXV XXVI

Cl OCH$_3$ Cl Cl

Anti-Auxins

Figures 72 and 73, describing the effects of synergists with auxins, also indicate that a variety of compounds can inhibit growth in the presence of auxin. Such inhibition effects serve to reduce the effectiveness of the auxin, but it is not clear in the case of most synergists whether they are directly antagonizing the action of auxin or whether they are inhibiting growth through more indirect means.

Perhaps the first compound asserted to reduce auxin effectiveness more or less directly was γ-phenylbutyric acid (XXIV) (Skoog *et al*, 1942). Contemplation of the molecular structure led to the suggestion that this compound had approximately the correct configuration for auxin activity, but its low reactivity hindered its functioning as such. Consequently, it would become attached to the active sites where auxins act but would not readily consummate the auxin performance, and would result in a direct reduction of auxin effectiveness. Enzymology readily recognizes the inhibition of reactions by compounds of slightly different properties from those of true substrates.

The search for compounds which would antagonize auxins in plant growth was stimulated by Åberg's report (1950) that two derivatives of naphthalene could reduce the inhibition of roots by auxin. There followed a report by van Overbeek *et al* (1951) that *trans*-cinnamic acid, which lacks auxin activity because of its spatial configuration, inhibits growth, and the inhibition may be reversed by auxin. The *trans*-cinnamic acid effect is illustrated by figure 74, in which it can be seen that a given amount (15 mg./l.) is inhibitory at low auxin concentrations and the inhibition disappears at higher auxin concentrations. A summary of the large number of anti-auxins reported in the following three years is given by McRae and Bonner (1953).

Modes of Action. The evidence concerning the molecular requirements for auxin activity has led to the general conclusion that auxins act by becoming attached to other materials at two points. Thus an auxin must have an unsaturated ring which can be attached to some receptor (at the *ortho* position in the case of phenoxyacetic acids), and there must be an acid group which can combine with some receptor. By assuming that the ring and the acid attach to the same receptor, Foster *et al* (1952) can account for the spatial configuration requirement as well.

A provocative theory of the means of anti-auxin actions has been proposed by McRae and Bonner (1953). In their theory, anti-auxins are compounds which have some of the three requirements for auxin activity but fall short of having all three. Three types of anti-auxins

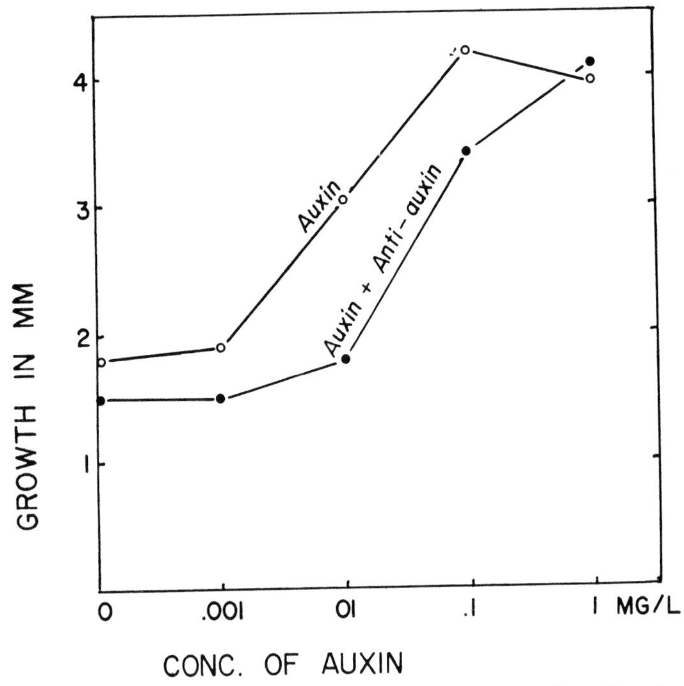

Fig. 74. An interaction between an auxin (naphthaleneacetic acid) and an anti-auxin (*trans*-cinnamic acid) in the pea straight-growth test, showing the inhibition of growth at low auxin concentrations by the anti-auxin (15 mg./l.), and the reversal of this inhibition by the presence of larger amounts of the auxin (van Overbeek *et al,* 1951).

are schematically portrayed in figure 75. Assuming that both points of attachment of auxins are on the same receptor substance, a true auxin can satisfactorily fill both (figure 75 *A*). If the ring attachment is obstructed, incomplete attachment results (*B*). If the appropriate acid group on the side-chain is lacking, incomplete attachment again occurs, as shown in *C*. If both ring and acid groups are satisfactory but a steric hindrance exists for the two-point attachment, attach-

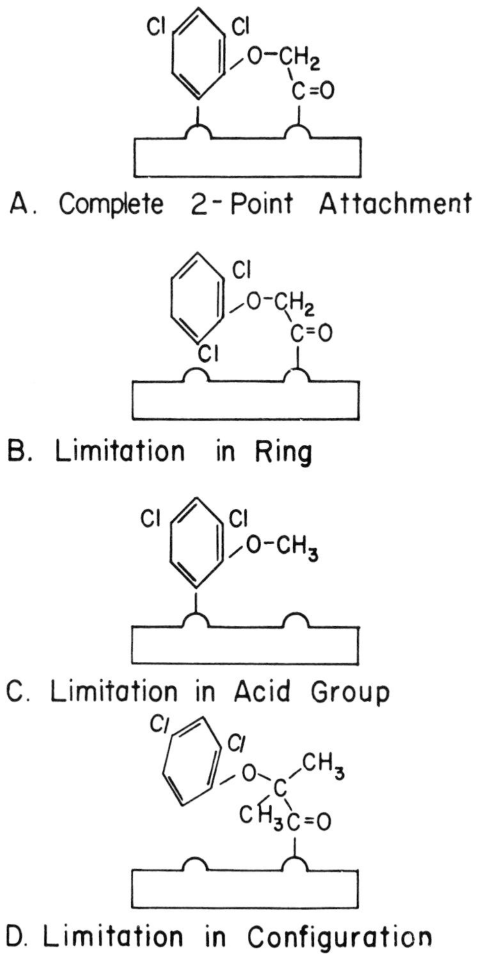

A. Complete 2-Point Attachment

B. Limitation in Ring

C. Limitation in Acid Group

D. Limitation in Configuration

Fig. 75. Diagrammatic representation of the two-point attachment scheme of auxin and anti-auxin action. *A* represents a complete auxin which completes both attachments. *B*, *C* and *D* represent anti-auxins which complete only one point of attachment because of structural limitations (redrawn from McRae and Bonner, 1953).

ment is incomplete as shown in *D*. A few examples of each of these types of anti-auxins are given in table 9.

TABLE 9

Examples of Auxins and Anti-auxins Belonging to the Classes in Figure 75
(Adapted from McRae and Bonner, 1953)

Class	Examples	Reference
A. Complete 2-point attachment	4-chlorophenoxyacetic acid	—
	2,4-dichlorophenoxyacetic acid	—
	2,4,5-trichlorophenoxyacetic acid	—
B. Limitation in ring structure	2,6-dichlorophenoxyacetic acid	McRae & Bonner, 1952
	2,4,6-trichlorophenoxyacetic acid	McRae & Bonner, 1952
C. Limitation in acid group	2,4-dichloroanisole	Bonner, 1949
D. Limitation in configuration	4-chlorophenoxyisobutyric acid	Burström, 1951
	2,4-dichlorophenoxyisobutyric acid	Burström, 1951
	(*L*)-α-(2,4-dichlorophenoxy)-propionic acid	Smith *et al*, 1952
	indoleisobutyric acid	Burström, 1951
	trans-cinnamic acid	van Overbeek *et al*, 1951

A compound which lacks both a reactive ring position and the proper acid group will not be an anti-auxin. If it does not react at either of the points of attachment, it will obviously not interfere with auxin molecules doing so. An excellent example of this has been cited by McRae and Bonner (1953) in the case of 2,4,6-trichloroanisole (XXVI), in which the *ortho* positions of the ring are both occupied and there is no acid group.

A fourth type of anti-auxin recognized by McRae and Bonner (1953) is the type which can apparently fill both of the points of attachment satisfactorily but whose activity in that position is weak. Perhaps the most clearcut examples of this type are γ-phenylbutyric acid (XXIV) (Skoog *et al,* 1942) and phenoxyacetic acid (Ingestad, 1953). It is believed that these compounds have strong affinities for one or both of the two points of auxin attachment, but that they show only weak activity in the final auxin function. Many of the anti-auxins show weak auxin activity, for example the two compounds cited as belonging to this class, and 2,6 and 2,4,6 chlorophenoxyacetic acids and most of the α-phenoxypropionic acids (Thimann, 1952; Smith *et al,* 1952). The very fact that they are such weak auxins is undoubtedly partly responsible for their anti-auxin properties. They are excellent examples of compounds which probably have good affinity for the receptor but poor activity after being attached.

Anti-auxins can antagonize auxin action in a wide variety of functions. Not only can they inhibit auxin-induced growth, but they can alleviate auxin inhibitions (Åberg, 1950), prevent respiratory responses to auxins (Bonner, 1949), remove the apical dominance effect of auxins, prevent tropic responses, and even protect against the epinastic responses to auxin sprays (Hoffmann, 1953).

Kinetics of Anti-auxin Action. A method of study of auxin and anti-auxin action which has yielded much valuable evidence of the mechanism of action has been the kinetic method devised by Lineweaver and Burk (1934) for the study of enzyme action. This method of analysis, described in chapter VIII, was adapted to the study of auxins by Foster *et al* (1952) and of anti-auxins by McRae and Bonner (1952, 1953) and Ingestad (1953). For the purposes of the present discussion the method will be discussed only briefly.

In studies of simple enzyme systems, if one measures the velocity of a reaction when the enzyme is supplied with various amounts of substrate, one can estimate the maximal rate of the enzymatic action under the conditions of the tests. This maximum velocity is constant under conditions in which only the substrate concentration is varied. If an inhibitor is added, the velocity at most of the substrate concentrations is reduced, of course. Now if the inhibitor is acting competitively with the substrate, that is, if the inhibitor is combining with the enzyme at the same position as the substrate, the maximum velocity obtainable is unchanged. On the other hand, if the inhibitor is acting non-specifically to lower the effectiveness of the enzyme, the maximum velocity obtainable is changed. In this way, one can test to determine whether an inhibitor is combining with the enzyme at the same point as the substrate by matching the maximum velocities obtainable with and without the inhibitors.

Assuming that auxins combine with some receptor in a manner like the combination of a substrate with an enzyme, one can test whether an anti-auxin competes for the same point or points of attachment by this kinetic analysis. Measurements of the velocities of growth with different auxin levels using the *Avena* straight-growth test have given the results shown in figure 76 *A*. By the device of Lineweaver and Burk (1934), one plots the inverse of the velocity (growth rate) on the ordinate and the inverse of the substrate concentration (auxin) on the abscissa; the point at which the line obtained intercepts the ordinate is the maximum velocity. Addition of a constant amount of an anti-auxin to each auxin concentration should not alter the point of intercept (maximum velocity) if the anti-auxin specifically competes with auxin for the active points of attachment.

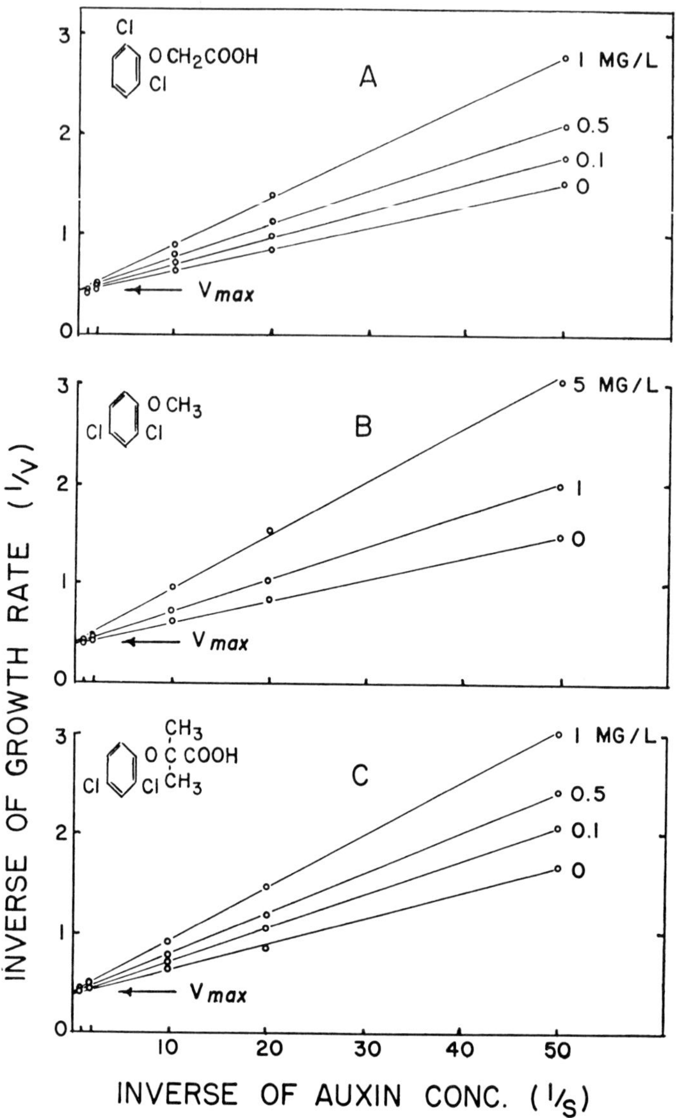

Fig. 76. Kinetic analyses of three anti-auxins with indoleacetic acid, showing unchanged maximum growth rate (V_{max}) in the presence of the inhibitors. *A*, 2,6-dichlorophenoxyacetic acid; *B*, 2,4-dichloroanisole; *C*, 2,4-dichlorophenoxyisobutyric acid (McRae and Bonner, 1952; 1953).

Examples of each of the first three types of anti-auxins are given in figure 76, including 2,6-dichlorophenoxyacetic acid which has an obstruction in the ring (*A*), 2,4-dichloroanisole which lacks the acid group (*B*), and 2,4-dichlorophenoxyisobutyric acid which has a steric obstruction in its configuration (*C*). With each of these inhibitors it is evident that the maximum velocity of growth is unchanged, and hence the observations are consistent with the assumption that these anti-auxins compete with auxins for the same points of attachment to the receptor substance or substances.

Precisely the same results are obtained with anti-auxins of the fourth type which have good affinity for the receptor but low activity after becoming attached. This has been demonstrated for phenoxyacetic acid by Ingestad (1953).

Other Inhibitors of Auxin Action

Some other growth inhibitors fail to show the unaltered maximum velocity of growth. These include maleic hydrazide, 2,3,5-triiodobenzoic acid and coumarin (McRae and Bonner, 1953; McCune

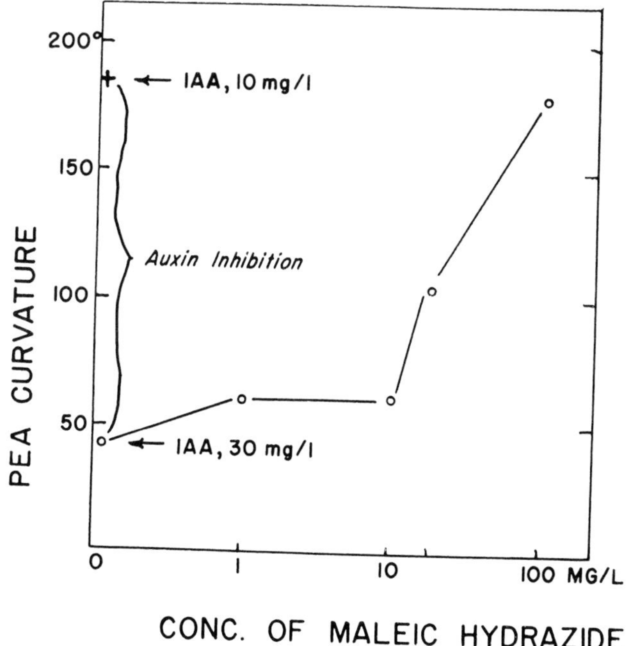

Fig. 77. The reversal of auxin inhibition of growth by maleic hydrazide in the slit pea test. The optimum auxin concentration for growth was 10 mg./l. indoleacetic acid and the presence of 30 mg./l. resulted in a 145° inhibition. The further addition of 100 mg./l. of maleic hydrazide restored optimal growth (Leopold and Klein, 1952).

and Leopold, unpublished; Bonner and Bandurski, 1952); hence these substances cannot be classified as anti-auxins in this specific sense. It is not certain that they inhibit growth by a direct competition with auxin for the same points of attachment.

Maleic Hydrazide. This interesting compound (XXVII) was first reported as a growth inhibitor with the remarkable property of retarding overall plant growth without causing epinastic or other obvious morphological abnormalities (Schoene and Hoffmann, 1949). The fact that it broke apical dominance as well as inhibited growth suggested that it might lower auxin effectiveness. Experiments indicate that it inhibits growth in standard auxin assays, and that its inhibition effects can be removed by the presence of additional auxin. Conversely, the inhibition effects of excess auxin can be reversed by addition of maleic hydrazide as shown in figure 77 (Leopold and Klein, 1952). This property of antagonizing auxins has been utilized for preventing the auxin stimulation of respiration and ripening of fruits (Smock *et al,* 1951), and in development of spray techniques for breaking apical dominance in floral crops (Beach and Leopold, 1953). The reduction of auxin effectiveness by maleic hydrazide may be explained in part by the finding that it can bring about increased enzymatic destruction of indoleacetic acid (Andreae and Andreae, 1953). A synergistic effect with auxin has also been reported (Gautheret, 1952). The rather startling effects of maleic hydrazide on dormancy are described in chapter XV. It also finds some use as an herbicide, and has been shown to alter flowering and growth in many plants (Zuckel, 1952; 1953).

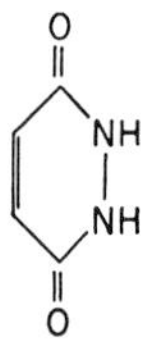

XXVII 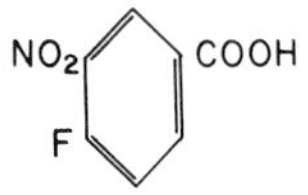 XXVIII

2,3,5-Triiodobenzoic acid (XXIII) was first shown to inhibit growth in the presence of auxins by Galston (1947). Its synergistic effects with auxins have been discussed in the preceding section. A variety of halogenated benzoic acid derivatives have been found which relieve the auxin inhibition of root growth (Minarik *et al,* 1951); the most active of these is 3-nitro-4-fluorobenzoic acid (XXVIII). 2,3,5-triiodobenzoic acid is the most active of the benzoic series tested for causing abscission (Weintraub *et al,* 1952), a property which may be a consequence of an antagonism with auxin. It has also been found to have some effects on flowering (Galston, 1947; Bonner, 1949) which may be interpreted as possible reductions in auxin effectiveness.

Coumarin (XXIX) and other unsaturated lactones have long been known to inhibit growth and germination. The synergistic effects with auxin were discussed in the previous section. The inhibition of growth is thought to take place through interference with some step closely allied with auxin action (Thimann and Bonner 1949), and the inhibition was effectively vitiated by a sulfhydryl protecting agent, as mentioned above. The concept of coumarin interfering with auxin action through a sulfhydryl effect has been criticized by Mayer and Evanari (1951; 1952) who found that coumarin increased the inhibition of germination by auxins.

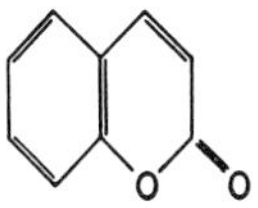

XXIX 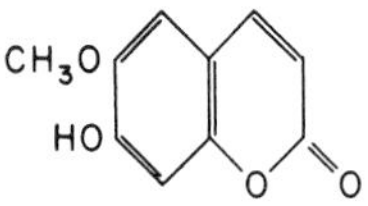 XXX 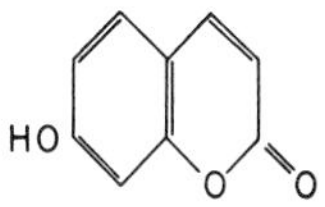 XXXI

Other lactones may have very diverse effects on auxin action. Scopoletin (XXX) inhibits the destruction of auxin by indoleacetic acid oxidase (Andreae, 1952). Kinetic analysis of the interaction by the Lineweaver and Burk (1934) method indicates that the lactone may be a competitive inhibitor against the auxin, an observation which suggests that if the auxin and the lactone have so much in common in the one enzymatic reaction one might almost expect a similar interaction with the auxin receptor itself. It is curious that competitive inhibition has not been found in the growth interactions. Another lactone, umbelliferone (XXXI), has been observed to do quite the opposite of scopoletin, and actually increases the enzymatic destruction of indoleacetic acid (Andreae and Andreae, 1953).

Besides the lactones, a wide variety of other naturally occurring auxin inhibitors has been found, including those compounds discussed above as auxin synergists plus a host of unidentified inhibitors. These compounds may play key roles in such phenomena as dormancy, seed germination and even the ecological relationships controlling plant distribution (see review of Bonner, 1950).

The general subject of anti-auxins is a very interesting one and one which can be expected to find many applications in the near future. The possibility of applying an anti-auxin to lower the effective auxin level in a plant is now a reality. Anti-auxins may find important uses in the modification of any of the many auxin functions in plants such as abscission, flowering, apical dominance, prolonging dormancy, and modification of herbicide effects.

An interesting possibility is the use of anti-auxins as systemic fungicides. The work of Crowdy and Wain (1950, 1951) indicates that several materials, such as isobutyric derivatives of phenoxy acids, and 2,4,6-trichlorophenoxyacetic acid, are effective in preventing infection by some virus and fungal pathogens. These anti-auxins may themselves be toxic to the pathogen or they may modify the constitution of the plant in such a way as to prevent infection.

Epinasty Agents

Compounds which cause swelling of cells along the vascular strands of leaves, stems and roots are commonly spoken of as *epinastic agents.* An example of such distortion—the *epinastic response*—is shown in figure 54. These agents include compounds such as carbon monoxide, unsaturated hydrocarbons (ethylene, acetylene), and many auxins and related compounds. Epinastic agents which are not auxins can often bring about responses which are commonly thought of as being auxin functions. For example, ethylene can stimulate root formation, can induce parthenocarpic fruit-set in tomato, and can stimulate flower initiation in the pineapple plant, as well as cause epinastic distortion of leaves and stems. Ethylene, however, cannot stimulate growth in the absence of auxin. Epinastic agents, then, are not necessarily functional as auxins.

Many auxins, particularly some of the chlorinated phenoxyacetic acids, are powerful epinastic agents. It should be noted that epinastic activity of different compounds will vary from one species to another. For example, 2,4-D produces strong epinastic effect upon tomato foliage, but is much less active on the foliage of tobacco (Zimmerman, 1951).

The nature of the epinastic effect is not at all clear. It may sometimes be the stimulation of a general swelling of cells in contrast to an orderly linear elongation, and sometimes only a poisonous effect in altering cell size. From the evidence of the effects of ethylene on the pea test (Michener, 1938), it appears that auxins must be present for epinastic responses to at least some compounds.

CHAPTER VIII

Theories of the Mechanism of Auxin Action

It is clear that many functions are involved in growth, and to ascribe the full responsibility for growth to any one function would appear to be an over-simplification. Similarly the action of the growth hormone in controlling growth appears to be a complex of many functions. Although the mechanism of growth hormone action may be partly explained by each of these functions, it seems that none of them known today can entirely account for the effects of auxin on growth.

In the last twenty-five years many extremely interesting facts have been set forth bearing on the mechanism of auxin action and many of these have contributed materially to our understanding of the physiology of growth and the growth hormone.

For convenience, discussion of the theories concerning the mechanism of auxin action will be grouped into five sections. First those theories concerning the molecular behavior of auxins will be discussed, then those concerning enzymatic effects, osmotic phenomena, cell wall effects, and finally theories of toxic metabolism.

MOLECULAR REACTION THEORIES

The first specific suggestion of a molecular reaction into which auxin might enter in causing growth was made by Skoog *et al* (1942). They postulated that auxin may act as a sort of coenzyme, serving as a point of attachment for some substrate onto an enzyme controlling growth. The molecular configuration and reactivity of auxins would affect activity through altering the fit and the functioning of this molecular union. The anti-auxin effects of very weak auxins such as γ-phenylbutyric acid (discussed in the preceding chapter) could be explained as resulting from proper molecular configuration for attachment but insufficient reactivity. The inhibition of growth by high auxin levels would be owing to separate molecules combining with the enzyme and with the substrate; thus the proper union of the two by an auxin molecule would be prevented.

Veldstra (1953) has suggested a different role for auxin. He found that the degree of fat solubility as influenced by the ring structure and the water solubility as influenced by the side-chain structure could be correlated with auxin activity. The correlation was rather complex, and it was concluded that auxin activity was greatest when the lipophilic and the hydrophilic properties were balanced. Having also compiled an immense amount of information indicating that the ring and the side-chain should be in different spatial planes for effective auxin activity, he conceived of the auxin action as being something of a physical bonding of some lipoidal material to some more aqueous phase. The identity of the two materials has not been established.

A third suggestion about the reactions of auxin has sprung from the suggestion of Muir *et al* (1949) that auxins of the phenoxy acid type may combine with some material (presumably proteinaceous) at the *ortho* position of the ring. Conceiving, then, of an auxin as reacting with some material in the cell at two positions, (a) at some position in the ring (*ortho* in the phenoxy acids) and (b) at the acid group of the side-chain, Foster *et al* (1952) advanced a theory of auxin action by two-point attachment. They supported the theory with a variety of kinetic evidence.

Kinetic Considerations

With the increasing importance of kinetic evidence in relation to auxin performance, a brief description of conventional kinetic methods would be in order here. The kinetic methods have been adopted directly from enzyme studies, based on the work of Michaelis and Menton (1913) and Lineweaver and Burk (1934). It is assumed that enzymes attach to a substrate to form an enzyme-substrate complex, and that this complex may further break in such a way as to produce the end product of the reaction and regenerate the enzyme again. Considering the enzyme to be the material with which auxin reacts. the reactions are formulated as follows:

$$E + S \overset{K}{\rightleftharpoons} ES \overset{k}{\longrightarrow} \text{growth} + E$$

where E is the auxin receptor, S is the auxin, ES is the complex of the two, K represents the attraction of the auxin for the receptor, and k the reactivity in growth.

For the purposes of this brief discussion, two kinetic values of interest may be obtained. One is the value of K and the other is the maximal growth rate attainable, each of which will vary from one auxin to another, all other factors being held constant. The method of obtaining the values is based on an elaboration of the assumptions made in the equation given. The derivation methods are described clearly by Foster *et al* (1952) and by Bonner (1953). By measuring growth rates over a range of auxin concentrations, and plotting the results by the double inverse method of Lineweaver and Burk (1934), the maximal growth rate may be estimated as the intercept of the plotted line with the abscissa. The method is illustrated in figure 78. The K value may be estimated by the slope of the plotted line. An auxin with a weak attraction for the receptor should have a relatively steep slope of the plotted line. Also a weak auxin should yield a low maximum velocity of growth, *i.e.* the intercept of the plotted line with the abscissa should be high, the growth rates being plotted on an inverse scale.

Maximal growth rates and K values have been measured for several auxins by Foster *et al* (1952), who found that auxins which produced the greatest maximal growth rates also had the highest affinity for the

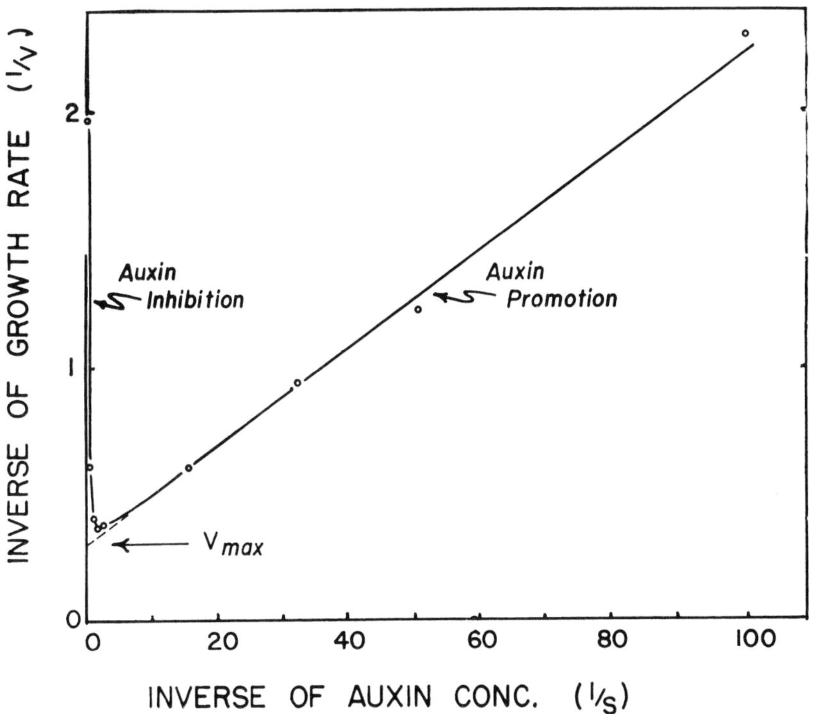

Fig. 78. The promotion and inhibition of growth by indoleacetic acid plotted by the double inverse method. Growth rate of *Avena* coleoptile sections as inverse of mm. per 12 hrs., auxin concentration as inverse of mg. per l. (from Foster *et al,* 1952).

hypothetical receptor. The kinetic studies of auxins and anti-auxins described in the preceding chapter further indicate that the affinity of the auxin for the receptor can be competitively inhibited by anti-auxins (see figure 76). Thus the use of K values and maximum growth velocities have permitted a new level of definition of auxin activities.

Returning to the concept of two-point auxin attachment, it was found that if the algebraic expressions were modified to fit the assumption of two points of attachment between E and S in the given formula, an inhibition of growth by high concentrations of S (auxin) could be predicted. This would result from two auxin molecules becoming attached to the receptor substance, one at each of the two points of attachment, each preventing the effective functioning of the other. In this way, the inhibition of growth by high auxin concentrations envisaged earlier by Skoog *et al* (1942) has found more graphic expression. The two phases of the auxin curve are shown in figure 79. A numerical expression of the inhibitory effects of an auxin can be taken from the slope of the inhibitory section of the growth curve given in figure 78.

Two reservations should be kept in mind concerning the kinetic

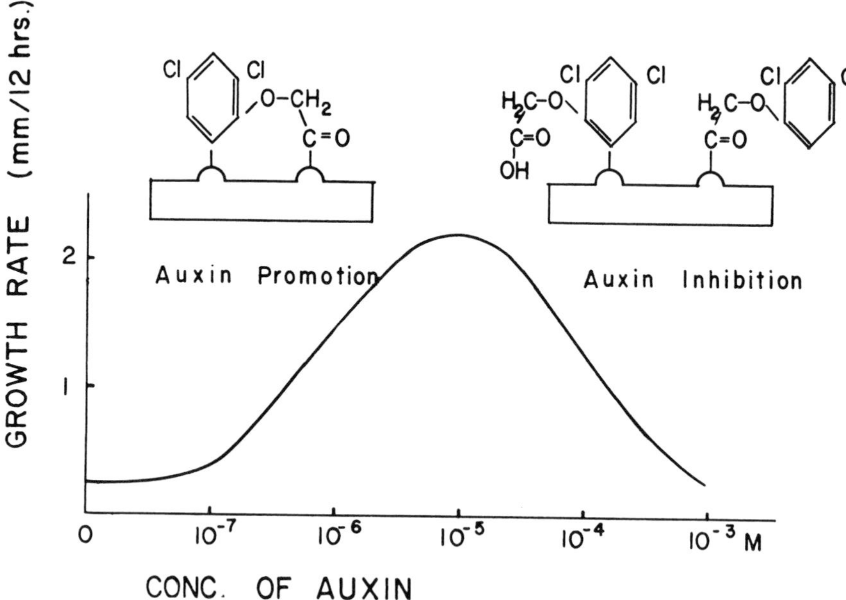

Fig. 79. The promotion and inhibition of growth by 2,4-D as interpreted by the theory of 2-point attachment. At low concentrations, both attachments are completed and growth is promoted. At high concentrations the auxin competes with itself for the two active sites and inhibition results (adapted from Foster *et al,* 1952).

evidence of the nature of auxin action. First, these kinetic analyses are based on the assumption that the velocity of the reaction being measured is dependent upon such an *equilibrium* as that in the prior equation, whereas in systems as complex as growing cells it is possible that the velocity is controlled by steady state conditions instead. Second, the agreement of the kinetic performance with that predicted by the assumption of two-point attachment does not prove the assumptions. Nevertheless these kinetic analyses are certainly the best evidence yet obtained as to how auxin acts. It will be critical for the theory to establish the identity of the receptor complex or complexes.

Suggested Auxin Receptors

Two lines of evidence as to the possible nature of substances which may form complexes with auxin have appeared almost simultaneously.

In studies of the disappearance of indoleacetic acid in pea brei, Siegel and Galston (1953) observed that some of the auxin was bound to a protein fraction in the brei. This bound auxin was detectable by the ferric chloride color test for indoleacetic acid which gave a red color with precipitated protein. The auxin-protein complex was stable to acid and alkali. In the presence of adenosine-triphosphate the binding reaction was facilitated, suggesting that energy might be consumed in the reaction. It is tempting to hope that this auxin-protein complex may be the auxin-receptor complex postulated by Foster *et al* (1952).

In studies of the reaction of some organic acids with coenzyme A (CoA) in the presence of tomato mitochondria it was found that the presence of several compounds which are auxins could bring about the enzymatic disappearance of the free sulfhydryl of CoA (Leopold and Guernsey, 1953). An interesting aspect of the study was the finding that the most active auxins were the most effective (e.g. 2,4-D, indoleacetic acid), weak auxins were less effective (e.g. *p*-chlorophenoxyacetic acid, indolebutyric acid), and compounds closely allied to auxins but lacking auxin activity were ineffective (e.g. cyclohexaneacetic acid, 2,4-dichlorobenzoic acid). The relative effects of some of these acids in the CoA reaction are shown in figure 80. A further parallelism between the auxin effects on this reaction and on growth is the inhibitions by higher auxin concentrations. It can be seen in figure 80 that at high concentrations each of the auxins inhibited the disappearance of CoA.

As in the protein reaction of Siegel and Galston (1953), adenosine-triphosphate facilitated the reaction.

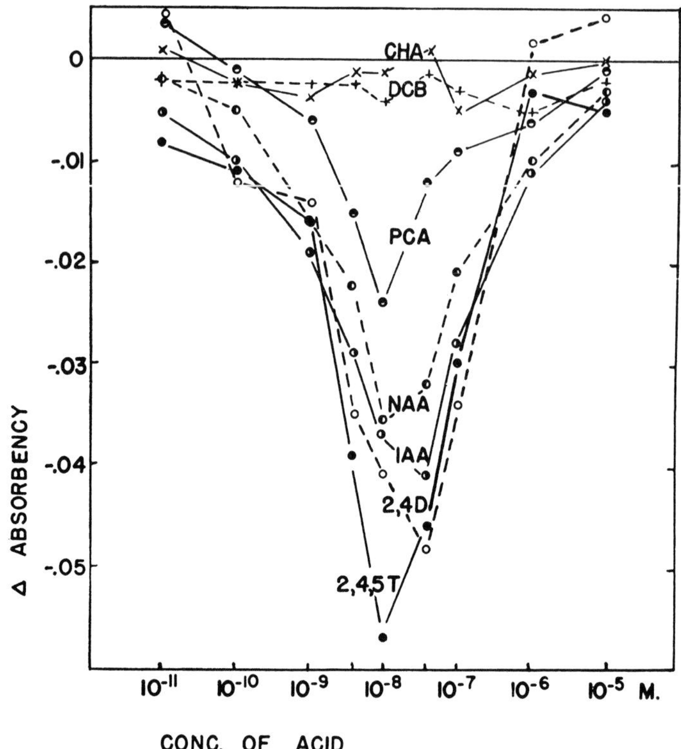

Fig. 80. The effects of some auxins and related compounds upon the disappearance of free sulfhydryls of coenzyme A (Leopold and Guernsey, 1953).

2,4,5-T:	2,4,5-trichlorophenoxyacetic acid
2,4-D:	2,4-dichlorophenoxyacetic acid
IAA:	indoleacetic acid
NAA:	naphthaleneacetic acid
PCA:	*p*-chlorophenoxyacetic acid
DCB:	2,4-dichlorobenzoic acid
CHA:	cyclohexaneacetic acid

The suggestion was made that auxin may form a thiol ester with CoA. The proposed reaction might be expected to be as follows:

$$\text{(indole)}\text{-}CH_2COOH + \text{CoA-SH} \xrightarrow[\text{ATP}]{\text{enzyme}} \text{(indole)}\text{-}CH_2C(=O)\text{-S-CoA} + H_2O$$

The auxinyl-CoA would be expected to be a high-energy bond, just as are the esters of CoA with other organic acids.

The theory that auxin may act through an ester with CoA is further supported by the findings that CoA and adenosine-triphosphate can increase auxin-induced growth in the pea straight-growth test, and that the greatest enzymatic activity for this reaction appears to be associated with tissues in the most rapid state of growth (Leopold and Guernsey, 1954). The theory may be criticized on the basis that the amount of auxin added is considerably less than the amount of CoA which disappears. The isolation of the proposed ester will be critical to proving the scheme.

Several interesting points are brought up by the auxin-CoA theory. The release of bound auxin by alkali has been known for many years (e.g. Berger and Avery, 1944), and the breaking of thiol esters by alkali is similarly well established (Lynen *et al,* 1952). The proposed ester would be a high-energy bond, which suggests that auxin may control a high-energy bond system in plants. This has already been suggested by Rhodes and Ashworth (1952) as possibly occurring through the formation of high-energy phosphate bonds on the auxin itself. The ability of CoA to remove the auxin from the protein complex of Siegel and Galston (1953) is also suggestive of an auxinyl-CoA product.

Because CoA is a key compound in the metabolism as well as in the synthesis of organic acids, fatty acids and steroids (Lipmann, 1951), auxin may control these diverse processes of metabolism and hence of growth itself through its influence on CoA. This would be a case of a hormone having its action through a coenzyme.

THEORIES OF ENZYME EFFECTS

The fact that auxins could inhibit enzyme activity was known for many years, but the realization that specific enzymes could be stimulated by auxins was not entirely appreciated until 1942 when Berger and Avery demonstrated that under certain circumstances some dehydrogenases could be stimulated by auxin. Treatment of growing tissues with auxin has been found to increase directly or indirectly the activity of a variety of enzymes as described in chapter V.

A provocative theory to explain auxin action has been proposed by Northen (1942). Having observed that auxins cause decreases in cytoplasmic viscosity, he suggested that auxins bring about dissociation of the protein constituents of the cytoplasm. The dissociation effect would increase water permeability, increase the osmotic value of the cytoplasm, and possibly also bring about increased enzymatic activity. It has been shown that gentle protein dissociation can sometimes activate enzymes (Hand, 1939), and such dissociation might increase the availability of substrates for the enzymes as well. Consequently one would expect that increased respiratory activity and growth might follow. Northen also pointed out that if dissociation activities are carried to the extreme, the stimulation effects upon enzymes in respiration would be reversed by dissociation of essential constituents from enzymes, and he proposed that this may be the nature of inhibition of growth by auxin and the concomitant inhibition of respiration.

If the auxin-induced decrease in cytoplasmic viscosity is due to a hydration of the protein constituents, one might expect an increase in the water of hydration in cells exposed to auxin. Levitt (1948) has not been able to find such an increase. A further criticism is found in the work of Blank and Deuel (1943) who were unable to detect protoplamic viscosity changes at some of the lower auxin concentrations even though growth was still being stimulated by the auxin.

Another theory of auxin action through enzymic mechanisms has been proposed by Thimann (1951). He points out several lines of evidence indicating that a sulfhydryl containing enzyme may be very intimately involved in growth and that poisons which attack sulfhydryl enzymes also antagonize auxin action. He has suggested that auxins may act, not as enzyme-activating agents, but as agents protecting growth enzymes from inactivation. On this basis, the structural requirements for an active auxin may be explained on the basis of structural specificity to antagonize enzymic inhibitors.

Another suggestion as to the nature of auxin action in growth has been made by Bonner (1949) and expanded by Bonner and Bandurski (1952). They cite a considerable amount of indirect evidence to suggest that auxin may serve in some manner to couple or mesh together the respiratory processes with the growth processes. By this scheme auxin would act in some role which would make the energy formed in respiration available to the growth processes. They point out several indications suggesting the participation of auxin in phosphorylation and energy transfer reactions. Such indications may be listed as (1) the ineffectiveness of auxin in the presence of agents which uncouple phosphorylations (such as arsenate and dinitrophenol), and (2) the evidence that phosphorylation reactions commonly limit growth. The suggestion is a very interesting one, but needs some direct evidence to support it.

THEORIES OF OSMOTIC EFFECTS

In the process of growth, increases in cell volume may be largely accounted for on the basis of water uptake. Consequently a great deal of attention has been given to the water uptake mechanism as a possible means of describing growth in its simplest form. The uptake of water could be due to changes in the cytoplasm itself, especially changes in osmotic value; or it could be due to changes in the properties of the wall and the cell membranes, particularly with respect to extensibility and permeability. Each of these two factors in water uptake has been defended as a possible mechanism through which auxin may bring about growth.

Changes in the osmotic value of the cytoplasm were first proposed by Czaja (1935) to account for water uptake. Essentially his idea was that auxin may increase the osmotic value of the sap which would result directly in water uptake and growth. A basic limitation to this concept lies in the fact that growth is not necessarily associated with an increase in osmotic value. In fact, van Overbeek (1944) and Hackett (1951) have been able to obtain growth with an associated decrease in osmotic value.

Changes in the cytoplasm do occur, however, following auxin treatment. Among these changes there appear to be decreases in cytoplasmic viscosity (Northen, 1942). There is some quantitative relationship between viscosity changes and auxin treatment, but the effect is not specific for auxins, and some active auxins do not produce these viscosity changes.

A very interesting suggestion has been made by Commoner *et al* (1942-3) who pointed out that since water uptake in growth may be linked with a respiratory mechanism, one might explain growth as being due to the osmotic uptake of water activated by a respiration-induced uptake of salts. By this theory auxin may stimulate the respiratory uptake of salts, and the resultant increase in the osmotic value of the cell sap would cause water uptake and hence growth. The major objection to this theory is van Overbeek's observation, already mentioned, that under some circumstances growth, associated with a drop in osmotic value, can occur in potato slices. Clearly such growth cannot be a function of salt accumulation bringing about an increased osmotic value. Another fact which contradicts the theory is that auxin-induced growth can occur in pure water in the absence of salt uptake (Reinders, 1942). On the other hand the presence of salts in the water can greatly facilitate growth (Steward *et al,* 1940).

In an effort to establish whether auxin-induced growth was a function of water uptake, Reinders (1942) has measured the effects of auxin on the uptake of water (measured by weight) of potato slices. Auxin does induce growth of these tissues, so of course she found a similar increase in water uptake. She further established that the water uptake response was strictly dependent upon the aerobic respiration of the tissues, for in anaerobic conditions the uptake essentially ceased. The application of respiratory inhibitors also prevented the water uptake. These studies and the subsequent ones of Hackett and Thimann (1952) establish that water uptake in response to auxin is dependent upon oxidative metabolism. Bonner *et al* (1953) have shown in addition that dinitrophenol could block water uptake without inhibiting respiratory rate, and suggest that phosphorylation reactions provide the energy for water uptake phenomena. These characteristics of water uptake are precisely similar to the characteristics of growth.

There seems to be no doubt that water uptake is an integral part of growth, and yet there is some difficulty in determining whether water uptake is the cause or only the consequence of growth. Burström (1953) has attempted to distinguish between reversible and irreversible water uptake (growth) by a comparison of the behavior of roots in solutions of various osmotic values. Water uptake which could be reversed by plasmolysis was subtracted from that which was essentially irreversible. The irreversible uptake in hypotonic solutions was found to be independent of the osmotic value of the external medium, which leads Burström to conclude that water uptake is a consequence and not the cause of growth.

Levitt (1947) has leveled another criticism at the concept that the driving force of growth is an active water uptake. He calculates that the energy required for the assimilation of water by some secretion mechanism against an osmotic gradient would require energy utilization far beyond the capacity of the cells to supply. Thus, for beet cells to maintain a turgor of 5 atmospheres, Levitt calculated that the entire dry matter of the beet would be utilized in three months, assuming that all of the respiratory energy was applied to the water uptake mechanism.

It seems difficult to expect, then, that plant cells may grow by means of an active uptake of water against an osmotic gradient. And if the theory of Commoner *et al* (1943) that water is taken up by an osmotic mechanism driven by respiration is not accepted, it becomes difficult too to expect that growth may be driven by an osmotic water uptake. If water uptake forces other than simple osmotic ones may be found, then the concept of growth as a function of such forces may be reopened.

THEORIES OF CELL WALL EFFECTS

Heyn (1932) has observed that auxin applications cause a pronounced increase in flexibility and extensibility of cell walls. He proposed that such an increased extensibility would result in a drop of wall pressure around the cell and would permit water uptake due to this simple drop in turgor pressure. By this concept, growth is attributed to a dynamic function of the cell wall, as contrasted to the dynamic function of the cytoplasm *per se*. The concept has been criticized by Commoner and Mazia (1942) who demonstrated that apparently flaccid cells would still take up water in response to auxin.

The stand that cell growth is primarily a function of the cell wall has been supported further by the work of Burström (1953). After a critical study of water uptake, as mentioned in the previous section, he concluded that the cell wall attains a plastic quality during growth, and that water uptake only follows the changes in the wall. As evidence for this he cited the finding that root cells which are at the appropriate stage for elongation attain a plastic quality in the walls. This plasticity can be observed whether the cells are permitted to enlarge and take up water or whether they are essentially prevented from growing by immersion in hypertonic solutions. If the wall plasticity is the primary action of growth, then cells should be strictly unable to grow in isotonic or hypertonic solutions. Some careful experiments on this aspect indicate that neither wheat root nor Jerusalem artichoke cells may grow in such osmotic conditions (Burström, 1953). By his concept, then, the effects of auxin and respiration upon growth are attained primarily through an activation of cell wall growth. The wall is thought to be made plastic enough for cell extension, and then the active deposition of new wall material causes cell enlargement. The cytoplasm must be capable of taking up enough water osmotically to keep up with the growing wall or else growth will cease, as it apparently does in hypertonic solutions.

TOXIC METABOLISM

There is reason to believe that the inhibitory or toxic effects of auxins may be physiologically distinct from the growth promoting effects (cf. Burström, 1951). If the promotive effects and the toxic effects are truly distinct, then the mechanism of the toxic actions of auxins may be sought in functions other than those thought to be responsible for growth.

From a survey of root inhibition effects of various phenoxyacetic acid derivatives, Leaper and Bishop (1950) have found that the most inhibitory materials are ones in which two positions *para* to one another on the ring are left unsubstituted. They point out that it would not be difficult for two such positions to become oxidized to quinonoid structures. Quinones in general are, of course, highly toxic. If phenoxyacetic acids are converted into quinones as Leaper and Bishop suggested, it would be reasonable to expect that they would be toxic. The toxic effects of maleic hydrazide and N-phthalamic acid derivatives may be due to their quinonoid structures also. This theory has been criticized on the basis that the benzoic acid auxins never have open positions *para* to one another (Thimann, 1952), and they are effective herbicides.

Van Overbeek *et al* (1951) have proposed that growth regulator toxicity may be a result of an alteration of metabolism such that unsaturated lactones are accumulated in the plant tissues. Such lactones as coumarin, scopoletin, and umbelliferone are toxic to plants when applied in high enough quantities, and it has been observed that such compounds may accumulate in plant tissues following application of herbicidal concentrations of 2,4-D (Fults and Johnson, 1950). Such materials have been found to be more toxic to some dicotyledonous plants than to monocotyledonous ones (Hamner and Sell, 1950). This suggests the possibility that stimulation of such toxic metabolism may account at least in part for herbicidal selectivity of auxins.

In conclusion it may be said that the mechanism of auxin action remains unsolved, but a variety of promising lines of evidence seems to be emerging. Auxin has been found actually to react with some proteinaceous material in a manner which is suggestive of a constructive step in growth. Evidence has appeared that auxin may form high-energy ester bonds with coenzyme A, which is suggestive of an energy-controlling action by the growth hormone. A picture of how auxin may react with its receptor compound has come from kinetic studies, as well as a picture of the means by which other compounds may alter auxin action. The means by which auxin may finally bring about cell enlargement is being hotly debated between those who feel that the action is principally based upon the cytoplasmic uptake of water and those who feel that it is principally based upon the growth of the cell wall.

The clarification of this important problem will not only be extremely interesting, but no doubt will greatly accelerate the advance of practical and theoretical knowledge of auxins and growth.

■ PART TWO

AUXINS IN AGRICULTURE

CHAPTER IX

Methods of Applying Auxins and Their Persistence in Plants and Soils

In the experimental use of auxins, certain precautions must be followed in making up solutions or other auxin preparations. A variety of methods may be employed in applying the auxin preparations. The experimenter needs to have a working knowledge of these techniques, as well as an appreciation of the persistence of auxins in plants, in soils, and in the greenhouse after application.

SOLVENTS AND SOLUTES

The usual means of applying auxins is in aqueous solution. Some salts of the acids are considerably more soluble in water than the free acids themselves. For this reason, the salts are ordinarily used in experiments requiring high concentrations of auxins.

The acidity of a solution of auxin greatly influences its effectiveness as well as its solubility. This influence of acidity appears to be twofold—affecting the entry of the auxin into plant cells, as well as the action of the auxin inside the cells. The distinction between these is difficult to draw.

Tests of the relative effectiveness of auxin solutions of various pH values in stimulating the growth of *Avena* coleoptile cells have shown that greatest influence is obtained under very acid conditions, and the effectiveness drops as the acidity is decreased (Bonner, 1934). Since the drop was most rapid in the range of acidity at which dissociation of the auxin takes place, it was believed that the auxin functions in growth as the undissociated molecule. More recently, however, it was found that the effects of auxins upon the growth of wheat roots could be precisely correlated with the calculated amount of auxin anions present at the surface of the cells (Lundegårdh, 1949). Thus the question of whether auxin acts in growth as the intact acid or as the anion is not settled, but it is quite clear that applied auxins are generally most efficacious in acid solutions of a pH from 3 to 5.5.

It is not clear whether the acid conditions are superior because of the relative abundance of anions or of undissociated molecules or alternatively because of a more ready entry by the auxin into the cell.

Advantage was taken of the superior effectiveness of acidic solutions of auxins by Lucas *et al* (1948), who buffered auxin spray preparations at an acid pH and observed that the spray was more effective. Hard water with its rather alkaline condition has been reported to be quite detrimental to the effectiveness of an auxin spray (Burg *et al,* 1946; Zussman, 1949).

In weighing out the crystalline auxin, care should be taken that the water of crystallization is accounted for in the weight. This is particularly important in the case of the sodium salt of naphthaleneacetic acid, for Gortner (1952) has shown that an error of 35 per cent in weight can be introduced if one does not take into account this possible error. In humidities ranging from 30 per cent to 90 per cent, four molecules of water are taken up by each molecule of the sodium salt, increasing its molecular weight from 208 to 280. At higher humidities, even more water is taken up. The potassium salt takes up one molecule of water under similar conditions, and the free acid takes up none.

Impurities in the crystalline auxin preparation can distort experimental results. This is particularly true if a technical grade of auxin is used. Hansen (1951) has shown, for example, that technical methoxone (2-methyl 4-chlorophenoxyacetic acid) contained as much as 53 per cent of other auxins and toxic materials. Even recrystallized 2,4-D of analytical grade contains quite large amounts of 2,4-dichlorophenol, a compound which is strongly active in uncoupling oxidation from phosphorylation in the manner of dinitrophenol, and also in activating indoleacetic oxidase (Goldacre *et al,* 1953). The significance of agents of this sort was discussed briefly in chapter VIII.

Some difficulty is commonly encountered in getting the crystalline auxin directly into an aqueous solution. To facilitate this step, a few milliliters of ethyl alcohol are often used to dissolve the crystals, and then large amounts of water are added to bring the solution up to volume. Three or four milliliters of alcohol will be sufficient to dissolve one tenth gram of crystalline indoleacetic acid. An alternative method is to dissolve the crystals in a few milliliters of concentrated NH_4OH, then dilute to volume and neutralize with a mineral acid.

In cases where very high concentrations of auxins are needed, organic cosolvents are commonly used with water. For example, in 50 per cent alcohol one can successfully dissolve at least ten times as much 2,4-D as could be dissolved in water alone.

Carriers are often very helpful in applying auxin solutions to foliage. Some examples of such carriers are carbowax (a mixture of polyalkalene glycols), detergents, or wettable powders. Employment of carriers not only permits the use of high concentrations of auxins, but also can increase the absorption of the materials into the plant tissues. This effect on absorption has been discussed in chapter VI.

Instead of organic carriers, emulsions are sometimes utilized, such as the lanolin emulsion described by Withrow and Howlett (1946) consisting of stearic acid, lanolin and water. Such elaborate preparations are not in wide use now, however, since the advent of good organic carriers for water solutions.

A helpful means of applying growth regulator sprays is with a freon or aerosol bomb type dispenser. For this purpose, the growth regulator is used as an ester derivative, since such derivatives are soluble in the freon solution, whereas most other derivatives are insoluble.

Instead of true solutions, auxins are often applied as pastes or talcs. The commonest type of auxin paste in use today is the lanolin paste in which a purified lanolin is simply melted over a water bath and the auxins are mixed in. It has been found that if the crystals are directly dissolved into the lanolin a solution was obtained which was ten times less effective than if the crystals were first dissolved in a small amount of alcohol or ether (Michel, 1951). Redemann *et al* (1950) expressed the additional caution that some crude lanolin pastes are capable of oxidizing indoleacetic acid and, for that reason, a purified lanolin is recommended. Talc dusts are commonly employed in the rooting of cuttings. To prepare such dusts one simply dissolves the auxin crystals in a small amount of alcohol or ether and mixes it thoroughly with talc to make a paste. After the auxin and talc have been intimately mixed together, the solvent is evaporated off, and the dry talc preparation is left.

METHODS OF APPLICATION

A wide variety of techniques has been developed for applying auxins to growing plants. These may be grouped into four categories: a) spraying solutions on the foliage, b) infiltration into leaves, c) injection into fleshy parts, and d) the immersion of plant parts into auxin solutions.

A direct spray on the foliage is the simplest method of application, but has some disadvantages in that the effective quantity of auxin is not well controlled. The effectiveness of foliage sprays may be strongly influenced by the ability of the auxin to penetrate through the cuticle and into the cells of the leaf, and there is no means of accurately controlling how much auxin is finally able to enter the plant. Furthermore, it is difficult to measure the residue that is left on the surface of the leaf, except in a small carefully controlled application.

A more quantitatively accurate method of application is by infiltration of the auxin solutions into the leaves. Some means of infiltrating solutions into leaves include forced infiltration by a sudden increase in pressure (e.g. Claes, 1952), or alternatively gradual infiltration through the cut ends of leaves (Leopold and Thimann, 1949) or through leaves submerged in the solutions (Bonner and Thurlow, 1949). Forced infiltration can be done easily by placing the plants in a bell-jar or desiccator with leaves in contact with the solution to be infiltrated. The chamber is evacuated by suction, and then the suction suddenly released. Each of these techniques permits the application of auxin solutions in such a manner that the total amount of solution which has been taken in by the leaf can be measured quantitatively. These techniques, of course, do not lend themselves to large-scale or field type of experiments.

Another means of auxin application is through injection of solutions into fleshy parts of the plant. This can be done either with a hypodermic needle (Galston, 1947), or by a vial with the end drawn out into a capillary which is inserted into the plant at the position to be treated as in figure 54, p. 121 (Zimmerman and Wilcoxon, 1935). Another method is the insertion of one end of a wick into the plant, and the other end into a reservoir of auxin solution. These injection techniques are again fairly good quantitatively and have an additional advantage in that the auxins can be applied to rather restricted plant parts where localization of the application is of interest.

Simple immersion of the plant part directly into the auxin solution has been done in many instances. Intact leaves, seeds or cuttings from plants have been successfully treated in this manner. The immersion of roots in auxin solutions over extended periods of time has been used as a method of studying quantitative effects of various auxins on seedling growth. Burström (1950) has found that wheat roots can gradually adapt themselves to grow successfully in solutions of aliphatic acids which initially may be toxic. It is interesting to note that the response of roots or seedlings to immersion in auxin solutions may be quite different during the time of immersion than after such immersion treatment has ended. This was first noticed by Thimann and Lane (1938), who found that auxin concentrations which inhibited the growth of oat roots immersed in them showed a subsequent stimulative aftereffect after the roots were removed from the solutions.

Various other methods of application of auxins have been described for special purposes, including the overall application of auxins to greenhouse crops by volatilization of esters (Zimmerman *et al*, 1939), and the incorporation of auxins into sprays such as fungicides, insecticides, and fertilizers. Auxins appear to be compatible with most ordinary spray materials provided they do not contain lime or other cations which would form insoluble salts with the auxin.

The use of a lanolin paste of auxin has advantages for some types of treatments. Unlike the water sprays, lanolin provides a fairly continuous supply of auxin to the treated plant part. Where an effect of long duration is desired, lanolin pastes are very good.

AUXIN PERSISTENCE AND DESTRUCTION

Indoleacetic acid is spontaneously inactivated to a certain extent in solution and, to a lesser extent, even in the dry crystalline state. Crystalline indoleacetic acid in time breaks down and turns brown as it does so. For this reason, storage of the dry crystals for more than two or three years tends to lower purity and activity. In solution the breakdown is much more rapid, and noticeable changes are observed in ten days' time even under refrigeration. For this reason it is worthwhile to discard stock solutions of indoleacetic acid after one week. Breakdown of auxins other than members of the indole series is generally much slower and storage precautions are less important.

Persistence in Plants

The persistence of auxins applied to the plant varies widely with the auxin which is applied. The currently recognized enzyme systems of the plant which destroy auxin are more or less specific to indoleacetic acid as described in chapter III, and for this reason such auxins as naphthaleneacetic acid and 2,4-D are often more effective and persistent than indoleacetic acid over periods of time. For example, it is known that sprays of many auxins will force flower initiation in the pineapple plant, but indoleacetic acid sprays are notably ineffective, even though the bulk of the growth hormone in the pineapple plant is indoleacetic acid. Consequently pineapple growers employ sprays of naphthaleneacetic acid or sometimes 2,4-D. Another example of the poor efficiency of indoleacetic acid is in the case of induction of parthenocarpic fruit-set in the tomato. Spraying with indoleacetic acid is very much less effective than applying many other auxins to stimulate fruit-set. Some auxins which are highly effective in setting fruit in the tomato are very much weaker in growth activity than indoleacetic acid, but one may assume that their persistence in the plant is considerably longer.

Auxins which have been applied to foliage generally remain active in the plant for only a limited time. Experiments in which applied auxins were recovered from plants by extraction suggest a rapid loss of the auxins in plants. For example naphthaleneacetic acid has been applied to cocklebur plants through the nutrient solution for different intervals of time, and the leaves extracted with ether and assayed. It was found that small increases in the amount of free auxin in the leaves were detectable for the first ten days, but that after that no increase was evident (Bonner and Thurlow, 1949). In an effort to determine how long 2,4-D persisted in plants in an active form, Dhillon and Lucas (1950) made water extracts of leaves at intervals of time after localized treatment of leaves. They found that the auxin could not be detected by epinasty tests even one day after application to bean, corn and oat plants, though it was detectable in tomato plants for five days. When large amounts of 2,4-D were placed in a reservoir in a tomato stem, the auxin could be detected for as long as 26 days in the tissues. Hay and Thimann (1954) also studied the persistence of 2,4-D in beans and they were able to recover 90% of the applied auxin 6 hours after application and only 44% after 48 hours.

Morphological evidence indicates that the growth effects of 2,4-D seem to be established in a relatively short period of time in most species. There has been considerable discussion in the literature about the length of time for which 2,4-D may exert morphological effects in plants. The bulk of evidence indicates that morphological irregularities or distortions in response to the treatment are usually all established within a few days after the application of the spray. This has been explained in some detail by Eames (1951). Some evidence for such a generalization can be seen in the description of morphological responses to 2,4-D described in chapter V. Morphological irregularities which are brought about in buds may not become evident for as long as a year after the 2,4-D application (Tullis and Davis, 1950). Morphological irregularities in young developing seeds likewise may not *appear* until the next growing season when the seeds germinate (Pridham, 1947); nevertheless, the evidence at hand indicates that the irregularities induced by 2,4-D have been essentially established even in these tissues within a very short period of time after the application (Eames, 1950).

Exceptionally long persistence of 2,4-D in cotton plants has been reported by McIlrath and Ergle (1953). They found that leaf abnormalities occur on many more leaves than were present in the bud at the time of treatment. It is estimated that ten leaves which were differentiated after the 2,4-D spray were so affected, and estimating the time of differentiation of each leaf at 2.5 days, one can calculate the persistence of the auxin in cotton plants to have been up to 25 days. When 2,4-D was applied in lanolin it was still extractable from the foliage after 3 months, but of course the lanolin is a source of the auxin continuing in time.

The persistence of auxin effects in plants varies a great deal with the auxin. For example, naphthaleneacetic acid is effective in preventing pre-harvest drop of apples for up to fourteen days, whereas 2,4-D and 2,4,5-TP are effective for 30 to 50 days. In the citrus species these latter auxins provide effective control of abscission for as long as seven months! It is not clear whether the auxins themselves persist in the plants for this length of time or whether the effects which they generate carry on after the auxins are metabolized away.

Persistence in Soils

The persistence of auxin in soils is a subject of very widespread interest, particularly with respect to soil or pre-emergence herbicidal applications. Such persistence appears to be dependent upon three major factors: auxin adsorption, leaching, and destruction by microorganisms.

Adsorption. Since the time when auxins were first used as pre-emergence herbicides applied to the soil, it has been recognized that some of the auxin so applied may become adsorbed in the soil. The adsorbing capacity can be observed as a reduced mobility of the auxin in the soil solution. Sample data demonstrating this phenomenon can be seen in figure 81 in which the distribution of 2,4-D in the soil profile is shown after the application of two inches of water. The first curve demonstrates the high mobility, and hence low adsorption, of 2,4-D in a fine sand soil. The second taken from a silt loam soil shows a concentration of the auxin near the surface due to greater adsorption. And the last curve shows an even greater restriction of the auxin to the surface in an organic muck soil.

Adsorption or degree of immobility of auxin varies with soil type and varies too with different auxins. Some observations have led to the suggestion that adsorption is a function of the organic matter content of the soil (Hernandez and Warren, 1950). However, other workers have observed less adsorption in high organic soils than in some mineral soils (Arakeri and Dunham, 1950). It has been suggested by Weaver (1947) that exchange capacity of the soil colloids was responsible for adsorption. A correlation between auxin adsorption and exchange capacity has been found for a diverse group of soils by Ogle (1953). However, exchange capacity is measured as the attraction of a colloid for cations, and auxins will probably be adsorbed as anions. It would seem more likely that adsorption is proportional to the free colloidal surface in a soil, which will be reflected in turn by the exchange capacity. Thus soils with large free colloidal surfaces will be highly effective in adsorbing auxins and will also have high exchange capacities. It seems probable that auxin adsorption by soils is a consequence of van der Waals' forces. These are forces which attract molecules to each other, and they are a function of electric charges on the molecules. Auxins are probably adsorbed as intact anions.

Because of the capacity of colloidal materials to adsorb auxin, it has been found possible to protect plants from auxins in the soil by the application of colloidal materials such as activated carbon (Arle *et al*, 1948). This method has been extended by Weaver (1948) who found that activated carbon could be used to protect sensitive plants against a large number of auxins by simple localized applications in the soil. It appears that adsorbed auxins are still active as growth

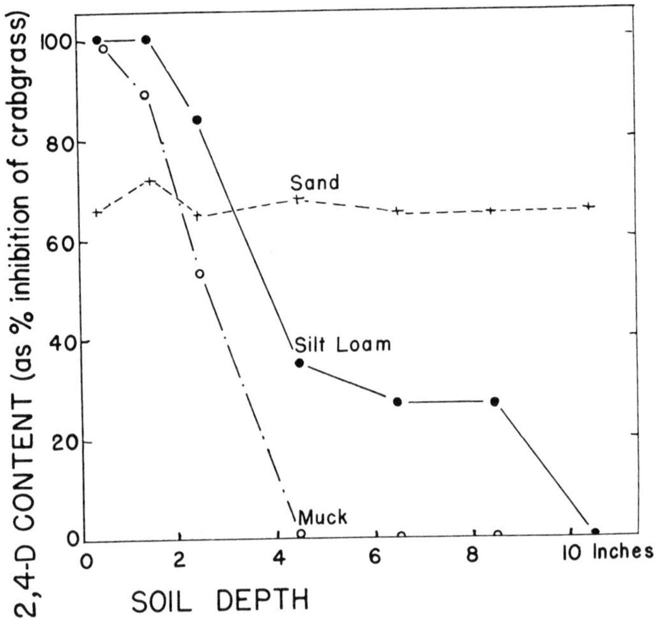

Fig. 81. The distribution of 2,4-D at various depths of the profiles of three different soils following the application of two inches of water. The 2,4-D is quantitatively estimated by the inhibition of growth of crabgrass seedlings (Ogle, 1953).

inhibitors (Audus, 1951) and consequently the protective effect appears to be due to the prevention of auxin from outside the root zone entering into contact with the root.

The effectiveness of activated carbon as an adsorptive agent to remove residues from spray equipment has been demonstrated by Lucas and Hamner (1947).

Leaching. The second major factor in the persistence of auxins in soils is that of leaching. Obviously the ease with which a material can be leached from a soil will be strongly influenced by adsorption, as we have discussed in the previous paragraphs, and the adsorptive properties will vary with soil type. Besides adsorption, the solubility of the auxin will play a role here. Early observations indicated that liming or an excessively calcareous condition would retard leaching of auxins (Kries, 1946; Muzik *et al,* 1951). This would presumably be accounted for on the basis of the formation of auxin salts such as the calcium salt which are relatively insoluble. Other reports have failed in several instances to confirm that liming or calcareous conditions retarded leaching (Hanks, 1946; Akamine, 1951), but the experimenters have seldom distinguished between adsorption and leaching and,

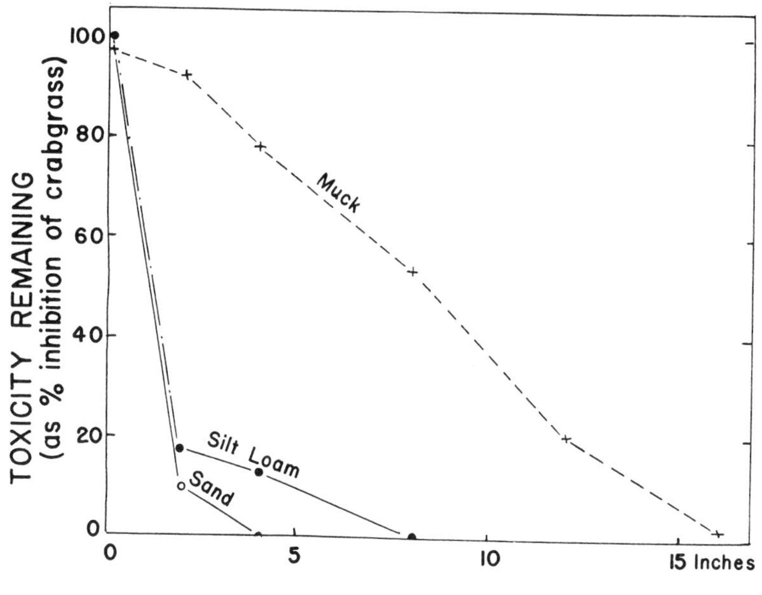

Fig. 82. The relative rates of leaching of 2,4-D from the surfaces of three different soils by various amounts of leaching water. The amount of 2,4-D remaining was quantitatively estimated by the inhibition of grabgrass seedlings (Ogle, 1953).

with the use of different soils, adsorptive differences might mask true leaching effects.

Leaching characteristics can be visualized rather graphically from results of experiments on the complete leaching of auxins from soils. For example in figure 82 it can be seen that the amount of water required to leach 2,4-D completely from three different soils varied immensely with the soil type. Four inches of water completely removed the toxic effects of the auxin from the surface of a sand soil; eight inches of water were required to do the same for a silt loam, and sixteen inches for a muck. Here again the distinction between adsorption and leaching is not clear, but differences in ability of the auxin to move are very clear. The leaching characteristics of various auxins and other growth regulators are quite different from one another and it may be tentatively presumed that such differences are owing to the adsorptive differences and the solubility differences between the auxins. Thus naphthyl pthalamic acid is much less easily leached than 2,4-D (Ogle, 1953) and consequently lends itself more readily to some pre-emergence types of application. This is discussed in more detail in chapter XVI.

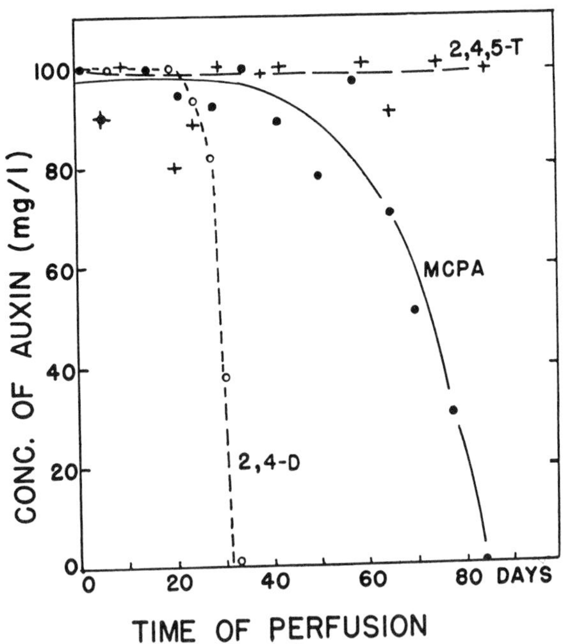

Fig. 83. The time course of destruction of three auxins in soil. Solutions of 100 mg./l. of the auxins were continuously perfused through the soil and assayed in the leachate by the cress root test (Audus, 1951).

Destruction. The third major factor in persistence of auxins in soils is the destruction of the auxin by microorganisms. The earliest workers on auxin persistence in soils concluded that the destruction was due to microorganism activity, for autoclaving prevented destruction, and moisture and temperature conditions suitable for microorganism growth were found to be necessary for auxin destruction (DeRose and Newman, 1947; Brown and Mitchell, 1948). An ingenious extension of this point has been made by Audus (1951) who found that respiratory poisons were likewise effective in preventing destruction. This same worker (1950) isolated the first microorganism which was found to be capable of destroying 2,4-D, and it turned out to be a gram negative bacterium of the *Bacterium globiforme* type. Subsequently Jensen and Peterson (1952) have isolated another microorganism capable of destroying 2,4-D, *Flavobacterium aquatile.*

The time course in the destruction of some auxins in the soil is shown in figure 83. Audus (1949, 1951) has shown that the rate of destruction varies greatly with the auxin used, 2,4-D being the most rapidly destroyed auxin which was tested and 2,4,5-T being the most persistent. Audus sometimes observed a small, immediate initial loss of auxin activity. He suggested that such an initial loss may be a result of adsorption of the auxin by the soil. The slow rates of microbial destruction in the early sections of each of the curves in figure

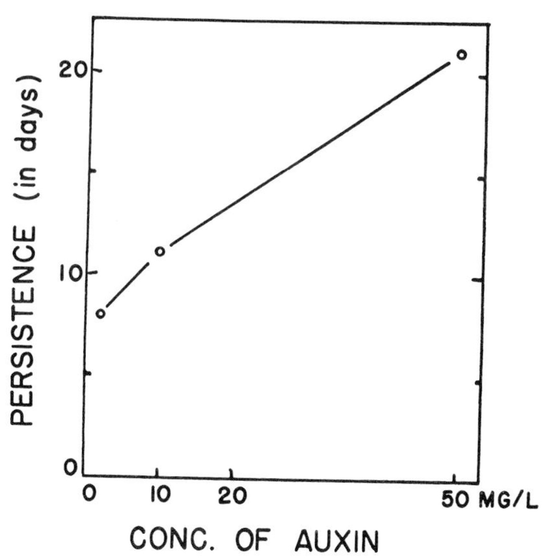

Fig. 84. The effect of various concentrations of auxin (2,4-D) upon the time of persistence of the auxin in the soil (Newman and Thomas, 1949).

83 is attributed to a latent period required for the adaptation of the microorganism to the new substrate.

The factors influencing the microbial destruction of auxin include the nature and quantity of the auxin, bacterial activity, and environmental factors of moisture and temperature, plus of course the degree of adaptation of the microflora to auxin destruction. Audus (1951) has shown that a given culture of his microorganisms which had become adapted to the destruction of 2,4-D could readily attack MCPA, but required a long adaptation period before it could attack 2,4,5-T. The scant evidence available indicates that the larger the dose of auxin, the longer the period required for its destruction. Some data on this point are shown in figure 84 from which it may be deduced that, in the concentration range used, the bacterial activity or the capacity of the bacteria to attack the 2,4-D were limiting the destruction.

One of the factors which influence bacterial activity and consequently influence 2,4-D destruction is the soil type (Kries, 1946). Ogle (1953) has shown that under identical conditions and after identical treatments with 2,4-D, different soils may take from as little as 10 days to as much as 10 weeks to destroy the auxin. The addition of leaf

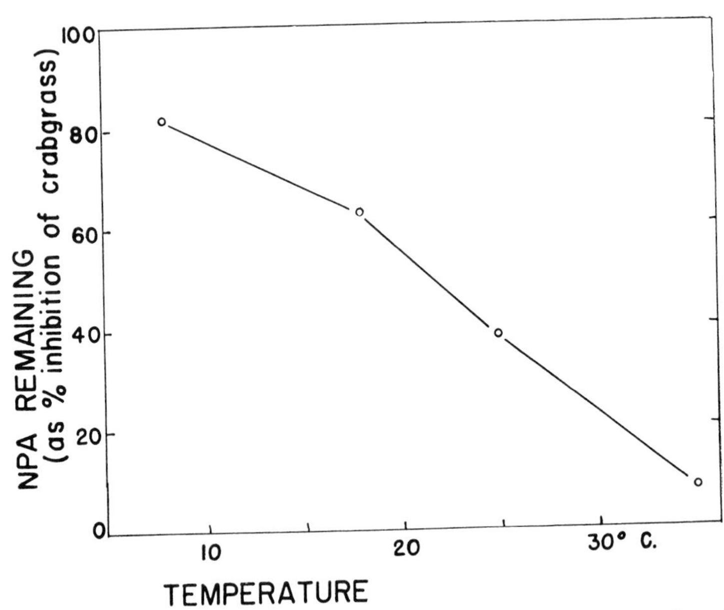

Fig. 85. The effects of different temperatures upon the persistence of naphthyl phthalamic acid in a fine sand soil. The herbicide was quantitatively estimated by the inhibition of crabgrass seedlings after 42 days (Ogle, 1953).

mold (Kries, 1946) or manure (Brown and Mitchell, 1948) to the soil have been observed to increase destruction. The previous application of auxin has been likewise shown to increase auxin destruction as a consequence of the enrichment of the soil with microorganisms adapted to auxin destruction (Audus, 1951).

Among environmental factors, moisture has been shown to be important in the destruction of 2,4-D. Excessively dry conditions clearly retard destruction as seed germination tests of Mitchell and Marth (1946) indicated, and increasing moisture results in more rapid breakdown. Very low temperatures also retard auxin destruction and lead to prolonged persistence (Jorgensen and Hamner, 1948). The responsiveness of the destruction of naphthyl phthalamic acid to various temperatures is shown graphically in figure 85. The temperature response again depends upon the soil type, being much more rapid in soils of high organic matter content (Ogle, 1953).

With respect to auxin persistence in general, not a great deal is known about the fate of auxins applied to plants, and the general means by which auxins are destroyed in the soil have only recently been outlined. Auxins applied to plants seem to disappear from effective loci in most plants by some quite rapid means. Some are undoubtedly metabolized into ineffective end products, but some seem to persist (Dhillon and Lucas, 1950) though perhaps not in a readily extractable form (Bonner and Thurlow, 1949). Auxins applied to soils may be lost by adsorption onto colloidal material, by leaching, or microbiological destruction. Consequently such factors as temperature, moisture, constitution of the soil and of the auxin may all alter auxin persistence in any one place. From the evidence at hand it would seem very unlikely that the common herbicidal auxins would persist in soils for more than one growing season, except under dry, sterile or very cold conditions.

CHAPTER X

Rooting

Before the discovery of auxins, many chemical compounds had been reported to increase the rooting of cuttings, including such diverse substances as permanganate (Curtis, 1918) and carbon monoxide (Zimmerman *et al,* 1933). A much higher order of effectiveness was found for auxin, however (Went, 1934), and in fact it was quickly discovered that auxin exerts a primary control over root formation in general (Thimann and Went, 1934). In the next year it was found that utilizing this property of auxins could be highly useful in the propagation of many horticultural species (Cooper, 1935; Laibach and Fishnick, 1935; Thimann and Koepfli, 1935; Zimmerman and Wilcoxon, 1935). Since that time, there have been well over 300 reports in the literature describing the uses of auxins for stimulating rooting.

It is interesting to note that Dutch gardeners have a centuries-old practice of embedding grain seeds into cuttings to promote root formation, and since we now know that germinating grains produce large amounts of auxins, it appears that this age-old custom has a sound basis in auxin physiology.

THE PHYSIOLOGICAL BASIS FOR ROOTING

An understanding of the physiological mechanisms responsible for root formation has gradually emerged during the last decade. The initial step in the formation of roots is the differentiation of a meristem into root primordia. The researches of Skoog (1944, 1948) have demonstrated that the type of differentiation that will occur in a meristem is dependent upon the proportion of auxins to certain other substances. He demonstrated, as has been described in chapter V, that when the ratio of auxin to some plant constituents (particularly purines such as adenine) is low, the meristem of tobacco stem sections will tend to form bud and leaf primordia. When the ratio is intermediate, simple callus will be formed. When the ratio is high (that is, when the auxin content is relatively high), root primordia will be evolved. The balance between auxins and other plant constituents as the control of differentiation is the physiological basis for the rooting of cuttings as we understand it today.

While it is not clear what the exact action of auxin in this process is, there are several established facts concerning the auxin function. The stimulation of root formation is not restricted to auxins alone, as similar responses can be obtained with compounds which increase auxin activity and with compounds which are epinastic agents. It is known that where roots are formed there is a pronounced increase in the auxin content. This increase occurs in each of the auxin fractions: the free auxin, bound auxin, and the neutral auxin (figure 86).

Some evidence about the nature of the substances which interact with auxin to control root formation has been brought to light through the observation that leaves strongly promote rooting of cuttings. Van Overbeek *et al* (1946) have analyzed the nature of the promotive materials which leaves provide for the cutting, and found that they could entirely replace the effect of leaves by supplying the

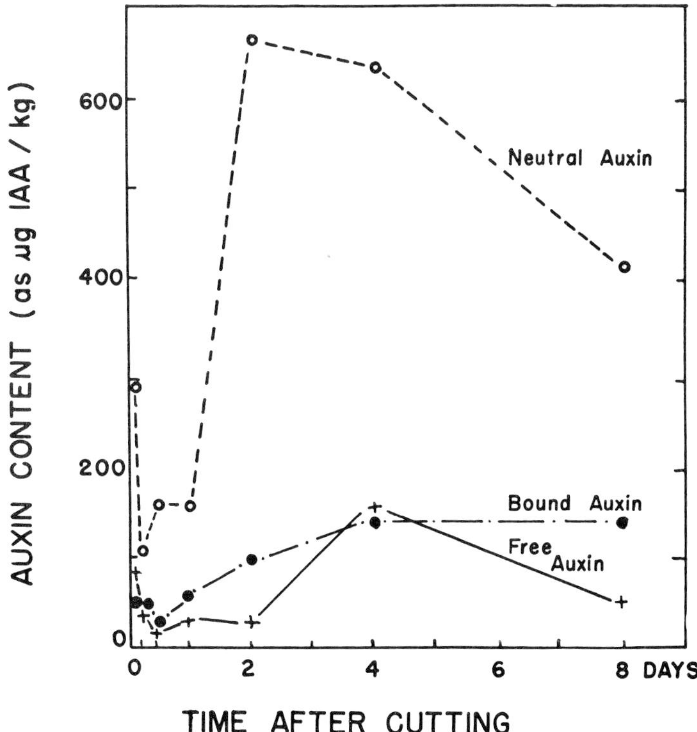

Fig. 86. The changes in content of neutral, bound, and free auxin in the basal ends of chicory root cuttings during root formation (Warmke and Warmke, 1950).

cuttings with sugars and nitrogenous compounds. In figure 87 it can be seen that there is a quantitative increase in roots formed in red hibiscus cuttings with the presence of leaves, and that the promotive effect can be entirely replaced by sucrose plus ammonium sulphate. It can also be seen that without the addition of auxin (indolebutyric acid) rooting is essentially absent whether these nutrients are provided or not. These same workers convincingly demonstrated that leaves do, in fact, supply the cutting with the same types of nutrient materials which had been added in the experiment described, namely sugars and soluble nitrogenous materials. Chemical analysis of cuttings with various numbers of leaves revealed that the content of reducing and non-reducing sugars and of soluble nitrogenous materials in the cutting was dependent upon the number of leaves. The nutritive effects of leaves are illustrated in figure 88.

Van Overbeek *et al* (1946) stated that organic forms of nitrogen

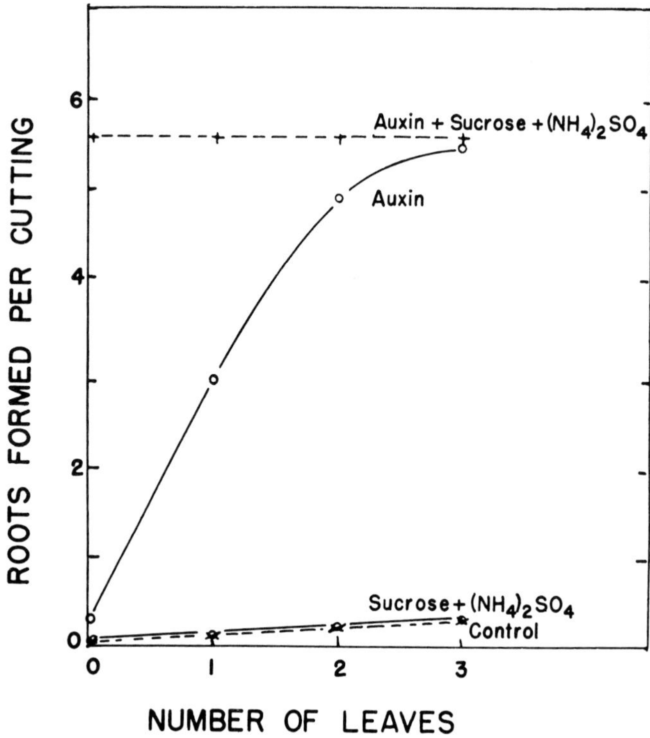

Fig. 87. The effect of leaves on cuttings of red hibiscus in permitting stimulation of root formation by auxin (2000 mg./l. indolebutyric acid). The promotive effects of leaves can be entirely replaced by supplying 4 per cent sucrose and 0.1 per cent ammonium sulphate (van Overbeek *et al,* 1946).

were more readily utilized than inorganic forms in the promotion of rooting. This is in agreement with previous reports that biotin (Went and Thimann, 1937, p. 239) and adenine (Thimann and Poutasse, 1941) were the most promotive of a variety of nitrogenous materials tested. Van Overbeek *et al* (1946) found that neither of these compounds was as good as arginine. It is entirely possible that the most effective organic form of soluble nitrogen varies from one species of plant to another.

Of course nutrient materials are of importance in rooting not only in relation to their ratio with auxin, but also in terms of the amount of substrate present for the actual growth of roots. It is not surprising to find that many workers have correlated ease of rooting with the carbohydrate reserve of a plant. When carbohydrate reserves are abundant, rooting is greatly facilitated (Kraus and Kraybill, 1918; Carlson, 1929). The relative level of soluble nitrogen materials in the cutting also has a bearing on ease of rooting, and the optimum level of these compounds is low in proportion to the carbohydrate level.

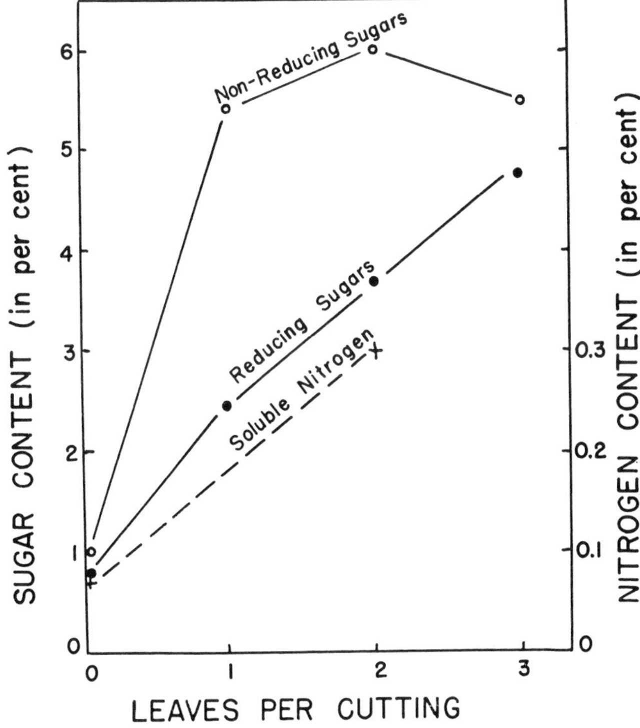

Fig. 88. The effects of leaves present on cuttings of red hibiscus upon some carbohydrate and nitrogen constituents of the cuttings (van Overbeek *et al,* 1946).

This has led to the generalization that the ratio of carbohydrate to nitrogen should be high for optimum rooting (Kraus and Kraybill, 1918; Pearse, 1943). The reports of many workers that nitrogen is detrimental to the rooting of cuttings (e.g. Knight, 1926) undoubtedly are explained by the requirement for an abundant supply of carbohydrate in proportion to the nitrogen. It is interesting to notice that in replacing the stimulatory effect of leaves, van Overbeek *et al* (1946) obtained the best results with forty times as much sugar as ammonium sulphate.

The rooting response to auxin is a quantitative one. The quantitative characteristic of the response can be seen in the data shown in figure 89. The use of auxin concentrations higher than optimum results in a reduction of rooting, but the evidence available suggests that this reduction may be owing more generally to the inhibition of growth of the root primordia rather than to a reduction in number of primordia formed.

It is evident that auxins stimulate the formation of roots by an interaction involving organic materials in the plants, particularly carbohydrates and nitrogenous materials. This interaction apparently controls the basic step of morphological differentiation at the cellular level.

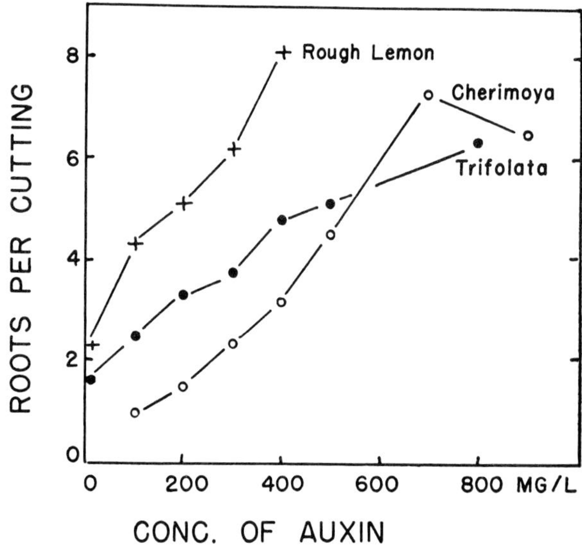

Fig. 89. The quantitative stimulation by auxin of rooting in cuttings of three varieties of citrus. The auxin used was indoleacetic acid (Biale and Halma, 1937).

METHODS OF TREATMENT

Selection of Auxins

A very wide variety of auxins has been used for the rooting of cuttings, but the one most commonly used with great success is indolebutyric acid. It appears probable that the success of this compound may be because its auxin activity is weak and it is slowly destroyed by the auxin-destroying enzyme system described in chapter III. Naphthaleneacetic acid and indoleacetic acid have also been used but with less uniform success. The former is quite a strong auxin and the latter is very readily destroyed. Because the phenoxyacetic acids are strong auxins they are highly effective in inducing the formation of root primordia. However, they are also very likely to inhibit bud and root growth (Hitchcock and Zimmerman, 1942) as well as cause leaf injuries. The phenoxy α-propionic and α-butyric derivatives, however, seem to be more promising as rooting auxins since they show less inhibitory characteristics. Several of these auxins with branched side-chains have been found to be superior even to indolebutyric acid.

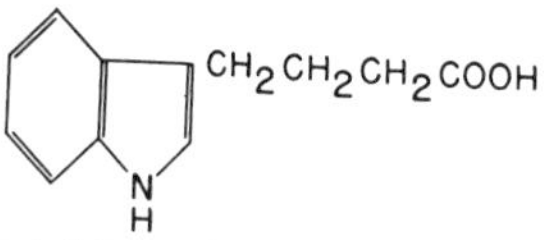

$CH_2CH_2CH_2COOH$ (N–H)

Indolebutyric Acid

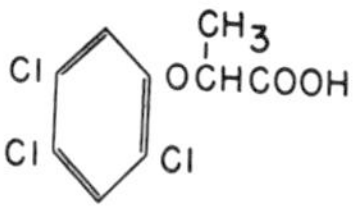

$OCH(CH_3)COOH$ (Cl, Cl, Cl)

α-2,4,5-Trichlorophenoxypropionic Acid

In selecting auxins for rooting, it seems that in general the strong auxins are undesirable as they inhibit bud and root development. Consequently weak auxins are generally selected. Another quality to select for is solubility, particularly since treatment of cuttings by dipping in auxin solutions requires high concentrations and consequently high solubilities. Because the acids are generally less soluble than the salts, the latter derivatives are more commonly used. The amide derivative has been used occasionally (Stoutemyer, 1941). It exhibits greater solubility and at the same time possibly more rapid penetration into the tissues. Mixtures of auxins have been found in some instances to be more effective than the one auxin alone (Hitchcock and Zimmerman, 1940). This interaction between auxins suggests synergistic activity. A striking improvement of rooting response to auxins in the presence of auxin synergists has been reported by van Raalte (1951).

Extensive compilations of reports concerning the relative effectiveness of different auxins in rooting of various species have been published by Avery and Johnson (1947), Thimann and Behnke-Rogers (1951), and Audus (1953).

Techniques of Application

The three commonest methods of application of auxins in the rooting of cuttings are the soak treatment, the dip treatment, and the talc treatment. In the first of these, cuttings are generally soaked for twenty-four hours in auxin concentrations varying from 25 to 100 mg./l. The dip treatment is essentially the same except that the time of exposure to the solution ranges from only a few seconds to a few minutes and the effective concentrations are much higher (1000 to 10,000 mg./l.). Because of the concentrations used, simple aqueous solutions often do not permit enough solubility and cosolvents are needed. The most common cosolvent is alcohol, and in concentrations as high as 50 per cent (Hitchcock and Zimmerman, 1939). The third common type of treatment involves the use of the dipping of the wet cutting into a talc containing the auxin (Stoutemyer, 1938) in concentrations ranging from 500 to 12,000 mg./l. This method is the simplest one for small operations, but in commercial practice it has the drawback of being less uniform when bundles of cuttings are used. Cuttings on the inside of a bundle are liable to receive insufficient coverage.

Stoutemyer and O'Rourke (1945) have reported good success with a pretreatment of the stock plant before the cuttings are made. Spraying the auxin onto the foliage a few days or a few weeks before the cuttings were made increased rooting ability of a dozen different plant species. This technique is both simple and effective.

If one treatment of auxin is not quite sufficient, retreatment of the cuttings can sometimes be used successfully (Cooper and Went, 1938).

In most cases where auxins are to be used in the rooting of cuttings it is not possible to find dependable reports of comparable previous experiments to aid one in determining what auxin concentration to use. For this reason, some preliminary experiments are desirable using a range of auxin concentrations. The first signs of injury due to excessive auxin concentrations are browning of the base of the cutting and inhibition of normal bud development and growth. Once one has determined the concentration at which these undesirable symptoms appear he can proceed with safety by using a lower and more beneficial concentration.

A method of causing root formation by utilizing the endogenous auxin in the plant instead of applied auxins has been common practice for many years. This method, called marcotting, involves ringing a stem and binding a moist medium such as peat moss around the ringed area. The ring interferes with the transport of auxin and other materials through the stem. Because of the polar nature of auxin transport and because transport can occur even against a large concentration gradient (as discussed in chapter III), auxin accumulates above the ring and stimulates root formation there. It is probable that other materials which are beneficial to root initiation and growth may also accumulate above the ring. These include sugars, nitrogenous materials, and growth factors such as thiamine which is formed in the leaves and is beneficial to root growth (Went *et al,* 1938). Marcotting is widely used by greenhouse operators for propagation of woody plants. The effectiveness of this treatment has been further improved by application of auxin above the ring to supplement the endogenous auxin (Cooper, 1944). Irradiation with large doses of x-rays also causes rooting above the treated zone (Christensen, 1954). It is probable that this treatment too is effective because of the interference of transport of auxins and other materials.

Another propagation technique which utilizes endogenous auxin is layering. Branches are bent to the ground and covered with soil to generate roots. This method of obtaining roots is also improved by ringing and by the addition of auxins above the ring (Gossard, 1941; Floor, 1951).

In many instances people have tried to use auxins to improve rooting in transplants. These attempts have been singularly unsuccessful with only rare exceptions such as the report by Neff and O'Rourke (1951), in which the roots were heavily trimmed back before auxin application. These observations find a ready explanation in that auxins applied to intact roots would be expected to inhibit root growth because of the extreme sensitivity of roots to auxin (cf. figure 46). The inhibitory effect would be expected to override any root-forming influence of the treatment. However, when the roots have been severely trimmed back as in the case reported by Neff and O'Rourke, or removed entirely, as is usual with cuttings, then the root-forming effects of auxins can become beneficial.

Selection of Structure

Nearly any plant organ is capable of forming roots. Not only stems but leaves, stolons, roots and even flowers and fruits can be rooted (e.g. Balansard and Pellissier, 1942; Warmke and Warmke, 1950; Bouillenne and Went, 1933; Erickson and De Bach, 1953).

Stems are generally an ideal rooting material because they usually have sufficient undifferentiated tissues to permit easy differentiation of root primordia and they also have buds already formed. As we have already pointed out, the work of Skoog (1944) indicates that auxin treatments which favor rooting do not promote bud formation; hence it is desirable to have buds already formed on propagation pieces. For these reasons stems are the commonest structures used in vegetative propagation.

It is interesting to note that woody stems are more susceptible to injury from auxin treatment than herbaceous stems. In fact, susceptibility to injury increases with increasing woodiness (Maxon *et al,* 1940).

In selecting woody stem material for rooting it is interesting to note that cuttings taken from the lower branches of trees quite commonly root more readily in response to auxin than do cuttings from the tops (Grace, 1939). This has been confirmed in the case of many species, and is probably due to nutritive differences in the stems.

The age of the wood from which a cutting is made has a real influence on rooting. Succulent new shoots are generally the easiest to root. Practically all experiments with woody plants seem to show consistently that one-year-old wood is the easiest to root. Besides the age of the cutting itself, the age of the stock plant from which the cutting is made also influences rooting capacity. Cuttings from older stock plants appear to be progressively more difficult to root with or without auxin treatment, even when uniform, one-year-old wood is taken for the cutting (Thimann and Delisle, 1942). An interesting observation has been made by Day (1932), that wounding of cuttings quite generally stimulates subsequent rooting capacity. Wounding seems to improve the rooting response to auxins as well (Thimann and Behnke-Rogers, 1950).

The beneficial effect of leaves has already been mentioned. Leaves themselves are often easily rooted, perhaps because of the abundant supply in the leaves of materials known to stimulate rooting (van Overbeek *et al,* 1946). The leaves of many plants root without auxin application as, for example, Kalanchoe, Saintpaulia, and Bryophyllum. Leaves of others such as pineapple, tomato, begonia, and Indian rubber will root in response to auxin treatment. Cutting the veins has been found to increase the rooting response of begonia and Indian rubber (Balansard and Pellissier, 1942), perhaps because of accumulation of growth substances at several points and consequent rooting there instead of just at the base of the petiole. Lily bulb scales have been used as propagating materials and respond well to auxin treatment (Avery and Johnson, 1947).

The use of leaves as propagating material requires the differentiation of both root and bud primordia. The application of auxins to leaf cuttings may be expected to improve root formation but to hinder bud formation for the reasons described in chapter V. This drawback to the use of auxins on leaf cuttings of Saintpaulia (Warner and Went, 1939) has been alleviated experimentally by the simultaneous application of adenine to encourage bud formation (Smith and Leopold, unpublished).

Stolons and roots are sometimes used as propagating material, but they have the limitation that buds are not present and the application of auxin certainly will not help overcome this limitation. The application of auxin has been found to hinder rather than improve propagation by stolon or root cuttings (Lindner, 1939). This seems reasonable since a low ratio of auxin to adenine is needed for bud formation, and the application of auxin will instead tend to increase the ratio. Very low concentrations of auxin have been found to improve rooting of root material provided that large pieces of stolon or root are used (Marth and Hammer, 1943; Warmke and Warmke, 1950).

FACTORS IN SUCCESS

Environmental Factors

The ability of cuttings to root in response to auxin applications is influenced by several environmental factors: the season of the year, the photoperiod exposure, and light, temperature, aeration and humidity conditions.

The *season* at which cuttings are taken greatly affects the ability of the cutting to take root, and the optimum season for taking cuttings varies immensely between species (Hitchcock and Zimmerman, 1930; Brandon, 1939). The succulent new growth appearing on fruit trees in June is favorable material for rooting although other woody plants generally are more easily propagated in the late summer or winter months. Many woody plants are easiest to root if cut in the winter before the buds are ready to break, for at this time the cutting may form callus and differentiate roots over a fairly long period during which there is no foliage to draw on the water supply.

The *photoperiods* experienced by the stock plant, or by the cutting after placement in the rooting bed, have a distinct effect on rooting. The photoperiods most favorable for rooting vary from plant to plant, with some species rooting best under long and some under short photoperiods (Stoutemyer and Close, 1946; Moskov and Koschezhenko, 1939). Some evidence suggests that the photoperiods most favorable for rooting are those in which carbohydrate reserves are accumulated in the cutting. While there is an interaction with nitrogen—that is, cuttings high in nitrogen will not show as good a response to carbohydrate accumulation in terms of rooting—still the photoperiod influence appears to be largely a consequence of its effect on the carbohydrates of the plant (Smith, 1926). The photoperiods experienced by the stock plant before the cuttings are made have a more profound effect on the ability of the cutting to root than the photoperiods experienced by the cutting itself (Pridham, 1942).

Light itself has an effect on root initiation. If the entire piece of plant material is exposed to light, root initiation commonly is inhibited and, furthermore, root growth is inhibited once root initiation has taken place (Went, 1935). On the other hand, if the cutting is embedded in a rooting medium and light is applied only to the parts above ground, a stimulation of rooting is sometimes produced (Stoutemyer and Close, 1946). For this reason, then, the application of light to leafy cuttings is often found to be beneficial. Stoutemyer and Close have found that red light is more effective in promoting rooting than blue light. It is curious to note that red light applied to the stock plant before the cutting is made has likewise been found to stimulate subsequent rooting ability (*ibid*).

The *temperature and aeration* conditions under which the cutting is kept, of course, have a strong influence on the rooting obtained. Low temperatures in general seem to promote the formation of callus tissue and, as one would expect, the development of root primordia on undifferentiated callus tissue is much easier than the formation of roots from well-differentiated tissues.

The growth of roots is favored by higher temperatures, so many rooting beds are heated from below. In commercial practice cuttings are often stored in cool places to permit callus formation and then are placed in warm rooting beds to facilitate the growth of the roots.

All known types of auxin stimulation of growth are aerobic in nature and hence it is not surprising that good aeration is essential to rooting of cuttings.

High *humidities* are helpful in rooting cuttings. Obviously the cutting is poorly equipped to obtain water for transpiration, so it is quite susceptible to damage by low humidity.

Physiological Factors

Several physiological factors inherent in the cuttings themselves are known to be important in the rooting of cuttings. One of these is the *polarity* of root formation. Since the movement of auxins in the stem is from the apex to the base, it is not surprising that root formation takes place preferentially at the base of the cutting where the auxins accumulate. Went (1936) has shown, however, that when high enough concentrations of auxin were applied to cuttings, some roots would be formed at the apex of the cutting. It is assumed that this phenomenon is due to a nonpolar auxin translocation at the high concentrations.

The role of *leaves* in rooting has already been described as providing certain nutritive materials beneficial to root formation. The dependence of rooting on the carbohydrate supply has been amply demonstrated (Pearse, 1943), and other materials such as vitamins and nitrogenous materials are supplied by the leaves as well. The beneficial effect of leaves may be accentuated by spraying a sugar solution on the foliage (Langston, 1954). It seems evident that leaves are beneficial to the rooting response to auxin for nutritive reasons.

The presence of *buds* on a cutting has a strongly promotive effect on rooting. Van der Lek (1934) found that root formation was almost absent if all the buds were removed from woody cuttings or if all the buds were entirely dormant. The same beneficial effect of buds has been found in auxin-treated cuttings. The application of auxin has not been found to entirely replace the presence of buds in causing root formation (Went and Thimann, 1937, p. 189). However, the basipetal polar transport of the substances from the buds strongly suggests that at least some of the effect is due to auxin production in the bud. It is interesting to note that O'Rourke (1942) found that in cuttings from some species at least flower buds strongly inhibit rooting in contrast to the promotive effect of vegetative type buds. It is possible that the inhibitory effect of flower buds may be related to the effects of flowers in removing auxin polarity described in chapter III. It has been pointed out by Dore (1953) that root and stem cuttings of most plant species are singularly poor at generating new roots if they are taken from the plant when flower buds are present. It seems that buds influence rooting through some hormonal influence rather than through nutritive effects.

Inorganic materials are influential in rooting, and most important among them appears to be the soluble nitrogen fraction in the plant. While some quantities of nitrogen are very beneficial to rooting, large quantities are very inhibitory. The lower the carbohydrate level of the plant, the greater are the inhibitory effects of high nitrogen levels (Pearse, 1943, 1946). Another inorganic nutrient which has a strong influence on rooting is boron. A lack of this nutrient in the rooting medium can entirely eliminate the capacity of the cutting to form roots (Hemberg, 1951). Although deficiencies of other inorganic nutrients such as phosphorus, potassium, calcium, and magnesium can lower the rooting response, there does not appear to be as marked a sensitivity to these ions as there is to nitrogen and boron.

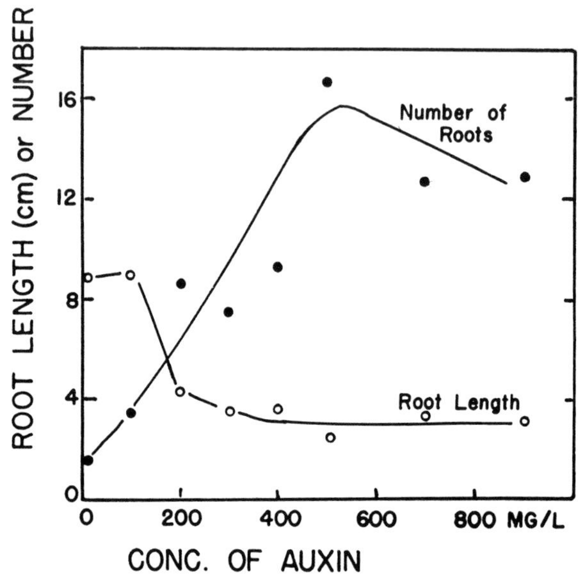

Fig. 90. The effects of auxin (indoleacetic acid) in stimulating the number of roots and the concomitant inhibition of root length in citrus cuttings (Biale and Halma, 1937).

It is well known that *root growth* is extremely sensitive to auxin levels, and that it is inhibited by even very dilute auxin applications. It is not surprising, then, that auxins applied to cuttings to improve root formation should sometimes retard the growth of the roots so formed. A particularly clear case of inhibition of root length associated with the stimulation of rooting with auxin can be seen in figure 90.

CHAPTER XI

Parthenocarpy

The capacity of some species of plants to set fruit parthenocarpically, *i.e.* without pollination, has been recognized for a very long time. The first indication that specific substances might be involved in this step came from the observation of Fitting (1909) that water extracts of pollen were able to prevent floral abscission in orchids and to produce ovary swelling which resembled fruit-set. Some years later Yasuda (1934) succeeded in producing parthenocarpic fruits by applying extracts of pollen to cucumber flowers. The fact that pollen extracts could exert such interesting effects led Thimann in 1934 into a study to identify the nature of the materials in such an extract. He found that there were auxins present. This information led Gustafson (1936) to attempt to induce fruit-set parthenocarpically by the application of synthetic auxins directly to the pistil of various flowers. He established that auxins could induce parthenocarpy in many species of plants, and his subsequent research has shown that parthenocarpy and fruit-set itself are brought about in nature by the growth hormone.

THE PHYSIOLOGICAL BASIS FOR PARTHENOCARPY

The Role of Auxins

If auxins play a crucial role in fruit-set in general, one would certainly expect that they should be present in large quantities when fruit-set occurs. This is the case, for Muir (1942) has shown that promptly after pollination a great increase in auxin content of tobacco ovaries occurs (figure 91). Without pollination such an increase is entirely lacking. The implication is that a large amount of auxin is released in the ovary by the consummation of pollination, and this auxin is the immediate cause of fruit-set. The upsurge of auxin content in the ovary is followed by the appearance of large amounts of auxin in the pedicel (figure 91), indicating that the auxin which is formed at pollination moves out of the ovary and into the rest of the plant. That this new supply of auxin moving into the plant may stimulate overall plant growth has been demonstrated by Wittwer (1943) in several species of plants.

Natural parthenocarpy takes place in ovaries which have naturally high auxin contents. This was found by Gustafson (1939), who showed that varieties of several fruits which set fruit parthenocarpically all contain much more auxin than closely related varieties which are not naturally parthenocarpic.

Since large amounts of auxin are released at the time of pollination and large amounts of auxin are present in ovaries that do not require pollination, it is hardly surprising that the application of auxins to flower ovaries can often artificially induce parthenocarpic fruit-set.

The change of auxin level in the ovary at the time of pollinated fruit-set is too great an increase to be accounted for simply on the basis of the auxin supplied by the pollen itself. Muir (1947) has shown that as much as one hundred times more auxin is formed in the ovary than is presented to the ovary by the pollen. Subsequent evi-

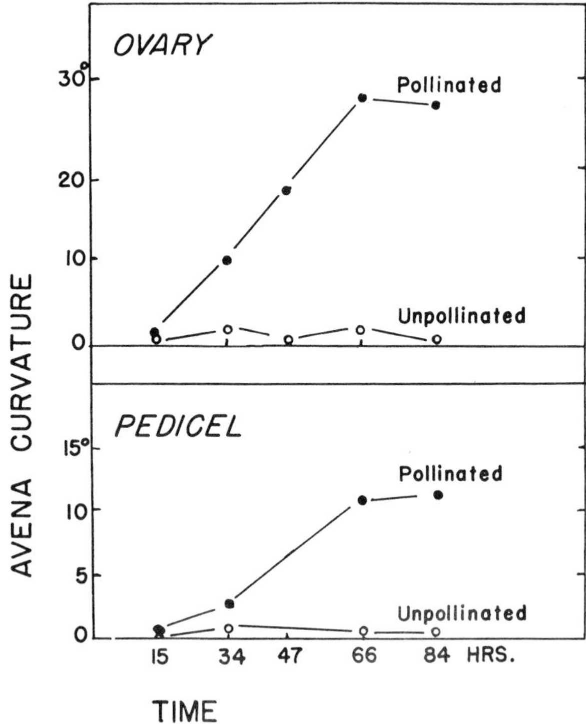

Fig. 91. Changes in diffusible auxin content of pollinated and unpollinated tobacco ovaries and of the pedicel below the ovary (data of Muir, 1942).

dence (Muir, 1951) has indicated that the enzymatic production of auxin is activated by pollination, possibly by increasing the availability of some precursor of auxin.

Thus it can be seen that, when fruit-set occurs by pollination, a source of auxin is made available to the ovary and stimulates the commencement of growth into a fruit. In parthenocarpic fruit-set, a sufficient source of auxin is supplied either by natural production in the ovary or by the application of auxin.

The Role of Nutrients

Fruit-set in general, either parthenocarpic or by pollination, requires something more than auxin alone. Leopold and Scott (1952) demonstrated that there is a requirement for organic nutrients or substrates for growth. They have shown that in the tomato there is a requirement for mature leaves, for with all the mature leaves removed from the plant there is no fruit-set. The presence of increasing numbers

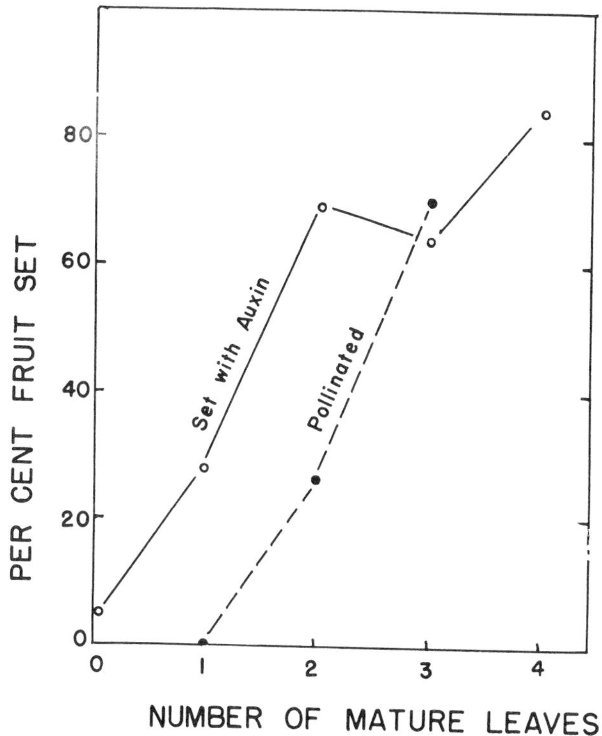

Fig. 92. The effect of leaves on tomato plants in permitting fruit-set as a result either of pollination or of treatment with auxin, 20 mg./l. *p*-chlorophenoxyacetic acid (Leopold and Scott, 1952).

of mature leaves permits a quantitative increase in the amount of fruit-set obtained (figure 92). It is interesting to note that the parthenocarpic fruit-set resulting from the application of auxin has a lower leaf requirement than fruit-set by pollination.

Investigations to determine the nature of the nutrients provided by leaves which are apparently essential for tomato fruit-set have not indicated that a specific substance or a specific group of substances is necessary, but rather that many different types of organic compounds can take the place of the mature leaves in this function. Experiments with excised flowers indicate that many sugars, organic acids, organic nitrogenous compounds and reducing substances can serve as the substrates for auxin-induced parthenocarpy. A possible reason for the non-specificity of this function appears in the suggestion by Leopold and Guernsey (1952) that the stimulation of some energy-producing reactions may account in part at least for the requirement for organic nutrients, and that a wide variety of organic materials stimulate such reactions in the metabolic scheme.

METHODS OF TREATMENT

Selection of Auxins

One of the species most readily set by auxins is the tomato, and in view of the economic importance of this crop the bulk of the information available on the induction of parthenocarpy is concerned with the tomato. Among the many auxins which have been used, PCA (*p*-chlorophenoxyacetic acid) and BNOA (*β*-naphthoxyacetic acid) have emerged as the most effective and most widely used. These are both fairly weak auxins and both produce relatively little deformation of tomato leaves. The search is still being carried on for other auxins which will be more effective in setting fruit, have less epinastic effects on the leaves, or bring about systemic fruit-setting.

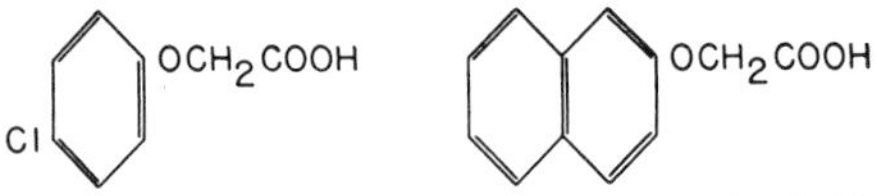

OCH_2COOH OCH_2COOH

Cl

p-chlorophenoxyacetic Acid *β*-naphthoxyacetic Acid

Indoleacetic acid is fairly ineffective in inducing parthenocarpy in tomatoes, presumably because of the ease with which it is inactivated by the natural enzymes of the plant. Redemann *et al* (1951) have shown that the relatively high effectiveness of pollen extracts in causing tomato fruit-set is due to the presence of the methyl ester of indoleacetic acid. They find that the ester is approximately one hundred times more effective in setting fruit than the free acid of indoleacetic acid. However, in view of the relatively weak action of indoleacetic acid, this does not make the methyl ester very high in activity. It is interesting to note that esterified auxins do exist in pollen and that they are quite effective in inducing parthenocarpy.

Another derivative of indoleacetic acid which is more active in fruit-set than the acid itself is indoleacetonitrile (Bentley and Bickle, 1952). The response to the nitrile is delayed for three weeks after application, which suggests that the material is inactive itself but is converted into an active substance in the plant. The conversion of the nitrile into the acid is discussed in chapter III.

A tentative report has been made (Wood and Fontaine, 1952) indicating that amide derivatives of 2,4-D with several *D*-amino acids are capable of setting fruit without producing epinastic deformations. Amide derivatives with *L*-amino acids on the other hand are strong epinastic agents like the 2,4-D acid itself.

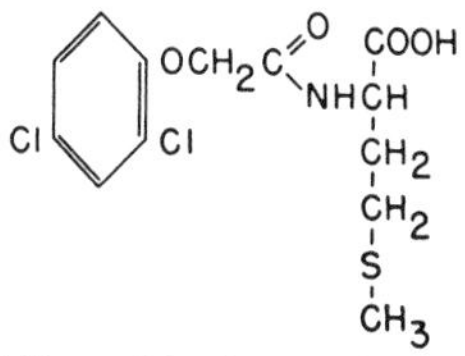

2,4-D-methionine amide

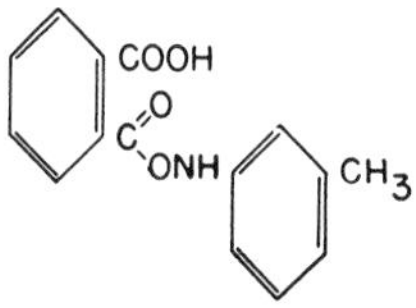

N-meta-tolylphthalamic Acid

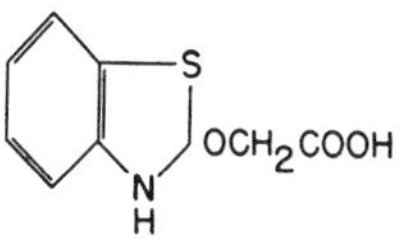

Benzothiazole-2-oxyacetic Acid

Epinastic agents which are not auxins are effective in fruit-set as well as auxins. Derivatives of phthalamic acid have been shown to induce fruit-set (Hoffman and Smith, 1949), as also have various benzoic acid derivatives (Zimmerman and Hitchcock, 1942). N-meta-tolylphthalamic acid has shown promising results as an overall plant spray for setting tomatoes (U. S. Patent No. 2,556,665). This is a highly desirable characteristic, for the application of sprays to the flower clusters only is costly in labor. N-meta-tolylphthalamic acid is not an auxin, but has synergistic activity with auxin in the pea straight-growth test (Leopold, unpublished).

The concentration of auxin used has a quantitative effect on fruit-set. Increasing concentrations of auxin give a comparable increase in percentage fruit-set obtained (figure 93) as well as in initial growth rate (figure 23). Although the optimum concentration for fruit-set varies considerably from one experiment to another, still the greatest percentage of fruit-set is generally obtained at concentrations between 30 mg./l. and 250 mg./l. of PCA or BNOA. The quantitative effect of auxin on the initial growth rate of tomato ovaries has been used as an assay for auxins as described in chapter II.

The selection of the auxin concentration to be used in practice must take into consideration the injurious effects that the spray may have on the plant and undesirable effects which the auxin may have on the fruit. Injurious effects to the tomato plant begin at 50 mg./l. of PCA if the spray is restricted to the flower cluster, and at much lower concentrations if an over-all plant spray is used (see figure 119). Also in many cases the fruit size and quality may be reduced by concentrations of PCA or BNOA of 50 mg./l. or above (cf. figure 96). For these reasons higher concentrations of auxin are avoided in practice and 25 to 50 mg./l. are generally accepted as the concentrations giving the best fruit-set with the fewest undesirable side effects.

The capacity of auxins to set parthenocarpic fruit in the fig has permitted another commercial use (Crane and Blondeau, 1949). In the Calimyrna fig the auxin application replaces the requirement for

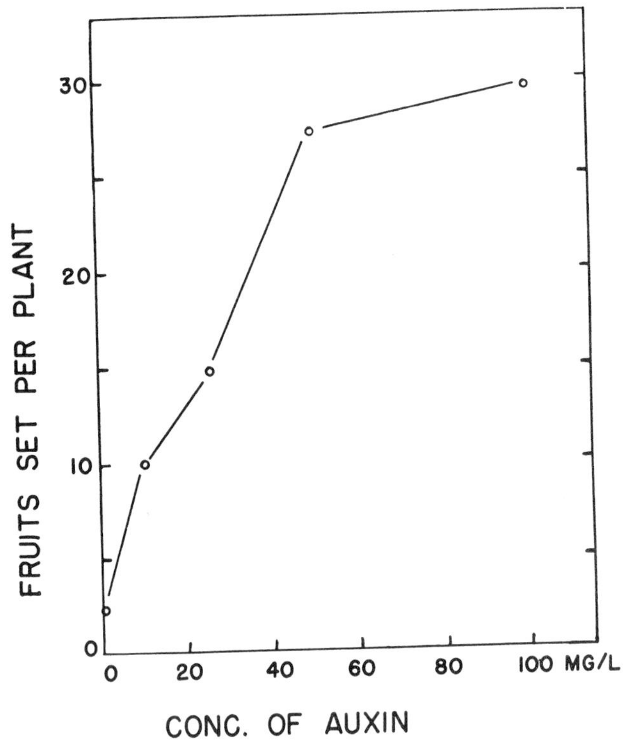

Fig. 93. Quantitative differences in effectiveness for forcing fruit-set of field tomatoes with various concentrations of auxin, *p*-chlorophenoxyacetic acid (data of Mann and Minges, 1949).

caprification (a specialized type of pollination) by the fig wasp. While auxins in general, such as 2,4-D and other phenoxyacetic acid derivatives, are very effective in this regard they have the disadvantage of producing seedless figs. Because consumers are so used to the presence of seeds in figs, it has become necessary to seek other auxins which might induce parthenocarpy and permit the development of at least the endocarp or seed coat. It has been found that benzothiazole-2-oxyacetic acid, a weak auxin, is capable of setting fruit in the fig and causing the development of the seed coat as well (Crane, 1952). This is a rather remarkable instance of different morphological responses to different auxins.

A good many other species of plants have been successfully forced to set fruit parthenocarpically by auxin application. These include many members of the *Cucurbitaceae* such as squash, pumpkin, watermelon and cucumber, several members of the *Solanaceae* such as tomato, tobacco, pepper and eggplant, and the holly, okra and fig. Each of these are fruits with many ovules per ovary.

Techniques of Application

Early experiments on fruit-set with auxins were carried out by severing the style and placing lanolin paste of auxin on the stump of the style. This exacting process has been found to be unnecessary, and instead a simple aqueous spray applied to the flower is entirely effective and much more convenient. It is not essential for the auxin spray to reach the stigma, the ovary, or even the face of the tomato flower, for it has been shown that auxins applied to the back of the flower, the pedicel, or even parts of the stem could induce fruit-set (Zalik *et al,* 1951). Randhawa and Thompson (1948) have succeeded in inducing fruit-set by applying growth regulators to the soil below the plant. This soil application is probably effective by translocation of the auxin through the transpiration stream to the floral parts.

The use of volatile esters of auxins to set tomato fruit in greenhouses without individual treatment of flower clusters has been used with moderate success (Zimmerman and Hitchcock, 1939). A quarter of a gram of a volatile ester of PCA per 1000 cubic feet of greenhouse space was found to be effective. Application in aerosol dispensers has been found to be both effective and convenient, using 1000 mg./l. of an ester derivative of BNOA or PCA (Howlett and Marth, 1946). Another technique which has been used successfully is the incorporation of the auxin into a fungicide dust. This has been found to be especially effective for snap beans using 2 p.p.m. 2,4-D (Wittwer and Murneek, 1949).

Time and Placement

Studies of the relative effectiveness of auxin sprays applied to tomato flowers at different stages of development show that fruit-set can be induced even in small, unopened flower buds (Roberts and Struckmeyer, 1944). The greatest relative effectiveness is obtained, however, when the petals have just begun to open. This is in contrast to responsiveness of the various flower stages to pollination, for of course no response to pollen is obtained until the petals have begun to open. Maximum response to pollen occurs several days later. These differences in responsiveness to parthenocarpic fruit-set and to pollination can be seen in figure 94. It is interesting to note that more flowers can be set with auxin than with pollen at every flower stage previous to full-bloom. The ability of tomato flowers to be set by auxin persists up to the time that the flower is abscissed from the plant, and even after abscission (Leopold and Scott, 1952).

The position of the flower on the flower cluster has been found to have a bearing on responsiveness to auxin treatment. The first

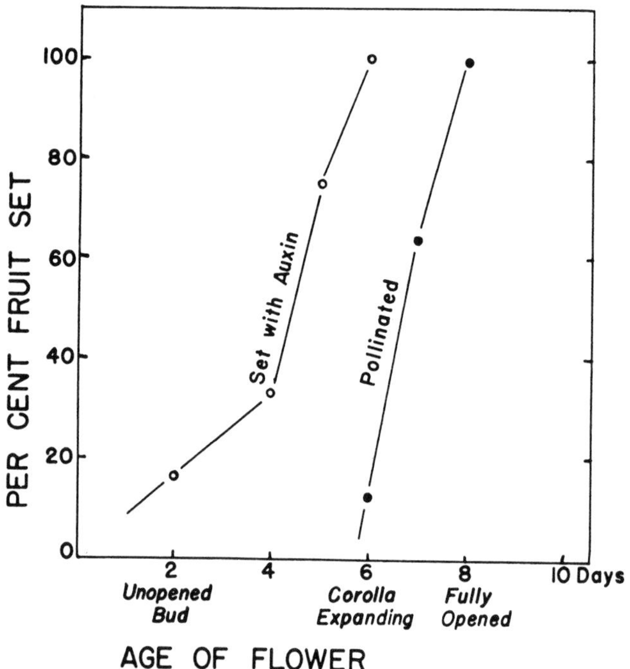

Fig. 94. The relative effectiveness of pollination and forced parthenocarpy with auxin (β-naphthoxyacetic acid) at various stages of flower development (data of Roberts and Struckmeyer, 1944).

flowers on a cluster to open respond best to auxin sprays, presumably because of the lack of competition for nutrients for growth. As more fruits are set and flowers further out on the cluster begin to open, the sensitivity to the auxin sprays is noticeably lowered (Roberts and Struckmeyer, 1944).

It has already been mentioned that auxins applied even at considerable distances from the flowers can influence fruit-set. It appears, however, that auxin sprays (PCA) applied to the face or front of the flower result in fewer fruit abnormalities than sprays applied at more distant points (Leopold and Guernsey, 1953).

Most workers who have studied the use of auxin sprays on tomatoes have found that although forcing fruit-set on the first 3 or 4 clusters is beneficial, auxin applications to flowers on higher clusters have very little effect. This is apparently attributable to differences in competition between fruits. When the plant is small and has few fruits, the application of auxins can act to overcome the limitation of fruit-set. On the other hand when the plants have many fruits already drawing on the food reserves of the plant, the application of auxin is usually of little value in forcing fruit-set.

FACTORS IN SUCCESS

The use of auxin in setting tomato fruits in commercial practice may be of benefit for the following reasons: (a) it can overcome certain limitations of fruit-set due to failure of pollination, (b) it can delay the loss of the flower through abscission, (c) it brings about an increase in the rate of maturation of the fruit, making possible an earlier crop, and (d) it can bring about an increase in fruit size.

Overcoming Limitations of Fruit-set

Certain physiological factors can limit the capacity of tomato flowers to set fruit. Since pollen is essential for natural fruit-set, those factors which limit the effectiveness of pollen—either in reaching the stigma or in affecting fertilization when it has reached the stigma—limit natural fruit-set.

Tomato plants grown in greenhouses are often so protected from wind and insects that normal pollen dispersion does not take place. Under circumstances in which self-pollination does not readily occur, forcing fruit-set with auxin can be beneficial.

Certain morphological limitations to pollination develop under conditions of weak light intensities, high nitrogen levels or high temperature (Howlett, 1939). Under these several circumstances the style of the tomato flower is prone to become excessively long. Such elongation begins before dehiscence of the anther sacs occurs, and consequently the capacity of the flower to pollinate itself is lost. In those cases where the pollen fails to reach the style, the forcing of tomato flowers with auxins can be very beneficial.

We know that sterile pollen is produced on tomato plants grown in weak light. Also, the temperature range for optimal pollen functioning is rather limited and when high or low temperatures are experienced, viable pollen becomes sterile (Smith, 1935). With regard to the influence of temperature, it is interesting to notice that the optimal temperature for pollen germination is around 85° F, whereas optimal fruit-set without pollen is obtained as much as twenty degrees lower, viz., 65° F. The effects of temperature on pollen germination and on the ability of ovaries to set fruit are plotted together in figure 95, where this difference in optima can be seen. In field tomatoes, auxins are very useful in forcing fruit-set when temperatures fall below 60° F (Wittwer *et al,* 1948; Odlund and Chan, 1950). This often permits the setting of the earliest flowers in the spring when low temperatures would normally prohibit fruit-set. These earliest fruits have the highest market value of the entire field crop. Curiously enough, when temperatures are excessively high, auxins again increase fruit-set (Mullison and Mullison, 1948). In the southern United States where temperatures become very high and light intensities are also high it has been found that shading tomato plants considerably improves the responsiveness to auxin (Moore

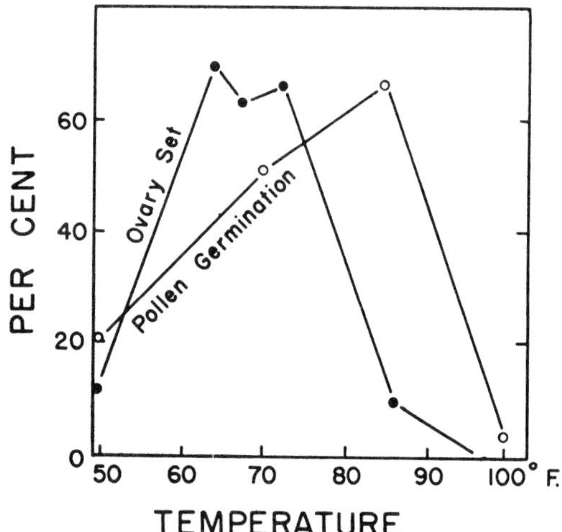

Fig. 95. A comparison of the effects of temperature upon pollen germination (Smith, 1935) and upon the capacity of tomato ovaries to set after forcing with auxin, *p*-chlorophenoxyacetic acid (Leopold and Scott, 1952).

and Thomas, 1952). Whether this improvement is owing to the lowered temperatures of the plant or to reduced light intensities is not clear. It is evident, then, that fruit-set may be limited by excessively high or low temperatures and light intensities, and that such limitations can be partly overcome by auxin treatment.

Lack of nutrient materials for growth may be another physiological factor limiting natural fruit-set. Since a number of mature leaves is essential for successful pollination, it is not surprising that tomato seedlings possessing only a few small leaves have difficulty in successfully pollinating the first cluster of flowers. As figure 92 shows, ovaries treated with PCA will set fruit with fewer leaves than those supplied with pollen. One of the most effective uses of auxins in commercial production of field tomatoes is to obtain fruit-set in the first clusters when there are few leaves on the young plants.

Plants in which carbohydrate availability is limited by weak light conditions, by disease, by high nitrogen levels or by the presence of a large proportion of fruits to leaves, may be unable to set fruit by normal pollination. In some of these instances where the inability to set fruit is caused by limitation of nutrients, a small beneficial effect may be obtained by forcing fruit-set with auxins (Murneek *et al,* 1944; Leopold and Scott, 1952). Low carbohydrate and high nitrogen situations frequently occur in greenhouses in winter when light intensities are low.

The Prevention of Abscission

It is well known that auxins applied to various plant organs prevent or at least delay abscission. The formation of an abscission layer in various organs is associated with the presence of weak auxin gradients or to a rather abrupt decrease in the auxin concentration (Shoji *et al,* 1951; Addicott and Lynch, 1951). Auxin production in flowers is largely centered in the maturing stamens (e.g. Wittwer, 1943) and ovaries (Katunskij, 1936). Once these have matured the auxin level in the flower may become quite low. Unless more auxin is added the level is frequently insufficient to hold the flower on the plant for any length of time. Flower abscission is encouraged by high night temperatures—above 78° F (Went, 1945), and by low nitrogen levels (Kraus and Kraybill, 1918). Since the flowers of tomato which are abscissed are still capable of fruit-set, the prevention of abscission would permit setting over a longer time period under conditions where abscission is prone to occur. It should be noted, however, that some workers have not obtained increases in fruit-set of tomatoes with auxin when abscission was active (Roberts and Struckmeyer, 1944).

Shortening of Time to Maturity

The fact that fruit growth may be started by forcing with auxin even before a flower is opened (figure 94) demonstrates one way in which auxin applications may shorten the time to harvest. A second way is the commencement of fruit growth 3 or 4 days sooner by auxin application than by pollination. Such earlier growth can be seen in the data of Roberts and Struckmeyer (1944) and of Singletary (1950). This may be because the time required for the release of the natural auxin-producing mechanism which follows pollination is eliminated when the auxin is added directly. Data from greenhouse experiments indicate that the use of auxins can cause production of mature tomato fruits approximately six days earlier than would occur naturally on the first flower cluster (Singletary, 1950).

The ability of auxin treatments to produce mature fruit in less

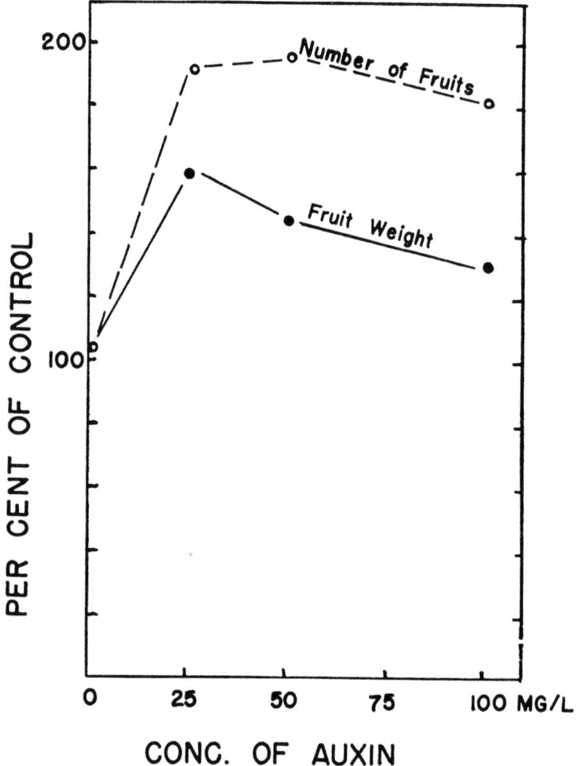

Fig. 96. The effects of various concentrations of auxin (*p*-chlorophenoxyacetic acid) upon the subsequent fruit-set and numbers of fruits harvested. The work was done with field grown tomatoes (data of Mann and Minges, 1949).

time can be a small but real advantage to commercial producers where early yields are financially of the highest value (Wittwer *et al,* 1948).

Increases in Yield

There appears to be considerable disagreement in the literature as to whether the use of auxins in setting tomatoes increases yield or not. The problem can be broken down into two parts: the first of these is the effect of auxins on fruit size, and the second is the question of auxin effects on early yield *vs* total yield.

At present five reports in the literature indicate that no increases in fruit size were obtained following the use of auxin and eight other reports show distinct gains in fruit size. The cases in which gains were found are all cases in which the auxin was applied locally to the flower cluster and not as an overall plant spray. Extensive tests reported by Mann and Minges (1949) show that significant gains in fruit size can

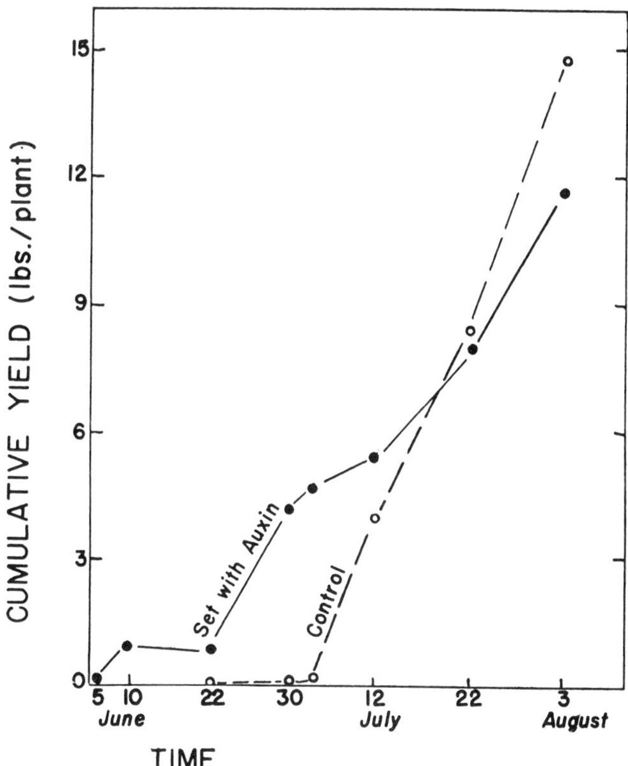

Fig. 97. The effects of forcing fruit-set in field tomatoes with auxin (*p*-chlorophenoxyacetic acid) upon the harvest pattern of marketable fruit (Mann and Minges, 1949).

be obtained by the use of 25 mg./1. of PCA on the flower cluster (figure 96). The use of higher concentrations does not result in any further gain in fruit size, but reduces the gain instead.

Many workers have reported immense gains in yield of tomatoes, as great as 400 or 500 per cent. These large gains are always cases in which the yield is an expression of the first pickings or the early yield. Auxin sprays can increase yields significantly only when limitations of fruit-set exist. Such conditions usually occur in the field primarily during the early stages of growth. A striking example of this fact is found in the report by Mann and Minges (1949), who followed the yields of field tomatoes through the picking season (figure 97). They found that while untreated vines produced fruit beginning on July 12, the vines treated with auxin were producing fruit more than a month earlier. The big increases in yield attributable to auxin treatment were restricted to the first month of production, for it is in the first month of flowering that field-grown tomatoes are most generally limited in their fruit-set by conditions which can be alleviated with auxin.

A limitation of the beneficial effects on tomato yield of auxins has been pointed out by the work of Hemphill (1949) who found that flower buds in the early stages of enlargement are inhibited in development by auxin sprays. As a consequence of this inhibition there may be a reduction in the number of flowers reaching maturity a week or two after auxin applications.

Large increases in the early yield of snap beans have been obtained through the use of auxin sprays to increase setting (Wittwer and Murneek, 1949). These sprays were beneficial only at high temperatures (above 90° F), presumably because pollination is limited under such conditions.

DIFFICULTIES RESULTING FROM FORCED PARTHENOCARPY

There are, of course, certain drawbacks to the use of auxin sprays to force fruit-set. One of these is damage to the foliage caused by the epinastic properties of the auxins which are commonly used for forcing fruit-set. Considerable damage can be done to the foliage and this can largely decrease yield if the damage is excessive. Not only epinastic curling of the leaves may be produced, but also abnormal development of leaves which are in the process of expansion at the time of treatment. Such damaged leaves fail to expand normally and give the appearance of leaves infested with cucumber or tobacco mosaic. Such distortions become evident about two weeks after spraying the flower clusters with PCA concentrations as high as 50 mg./1. or higher.

Another type of difficulty experienced is the production of deformed fruits. The auxin sprays force many abnormal flowers (which would naturally abscise) to set fruit instead. This results in a higher proportion of deformed fruits, particularly by setting of fasciated flowers with multiple ovaries (Mann and Minges, 1949).

Several reports indicate that hollow locules or puffy fruit are sometimes associated with auxin treatments as well as abnormally green locules (Howlett, 1949). Studies on nitrogen nutrition of the tomato have indicated that both puffiness and green locules are associated with excessive nitrogen fertilization, and the use of auxin sprays only accentuates these difficulties when the inherent condition for their expression already exists (Leopold and Guernsey, 1953). It was reported that restricting the auxin solution to the face or front of the flowers could considerably alleviate the tendencies toward deformed fruits.

There is some evidence that auxin treatments can actually cause the abortion of young embryos in the fruit and produce seedlessness in spite of pollination (Singletary, 1950). For this reason, use of auxins to force fruit-set in crops in which the seeds are important is seldom effective (e.g. seed beans and shell peas).

Another difficulty resulting from auxin treatments is the occurrence of relatively fragile carpel walls on the fruit. These walls make the fruit more susceptible to bruising, and for this reason there have been reports of "premature softening" of parthenocarpic tomatoes (Howlett, 1949). Marketed parthenocarpic fruit held at 70° F softened two to four days earlier than pollinated fruit; however, if pollen and auxin were both used to set the fruit then the condition of premature softening did not occur. There is indication that the use of different auxins may overcome the problem of thin-walled fruits as Howlett (1950) has reported. He found that α-2,3,5-trichlorophenoxypropionic acid may set fruit with walls as sturdy as pollinated fruits.

CONCLUSIONS

It may be said in summary that auxins will not increase fruit-set unless a limitation of fruit-set exists at the time of use. Recognized limitations which may make the use of auxins feasible are weak light, excessively high or low temperatures, high nitrogen content, low leaf areas, and conditions of excessive flower abscission. Auxins will increase early yields in tomatoes by overcoming these limitations of fruit-set which commonly exist in winter greenhouse conditions and in the early spring field plantings. Hastening of maturity of the fruits will also contribute to the production of early yields.

It is clear from the studies of fruit-set which have been carried out that not only is auxin essential to fruit-set, but nutrient substrates for growth are needed as well. Normally auxin is supplied by the pollen plus some auxin-forming mechanism activated by the pollen; the substrates for growth are apparently supplied by mature leaves. The application of auxin can replace the former requirement, and in some cases at least alleviate the latter. The interesting fact that auxins can alleviate what appear to be limitations in nutrients suggests that auxins may exert their effect in part by bringing about a mobilization of nutrient materials in the flower.

Although many species of plants have been caused to set fruit parthenocarpically by auxin sprays, the practice appears to be commercially feasible only in tomatoes and figs at the present time.

CHAPTER XII

Flower and Fruit Thinning

Many fruit trees produce such excessive quantities of flowers in one year that sustaining the large number of fruits causes the trees to fail to lay down normal numbers of new flower buds. Consequently, the trees become biennial in their bearing habit, producing excessive numbers of blossoms one year and few or none the next year. To alleviate the situation, growers have thinned flowers or young fruits by hand, but this tedious and expensive process has many disadvantages. Besides being expensive, hand thinning must be completed approximately three weeks after bloom in biennial bearing apples, for the primordia are initiated approximately three weeks after petal fall in mature trees (Murneek, 1943).

A second need for thinning is reduction of heavy fruit crops to aid in effective insect and disease control and to increase fruit size and quality. When excessive numbers of fruits are set in a tree it may become difficult to obtain complete coverage of the fruit and foliage with sprays, and the fruits harvested are prone to be low in quality and small in size. Excessive set may also cause damage to the trees as the fruits enlarge and weigh the branches down excessively.

Auchter and Roberts (1935) were the first to demonstrate that chemical sprays could be used effectively to thin apple flowers. From their work there has evolved the use of toxic substances such as phenols and cresols literally to kill off some of the blossoms. Burkholder and McCown (1941) were the first to find that an auxin such as naphthaleneacetic acid could be effectively used to thin flowers. Subsequent workers have found that auxins are effective in thinning of young fruits as well.

It seems rather paradoxical to find that in some cases auxin sprays applied to flowers will hold the flowers on the plant and cause parthenocarpic fruit development, whereas the same material sprayed onto other plants causes thinning of the blossoms and fruit. The difference in the effects obtained is apparently owing to differences in the ability of various species of plants to set parthenocarpic fruit. A particularly good example of such differences in behavior among tree fruits may be seen in the case of pears. Bartlett pears set fruit in response to auxin sprays and consequently an increased set is obtained from such treatment. On the other hand Anjou and other pear varieties do not set fruit parthenocarpically and are thinned by auxin sprays (Griggs *et al*, 1951).

THE PHYSIOLOGICAL BASIS FOR FLOWER AND FRUIT THINNING

The thinning of flowers and fruits by auxins appears to be a function of three physiological factors. These are (1) the thinning of flowers by the prevention of natural pollination, (2) the abortion of young embryos and a consequent dropping of the fruits, and (3) the direct forcing of abscission by alteration of the auxin gradient at the abscission zone.

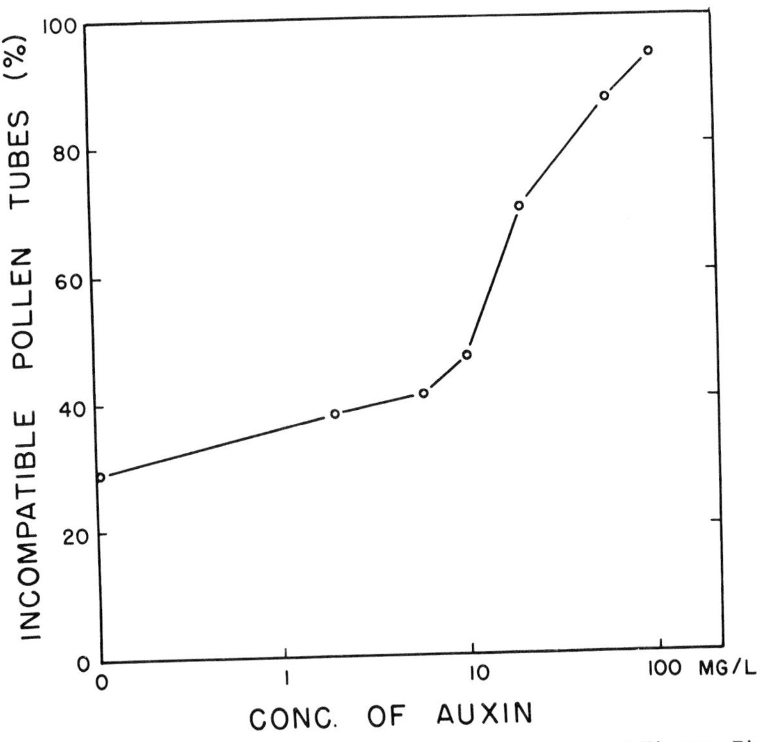

Fig. 98. The extent of incompatibility of pollen from untreated Kingston Bitter apple flowers when applied to styles of Crawley Beauty flowers which had been sprayed with various concentrations of naphthaleneacetic acid (data of Luckwill, 1953).

The Prevention of Pollination

For some time evidence has indicated that auxins may alter the germination and growth of pollen tubes. For example, in a synthetic medium Addicott (1943) obtained a small inhibition of pollen tube growth with indoleacetic acid, and a greater inhibition of pollen germination. In studies of the means by which auxins may thin apple flowers, Luckwill (1953) has treated flowers with various concentrations of naphthaleneacetic acid and subsequently introduced fresh pollen onto the stigmas. The inhibition of pollen germination following the auxin treatment is evident in figure 98. This action of auxin in thinning will of course apply only to flowers.

Flower thinning materials such as the cresols and phenols obtain their greatest effects through a toxic action on opened, unset flowers (Shepard, 1939; MacDaniels and Hoffman, 1941). For this reason, they

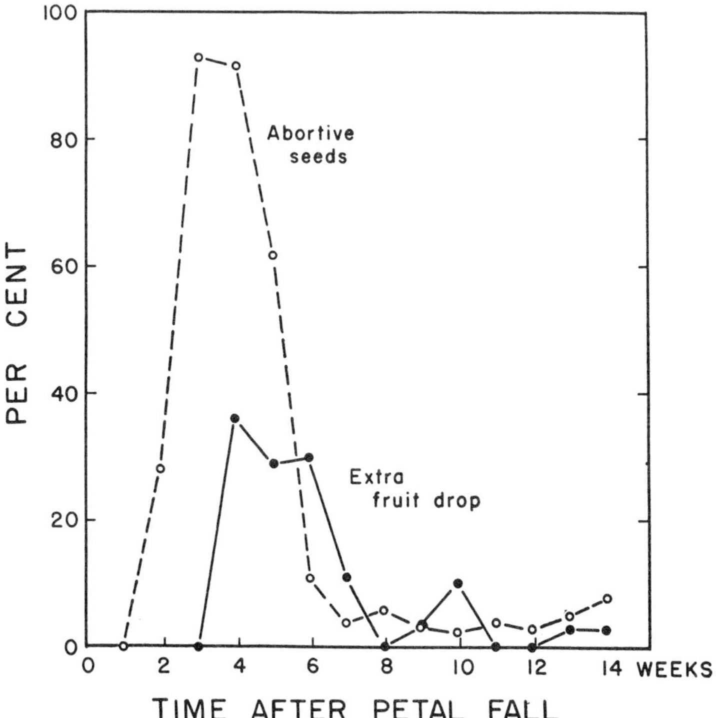

Fig. 99. The abortion of seeds in Crawley Beauty apples following a fruit-thinning spray with 40 mg./l. naphthaleneacetic acid at petal-fall, and the subsequent abscission of the fruits (Luckwill, 1953). Figures represent percentage differences from unsprayed controls.

are principally effective only until fruit-set has taken place. An advantage of auxin as a thinning agent is that there are other physiological means by which auxin may act as well.

The Abortion of Embryos

The capacity of auxins to cause the abortion of embryos in young fruits was first demonstrated by Swanson *et al* (1949) in *Tradescantia* fruits. In studies of the action of auxins in thinning apples, Murneek (1952) noted that the abscissed fruits uniformly contained aborted embryos, whereas the fruits remaining on the tree contained a large proportion of normal embryos. The tissue showing the most conspicuous deterioration in the abscissed fruits was the endosperm. Murneek (1952) proposed that the thinning action was a consequence of the abortion of the endosperm or perhaps of the inhibition of normal embyro growth (Murneek and Teubner, 1953). The endosperm tissue is the principal source of auxin to the young apple fruit (Luckwill, 1948), and deprived of its auxin supply, the fruit would be expected to abscise. Comparison of the frequency of aborted embryos and the shedding of young apple fruits in figure 99 indicates that a large wave of seed abortion occurs three weeks after auxin application at petal-fall, and this event is then followed one week later by a wave of fruit drop.

Direct Abscission Control

The two thinning mechanisms described above are each probably effective through interference with the auxin production in the flower or fruit. It is well known that abscission can be obtained either by lowering of the auxin supply distal to the abscission zone or by supplementing the auxin supply proximal to the abscission zone, as shown in figure 51 (page 112). A considerable body of evidence indicates that a third thinning effect of auxin involves supplementing of the proximal auxin supply.

In studies of the thinning of olive fruits, Hartmann (1952) has found that the application of auxin to the fruits was ineffective in thinning, whereas the application of auxin to the foliage of the tree resulted in the shedding of the fruits. Application to the foliage alone was actually more effective than an overall spray which covered both foliage and fruits. If the auxins were acting exclusively upon the flower or fruit one would certainly expect that direct application onto that organ would be more effective than applications to more distant parts. It is suggestive, then, that auxin applications may thin olive fruits by so altering the auxin gradient across the abscission zone as to force abscission.

Auxins are ineffective for thinning of peach flowers when there is no foliage. Approximately two or three weeks after bloom when the foliage has developed on peach trees, auxin sprays can effectively be used to thin fruits (Hibbard and Murneek, 1950) as shown in figure 101.

The situation with apples is not as clear as with olives. Auxin applied to the leaves is considerably more effective than applications to the fruits, but overall sprays are more effective still (Batjer and Thompson, 1948). There is some evidence that the initial effect of an overall auxin spray on apple trees is to retard abscission, even of fruit pedicels from which the fruits have been removed (Struckmeyer and Roberts, 1950; Murneek and Teubner, 1953).

Of course the auxin produced in the flower or fruit has a strong influence on the effectiveness of flower and fruit thinning sprays. If parthenocarpic fruits are set by the spray, as in the case of tomato or Bartlett pear, the auxin-producing mechanism described in the preceding chapter will be released within the ovary and a relatively high auxin content on the side away from, or distal to, the abscission layer will result. This auxin will prevent abscission and hold the flower on the plant. Apple and peach flowers do not readily set fruit parthenocarpically and hence any retarding of abscission by auxin sprays will be short-lived at best.

Struckmeyer and Roberts (1950) have proposed that auxins thin flowers by causing an excessive number of flowers to set fruit, resulting in such a competition for nutrients for growth between the young fruits that large numbers of them are forced to abscise for the lack of such nutrients. However, Batjer and Uota (1951) have been unable to confirm their observation that the auxin spray resulted in an initial increase in apples set.

METHODS OF TREATMENT

The sodium salt of naphthaleneacetic acid has been most generally used in auxin fruit-thinning work. The reason is not clear, but this auxin is certainly very effective and the sodium salt is convenient in that its solubility is much greater than that of the free acid. While most treatments are made by means of an aqueous spray, dust preparations have been used with good success (Southwick and Weeks, 1952).

Naphthaleneacetamide has also come into considerable commercial use for thinning apple flowers. This compound is considerably less effective than the salt of the acid, and hence concentrations of approximately twice the strength of acid sprays are used. The amide has the advantage of apparently causing less flagging of the foliage and less epinastic response. It is most effective when applied before petal fall.

Another auxin, 2,4,5-T, has been used successfully for thinning Anjou pears (Griggs *et al*, 1951), but comparative trials with various auxins on other fruits usually indicate that naphthaleneacetic acid is the best for thinning (Hartmann, 1952).

Various phenols and cresols are used as *flower* thinning sprays more generally than are the auxins. A compound which is finding considerable use as a fruit thinning agent is chloro-IPC (3-chloro-isopropyl-N-phenylcarbamate), which like auxin is effective in thinning both flowers and fruits.

The concentration of auxin considerably influences the effectiveness. Very few experiments have been published giving information on comparative effects of extensive ranges of concentrations, but experiments using small concentration ranges indicate that the response is usually quantitative. In figure 100 it can be seen that the percentage of fruits dropped from the tree increases with greater auxin concentrations. Southwick and Weeks (1952) have found, however, that some varieties of apples do not appear to give a quantitative response to the auxin.

The effectiveness of any given concentration is strongly dependent upon the vigor of the tree or branch, as more vigorous trees are less effectively thinned by a given concentration than weaker trees or

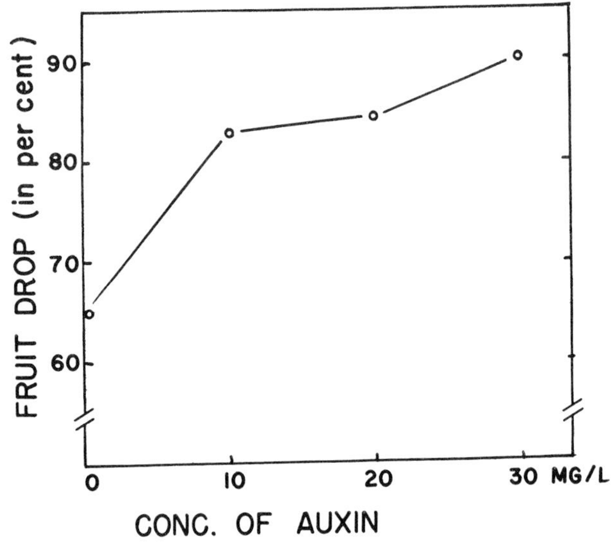

Fig. 100. Relative effectiveness of various concentrations of auxin (naphthalene-acetic acid) upon thinning of apples (Murneek, 1950).

branches (Murneek, 1950; Batjer and Uota, 1951). There are varietal differences in sensitivity as well: such varieties as Jonathan respond well to as little as 5 to 7 mg./l. sodium naphthaleneacetate and Golden Delicious apples respond well to 20 to 30 mg./l. Peaches respond only to higher concentrations of 40 to 60 mg./l. and olives to 100 to 125 mg./l. Spraying of apple trees from airplanes is done with much more concentrated preparations, usually 2400 mg./l. of the salt in a 40% oil emulsion (Batjer and Thompson, 1948).

The timing of auxin thinning sprays is much less crucial than the timing of caustic thinning sprays. Caustic sprays may be applied effectively only during the blossom period and after some fruit-set has occurred, whereas auxin sprays may be effective for four weeks

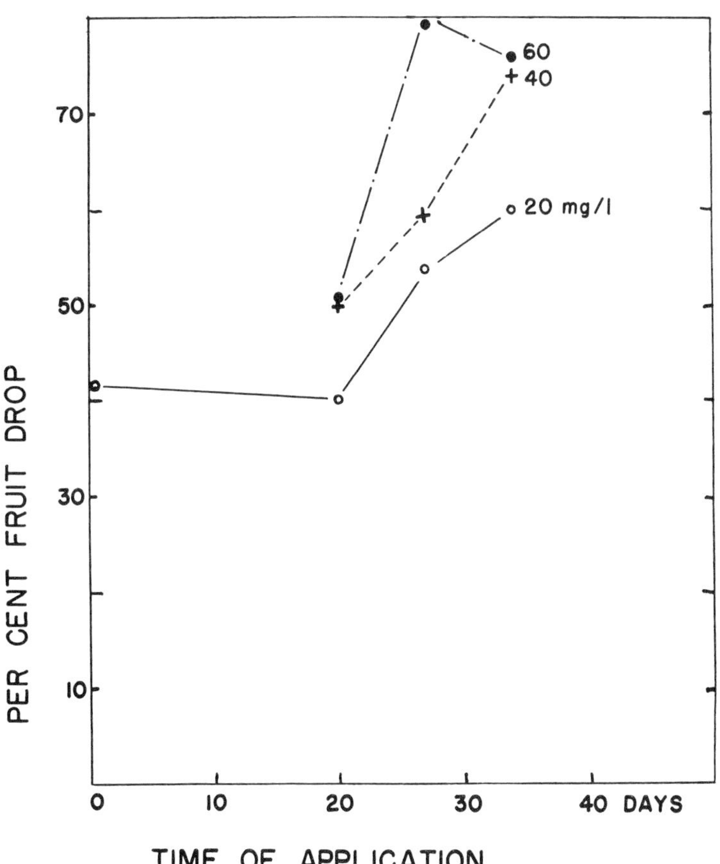

Fig. 101. The effect of time of application after full bloom upon the efficiency of thinning sprays of auxin (naphthaleneacetic acid) applied to peaches (data of Hibbard and Murneek, 1950).

after bloom. Peaches are more susceptible to late sprays than are apples. Only poor and irregular thinning of peaches can be obtained for the first three weeks after bloom, whereas good thinning can be obtained from 3 to 5 weeks, as shown in figure 101.

A very real advantage is the ability of auxin sprays to be used effectively for several weeks after flowering. This permits the grower to wait until there is less danger of frost and the degree of natural set in the trees can be estimated before any thinning operations need be started. Another advantage in late timing lies in the fact that the foliage of fruit trees becomes more resistant to damage from auxin sprays in the first few weeks after full bloom. This greater resistance with maturity of the foliage is entirely consistent with the increased resistance associated with age and increased differentiation discussed in chapter V.

FACTORS IN SUCCESS

Physiological Factors

Perhaps the most variable physiological factor affecting thinning sprays is the vigor of the tree. It has been found that large, husky spurs are more resistant to thinning sprays than are small weaker spurs (Murneek, 1950). Vigorously growing plants or limbs are more resistant to these sprays, whereas trees or limbs weakened by disease such as fire blight or by insect damage are more susceptible to thinning sprays. Much lower concentrations can be used effectively on such weakened trees than on healthy ones.

Again, more vigorous plants generally set a larger proportion of fruit, and it has been observed in many instances that when the fruit-set is great, relatively high concentrations of auxin must be used. More vigorous trees are also more resistant to leaf injury by auxin sprays.

The nitrogen level also influences abscission and thinning. Plants which are relatively rich in nitrogen generally shed fewer fruits by natural drop, and are more difficult to thin with auxins (Burkholder, unpublished).

Another physiological factor relating to the effectiveness of thinning sprays is that of the age of the fruit at the time of spraying. It has been pointed out that peaches become more susceptible three weeks after full bloom, and it is thought that apples become more resistant to thinning sprays after two weeks. After the fruit reaches the age of four to six weeks the large amount of natural abscission which is known as "June drop" is completed and after that even high concentrations of auxins are ineffective in removing any fruits at all from apples (Southwick and Weeks, 1950). Similarly, it has been found that olives can be thinned with auxins only until natural drop has stopped, and after that auxin sprays have no thinning effect (Hartmann, 1952). It is known that "June drop" of apples is associated with a low production of auxin (Luckwill, 1953), after which auxin production in the young fruit is relatively high (see figure 103).

Many workers have noted that auxin applications selectively thin the fruits on weak or small spurs preferentially. In fact, even on large, vigorous spurs the peripheral fruits are more susceptible to thinning, and the center or "king" fruits are the most tenaciously held (Batjer and Thompson, 1948).

The fruit thinning action of auxin sprays brings about an in-

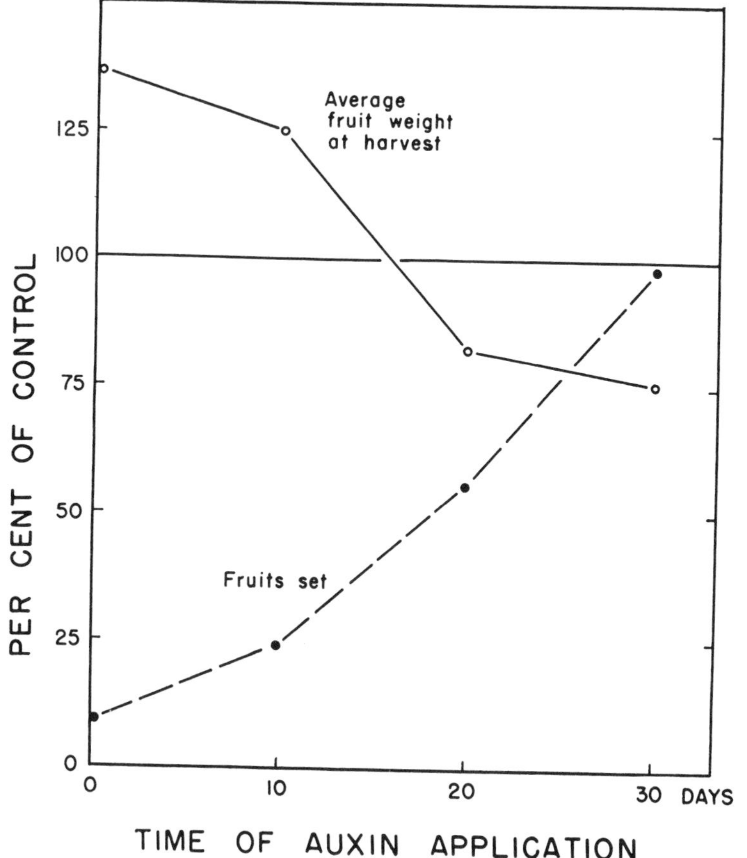

Fig. 102. The differences in fruit weight and in per cent of fruits set on Crawley Beauty apples obtained with various times of application after petal-fall of a fruit thinning spray (20 mg./l. naphthaleneacetic acid) (Luckwill, 1953).

creased fruit size. This is probably largely a result of fewer fruits remaining on the trees. Luckwill (1953) has studied the relationship between the thinning action and fruit size achieved as a function of the time of application of the spray. His data, given in figure 102, indicate that for the apple variety used, most effective thinning and greatest fruit size were obtained when the spray was applied at petal fall. Later applications appeared to cause rapid decline of the fruit size, until actual decreases in fruit size were obtained. The reduction in effectiveness in the thinning of the fruits was less rapid.

The thinning of fruits gives increased cold-hardiness of the trees in the succeeding winter season. This benefit from thinning is also obtained from auxin thinning (Edgerton and Hoffman, 1952).

Environmental Factors

Temperatures exert a strong influence on the shedding of flowers and fruits, both naturally and in response to auxin sprays. Many species of plants shed flowers at high temperatures. Apple trees have been observed to shed more at 70–75° F than at 55–60° F (Lu and Roberts, 1952). Temperatures near freezing also cause excessive drop of young apple fruits. The temperature regime will not only alter the natural drop, and hence the need for auxin sprays, but it will also alter thè effectiveness of spray treatment. Burkholder (unpublished) has observed that auxin thinning treatments were much less effective when applied in cold weather.

EFFECTIVENESS ON OTHER SPECIES

Besides the work with apples and peaches, some success in fruit thinning has been obtained with pears and olives. Anjou, Hardy and Winter Nelis pears have been successfully thinned with 100 mg./l. solutions of 2,4,5-trichlorophenoxypropionic acid (De Tar *et al,* 1950; Batjer and Uota, 1951). Some very interesting results have been obtained in thinning olives (Hartmann, 1952). If naphthaleneacetic acid is applied to the *flowers,* too much thinning results, but resistance to the auxin builds up as the young fruits begin growth. Use of 125 mg./l. naphthaleneacetic acid with a light oil in the spray gave good thinning after the fruits had grown to 3 or 5 mm. in diameter.

Some preliminary work has been done on the possible uses of auxins in removal of all fruits from ornamental trees which have obnoxious fruits (Chadwick *et al,* 1951).

CONCLUSION

Auxin sprays can be effectively used to remove excessive sets of apple and peach fruits after full bloom. Fruit trees which do not easily set parthenocarpic fruit in response to auxin sprays can be thinned in this way.

These treatments provide several advantages to the pomologist. They can be used to remove excess fruits several weeks after full bloom whereas most other chemical thinning agents can be used only at full bloom. This permits the grower to wait until the major threat of late frost has passed, and also to wait until the time that he can estimate the extent of loss due to natural fruit drop. The sprays offer the advantage of great saving in labor and permit much more accurate timing than hand thinning will permit. Such sprays can effectively break the biennial bearing habit and greatly increase the quality of the fruit harvested.

It is evident that fruit thinning with auxin sprays is not at all precise and small differences in the vigor of the tree will be largely reflected in the amount of thinning obtained. Therefore it is very difficult to predict how much thinning a given spray will bring about. Nevertheless, the growers find this treatment a useful one for biennial bearers, for even if excessive thinning does result, a larger crop can be expected the following year; and when insufficient thinning is obtained, the grower still reaps a higher quality crop and can expect a small, high quality crop in the off-year as well.

■ CHAPTER XIII

Control of Pre-Harvest Fruit Drop

A serious problem confronting growers of tree fruits is the loss of mature fruits by abscission from the tree before harvest. Perhaps the crop most seriously affected in this way is the apple. As the apple crop nears maturity, a spell of windy or hot weather can result in the abscission and loss of almost the entire crop. Essentially the same problem confronts the growers of stone fruits and citrus fruits. The fact that auxin could prevent abscission of leaves was demonstrated in 1936 by LaRue, and that this same control could be applied to mature apples was first shown in 1939 by Gardner *et al.* Their findings have led to the development of one of the most valuable new tools of the pomologist.

PHYSIOLOGICAL BASIS FOR PRE-HARVEST DROP CONTROL

With respect to abscission in general, it has gradually become apparent that plant organs have a general tendency to abscise, and that the auxin production within the organs suppresses the tendency. The retention of leaves, flowers or fruits on a plant are therefore dependent upon the auxin supply in the organ, and abscission occurs at times when the auxin production in the organ becomes low. In the case of the apple, auxin is produced in three waves: (1) upon fertilization, the ovary produces a flush of auxin, (2) in the fourth week of growth, the endosperm produces auxin, and (3) from the 8th to 12th week, the embryo in the seed produces a large amount of auxin. These waves of auxin production have been worked out in detail by Luckwill (1948, 1953), and he has shown that spells of fruit abscission occur between each of these production waves, and after the last one. A large drop in auxin production as maturity approaches is readily seen in figure 103. Each of the low ebbs in auxin production by the fruit would be expected to result in a weakened auxin gradient, and consequently in fruit abscission. Because the seeds are the apparent sources of the last two auxin waves, it is not surprising that as maturity approaches the fruits with the fewest seeds are the first to abscise (Heinicke, 1917).

It is possible that ethylene production by the maturing fruits may accentuate the tendency to abscise. Ethylene is produced by ripening apples (Gane, 1935) and also brings about abscission in general (Goodspeed *et al,* 1918).

The abscission of mature apple fruits takes place principally as a result of a weakening and ultimate fracturing of the middle lamella of cells in or near the abscission zone (McCown, 1943). Auxins applied to the fruit prevent the development of these changes in the middle lamella, possibly through inhibition of enzymes which render pectins soluble (van Overbeek, 1951). Inhibition of pectin methylesterase with auxin has been observed *in vitro,* but not *in vivo* (Bryan and Newcomb, 1954).

When auxin sprays are used to control pre-harvest drop in apples, auxins applied to the stem end of the fruit are most effective (Gardner *et al,* 1940). Application to this part would most logically produce the greatest effect in increasing the auxin gradient across the abscission layer, hence preventing abscission in the manner discussed in chapter IV.

Studies of abscission have shown that for the effective control of

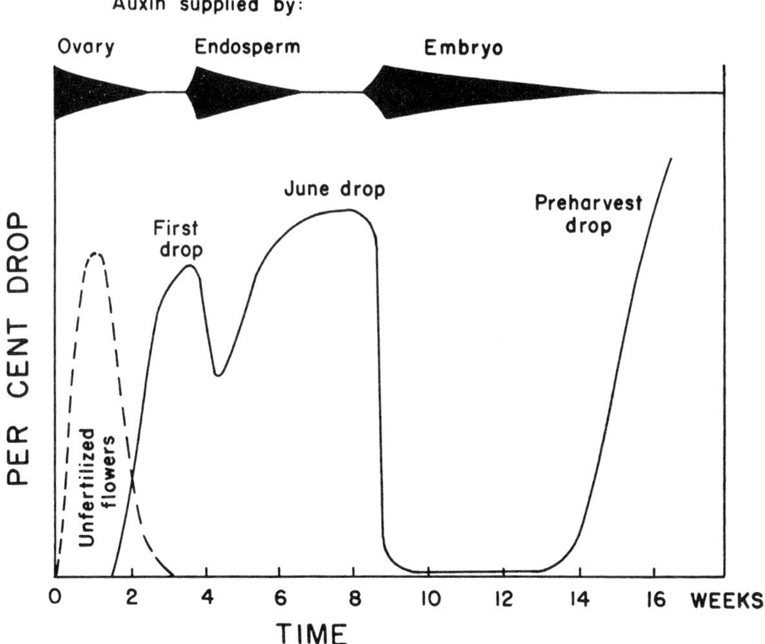

Fig. 103. Schematic diagram of the relationship between spurts of auxin production (above) and fruit drop (below) in apples (adapted from Luckwill, 1953).

abscission by auxin there must be a sufficiency of certain nutritive materials—especially carbohydrates (Livingston, 1950). Indirect evidence that this same factor has a bearing on pre-harvest drop control has been produced by Thompson (1951). He found that auxins applied to weak trees with yellowing foliage presumably low in carbohydrates, could not effectively prevent pre-harvest drop.

METHODS OF APPLICATION

Selection of Auxins

In the first study of pre-harvest drop control with auxins, Gardner *et al* (1940) found that of several different auxins tested, α-naphthaleneacetic acid was the best. The amide form of this same auxin performed essentially in the same manner. For more than a decade this auxin was the most effective one reported in the literature. After being sprayed on the trees it took 2 or 3 days to control drop, and effective control lasted from 7 to 14 days depending upon the variety of apple. In some instances there was an extremely effective reduction in fruit drop, as much as 78 per cent (Murneek, 1940). The major limitations of this auxin are (1) it is not effective on several varieties such as Rhode Island Greening, Jonathan and Delicious, and (2) its effectiveness on McIntosh is very short-lived, usually 7 or 8 days. This second limitation is unfortunate since McIntosh is particularly prone to drop its fruits and is one of the commonest orchard varieties in the United States.

The compound 2,4-D was found to be particularly effective on Winesap and closely related varieties (Batjer and Marth, 1949), but was much less effective on more distantly related varieties and has never achieved widespread use for this reason. This is an interesting case of a genetic specificity for an auxin, in that one group of closely related varieties responds well to a given auxin whereas other varieties do not.

2,4,5-T (2,4,5-trichlorophenoxyacetic acid) has more recently been found to be highly effective in controlling drop of McIntosh apples (Hoffman and Edgerton, 1952). This auxin effectively controls apple drop for the remarkably long period of 4 to 6 weeks after spraying and appears to be the best controlling agent for McIntosh apples.

2,4,5-TP (α-2,4,5-trichlorophenoxypropionic acid) is another very effective auxin for controlling drop on McIntosh apples (Edgerton and Hoffman, 1951), and while it does not produce as strong an effect as 2,4-D in controlling drop of Winesap apples, it has the advantage of affording effective control on most other apple varieties. Like

2,4,5-T, the effect lasts for from 4 to 6 weeks. This compound has essentially displaced all others in the control of pre-harvest drop of apples in the United States.

The amide of 2,4,5-T has been reported as being particularly effective in the control of fruit drop (Edgerton and Hoffman, 1953).

Not only do the phenoxy acid auxins show a longer lasting effect in the control of fruit drop, but they take a considerably longer time to begin their effects after spraying. Naphthaleneacetic acid holds fruits on after only 2 or 3 days from the spraying time, but 2,4,5-T and 2,4,5-TP do not generally control drop effectively for some 10 to 17 days after spraying. Such delays in effectiveness can be seen in the data of Erickson *et al* (1952). A few reports indicate a retarded fruit drop as early as 4 days after application of 2,4,5-TP (Southwick *et al*, 1953), but such early control is not general.

A good many other auxins have been tested for this use with less success. It may be of interest to note that β-propionic and β-butyric phenoxy acids are ineffective in prevention of fruit drop (Osborne and Wain, 1951).

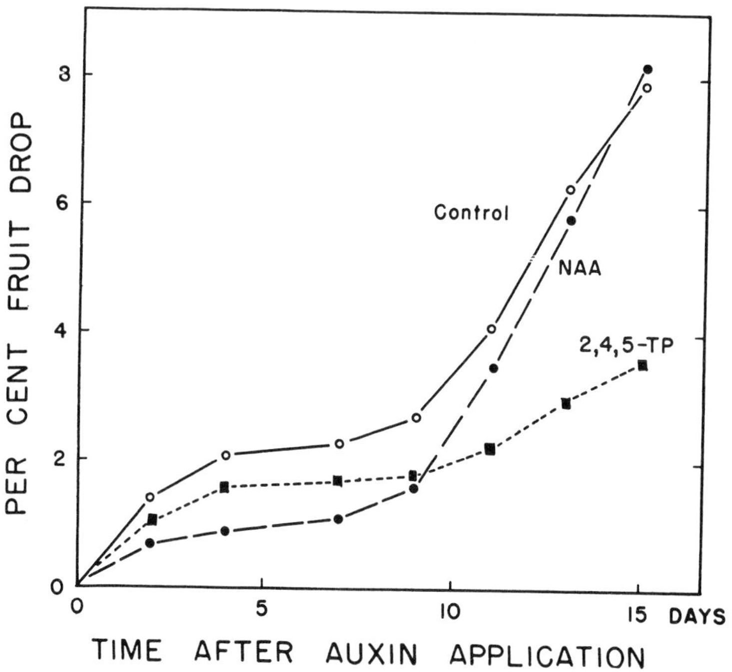

Fig. 104. The relative effectiveness of naphthaleneacetic acid (NAA) and α-(2,4,5-trichlorophenoxy)-propionic acid (2,4,5-TP) in controlling drop of McIntosh apples (Southwick *et al*, 1953), showing the more rapid control by NAA and longer duration of control by 2,4,5-TP. Both auxins used at 20 mg./l.

It is rather striking to observe that the effectiveness of an auxin in controlling pre-harvest drop of apples is not in proportion to its activity in growth. This has been pointed out by Edgerton and Hoffman (1951), and is a particularly interesting observation in view of the fact that there is no clear-cut concentration effect observable in the control of pre-harvest drop. The effects of auxin in nearly all its known functions show a quantitative increase in effectiveness with increasing concentrations. In the control of pre-harvest drop, however, there is no consistent difference between concentrations ranging from approximately 5 to 50 mg./l. Most consistent results have been obtained with concentrations of 10 to 20 mg./l. of these various auxins and, consequently, the use of such concentrations has become general.

The relative rapidity of effectiveness and the duration of the effect of naphthaleneacetic acid and 2,4,5-TP are compared in the data shown in figure 104. It can be seen that the naphthaleneacetic acid afforded good control of fruit drop from 2 to about 10 days after the spray was applied, and after that the dropping rate was as high or higher than with untreated fruits. The 2,4,5-TP, however, started to control drop effectively after 9 days, and was still giving excellent control 15 days after application.

Auxin sprays to prevent fruit drop have been used effectively on apricot (Hesse and Davey, 1942), pear (Davey and Hesse, 1942), orange (Stewart and Klotz, 1947), grapefruit (Stewart and Parker, 1948), lemon (Stewart and Hield, 1950), and almond (Serr and Forde, 1952). Its use has been attempted unsuccessfully on grape (Pentzer, 1941) and peach (Hesse and Davey, 1942).

Techniques of Application

The commonest method of applying auxins for pre-harvest drop control is in aqueous sprays. In their original study, Gardner *et al* (1940) showed that the auxin applied to the stem ends of the apple fruits was considerably more effective than auxin applied to the distal (blossom) end of the fruits or to the leaves. Later studies of the effects of different placement of the sprays have shown that not only are materials effective when applied to the fruits, but also some effect is obtained when applied to the leaves immediately adjacent to the fruits (Batjer and Thompson, 1948). The effectiveness of the spray is quite localized and is effective only for fruits within approximately 3 inches of the locus of application.

Another technique which has been reported to be effective is the use of dusts containing the auxin (Hoffman *et al,* 1942). Dust applications have not been uniformly successful, however, and have not received widespread use.

Other techniques that have been used include aerosol sprays (Tukey and Hamner, 1945) and concentrated solutions applied from airplanes, particularly in the large orchard areas of the Pacific Northwest.

Experiments with naphthaleneacetic acid have shown that repeated applications at intervals of from 3 to 7 days may somewhat prolong the effective control obtained (Gardner *et al*, 1940), but the more recent use of 2,4,5-T and 2,4,5-TP with their long periods of effective control have essentially obviated the need for repeated spraying.

The time of application of the spray is, of course, of great importance to its effectiveness. If the breakdown of the middle lamellae of cells of the abscission zone proceeds too far, no auxin application could be expected to prevent abscission. Therefore it is most important that the auxin be applied when the first signs of fruit drop appear or as soon as the grower realizes that a delay in picking time will be necessary.

FACTORS IN SUCCESS

Severity of Natural Drop

The usefulness of auxin sprays to control pre-harvest drop will obviously be a function of the severity of the fruit drop which would occur without the spray. Under particularly adverse conditions as much as 90 per cent of an apple crop may be lost by fruit drop.

Several environmental factors are recognized as playing a part in causing fruit drop. A spell of warm weather at or shortly before harvest time is the most common of these factors; also frost and windstorms can result in heavy drop (Roberts and Struckmeyer, 1943).

Several factors inherent to the tree itself are also recognized as favoring fruit drop. Among these are high levels of available nitrogen (Southwick, 1940), a particularly heavy apple crop (Southwick and Shaw, 1941), a low seed content in the fruits (Southwick, 1939) or trees weakened by disease, animals, or insects (Enzie and Schneider, 1941). Some varieties are recognized as more susceptible to fruit drop than others and these include McIntosh, Duchess, Delicious, Williams, and Winesap.

Delay in Picking Schedule

As apples mature and the auxin production in the seed drops lower and lower (figure 103), the tendency to abscise becomes greater and greater. Unless the fruits are picked before ripening proceeds too far, fruit fall can be expected to be excessive. Frequently growers are unable to harvest their fruit at the ideal stage of ripeness, and where delays are necessary an auxin spray finds its usefulness to hold the fruit on the tree. In some crops it is desirable to delay harvest in order to await a more profitable market. This is true in the case of lemons which are in greatest demand in the summer months. The fruits ripening in spring can be held on the tree with auxins until the more favorable marketing season has arrived.

Effectiveness of the Auxin Application

Fortunately, one of the commonest environmental conditions leading to severe fruit drop is apparently also a factor in increasing the effectiveness of pre-harvest drop sprays. That is high temperature, which not only increases fruit drop, but likewise may increase the effectiveness of a spray (Batjer, 1942). The experiments on this point are not entirely conclusive, however, for sprays applied at different times of day were used for the various temperature conditions. However, beneficial effects of high temperature have been confirmed in several other instances (Davidson, 1940; Overholser *et al,* 1943; Barlow, 1952). In autumn seasons with excessively high temperatures associated with drought conditions, auxins may be entirely ineffective in preventing abscission (Klackle, unpublished). The occurrence of low temperatures after application of auxin sprays may increase the duration of the effect in controlling pre-harvest drop.

Several physiological factors will likewise help to determine the effectiveness of a spray. It has already been mentioned that the extent of development of abscission processes at the time of spray application can make a late spray almost ineffective. The several factors listed as encouraging the natural drop of apples are all factors in the usefulness of a given spray. Each of them can be interpreted as either altering the carbohydrate or the auxin levels in the pedicel consequently affecting fruit drop. If the auxin and/or the carbohydrate level of the fruit pedicels drops too low to prevent abscission naturally, auxin sprays will be effective. However, in instances where the carbohydrate level drops excessively low as in the case of weak or dying trees, the auxin sprays will not prevent abscission of the fruits at all (Thompson, 1951; Griggs *et al,* 1951). It appears also that wormy or otherwise moribund fruits will not be retained on the tree by auxins (Erickson, 1951).

Varietal differences have been reported in several instances. It appears that fruit drop is more readily controlled in early than in late apple varieties (Vyvyan, 1946).

Side Effects of Auxin Sprays

A side effect of these treatments which has gladdened the hearts of apple growers is the increase in coloring of the fruits following auxin spray application. This increased coloring was observed by Gardner *et al* (1940) in their original study of the control of fruit drop. However the extensive use of naphthaleneacetic acid in the 1940's minimized the coloring effect, and only recently when the chlorinated phenoxyalkyl acids have been used (2,4-D, 2,4,5-T, 2,4,5-TP) have pronounced increases in color been obtained. More intense red coloration permits the sale of the fruit as a fancier product and at a higher price. The extent of color development is dependent upon the time of application in relation to the time of picking. If the fruits are picked within two weeks of the time of spray, color is not generally intensified, but longer periods of time between spraying and picking will result in greater color development in response to the auxin.

The development of greater coloration in apples is primarily useful for fruit which is to be sold without being stored, for encouragement of coloring and ripening by auxin application shortens the storage life of the fruits.

There are many conflicting reports in the literature on the question of whether auxin applied to prevent pre-harvest drop alters the ripening and storage performance of the apples. There is clear evidence that auxin causes an increase in the respiratory rate of the fruits, and if this increased metabolic activity is permitted to continue over a long period of time the fruits will necessarily ripen more rapidly (Smock and Gross, 1947). The conflicting findings of many different authors that auxins did or did not shorten the storage life were finally clarified by Gerhardt and Allmendinger (1945), who demonstrated that if the fruits were placed in storage within two weeks of the time of spraying with naphthaleneacetic acid there was no noticeable hastening of ripening or shortening of storage life. However, if the fruits remained on the tree or out of storage for more than two weeks from the time of auxin application, ripening was hastened and the storage life definitely shortened. The same situation appears to exist following treatment with 2,4,5-TP (Southwick *et al,* 1953).

A promising means of preventing the early ripening due to auxin treatments has been suggested by Smock *et al* (1951) who showed that incorporation of maleic hydrazide into the auxin spray effectively removed the stimulation of respiration by the auxin and yet did not interfere with the prevention of fruit abscission. The ability of maleic hydrazide to counteract auxin effects in growth have been discussed in chapter VII. The firmness of apple fruits was actually increased by maleic hydrazide and the early ripening effect resulting from the auxin treatment was essentially erased.

The effects of auxins in altering ripening and storage of fruits and vegetables is discussed in more detail in chapter XV.

Excessively high concentrations of auxins applied for pre-harvest drop control can result in excessive prevention of development of abscission tendencies. As a consequence harvesting the fruit can cause extensive breakage to the flowering spurs. This type of damage is not excessive if auxin concentrations of less than 20 mg./l. are used (Thompson, 1951). Another abnormal result which sometimes appears is excessive enlarging and radial cracking of the fruits.

PRE-HARVEST DROP CONTROL IN OTHER FRUITS

Oranges

Although the fruit drop problem with oranges is not as great as with apples, some orange groves are particularly prone to drop their fruit early and, as in the case of apples, the advent of warm weather before harvest will result in losses due to excessive drop. In contrast to the effect on apples, naphthaleneacetic acid has no effect on drop of oranges but 2,4-D has been found to furnish good control (Stewart *et al,* 1951). Of several derivatives tested, the isopropyl ester of 2,4-D has given the best results (Erickson, 1951). The duration of the effect is remarkably long, for these workers have found that sprays applied as early as October could effectively control drop until harvest in May. Whereas the first experiments were carried out by applying the auxins shortly before harvest time, it was soon discovered that applications made at or near the time of full bloom would not only control drop at harvest time but would also cause an increase in the yield of large-sized fruits. For this reason the 2,4-D is commonly applied either at full bloom or shortly before. The concentration used is 8 to 10 mg./l. in an ordinary aqueous spray, generally combined with a fertilizer spray of zinc or manganese (Stewart *et al,* 1951). In some orchards it is applied by helicopter spraying a concentrated solution of 2400 mg./l.

The auxin spray applied to oranges at the time of flowering stimulates the rate of growth of the individual fruits. Gains in fruit sizes as great as 13 per cent have been reported (Stewart *et al,* 1952). One factor which undoubtedly contributes to this stimulation of growth rate is the reduced set of flowers which open after the spray is applied. An additional benefit obtained is the prevention of water spot breakdown of the fruits after they are picked and placed in storage (Stewart, 1949).

Oil sprays are used in most large orchards in the insect control program and these sprays commonly cause the abscission of some leaves and some fruit stems. The auxin sprays sometimes can neutralize these effects (Stewart *et al,* 1951).

Some of the problems which have arisen from the use of auxin sprays in oranges include the development of rudimentary seeds, of navels in Valencia oranges or excessively large navels in the Washington navel orange, and the development of abnormally large oil glands on the surface of the fruit (Stewart *et al,* 1951, 1952). It has been found that these abnormalities are held to a minimum if concentrations of 10 mg./l. or less of the auxin is used. As in the case of apples, defective fruits are not held on the tree by auxin sprays (Erickson, 1951) and hence the spray does not increase the percentage of defective fruits harvested.

In using 2,4-D to prevent fruit drop of Washington navel oranges, experimenters have found that increases in fruit size are obtained when the spray is applied six weeks before bloom. In this curious instance, auxin applied before the flowers have opened stimulates the subsequent fruit growth rate as well as prevents pre-harvest drop. Thus the auxin effect is exerted over a period of seven months (Stewart *et al,* 1951).

The 2,4-D sprays on Washington navel oranges were found to have another beneficial side effect by reducing the amount of fruit stem dieback which normally occurs in this variety. This appears to be a case of actual abscission of stems which occurs naturally, and such abscission is effectively prevented by auxin sprays.

Lemons

The pre-harvest drop problem in lemons is slightly different from that in oranges, for the lemon continues to flower over a long period of time, and the fruits on a tree are of diverse ages. Stewart and Hield (1950) have found that 2,4,5-T sprays can effectively hold the fruit on the tree even though the fruit is mature. In this way the sprays make it possible to hold fruit on the tree until the desirable summer market for lemons is at hand. Concentrations of from 5 to 8 mg./l. of 2,4,5-T are apparently optimal. The diethanolamine salt is the most effective preparation, having a longer effect than the simple salts or the esters. The spray does not prevent the fall of immature fruits, but curiously limits its effects to the larger mature fruits.

As with oranges, an increase in fruit size of lemons can be obtained if the spray is applied sufficiently far ahead of harvest time. Stewart and Hield (1950) recommend the application of the spray seven months before the harvest to increase fruit size.

The lemon tree grows in spurts throughout the year and if the auxin spray is applied during a growth spurt, fairly great dieback of the new growth will occur. If the spray is applied between the growth spurts, when the amount of immature tissues is at a minimum, such injury is essentially prevented. From the studies of the effects of auxins on tissues of different ages discussed in chapter V, this is precisely what one would expect.

Other Fruits

Fruit drop in the grapefruit can be effectively controlled by 2,4-D (Stewart and Parker, 1948). Fruits sprayed in June are held on the tree until December.

Pre-harvest drop in the Stewart apricot is a serious problem, apparently owing to abortion of the embryo at various stages in the growth of the fruit. The embryo is a major source of auxin in maturing fruits and the abortion of the embryo would be expected to result in a strong decrease in auxin production within the fruit. Fruit drop due to this curious circumstance in apricot can be effectively suppressed by spraying with 10 mg./l. naphthaleneacetic acid. Hesse and Davey (1942) reported that when untreated controls dropped 25 per cent of the fruit, the spray reduced this drop to 8 per cent. It is interesting to note that after the application of naphthaleneacetic acid to apricots ten days is required for a difference in the rate of fruit drop to appear.

In apricots, the use of 2,4,5-T for control of fruit drop has also been noted (Crane, 1953). The auxin is effective in preventing abscission for the remarkably long period of 50 to 60 days.

Control of fruit drop in Bartlett pears with naphthaleneacetic acid is a general practice in California. Good control can also be obtained with 2,4-D, but with greater chance of injury effects (Batjer *et al,* 1948).

No stone fruit other than the apricot has been found to respond to auxin sprays to prevent pre-harvest drop. Peaches and olives have been treated without success. Attempts to prevent dropping of grapes from picked clusters have met with no success.

■ CHAPTER XIV

Flowering

Several different paths have led to the discovery that auxins can alter flowering behavior in plants. The influence of auxin on flowering suggests the ultimate possibility of using growth regulators to control or alter flowering in agricultural crops.

The first demonstration that auxins can affect flowering was by Hitchcock and Zimmerman (1935) who found that flowering of tobacco could be slightly hastened by auxins. The first and only species which has been found actually to be induced to flower by auxins is the pineapple (Clark and Kerns, 1942), although auxins have been found to alter slightly the threshold daylength required for the photoperiodic induction of some long-day species (Liverman and Lang, 1953).

There have evolved three different types of auxin applications to influence flowering. In the case of the pineapple, auxins are sprayed on the foliage of vegetative plants, and by this treatment flowering is actually induced. A second method, the foliar application of auxin sprays at the time of normal flower initiation or shortly thereafter, can quantitatively increase or decrease the flowering behavior. In this way the litchi tree can be made to flower more profusely (Shiguera, 1948), and the bolting of the sugar beet may be delayed (Price *et al,* 1950). A third method of applying auxins is by soaking seeds in an auxin solution, a technique originally described by Cholodny (1936).

THE PHYSIOLOGICAL BASIS OF FLOWERING EFFECTS

There is some evidence that floral initiation is controlled by a hormone. Perhaps the most salient evidence for the existence of a flowering hormone is the fact that photoperiodic stimuli are perceived by the leaves and are thence translocated to buds where the response takes place (Cajlachjan, 1936; Moskov, 1936). The suggestion that a hormone was responsible for photoperiodic induction was made by Cajlachjan (1936). He rather guardedly suggested that the flowering hormone might be auxin, but that has not proved to be the case. Several characteristics of the flower-inducing stimulus have been elucidated experimentally. For example, the stimulus moves principally in the phloem (Cajlachjan, 1938), either up or down a stem (Moskov, 1939), its rate of movement can be retarded by low temperatures (Borthwick and Parker, 1941), it can move only in living tissues as indicated by the fact that it can cross graft unions only when living connection has been made (Withrow and Withrow, 1943), and finally, the stimulus of long-day, short-day and indeterminate species has been found to be identical (Lang, 1952).

In analyzing the physiological characteristics of auxins and the hypothetical flowering hormone, it seems clear that the two are not identical. Several distinctions between them can be drawn: auxins are principally polar in movement whereas the flowering stimulus is not; auxins are diffusible, the flowering stimulus apparently is not; and lastly, compounds which are not auxins can force flowering in pineapple in a manner very similar to auxins (Rodriguez, 1932; Lewcock, 1937). This latter point suggests that even in pineapple the flowering response may not be specific for auxins.

There have been several suggestions as to the means by which auxins may modify floral initiation. Galston (1947) has suggested that the flowering hormone and the growth hormone may be antagonistic to one another and consequently the application of auxins inhibits flowering. Bonner (1951) has suggested that auxins modify photoperiodic responses of plants by interfering with the night reaction in the leaf. While these suggestions may be valid for inhibitions of floral induction they cannot apparently account for promotions of flowering by auxins. Some evidence mentioned in chapter IV indicates that the effects of auxins on flowering involve an interaction with other plant materials. For example, addition of auxins alone may inhibit flowering, but the addition of auxins in the presence of other added materials such as sugars or organic acids may promote flowering (Leopold and Guernsey, 1953). There is a rather striking parallel between these effects and the interaction of auxins and other materials in the control of differentiation of buds (cf. figures 48 and 49, pp. 104, 108).

CONTROL OF FLOWERING IN PINEAPPLE

Rodriguez (1932), having observed that brush fires adjacent to pineapple fields stimulated flowering, was led to the discovery that smoke, and specifically unsaturated gases such as ethylene in smoke could bring about flower initiation. In the following year similar experiments in Hawaii revealed that acetylene gas, too, would initiate flowers. This latter material found its first field use for that purpose in 1935. The data were published later by Lewcock (1937). The discovery that auxins could also force flower initiation was first made in Hawaii in 1937, and was published five years later (Clark and Kerns, 1942). These workers found that the application of small amounts of auxin onto vegetative pineapple plants caused the formation of flower buds, and the application of relatively large amounts of auxin onto plants which would normally be expected to flower prevented flowering. These opposite qualitative responses to auxin are shown in figure 105. It can be seen that plants treated with 10 or 50 mg./l. of naphthaleneacetic acid in August came into flower whereas the control

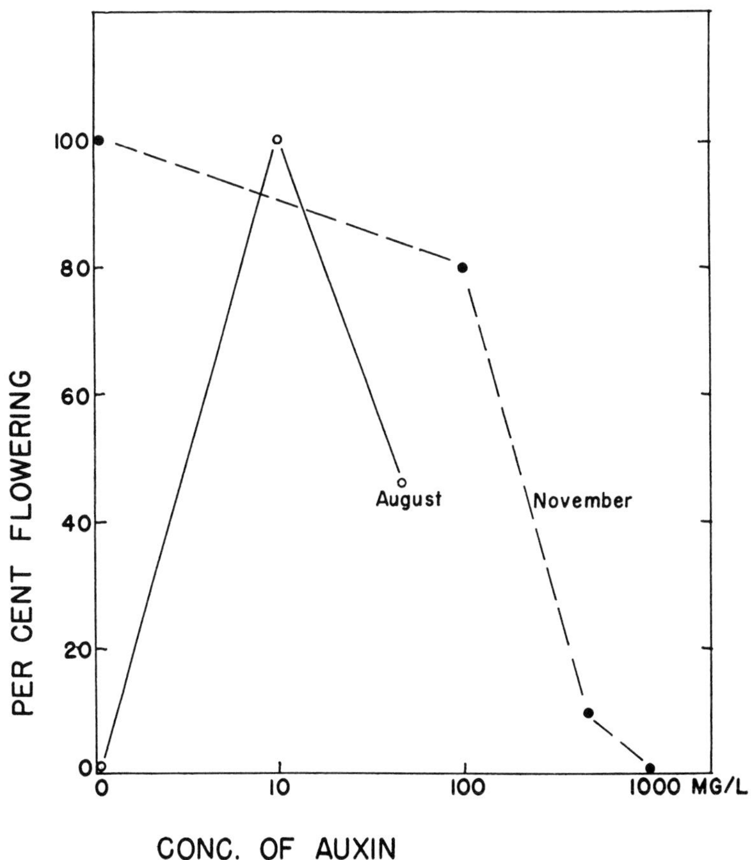

Fig. 105. The effects of sprays of various concentrations of auxin (naphthaleneacetic acid) upon flower initiation in the pineapple, showing 100 per cent forcing of flowering by weak concentrations applied in August, and complete inhibition by strong concentrations applied in November (data of Clark and Kerns, 1942).

plants did not. In November, when pineapple plants normally initiate flowers, the application of relatively concentrated auxin sprays (500 to 1000 mg./l.) inhibited or entirely prevented flowering.

The pineapple normally initiates flowers when temperatures are low and photoperiods are short. Each of these environmental factors influences flower initiation, but temperature appears to be the stronger control (van Overbeek and Cruzado, 1948).

It has been proposed that flowering in pineapple is brought about both naturally and artificially by the accumulation of auxin at the stem apex. Some neat evidence to support this concept is the finding that a pineapple plant placed horizontally will be induced to flower (van Overbeek and Cruzado, 1948). Presumably the reorientation of auxin at the stem apex associated with the geotropic response produces a net increase in the auxin present on the nether side, and the increased auxin level results in floral initiation. The theory is in agreement with the finding that auxin sprays can induce flowering. However, the effectiveness of ethylene and acetylene is unsettling to the theory, especially in view of the fact that no increase in auxin content of the stem tip has been found following ethylene treatment (Leopold, 1949).

Methods

Ethylene has been used extensively to force pineapple plants to flower in Hawaii. The method of application involves 4% ethylene adsorbed on a Bentonite suspension in water. The gas is bubbled through the Bentonite suspension, becoming adsorbed on the clay particles, and the mixture is subsequently sprayed on the foliage. Acetylene has been applied in a water and clay suspension as well, but a much simpler method is by the application of dry calcium carbide. Approximately one gram of the calcium carbide powder is dropped into the heart of each pineapple plant where there is commonly a small reservoir of rain-water. The calcium carbide reacts vehemently with the water producing liberal amounts of acetylene, and forcing the plant into floral initiation.

The use of auxin to force flowering in pineapple can be effectively carried out with any of a large variety of auxins such as naphthaleneacetic acid, indolebutyric acid, and 2,4-dichlorophenoxyacetic acid. Indoleacetic acid is almost entirely ineffective in forcing flowering, presumably because of the presence of large amounts of auxin-destroying enzymes in pineapple tissue as reported by Gordon and Nieva (1949). In Puerto Rico, 2,4-D in concentrations of from 5 to 10 mg./l. has been recommended (van Overbeek, 1946) and in Hawaii 25 to 30 mg./l. naphthaleneacetic acid are commonly used. The concentration of the auxin solute does not have a large effect on the results obtained, but the governing factor is rather the actual amount of auxin which reaches the plant. Van Overbeek (1946) has shown that several different concentrations of auxin would be effective, provided only that approximately 0.25 mg. of actual auxin was applied to each plant.

Factors in Success

As in all of the other uses of auxins in agriculture, the condition of the plant plays a very important role in the success of flower forcing. Pineapple plants high in carbohydrate are the most uniform in their response to auxins. The time of day at which the auxin is applied has a strong influence upon its effectiveness (Nightingale, unpublished).

It was seen in chapter VI that light and temperature have a profound effect on the absorption and translocation of growth regulators, and these two factors likewise strongly modify the spray's effectiveness. Of the two, light may be the most crucial, for unpublished experiments by Nightingale have revealed that on cloudy days the effectiveness of the auxin spray in Hawaii may be reduced 50 per cent.

Several side effects have been observed following the use of auxin sprays. The first of these is the abnormal elongation of the peduncle. This tall, thin structure is often unable to sustain the pineapple fruit following auxin forcing, and consequently excessive bending or even breaking of the peduncle under the ripening fruit frequently occurs. Another auxin spray developed to strengthen the peduncle is described in chapter XVII.

A second side effect is that of reducing the slip production. Because pineapple plants are propagated by the lateral peduncle buds, or slips, such a reduction can have important implications for pineapple plantation operations.

A third side effect is the reduction in size and quality of the fruit due to the forcing procedure. Pineapple fruit size and quality are intimately related to the size of the plant and its stage of development (van Overbeek, 1946). It is not surprising then to find that when all plants are forced to flower regardless of whether or not they are large enough to flower naturally, the average fruit size and quality are reduced.

A fourth and extremely important side effect of forcing flowering is the production of fruits ready for harvest almost simultaneously over the entire field.

SPRAYS TO MODIFY FLOWER INITIATION

Whereas auxins can induce flower initiation only in the pineapple, they can exert a quantitative modification of flower initiation in a large number of plants. There are two techniques which have been used to bring about such a modification, one being the application of auxin to the growing plant and the other being the soaking of seeds in auxin solutions.

Some early reports indicated that auxins may slightly hasten (Hitchcock and Zimmerman, 1935) or strongly inhibit flowering (Dostal and Hosek, 1937). Subsequent research has confirmed that the

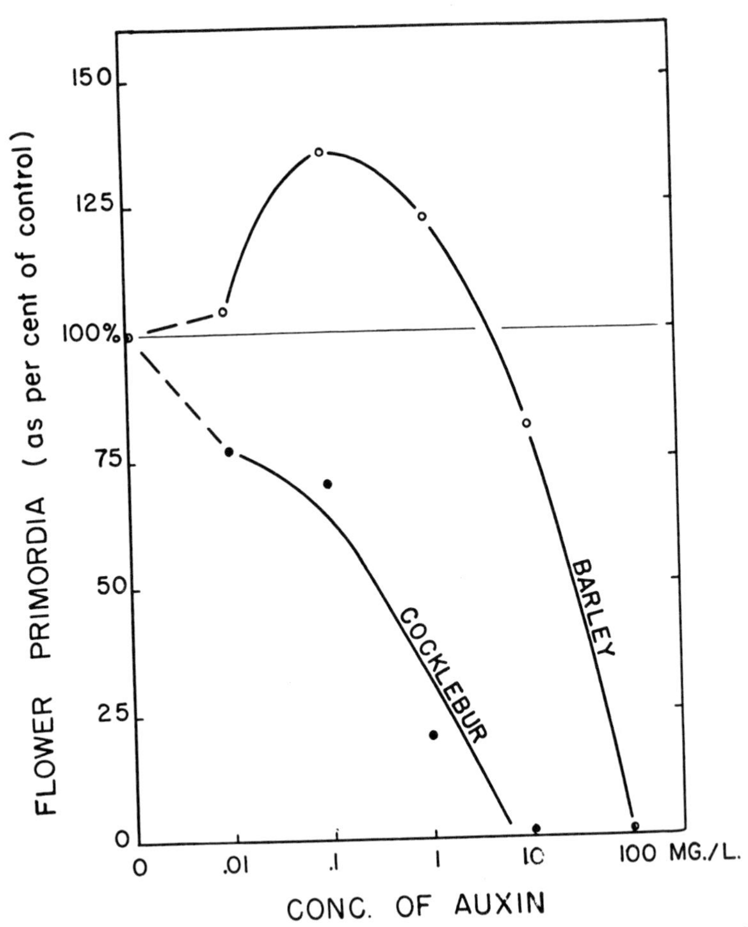

Fig. 106. The quantitative modification of photoperiodically induced floral initiation in Wintex barley and cocklebur by various concentrations of naphthaleneacetic acid (Klein, 1951).

inhibitory effects may be especially pronounced. In fact flower initiation may be prevented in many species, including species sensitive to photoperiodism or to vernalization and indeterminate species (Obsil, 1939; Leopold and Thimann, 1949; Bonner and Thurlow, 1949; Leopold and Guernsey, 1953). In addition, some compounds which antagonize auxin can have the reverse effect, and quantitatively increase flowering in many of the same species (Zimmerman and Hitchcock, 1942; Galston, 1947), or relieve the inhibitory effects of applied auxins (Bonner and Thurlow, 1949).

The quantitative effects of auxins on flower initiation are not always inhibitory, for, as already mentioned, auxin applications can promote initiation of some species as well. These promotive effects appear to be most readily obtained with species in which flower initiation is photoperiodically induced by long days (Leopold and Thimann, 1949; Claes, 1952; Liverman and Lang, 1953), although short-day and indeterminate species may also be promoted by auxin after experiencing conditions of low temperatures (Leopold and Guernsey, 1953). At relatively high concentrations, auxins have been found to inhibit flowering of all species tested.

The comparative effects of auxin applications to the foliage of a species which is promoted and a species which is only inhibited are shown in figure 106.

The effects upon flowering of agents which antagonize auxin have been studied in some detail, indicating that different agents of this category may have very divergent effects. TIBA (2,3,5-triiodobenzoic acid, an auxin synergist) was the first such compound found to alter flowering (Zimmerman and Hitchcock, 1942). Increased flowering has been obtained with this compound in each of the different photoperiodic classes of plants. Both TIBA and DCA (2,4-dichloroanisole, an anti-auxin) have been found to increase flower development in cocklebur, and in fact the latter compound can actually overcome the inhibitory effects of small quantities of auxin applied during photoinduction of cocklebur (Bonner and Thurlow, 1949; Bonner, 1949). Maleic hydrazide is another compound which can generally alter flowering, but in contrast to TIBA and DCA this material generally inhibits flowering. Since the first report of flowering inhibition by maleic hydrazide (Naylor, 1950), it has been found to *inhibit* flowering in each of the photoperiodic classes. It has been suggested that the inhibiting effect of maleic hydrazide on flowering may be a result of growth inhibition rather than a direct effect upon the flowering stimulus (Klein and Leopold, 1953).

Although the properties of auxins and auxin antagonists in

modifying floral initiation have been fairly well worked out, the applicability of the information to agricultural crops has been very limited. Attempts to inhibit flowering of some field crops by foliar auxin application have damaged the crops without producing a control of flowering (Rice, 1950). While some control of celery flowering has been obtained with auxin, the effects were inconsistent (Wittwer *et al,* 1947; Clark and Wittwer, 1949). Evidence of a more complete control with maleic hydrazide has been indicated (Wittwer *et al,* 1954). An effective inhibition of bolting of sugar beets with auxin has been reported (Price *et al,* 1950).

Curiously enough, auxins not only can alter the number of flowers, but they can also alter the sex of flowers. Laibach and Kribben (1950) have reported that auxin treatment of gherkin flowers caused an increase in the number of female flowers and reduction of male flowers. A differential sensitivity of male and female flowers to growth regulators has led to the development of sprays to cause the abortion of male inflorescences. For example, Naylor (1950) and Moore (1950) have successfully used maleic hydrazide to induce male sterility in corn plants, suggesting that the chemical treatment could substitute for detasseling in the production of hybrid corn seed. The technique has been extended to some cucurbits and tomato (Rehm, 1952).

A promotion of flowering by auxin treatment has been reported by Shigeura (1948) for the litchi tree. This crop is limited in productivity in Hawaii by irregular flowering, a situation which may be alleviated somewhat by auxin sprays.

SEED TREATMENT WITH AUXIN

Following the reports by Cholodny (1936) and Thimann and Lane (1938) that short-term auxin treatments of seeds could produce increases in earliness and vigor of grains in a manner suggestive of vernalization (see figure 52, p. 115), many attempts were made to utilize such a treatment to increase earliness of crop plants. Results of such experiments have not generally been promising. A few laboratories reported gains in flowering (Stier and DuBuy, 1938; Borgström, 1939; Tang and Loo, 1940), but the great majority of such attempts found no consistent beneficial effect (e.g. Barton, 1940; Stewart and Hamner, 1942). More recently it has been found that differences in temperature experience of soybean seeds following the auxin treatment can result in opposite flowering responses to the treatment. This effect of temperature can be seen in figure 107. The application of auxins to seeds followed by a period of low temperature incubation can sometimes produce a strong gain in early flowering. Such gains are measurable as greater numbers of flowers and the differentiation of the first flower at a morphologically earlier stage. The large gains in numbers of flowers and in earliness following auxin and low temperature treatments are consistently obtained in winter greenhouse conditions, but not always in summer field conditions of optimum sunlight and temperature. Some compounds which are not auxins, produce the same effect, and it appears to be related to some physiological process which is dependent upon carbon dioxide, presumably a non-photosynthetic fixation process (Leopold and Guernsey, 1954).

The method by which these treatments are applied has been worked out primarily by using naphthaleneacetic acid. Soaking seeds for twenty-four hours in solutions of from 0.01 to 1 mg./l. produces gains in earliness if followed by temperatures of 3 to 10° C. In Alaska pea the low temperature incubations may be terminated in four days, whereas in the tomato, the low temperature incubation must proceed for about two weeks (Guernsey and Leopold, unpublished). A wide

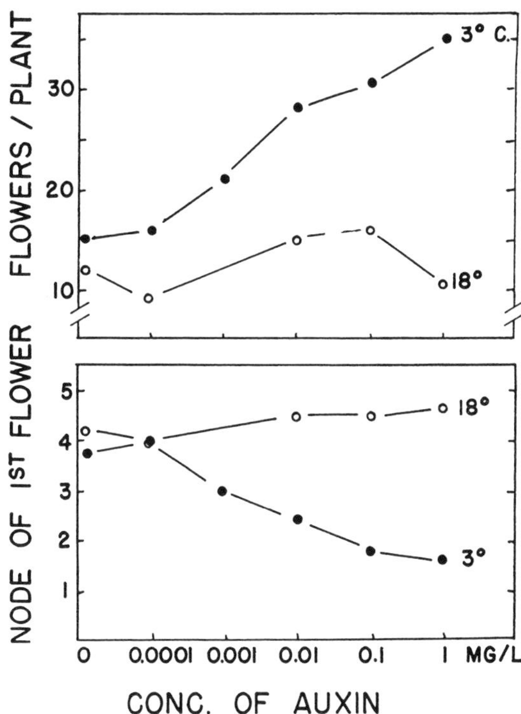

Fig. 107. The modification of flowering of Biloxi soybean by the treatment of seed with auxin (naphthaleneacetic acid) followed by a two-week incubation at 3° or 18° C (Leopold and Guernsey, 1953).

variety of species has been tested and found to respond to such treatment (Leopold and Guernsey, 1953). Many other methods and the results obtained have been carefully reviewed by Kruyt (1954).

Field experiments using auxin and low temperature treatments have yielded large increases in pea and tomato crops, though the gains may not be consistent from year to year (Leopold *et al,* 1953).

In conclusion, the use of auxins to modify flowering, either by spray treatments or by seed treatments, is not yet sufficiently well understood for field use. Appropriate advances in physiological understanding of the role of auxin in flower initiation may ultimately make such auxin treatments practicable.

■ CHAPTER XV

Dormancy and Storage

Dormancy, storage, and ripening of plant materials are essentially expressions of growth and respiratory phenomena. In view of the powerful influence of auxins upon both growth and respiration, it is not surprising that auxins should be able to exert considerable influence upon dormancy and storage characteristics of plant crops. The first demonstration of the possibility of using auxins in controlling dormancy was made by Guthrie (1939), who effectively prevented the sprouting of potatoes in storage by application of naphthaleneacetic acid. Making use of the same principle, Winkelpleck (1937) reported some success in delaying bud growth in woody plants by auxin treatment. The possibility of improving the storage quality of citrus crops with auxin sprays was first demonstrated by Stewart (1949). This last effect of auxins is essentially an indirect one, since the auxin apparently acts more to limit the activity of pathogens on the fruit than to alter the fruit *per se.*

CONTROL OF DORMANCY

For many decades empirical research has sought for chemicals and types of treatments to break dormancy or induce dormancy in stored agricultural products. A good many treatments have been found which can alter dormancy, but only in the last few years has there begun to evolve the semblance of a physiological understanding of dormancy and how it can intelligently be controlled.

The Physiological Basis for Dormancy

In discussing the rather large question of the physiological basis of dormancy, attention will here be focused only upon dormancy in relation to the biochemical environment of meristems. In many instances, particularly in seeds, dormancy may be caused by mechanical factors, especially in the seed coat, but these are not to be considered here.

For many years it has been known that auxins can promote bud growth, and that more generally they inhibit bud growth—particularly through the phenomenon spoken of as apical dominance. The dualism of the effects of auxin on bud growth has been clearly pointed out by Thimann (1937) (see figure 46, p. 95). The response of buds to auxins is essentially like the response of stems, but with the optimum concentration much lower. A specific case showing the dual action of auxin on bud growth is seen in the data of Skoog (1939), given in figure 108. Small amounts of auxin promoted bud growth, whereas larger amounts inhibited or entirely prevented it.

At about the same time, Guthrie (1939) discovered that the treatment of potato tubers with auxins could prolong dormancy in stored tubers. Sample data showing the quantitative inhibitory effects are given in figure 109. This experiment was carried out with the methyl ester of naphthaleneacetic acid placed on paper shreds which were scattered among the tubers. It is interesting to note that at lower temperatures (10° C) higher concentrations of the auxin were necessary to control sprouting. Also it is of particular interest to notice that even in this first report Guthrie observed that under some circumstances, not then clearly defined, auxin treatment could actually stimulate sprouting of potatoes. This stimulation is seen in the data for tubers held at 22° F in figure 109. In some of the experiments

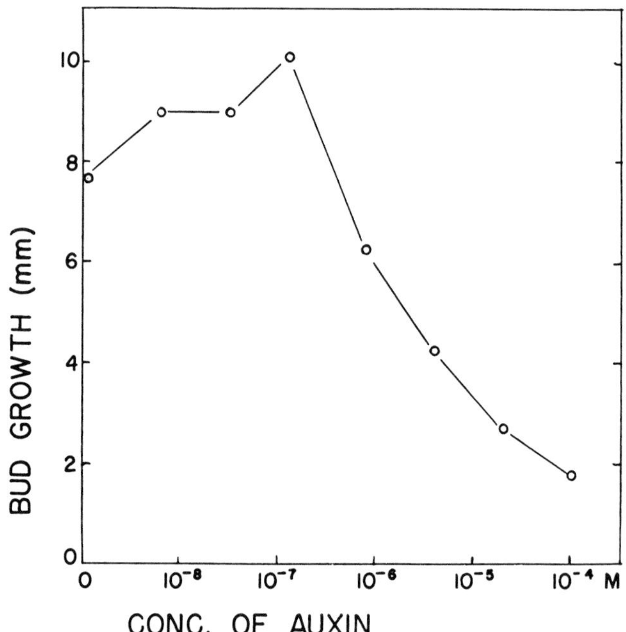

Fig. 108. The effects of various concentrations of auxin (indoleacetic acid) on the growth of pea buds in excised culture (Skoog, 1939)

reported by Guthrie, 2 mg. of the auxin gave four-fold increases in the number of sprouts over the control tubers. Perhaps one can say that the effects of auxin on dormancy as on bud growth may be either promotive or inhibitory; that is, they may encourage the breaking of dormancy or they may accentuate dormancy.

Although suggestions have been made that auxins may be actually responsible for dormancy in a manner similar to their action in apical dominance (Michener, 1942), more recent evidence now indicates that this is very improbable. Dormant tubers and buds generally lack auxin or contain only very small amounts, surely too little to inhibit bud growth. In many cases measurable amounts of diffusible auxin appear in the buds only after dormancy has passed. This has been shown for potatoes (Guthrie, 1939), some tree species (Bennett and Skoog, 1938), and in other instances cited in chapter III. Careful separation of auxins from growth inhibitors has led Hemberg (1949, 1952, 1954) to conclude that as the potato emerges from dormancy there are either no changes in auxin content or the auxin content may rise somewhat. His evidence is directly opposed to the concept that auxins are immediately responsible for dormancy.

A great many inhibitors of germination and growth have been found to be present in various plant parts. The very wide distribution

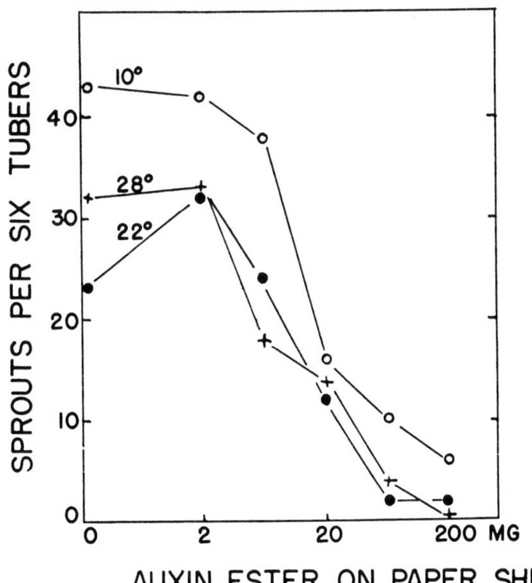

Fig. 109. The effect of methyl ester of naphthaleneacetic acid on sprouting of potato tubers in storage at three temperatures (Guthrie, 1939).

of such inhibitors has been ably reviewed by Evanari (1949). The specific demonstration that growth inhibitors are directly involved in dormancy has been made only recently by Hemberg (1949). He has found that dormant potatoes and dormant tree buds contain substances which are strong inhibitors of growth, as analyzed in the *Avena* test. Furthermore these inhibitors disappear from the plant as dormancy is broken either naturally or artificially. The presence of inhibitors of growth in dormant ash buds collected in October can be seen in figure 110. In February as the bud emerges from the dormant condition, the inhibitors disappear. The same situation has been found to exist in potato tubers (Hemberg, 1952). Furthermore, chemical treatments which break dormancy likewise cause the disappearance of these growth inhibitors. A striking example of this induced disappearance following ethylene treatment to break dormancy is shown in figure 111. Extracts of peelings from dormant potatoes produced a fairly constant inhibition of *Avena* curvature during the test period, but extracts from ethylene treated potatoes showed a nearly complete disappearance of the inhibition effect in a period of six days after treatment.

Guthrie (1940) has found that the ethylene treatment of potato tubers breaks dormancy and causes the appearance of relatively large amounts of glutathione. Glutathione has been shown by Hemberg (1950) to cause the disappearance of the growth inhibitors associated

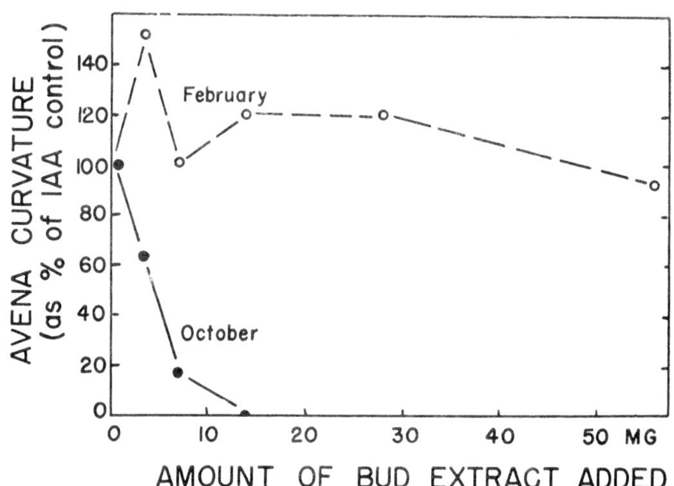

Fig. 110. The inhibitory and non-inhibitory effects of extracts of dormant (October) and non-dormant (February) ash buds as measured by the *Avena* test. The samples were added to a constant amount of indoleacetic acid (data of Hemberg, 1949).

with dormancy in a manner very much like their disappearance at the end of natural dormancy. Glutathione has been demonstrated in many instances to break dormancy (potatoes, pears, peaches, and oat seeds). These observations linked with the finding that the glutathione content increases as potato tubers emerge from dormancy (Emilsson, 1949), suggest that this compound or related compounds may play a key role in the breaking of dormancy in general.

Judging from all of the information available at present, it appears that dormancy is a result of the presence of acidic inhibitors in the buds or seeds. In the presence of these inhibitors the endogenous auxin is ineffective. As dormancy is lost, glutathione may be formed and an associated disappearance of the inhibitors occurs; the auxin content becomes effective and growth commences.

Recent evidence of Elliott and Leopold (1953) indicates that dormancy in oats may be due to inhibitors which antagonize or form complexes with sulfhydryl-containing enzymes such as the amylases. Apparently by protecting the sulfhydryl enzymes from these inhibitors such substances as glutathione and British Anti-Lewisite (1,2-di-

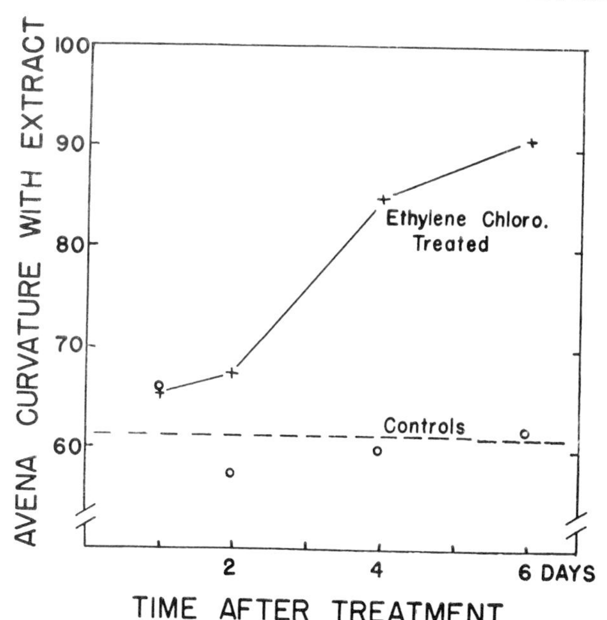

Fig. 111. The inhibition of growth in the *Avena* test by extracts of peelings of dormant potato tubers, and the regression of that inhibition following treatment with ethylene chlorohydrin to break dormancy. Extracts of 80 mg. of peeling were used in each instance and tested with a constant, unspecified quantity of indole-acetic acid. Curvature expressed as a percentage of auxin control (Hemberg, 1949).

thiopropanol) break dormancy. Looking back at the early searches for substances which can break dormancy of seeds and tubers, all the effective materials are either unsaturated hydrocarbons like ethylene—which causes glutathione formation (Guthrie, 1933)—or they are compounds containing divalent sulfur, such as thiocyanates, thiourea, thiosemicarbazide, thioacetamide and a host of others, or glutathione itself (Guthrie, 1940; Miller, 1933; Thompson and Kozar, 1939; Tukey and Carlson, 1945). These materials would be expected to protect sulfhydryl enzymes by simple competitive effects. It may be, then, that the inhibitors of growth which are supposedly responsible for dormancy are inhibitors of sulfhydryl enzymes essential to growth. One cannot help recall at this juncture the evidence discussed in chapter VIII indicating that the stimulation of growth by auxin may be intimately involved with sulfhydryl enzymes or coenzymes.

Although the bulk of evidence now indicates that dormancy is essentially a function not of auxins but of growth inhibitors, it is clear that auxins themselves can exert an effect on the capacity of a potato or a deciduous tree bud to commence growth. The work of Guthrie (1939) has clearly shown that moderately strong dosages of auxins can inhibit sprouting and thus prolong apparent dormancy. It must be remembered however, that low concentrations of these same materials may have stimulatory effects upon sprouting as the primary control of dormancy is removed. This makes the use of auxins for prolonging dormancy a sometimes unpredictable and not completely satisfactory technique.

In recent years an alternative method of prolonging dormancy has been suggested by Wittwer and Sharma (1950) in which a growth inhibitor is used instead of an auxin. These workers have found that maleic hydrazide can effectively prevent sprouting of onions in storage. This technique would seem to be a sounder approach to the control of dormancy from a physiological point of view, since the maleic hydrazide would probably accentuate the natural inhibitor system thought to control dormancy instead of superimposing an auxin inhibition system instead.

Methods of Treatment

Of the various auxins that have been used for prolonging dormancy, the methyl ester of naphthaleneacetic acid has achieved the widest use. In preventing sprouting in potatoes the original recommendations of Guthrie (1939) have been most commonly followed. The potatoes are mixed with paper shreds or with talc containing the esterified auxin at rates such that approximately one gram of auxin is applied per bushel of potatoes. Smith *et al* (1947) have more recently found that auxins applied to the foliage of the plants before harvest will reduce sprouting of root and tuber crops. The methyl ester of naphthaleneacetic acid appears to be effective in this technique. Recent reports indicate that maleic hydrazide can also effectively be used on potatoes, especially as a foliar spray before harvest. The effects of varying concentrations of maleic hydrazide have been reported by Paterson *et al* (1952) as shown in figure 112. It is rather interesting to note that maleic hydrazide, which antagonizes auxin, is more effective in prolonging dormancy at lower temperatures whereas the naphthaleneacetate ester, an auxin, may be less effective at lower temperatures (cf. figures 109 and 112).

Prolonging dormancy in carrots has been done successfully with the methyl ester of naphthaleneacetic acid dusted onto the roots in storage (Dallyn and Smith, 1952) or by spraying auxins or maleic hydrazide on the foliage before harvest (Wittwer and Sharma, 1950).

The effective treatment of onions is made more difficult by the protected position of the growing point inside the onion bulb; con-

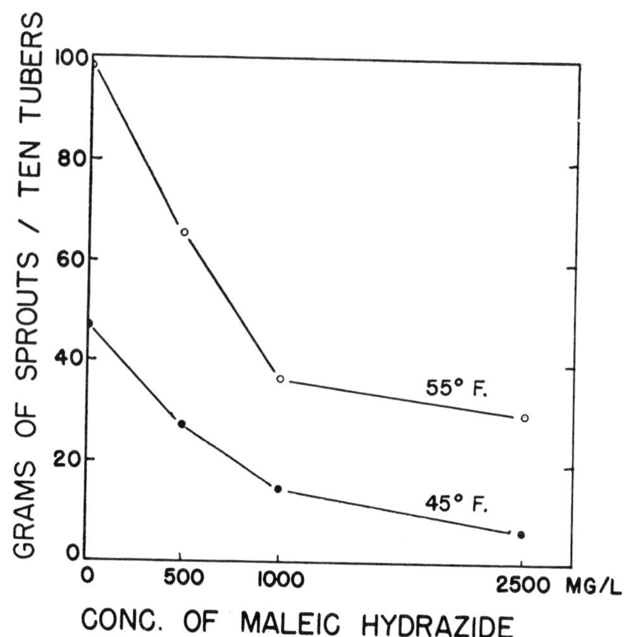

Fig. 112. Effects of foliar sprays of maleic hydrazide on sprouting of potatoes in subsequent storage at two temperatures (Paterson *et al*, 1952).

sequently the only successful treatments have involved foliar applications. Maleic hydrazide has so far given the best results (Wittwer and Sharma, 1950).

Prevention of sprouting of nursery stock of trees and shrubs during storage has been obtained with the methyl ester of naphthaleneacetic acid applied in a wax emulsion (Marth, 1942). The effects of various auxin concentrations can be seen in figure 113. It is interesting to note that at lower storage temperatures the inhibitory effects of this auxin are much reduced and the typical stimulation-inhibition curve for the effects of auxin on bud growth is obtained. These responses are strikingly parallel to the classic type shown in figure 108.

Naphthaleneacetic acid applied as an emulsion, an ester vapor, a spray and a dip treatment has been tested on several types of tree nursery stock (Ostrom, 1945; Way and Maki, 1946). They found that the growth of buds in storage could be reduced in several different types of tree seedlings if the proper concentration of auxin were used. Effective concentrations varied considerably from species to species.

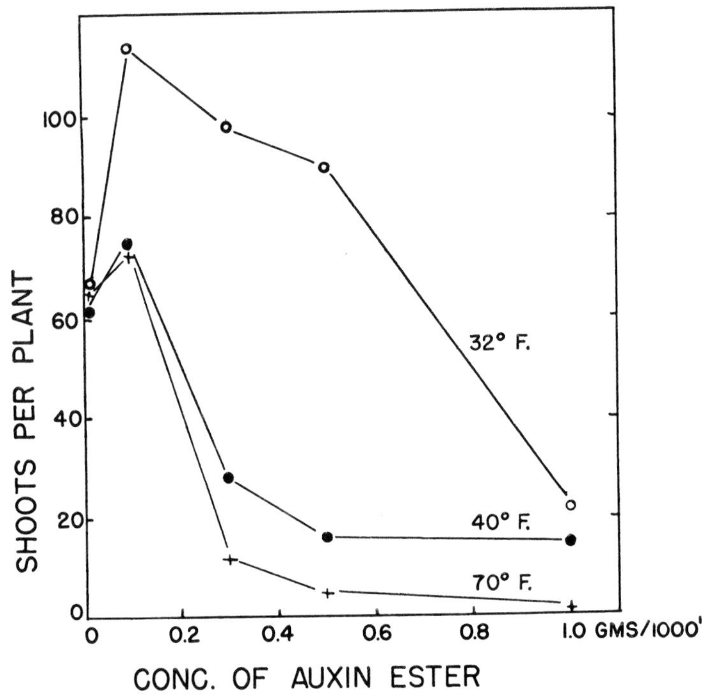

Fig. 113. The effects of brief treatment with the methyl ester of naphthaleneacetic acid on subsequent sprouting of rose bushes in storage at three temperatures (Marth, 1942).

Tentative reports of success with maleic hydrazide to prolong dormancy of woody plants in storage have also been made (Fillmore, 1950).

Attempts to prolong dormancy of fruit trees in the field have generally involved using salts of naphthaleneacetic acid, either during the previous growing season (Hitchcock and Zimmerman, 1943) or shortly before growth would be expected to begin (McCartney, 1948). Although only one auxin has been tested, the results do not appear to be very promising.

Attempts to prolong dormancy of sweet potatoes in storage or of some shrubs and trees have been unsuccessful (Simons and Scott, 1952; McCartney, 1948; Way and Maki, 1946).

Factors in Success

Since buds can be either stimulated or inhibited in growth by auxins, it is not surprising that attempts to use auxins to prevent bud growth are not always effective. From the experimental data which have been accumulated it would seem that two types of difficulties may be involved, one being to achieve the penetration of the auxin to the growing point in sufficient quantities to inhibit bud growth, and the second being to maintain a sufficiently high auxin level over a period of time to sustain that inhibition. Treatment of dormant materials with esterified auxins probably owes its success to the ability of esters to penetrate the buds more readily and to continue penetration over a long period of time. There are many instances in the literature which demonstrate that inhibitory auxin levels maintained for only a short time can actually result in a stimulatory aftereffect. A clear example of this is reported by Skoog (1939). Consequently, if applied auxins are destroyed in the dormant buds, and are not continuously renewed, they may produce stimulatory aftereffects.

Aside from the factors of penetration and maintenance of high auxin levels in the bud, effective prevention of sprouting shows a strong interaction between auxin concentration and temperature. A striking example of this can be seen in figure 113, where sprouting of rose bushes was effectively prevented by the auxins at higher temperatures but the inhibition was largely lost at lower temperatures. The control of sprouting of potatoes does not show as clear a temperature interaction, but there are several instances reported in the literature which suggest less effective control at lower temperatures (for example, see figure 109). As already mentioned, maleic hydrazide seems to be more effective at lower temperatures (Paterson *et al,* 1952).

The importance of penetration of the applied auxin into the

bud is perhaps responsible for the fact that foliar sprays are much more effective than dust treatments of the tubers and roots themselves. Auxins applied to the foliage before the plant dies down are translocated into the storage organs where they can effectively inhibit sprouting in storage. It appears that in general early foliage applications are more effective in controlling sprouting than are late applications, but unfortunately early applications are also more damaging to the plants. The success of such applications in each crop is dependent upon the finding of a time of application which will minimize damage and still give effective sprouting control.

STORAGE QUALITY

Applications of auxins to prevent sprouting of tubers and bulbs can have rather important effects on the quality of the stored product. It has been reported that pre-harvest foliar sprays of auxins on potatoes decrease the specific gravity of the tubers and increase the occurrence of potato scab (Smith *et al,* 1947). The high incidence of scab is apparently associated with the normal scabies pathogen, and somehow the tuber is simply more susceptible to its attack (Wood and Ennis, 1951). Such sprays also lower the amount of reducing sugars in the potato, which is a desirable characteristic. It has been found that tubers from auxin-treated plants are perfectly effective for seed stock the following year (Ellison and Smith, 1948).

The control of sprouting in carrots with auxin treatment of the roots in storage is generally damaging, although the use of methyl ester of naphthaleneacetic acid appeared promising (Dallyn and Smith, 1952). The auxins are very prone to cause callus formation and sprouting of secondary roots from the carrot. Foliar sprays of auxins can sometimes overcome this quality limitation (Wittwer *et al,* 1950).

The effects of maleic hydrazide on storage quality are not as well defined as are the effects of auxins. Potatoes from plants receiving foliar sprays of maleic hydrazide have been found to contain a low sugar content (Paterson *et al,* 1952). Onions treated similarly have shown no change in either carbohydrate content or in soluble nitrogen fractions (Wittwer and Sharma, 1950). The storage quality of beets has been reported to be improved by maleic hydrazide treatment, not through effects on sprouting but rather by prevention of sugar loss during storage (Wittwer and Hansen, 1951).

The effect of maleic hydrazide in improving storage quality of apples which have been treated with auxin to control abscission is discussed in chapter XIII.

Another means by which auxins can alter storage quality is through the inhibition of molds and pathogens. It was reported in 1945 by Stevenson and Mitchell that 2,4-D would selectively inhibit the growth of certain bacteria without inhibiting fungal growth. The selectivity of auxin inhibition of bacteria and molds offers real possibilities for using auxins in the culture of molds in industrial processes where specific strains of mold may be wanted. If the desirable strain is not inhibited by auxin, then auxin may be added to the substrate to inhibit the growth of contaminating molds.

The development of molds on stored stock plants of shrubs and trees is responsible for considerable damage to these materials. Apparently dipping or spraying nursery stock with auxins can greatly retard mold development during storage (Marth, 1942; Way and Maki, 1946).

Mention has been made of the finding by Stewart (1949) that citrus fruits treated with 2,4-D are less susceptible to Black Button, a rotting of the stem end of the fruits. This type of breakdown of the fruits in storage is due to the development of Alternaria rots and is effectively controlled by pretreatment of the fruits with 500 mg./l. of either 2,4-D or 2,4,5-T (Stewart *et al*, 1952). Curiously enough, not only is the Black Button type of rot prevented but also, in the case of lemons, the auxins appear to retard the yellowing and ripening processes in storage.

■ CHAPTER XVI

Herbicides

The first recognition of selective herbicidal properties of auxins was made in England by Slade *et al* (1945). These workers observed that naphthaleneacetic acid killed Yellow Charlock in a stand of oats without injuring the oats. The first experiment was carried out in 1940 and was followed by a long series of researches under the auspices of the Agricultural Research Council and under military secrecy. For security reasons, their work was not published until 1945. Quite independently, Kraus in this country began investigating herbicidal qualities of auxin in the fall of 1941. This work likewise was carried on under military secrecy during the war, in the course of which it was found again that auxins were not only herbicides, but they were also selective in their action (Kraus and Mitchell, 1947). Two other research teams participated in the work in England, Nutman *et al* (1945), and Blackman (1945).

The first work was done with naphthaleneacetic acid, but while the early experiments were being carried out Zimmerman and Hitchcock (1942) published the finding that some chlorinated phenoxyacetic acids were much more powerful auxins and this led to the discovery that such compounds were much more powerful selective herbicides as well.

The use of auxins as herbicides has four major advantages: 1) the herbicidal action is highly selective and differences in molecular structure of the auxin, species or status of the plant lead to pronounced differences in selectivity; 2) the herbicidal action is not permanent in the soil, and after the passage of a few weeks no toxic residue usually remains; 3) auxins exert their effects at extremely low concentrations making their use economical and 4) auxins are nontoxic to animals and humans.

PHYSIOLOGICAL BASIS OF HERBICIDAL ACTION

For auxin materials to be effective in killing plants, the materials must succeed in carrying out three steps. They must first enter the plant, then be translocated through the plant, and finally carry out the toxic reaction. Having discussed these steps in chapter VI, attention here will be centered on the physiological basis for the toxic reaction itself.

Possible Mechanisms of Toxic Action

Once distribution of the auxin through the plant has been obtained, some toxic action at the cellular level occurs. The nature of this action is not yet established. There are five major theories to explain the herbicidal action of auxin and most of these are closely related to the theories of auxin action in growth described in chapter VIII. These theories attempt to ascribe the herbicidal action to respiratory depletion, cellular proliferation, the formation of toxic materials, an activation of phosphate metabolism, and lastly the dissociation or hydrolysis of proteins.

The first of these theories, that the herbicidal effects of auxins are caused by respiratory depletion, was suggested by Mitchell and Brown (1945) who found that 2,4-D applied to morning glory at sub-lethal dosages would cause respiratory increases and a depletion of the carbohydrate reserve of the plant. This action was studied in some detail by Rasmussen (1947) who concluded that the rather large weight losses in dandelion tissue following 2,4-D application would indeed be accounted for by respiratory increases. However, neither the weight loss nor the respiratory changes were proportional to the herbicidal effects observable. The conclusion that the weight loss could not account for the killing action was independently reached by Taylor (1947).

The possibility that cellular proliferation induced by auxins may be responsible for their herbicidal action was pointed out by Struckmeyer (1951). She suggested that the selectivity of auxins against dicotyledonous plants might be accounted for on the basis that potential cambial layers are abundant in the dicotyledonous stem and are generally in a ring-like pattern which passes close to each group of phloem cells in the stem. Presumably proliferation of these weakly differentiated cells would destroy the phloem system of the stem. Eames (1950) has demonstrated that this phloem destruction actually takes place after auxin application. Struckmeyer points out that in contrast to the dicot, the less sensitive monocotyledonous stem does not have potential cambial layers or weakly differentiated cells adjacent to the phloem, which may account in part for the fact that most monocots are less sensitive to auxin herbicides.

Van Overbeek *et al* (1951) suggested that herbicidal killing may be due to the production of toxic substances through abnormal metabolism induced by the presence of large amounts of auxin. They suggested that such toxic substances might be either lactone compounds or perhaps amino acids or other protein fragments. It is well known that subsequent to 2,4-D application, large quantities of amino acids do accumulate in some plant parts (Sell *et al,* 1949). Accumulations of a toxic lactone compound, scopoletin, have also been observed to occur following 2,4-D application in some susceptible plants (Fults and Johnson, 1950).

Another suggestion by Bonner and Bandurski (1952) was that herbicidal action may be a result of the activation of phosphatase systems. Such an activation might lead to the destructive hydrolysis of high-energy phosphate bonds, resulting in a considerable increase in catabolic activity which could essentially prevent growth or anabolism in the cell. Some evidence that auxins and some related compounds may alter high-energy phosphate systems was discussed in chapter VIII. Supporting evidence for such a mode of action comes from the work of Loustalot *et al* (1953) indicating that large amounts of inorganic phosphate appeared in bean plants as the lethal action of 2,4-D set in. Such increases are just what one might expect if phosphatase activity were involved in the herbicidal function.

It has been suggested by Northen (1942) that the essential action of auxins may be an hydrolysis of protein materials in the cell. Auxins generally bring about a decrease in the viscosity of cell cytoplasm which may be a reflection of protein hydrolysis. High concentrations of auxin may cause extreme hydrolysis and retard or destroy essential enzymatic activities. It may be that the increases in amino acids observed by Sell *et al* (1949) are a consequence of such an hydrolytic action.

Another suggestion about the possible mechanism of herbicidal action of auxins is the suggestion by Rhodes *et al* (1950) that auxins may kill by interference with potassium metabolism. The initial observations which led to this suggestion are cited in figure 62 (p. 135).

It seems entirely possible that the herbicidal action of auxin is a combination of several of these functions or other functions yet to be discovered, and in different situations any one of them may be responsible for the herbicidal effect. Thus some plants may finally succumb as a result of destruction of the phloem, others from the accumulation of toxic materials or depletion of mobile phosphate energy or to combinations of any of these. The reader will recognize, however, that no satisfactory explanation of auxin toxicity has yet been proposed and supported by convincing experimental evidence.

FACTORS IN SUSCEPTIBILITY

Stage of Development

Perhaps the most outstanding factor which influences the susceptibility of plants to auxin herbicides is the stage of development of the plant at the time of treatment. Judging from the work on susceptibility by Blackman's group (summarized by Blackman, 1950) and the work in America pioneered by Shaw and Willard (1949), it would appear that susceptibility of grains follows a consistent general pattern during the various stages of growth. Such a pattern is presented in a diagrammatic fashion in figure 114. There is a very low degree of susceptibility in the ungerminated seed. Upon germination and the commencement of growth, sensitivity to auxins increases at once and an extremely high sensitivity is maintained through the early stages of seedling growth. This high degree of sensitivity falls off in the case of corn at the 6- to 8-leaf stage (Rodgers, 1952), in the case of oats, wheat and barley at the time the plants are five inches in height and have two leaves (Olson *et al,* 1951). During the tillering stages of wheat and barley, susceptibility remains low. Upon flower initiation susceptibility becomes rather high again and remains so until the stages of rapid growth associated with bolting have passed. After heading the susceptibility again drops off.

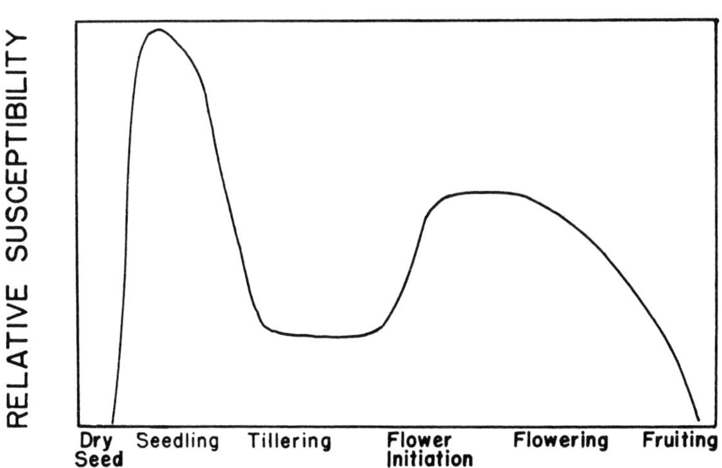

Fig. 114. A schematic diagram of changes in relative susceptibility of grains to auxin herbicides applied at various stages of development.

In the generalized graph for grains given here the ordinate might be an expression of the percentage of plants killed with a given dosage of an herbicide, or it might be an expression of the degree of crop injury or the reduction in yield following the application of the herbicide at a low concentration. In several instances small gains have actually been reported to follow applications of weak auxins during the period of low sensitivity prior to flowering (Shaw and Willard, 1949).

A generalization seems much more difficult in the case of dicotyledonous plants. A remarkable degree of variation in susceptibility with stage of development is pointed out by Blackman (1950). He has found that the susceptibility of pepperwort and dandelion can vary in strikingly heterogeneous patterns depending on the growth regulator used. For example, as the growing season progresses pepperwort becomes less and less susceptible to MCPA (2-methyl-4-chlorophenoxyacetic acid). Yet it shows an increasing susceptibility to 2,4-D until flowering time followed then by decreased susceptibility. The dandelion shows only small changes in susceptibility to MCPA during the growing season, whereas its susceptibility to 2,4-D increases progressively from April to October. We may conclude then from Blackman's work that susceptibility in dicotyledonous weeds may change in any of several different possible fashions during successive stages of development.

It appears to be safe to say that almost all plants undergo a period of maximum susceptibility in the early seedling stages, and of low susceptibility after fruiting has occurred. This was first pointed out by Lee and Bewick (1947). The susceptibility of a plant between early seedling stage and fruiting varies with the species and the herbicide used, but in general it would seem that many plants show a trend toward decreased sensitivity as the plant grows older.

In a study of changes in sensitivity of excised epidermal tissues taken from plants at various stages of development, Biebl (1953) found that tissues from seedlings were generally more susceptible to 2,4-D than similar tissues from older plants. No changes in susceptibility were found in later stages, suggesting that susceptible stages other than the first one were due to morphological differences within the plant rather than to overall differences common to all tissues.

Growth Rate

Another factor in susceptibility is the growth rate of the plant. In discussing the anatomical effects of auxin applications in chapter V, it was pointed out that cells which are young and weakly differentiated are much the most responsive to auxin applications. The changes in susceptibility of the plant from one stage of development to another may be due in large part to differences in growth rate and the associated proportion of young, weakly differentiated tissues in the plant. Thus seedlings, which are almost universally highly susceptible, are made up primarily of meristematic and young expanding tissues with a rapid growth rate. When flowering has been completed the plant is generally quite resistant to auxins and is primarily made up of mature, well differentiated tissues in a static condition with respect to growth.

Changes in growth rate forced upon the plant by environmental factors may greatly alter the susceptibility to auxin herbicides. Derscheid (1952) has pointed out that differences in susceptibility in some instances may be more accurately correlated with growth rate than with stage of development. It has commonly been observed that plants experiencing a condition of very low moisture availability are much less susceptible to auxin herbicides than plants with normal moisture and experiencing normal growth (Erickson and Gault, 1950). It has also been observed in several instances that plants suffering from nutrient deficiencies are likewise less susceptible than normal plants (Freiberg and Clark, 1952). These and other factors in the environment which alter growth rate may likewise alter susceptibility to herbicides.

Environmental Factors

The effects of various environmental factors on auxin effectiveness have been discussed in chapter VI, bringing out the particular importance of light, temperature and nutritive status of the plant.

Morphological Factors

A fourth category of factors of susceptibility relates to the morphology of the plant. The greater susceptibility of dicots compared to monocots has been asserted to be partly attributable to the fact that the buds of dicots are in a more exposed position morphologically and hence more easily damaged by the spray. Roberts and Blackman (1950) have pointed out that leaf shape can have a considerable influence on susceptibility, particularly with respect to leaves which are cupshaped at the base permitting accumulation of the auxin solution over the tender buds at the axils of the leaves. Experiments with several varieties of peas are cited in support of this suggestion. This has been at least partly discredited by Willard (1947) who states that he has filled the cup-like leaf sheaths around the apical bud of a corn plant with a solution of 2,4-D and failed to get any more severe response than if he simply sprayed the auxin on the foliage.

The wettability of the leaf is another morphological factor which can alter susceptibility. Fogg (1947) has observed that diurnal changes occur in the wettability of the leaves of *Sinapsis arvensis* and has associated these changes with the water content of the leaves. As leaves dry out they are less readily wet by a spray. He also pointed out that the mechanical nature of the leaf surface has a strong influence on the resulting droplet size, a factor which has considerable influence on toxicity of 2,4-D sprays. Large droplets are more effective than small ones (Loomis, 1949). Pubescence of leaves in some cases can increase spray retention from 10 to 100 per cent, and even the angle of orientation of the leaves can alter spray retention considerably (Ennis *et al,* 1952).

Genetic Factors

There are genetic differences in susceptibility characteristics of various species and varieties. Willard (1947) has reported that an inbred line of corn has been found which is much more sensitive to 2,4-D than other corn varieties. Such an inherent difference in sensitivity even in closely related species and varieties has been reported for many crop plants, especially among the grains. These differences in response, presumably at the cellular level, remind one of the differences between more and less susceptible species with respect to respiratory responses reported by Kelly and Avery (1949), the differences in potassium metabolism reported by Rhodes *et al* (1950), and the differences in susceptibility of enzyme preparations to 2,4-D inhibition as reported by Kvamme *et al* (1949).

FACTORS IN SELECTIVITY

Some suggestions have been made concerning the physiological mechanism of selective herbicidal action. Several of these have been mentioned above in the discussion of the possible mechanisms of toxic action. An interesting specific suggestion has been made by Brian and Rideal (1952), who studied the adsorption of MCPA to a variety of materials spread as monolayers on a Langmuir trough. They found that the auxin anion is readily adsorbed onto materials rich in amines and ketones, and that such adsorptive materials are relatively abundant in wheat which is a resistant species as compared with tomato and cress which are highly susceptible species. The inference is drawn that the selective action of auxin herbicides may be related to the amount of exogenous auxin which is adsorbed on such proteins or lipoproteins in the plants. Thus the relative resistance of wheat may be owing to the strongly adsorptive action of such materials toward auxin. Auxin molecules which are adsorbed in this manner would be unavailable for participation in metabolic events.

Gallup and Gustafson (1952) have observed that the absorption and translocation of a radioactive analogue of 2,4-D by grass species tended to be less than that by the broadleafed species tested. It was suggested that differences in absorption and translocation could well contribute to selectivity of auxin herbicides.

In approaching the question of selectivity one must recognize that all plants have a potential susceptibility to 2,4-D. That is, if a sufficient amount of the auxin is introduced into the plant death will follow. Selectivity is an expression of *differences* between plants in the capacity of an auxin preparation to enter, be translocated, or finally to express toxicity at the cellular level. Thus selectivity may be owing to differences in the ability of an herbicide to *enter* as in the case of peas compared with mustard. A salt of MCPA can evidently enter the mustard foliage more readily than the more waxy foliage of the pea. The ester derivatives of the same herbicide apparently enter the foliage of either plant equally well (Buchholtz, 1952), and consequently the salt of MCPA is selective between the plants and the ester is not. In other cases selectivity may be due to differences in *translocation,* as in the case of perennial species like Johnson grass

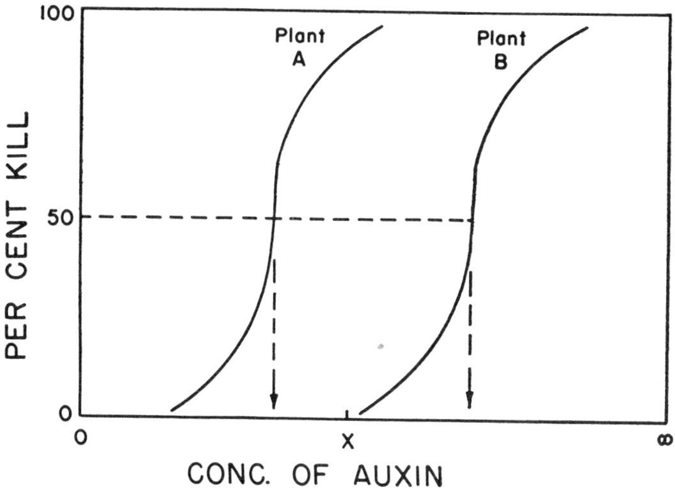

Fig. 115. Theoretical mortality curves for two different plant species sprayed with different concentrations of an herbicidal auxin. Arrows indicate relative concentrations required to kill 50 per cent of the plants of each species (modified from Woodford, 1950).

which apparently translocate insufficient amounts of auxin to kill the roots, whereas annual grasses such as foxtail apparently translocate amounts sufficient for lethal action much more readily. Selectivity may be the expression, finally, of inherent differences in the *toxicity* of the auxin at the cellular level as is the case of 2,4-D on oats and peas. Thus, excised tissues of oats are known to have much less metabolic susceptibility to a given level of 2,4-D than have comparable tissues of peas (Kelly and Avery, 1949), and the selectivity between these species may be accounted for in that way.

Selectivity, then, is an expression of differences in susceptibility between plants. It may be accountable as an expression of any of the factors altering susceptibility just enumerated. Thus differences in stage of development, growth rate, morphology or metabolic susceptibility of two plants can make possible a selective action of auxin herbicides.

Woodford (1950) has pointed out that, theoretically, mortality can be related schematically to auxin concentration in the manner shown in figure 115. In his original discussion he was comparing mortality curves between two herbicides, but the same plan can be modified to compare mortality curves between two species. Thus one would find that plant *A* would show a 50 per cent mortality at a lower concentration of a given auxin than plant *B*. Both will succumb if a sufficiently high concentration is given. By applying the concentration indicated in the figure as concentration *X* it is possible to kill selectively plant *A* without destroying any of plant *B*. This difference in sensitivity, whatever is the cause, makes selective killing possible.

In general it is not considered to be sufficient to kill 50 per cent of the weeds, but Woodford suggests that the concentration to kill 90 per cent of the weeds may be of greater value. As indicated in the curve, the final destruction of 100 per cent of the plants may require a much higher concentration than that required for a 90 per cent kill, hence the latter figure is probably more valuable and more economically utilized. The tenacity of the last 10 per cent of the weed population is evident in the data of van Overbeek and Velez (1946), which indicate that the amount of 2,4-D required for 100 per cent kill was as much as half again greater than the amount for 90 per cent kill.

SELECTION OF AUXINS

The most potent herbicidal materials among auxins appear to be 2,4-D, 2,4,5-T (2,4,5-trichlorophenoxyacetic acid), and MCPA (2-methyl,4-chlorophenoxyacetic acid).

2,4-D (2,4-dichlorophenoxyacetic acid: OCH_2COOH, Cl, Cl) — 2,4,5-T (OCH_2COOH, Cl, Cl, Cl) — MCPA (OCH_2COOH, CH_3, Cl)

The relative effectiveness of different derivatives of auxins is altered by the age of the plant. For example, it has been observed that esters and salts are essentially equally effective at the seedling stage, but as the plants become older the esters become more and more effective in comparison with the salts (Lee and Bewick, 1947). This is consonant with the generalization of Crafts (1948) that lipoidal or non-polar materials enter the plant more readily when the cuticular layers of the epidermis have matured, for these cuticular layers themselves are primarily made up of lipoidal, non-polar materials.

Comparison of different salts of auxins indicates that salts of low solubility are relatively less effective when applied to plants and conversely that those of high solubility are more effective. Some comparisons are shown in figure 116. Uniform quantities of the various salts

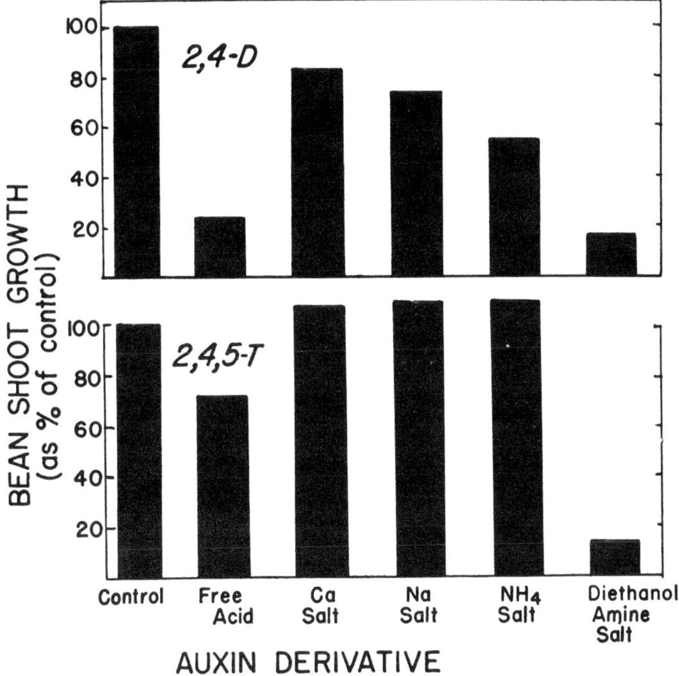

Fig. 116. Relative effectiveness of various salts of 2,4-dichlorophenoxyacetic acid and 2,4,5-trichlorophenoxyacetic acid in inhibiting bean shoot growth. All applications were of 6 micrograms of acid equivalent per plant (Mullison, 1951).

of 2,4-D and 2,4,5-T were applied to bean plants, and the resulting inhibition effects were measured. The strongest effects were obtained with the free acids and with the diethanolamine salts. The calcium salt is the least soluble of the ones tested, and produced the least effects on growth. The diethanolamine salt has been recommended as a derivative showing high solubility and high activity (McNew and Hoffman, 1948), and the di- and triethanolamine salts have subsequently become among the most widely used derivatives for aqueous formulations of 2,4-D.

Because of their more effective penetration, ester derivatives of auxin show greater contact toxicity to plants, although their translocation within the plant is considered to be poorer than that of the acids or salts (Robbins *et al,* 1952, p. 195). The possible difference in translocation between salts and esters was not confirmed by Hauser and Young (1952), undoubtedly because they injected the auxin into the transpiration stream.

The volatility of different esters is approximately inversely proportional to the size of the alcoholic part of the ester as shown in

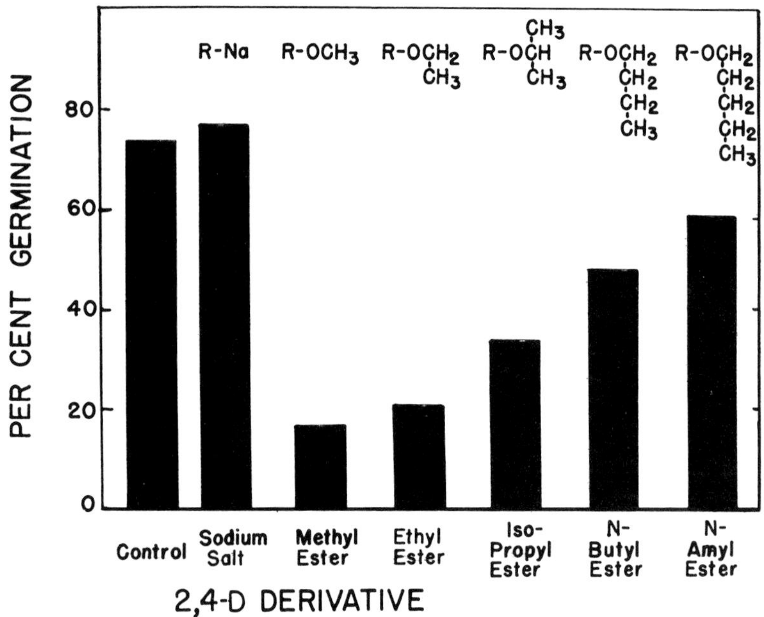

Fig. 117. Effectiveness of vapors of various esters of 2,4-dichlorophenoxyacetic acid in inhibiting germination of seeds of ten common species (tomato, bean, corn, cucumber, rye, wheat, turnip, cotton, pea, and squash averaged together) showing greatest volatility effect of the smallest ester derivatives (calculated from Mullison and Hummer, 1949).

the data given in figure 117. It is evident that the inhibition of germination of seeds when suspended over various esters of 2,4-D is much the greatest when the alcoholic group is small as in the methyl ester, indicating the greatest volatility for the small esters. Of course high volatility is a treacherous characteristic for an herbicide because of the danger of damaging plants away from the treated area. Although the volatility decreases as the size of the alcoholic group is increased, the toxicity is apparently unchanged (Robbins *et al,* 1952, p. 149). Esters with intermediate-sized alcohols such as the isopropyl derivative have achieved most widespread use in crops, and esters with much larger alcohol groups—such as butoxy-ethanol esters—are used generally for killing woody species. In the spraying of woody plants along roadsides or railroad right-of-ways, it is very important to insure against volatility which may result in damage to neighboring fields. The use of esters results in a strong reduction of selectivity (Alex *et al,* 1950) as we have already pointed out in another connection.

Besides the derivatives of the phenoxyacetic acids, quite another type of material has come into use as an herbicide, namely the phenoxyethyl acids. The commonest of these is 2,4-dichlorophenoxyethylsulfate (King *et al,* 1950). This material is not an auxin, nor does it have herbicidal activity. However, upon being applied to the soil it is converted into 2,4-D either by microbial action (Audus, 1952) or simply by acid hydrolysis (Vlitos, 1952). The 2,4-D thus formed can then be taken up by plants and exert the herbicidal effect. A delay in effect of five to fifteen days is caused by the necessity for conversion into 2,4-D. Similar effects are obtained for 2,4-dichlorophenoxyethylbenzoate. These materials are advantageous in that relatively large amounts can be applied to fields without foliar damage to the crop, and upon conversion into 2,4-D they can effectively control the germinating weeds at the surface of the soil.

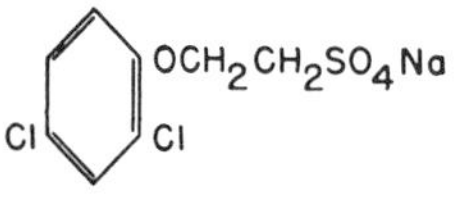

$OCH_2CH_2SO_4Na$ Cl Cl

Sodium
2,4-dichlorophenoxyethyl
sulfate

$OCH_2CH_2CH_2CH_2CH_2CH_2CH_2CH_3$ Cl Cl

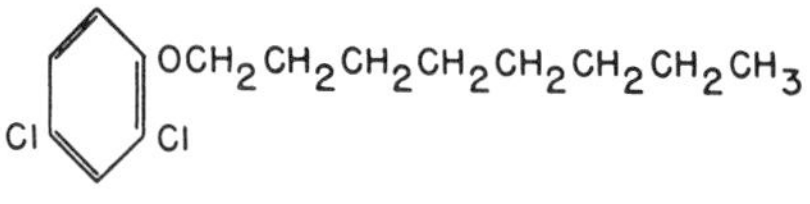

2,4-dichlorophenyl
octanoic ether

Another group of herbicidal compounds which probably act through auxin mechanisms are the chlorinated benzoic acids. Some compounds in this group with three chlorine substituents are auxins, as described in chapter VII. They produce leaf distortions and epinasty in the manner common to most auxins (Zimmerman and Hitchcock,

1951). The tetra- and penta-chloro derivatives are apparently not auxins, but they are effective herbicidal materials. They bring about a stasis of growth without much leaf distortion (Miller, 1952). One of the most outstanding characteristics of the benzoic acid herbicides is their extensive persistence, both in plants and in soils. Whereas 2,4-D persists in bean plants only long enough to cause extreme distortion to 3 or 4 leaves, the substituted benzoic acids persist long enough to distort up to 11 leaves (Minarik *et al,* 1951). Field observations similarly indicate much longer persistence in soils.

In 1953 it was reported that halogenated phenyl alkyl ethers produce strong distortion effects on plants after a delay in time, and these compounds show some promise as herbicides (McLane *et al,* 1953). Structurally these materials are comparable to 2,4-D except that they have long straight side-chains with no acid group at the end. Only even-numbered carbon side-chains are active, and the side-chain must be from eight to twelve carbon units in length for herbicidal activity. This strongly suggests that the alkyl ethers are metabolized down to 2,4-D, for biological ω-oxidation of straight-chain hydrocarbons to produce a terminal carboxyl is known to be limited to those of eight to twelve carbon lengths, and only the even numbered side-chains would result in an acetic acid final derivative, because fatty acids are broken down in two-carbon fragments.

Solvents

For approximation of herbicidal amounts and concentrations it is convenient to know that when a solution is applied at the rate of 100 gallons per acre ("to runoff"), a concentration of 1000 mg./l. will furnish an application of almost exactly one pound per acre. When concentrate sprays are applied at the rate of five gallons per acre, a concentration of 20,000 mg./l. (2%) will result in an application of one pound per acre.

The use of various solvent carriers has been discussed in chapter IX. The use of polyalkylene glycols (Carbowax) to increase solubility and effectiveness of 2,4-D originated with some of the early herbicidal auxin studies (Mitchell and Hamner, 1944). Detergents in general similarly increase herbicidal effectiveness (Staniforth and Loomis, 1948), undoubtedly by facilitating entry of auxin into the plant in the manner described in chapter VI. The use of oil carriers for esters is common practice and light oils have been consistently more effective than heavy oils (Kraus and Mitchell, 1947). The use of oil or diesel fuel carriers permits the use of very high concentrations of auxin such as the 44% 2,4-D commonly used in airplane applications.

Foliar Applications

The herbicidal effects obtained are strongly dependent upon the concentration or the amount of auxin applied. A comparison of concentration effects for three species is shown in figure 118. These curves fit very well with the generalized scheme of Woodford shown in figure 115. The effectiveness of different concentrations on mortality can be appraised only in the light of the injurious effects which may result to the crop itself. For example, in figure 118 it can be seen that the weight of tomato plants was seriously reduced by concentrations which were one hundred times more dilute than the lethal level. In contrast pigweed showed no change of plant weight until the lethal

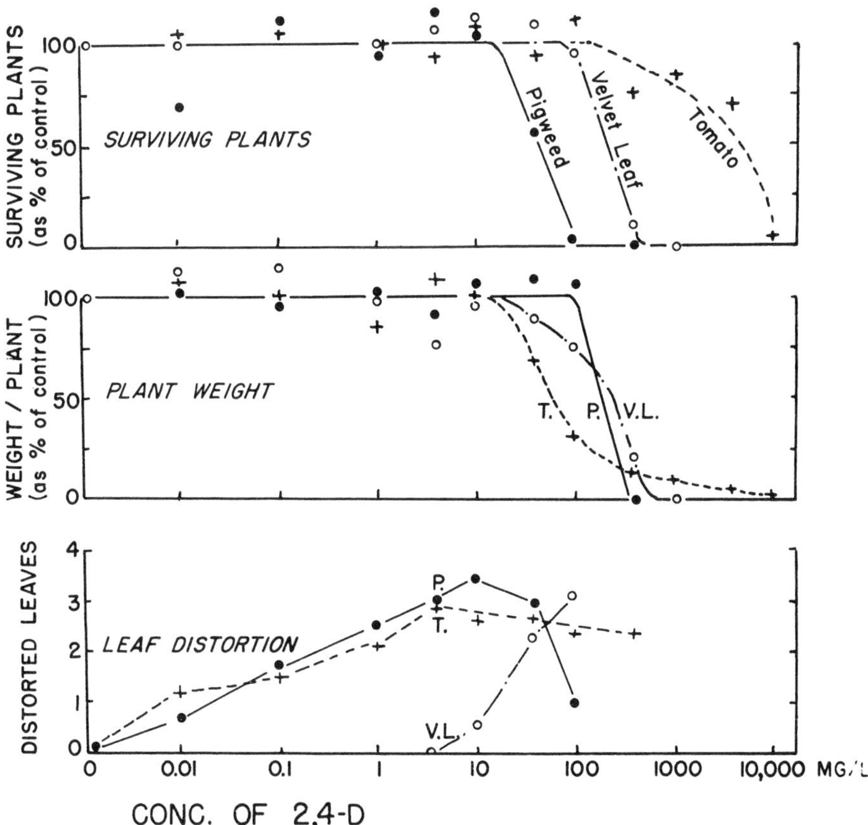

Fig. 118. The effects of various concentrations of 2,4-D on kill, plant weight, and number of distorted leaves of three plant species. Plants were four weeks old at time of spraying, seven and one-half weeks at end of the experiment (Warren and Leopold, unpublished).

level had been reached. Another expression of plant injury is the distortion response of leaves, and in figure 118 it can be seen that these may appear at concentrations a million times more dilute than the lethal concentration in the case of tomato and pigweed. In the velvet leaf, distortion responses did not appear until near-lethal levels were applied.

Herbicidal responses to increases in concentration of auxins are more precipitous than are many other auxin effects. For this reason most herbicidal work is done over very narrow concentration ranges, such as comparison of 1/4, 1/2, and 1 pound per acre of 2,4-D or of other experimental ranges equally narrow.

At the time of the discovery of the herbicidal action of auxins, the majority of herbicides then available had to be applied at concentrations many times greater. For example, arsenical herbicides were applied at rates as high as 1500 pounds per acre which represents quite a contrast to 2,4-D which kills most annual broad-leafed plants at rates of less than two pounds per acre. It has been commonly observed that the effectiveness of herbicidal auxin sprays does not continue to increase as the concentration is raised, for the application of very high concentrations may lead to the rapid killing of the foliage before the herbicide has been translocated into the remainder of the plant. This concentration phenomenon limits the usefulness of some auxins like 2,4-D in killing deep-rooted or perennial species. The concentration curve of herbicidal effectiveness of auxins for many plants shows a reduction in activity if very high concentrations are used because of this obstacle to translocation.

The quantity of auxin solutions applied varies greatly. Almost all early herbicidal applications were made using one hundred gallons or more of solution per acre. This volume represents approximately the amount which can be retained on the foliage without excessive runoff. Low-volume concentrate sprays are being used more and more frequently, in many instances at volumes as low as four to six gallons of solution per acre (Foster, 1952) or even one to two gallons per acre when applied in oil by airplane. There is some evidence that the selectivity of auxin herbicides is somewhat reduced by the use of low-volume sprays (Miller and Dunham, 1950), but the economy of the method often makes it worth while.

It seems quite clear that in the majority of cases the concentration of auxin applied means very little *per se,* but rather the actual amount of auxin which is applied determines the herbicidal effect (Robbins *et al,* 1952, p. 170).

A difficulty encountered with Canada thistle is that the leaves are readily killed by moderate auxin applications, and translocation of the auxin to the roots is not obtained. Consequently the control of thistle is particularly difficult. A clever means of partially circumventing this translocation obstacle is the repeated application of weak auxin concentrations in order gradually to accumulate a lethal level in the roots (Hill and Willard, 1952).

In some instances with the use of maleic hydrazide as an herbicide it has been found that damaging the plant mechanically after spraying may increase the injury obtained. For example, plowing under or mowing perennial weeds after spraying with maleic hydrazide can increase the herbicidal effect (Hoffman and Sylwester, 1950, 1953).

Mixtures of auxins are very generally used. Striking results have been obtained with mixtures of 2,4-D and phenylacetic acid (King, 1946) and especially with mixtures of 2,4-D and 2,4,5-T (Offord and Moss, 1948). The latter is commonly used against woody species.

After extensive evaluations of the effects of herbicides on various plants, researchers in the field are now able to classify a wide variety of herbicides as to their effectiveness in killing specific weeds and as to the tolerance of each crop plant to them. Using this array of information, combinations of herbicides can be tailored to which the crop is tolerant and which will destroy each of the particular weed species expected in a given field (Warren and Larsen, 1952).

Besides foliar applications, auxin herbicides are highly effective in killing trees when applied to the bark. Because of the corky nature of the bark, esters must be used, and generally in oil. The lethal effect can be increased by stripping off a section of bark at the base of the tree and applying the auxin to the inner bark and cambial layers.

Herbicides Applied to Soils

Slade *et al* (1945) first demonstrated in England that the application of auxins to the soil could be effectively used as an herbicidal treatment. This method has achieved widespread use. Its effectiveness is obtained first through exerting a positional effect against the seeds germinating at the surface of the soil and, second, by utilizing the same selectivity factors discussed earlier in this chapter.

The lethal dosage per plant for soil applications is generally somewhat lower than the amount required for killing by foliar application. However since the auxin is not concentrated on the plant more auxin in pounds per acre is required. The selectivity between species is somewhat different for soil applications, but in general approximately twice as much auxin is needed for effective soil application as for foliar treatment.

Soil herbicides applied before the crop plant emerges depend to a considerable extent upon positional selectivity. The herbicide is applied to the surface of the soil where the bulk of the weed seeds germinate, while the crop seed is at a lower depth. For this reason herbicides which are readily leached are somewhat less dependable than less mobile materials. If the chemical remains strictly on the surface of the soil, large amounts may be lost by volatilization in the heat of the sun, so some small movement into the soil is desirable.

Soil herbicides may also be applied after the crop plant has emerged. Most generally this is done by utilizing some device to keep the herbicide from excessive contact with the crop plant. In some cases the herbicide is sprayed onto the soil with nozzles held below the foliage level of the crop plants, or pelleted formulations are sometimes used to avoid retention of the herbicide on the foliage. The sodium 2,4-dichlorophenoxyethyl sulfate is advantageous for this purpose, as there is no contact injury sustained by the foliage.

FACTORS IN SUCCESS

The use of auxin herbicides to remove weeds selectively often represents something of a compromise between reduced competition by weeds, and injurious effects of the sprays on the crop itself. This has been pointed out particularly clearly by Woodford (1950).

Various types of injuries to crop plants have been observed subsequent to removal of weeds by auxin herbicides. An interesting set of observations by Andersen and Hermansen (1950) indicates that the

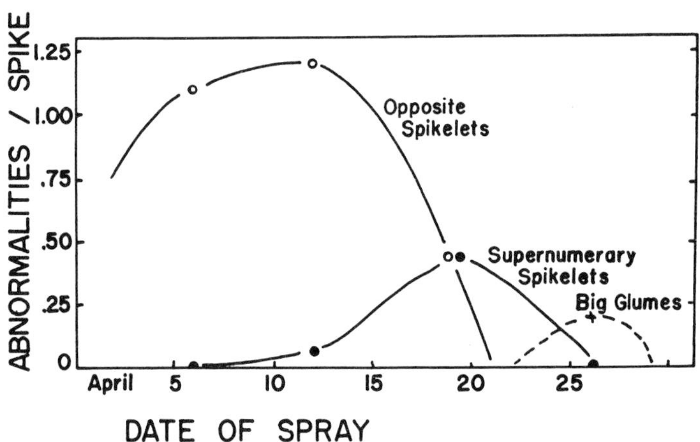

Fig. 119. Changes in the type and frequency of abnormalities in wheat with various dates of spraying of 2,4-dichlorophenoxyacetic acid, 0.75 lb./acre (Andersen and Hermansen, 1950).

type of injurious effects suffered by grains changes with different times of application. For example, in figure 119 it can be seen that spraying a stand of wheat in early April resulted principally in abnormal position of spikelets in the head. Sprays in mid-April resulted in the occurrence of supernumerary spikelets, and sprays in late April or early May induced abnormal glume formation. In the case of corn several different injurious effects have been described, including the production of brittle stems, seed of low viability, poor set of the kernels or distorted ears (Rodgers, 1952; Staniforth, 1952). These abnormalities, too, are a function of the time of spray application. Reductions in yield can be closely correlated with some of these injurious effects.

Sample data on reduction of yields in peas as a function of time of auxin application are shown in figure 120. It is evident that the germinating seed is most sensitive to the auxin application, for treatment at that stage reduced yields to almost zero. A second period of sensitivity occurs as flowering begins. The inverse relationship of this curve with figure 114 may be noted. Yield data for other crops do not always follow the same trend (Derscheid, 1952; Andersen and

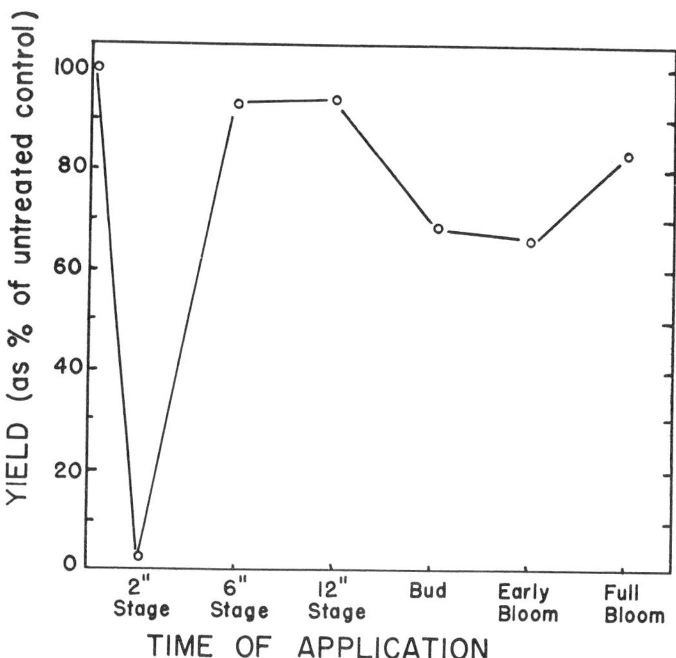

Fig. 120. The effects of an herbicidal spray of 0.5 lb./acre of MCPA (2-methyl 4-chlorophenoxyacetic acid) applied to peas at various stages of development upon subsequent yield (Buchholtz, 1952).

Hermansen, 1950). The high sensitivity of crop yields to auxins applied at the time of flower initiation is borne out by many workers.

In some instances moderately injurious effects to the crop can be tolerated in order to obtain larger beneficial effects in terms of removal of weeds. For example, Buchholtz (1952) recommends the application of approximately 0.17 lb./acre of MCPA to remove thistles from peas, even though this application will damage the peas, for the presence of thistles would be much more undesirable than the reduction of yield obtained.

The time at which auxin application is made will have a strong bearing on the success. It has been pointed out in several different contexts that the stage of growth at the time of auxin application has a strong effect on the susceptibility of a plant. Advantage can be taken of this point to remove weeds when the crop is least susceptible or when the weed is most susceptible. For example, orchard bindweed can be removed from a stand of apple trees in the fall when the apple trees have ceased growth and are not at a susceptible stage (Bryant and Rasmussen, 1951). Again, mustard weeds may be removed from clover at a time when the mustard is in bud or in flower and the clover is not (Fertig, 1952). The removal of weeds at an especially susceptible stage is advantageous not only because of the attendant greater selectivity of the auxin, but also because less herbicide need be applied to obtain the desired effect.

The effects of various environmental and physiological factors on the effectiveness of auxin applications have been described in chapter VI. It may be worth special note here that the moisture level in the soil is critical to the effectiveness of auxin herbicide applications (Buchholtz, 1948). Reports concerning irrigated crops show consistently more effective herbicidal action where irrigation has kept the moisture level high (e.g. Tafuro and Marshall, 1952). In general, low temperatures lead to reduced effectiveness (Marth and Davis, 1945), although some exceptions have been noted (Brown and Weintraub, 1952). As would be expected from the known effects of light on translocation, most effective herbicidal action has been obtained under high light intensities (Mitchell and Brown, 1945; Weaver and DeRose, 1946). An occasional exception to the light intensity factor has been noted (Robertson-Cuninghame and Blackman, 1952), perhaps because the auxin was not sprayed onto the foliage.

Simultaneously with the development of auxin herbicides, there has been rapid development of a variety of other herbicidal materials. Some of these are as highly selective between species as the auxins, for example the fractionated oils, the phenols, carbamates and trichloroacetic acid. Others are effectively transported in plants, as are the arsenicals and sulfamates. Auxin herbicides take their place among these materials as highly effective and highly selective killers which give weed control with remarkably low application rates and their property of ready translocation through plants particularly enhances their value.

Auxins find their greatest agricultural use as herbicides. With the 60,000,000 pounds of 2,4-D produced in the United States in 1952, it may be estimated that approximately 50,000,000 acres of land were treated with this herbicidal material.

CHAPTER XVII

Miscellaneous Uses of Auxins

Several of the minor uses of auxins relate to fruit growth and development and of these perhaps the most promising are the uses of auxins to increase fruit size and induce early maturation and coloration.

ALTERING FRUIT SIZE AND MATURATION

The first report that auxins could increase fruit size was made by Clark and Kerns (1943). These workers found that the application of naphthaleneacetic acid to growing pineapple fruits could increase the final size of the fruits as much as ten or twenty per cent. Some of their data are shown in figure 121, from which it can be seen that

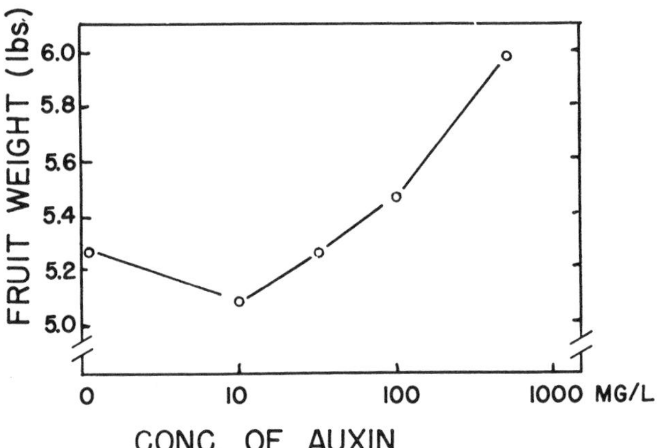

Fig. 121. The effect of auxin (naphthaleneacetic acid) applied during fruit growth upon the ultimate size of pineapples (Clark and Kerns, 1943).

concentrations of 100 and 500 mg./l. resulted in appreciable gains in fruit weight. Similar gains in fruit size have been reported for limes (Erickson and Brannaman, 1950), seedless grapes (Weaver and Williams, 1950), apricots (Crane and Brooks, 1952), strawberries (Zielinski and Garren, 1952), and possibly the fig (Crane and Blondeau, 1949). The procedure for pineapples has been worked out in detail by Krauss *et al* (1948). The application of auxins at the time of fruit-set or during early stages of fruit growth resulted in increases in size running from ten to thirty-five per cent in each of these fruits.

It is difficult to distinguish the effects of auxins on maturation and coloration from their effects on alteration of fruit size. In many instances both effects are obtained simultaneously in the same fruits. The first report of hastened maturation was made by Gardner *et al* (1940) who observed increased coloration and maturity in apple fruits which had been sprayed with auxins to prevent pre-harvest drop.

The physiological basis for the effect on fruit size appears to be two-fold, the auxin brings about an increased growth rate and an alteration of the time of maturity of the fruit.

In almost every reported instance the application of auxins to young fruits of the species listed above results in an immediate increase of the growth rate over that of the control. Clark and Kerns (1943) observed that sprayed pineapples increased in weight over the untreated controls very soon after the spray. They implied that the gain in size was largely owing to this stimulation. Some data reported by Marth *et al* (1950) on the effects of auxins upon the growth of peach fruits indicate that an immediate growth increase was obtained even though the final size was not increased. It will be remembered at this point that in the discussion of parthenocarpy in chapter XI it was observed that tomato fruits set with auxins showed a more rapid growth rate in the first five days after auxin application (Singletary, 1950).

The acceleration of fruit growth by auxins is apparently the greatest in cases where the fruits experience periods of retarded growth as in the case of the fig. In figure 122 the normal growth rate for the fig is plotted, showing two periods of rapid growth with a period of relatively slow growth in between. The application of 2,4,5-T at the beginning of the slow phase in growth resulted in maturation of the fruit in fifteen days instead of the sixty-five days normally required. It has been suggested by Zielinski *et al* (1951) from their work with prunes that such growth effects are caused by the reinforcing of low auxin levels in the fruit. A similar hastening effect is obtained with apricot fruits (Crane and Brooks, 1952). The apricot has three phases of rapid growth, and if 2,4,5-T is applied during the slower phases the fruits may be brought to maturity about two weeks early and with an increase in final fruit size.

Fruits which do not show cyclic fluctuations in growth may still obtain size increases with the application of auxins. An example of this is the strawberry which yields small increases in fruit size when sprayed during the early stages of fruit growth with β-naphthoxyacetic acid (Zielinski and Garren, 1952). Incidentally, it is interesting to note that the responsive stage in the growth of the strawberry is one in which the natural auxin production is low (Nitsch, 1950).

It is a little confusing to find that in some instances the application of auxins at the time of fruit-set may actually retard the growth rate. For example, Crane (1948) found that indolebutyric acid would set fig fruits and retard the growth rate. The same fruits sprayed with 2,4,5-T respond in quite the opposite way as figure 122 showed.

A hastening of maturity has been reported for apple (Gardner *et al,* 1940), peach (Southwick, 1946), seedless grapes (Weaver and Williams, 1951), prune (Zielinski *et al,* 1951), and apricot (Crane and Brooks, 1952). The opposite effect on maturity, a delay, has been reported for pineapple (Clark and Kerns, 1943), lemon and other citrus fruits (Stewart, 1949). As already mentioned fig has been reported to be sometimes hastened and sometimes delayed in maturity. Associated with the hastened maturity there is usually no gain in fruit size found for the apple or the peach, but in each of the other instances gains in size were obtained.

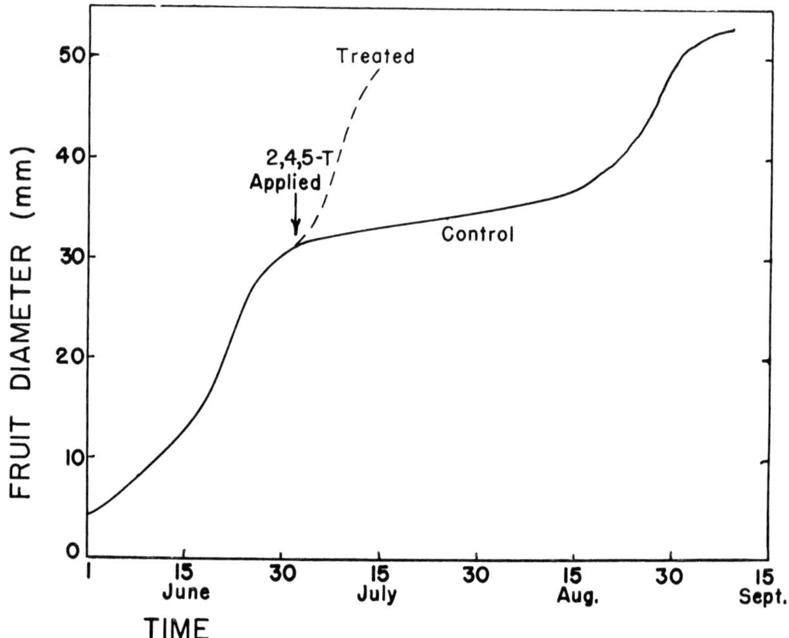

Fig. 122. The hastening of growth and maturity of Calimyrna figs by 2,4,5-trichlorophenoxyacetic acid (25 mg./l.) applied to young fruits (Crane and Blondeau, 1949).

The acceleration of maturation phenomena in the fruit can terminate growth before the fruits have reached full size. A clear case of this premature maturation is found in the peach. If this fruit is sprayed six or seven weeks before normal maturity, the fruits can be harvested some two weeks earlier than normal (Weinberger, 1951), but the growth rate is not maintained and the fruits are very small (Marth *et al,* 1950).

It seems generally true that the earlier the application of auxin, the greater the maturation effect; however, associated with this more rapid maturation is a greater frequency of distorted, undersized and otherwise objectionable fruits. The effect of time of application upon the maturation of peaches can be seen in figure 123. One might deduce from the data reported in this figure and data of other authors as well that fruits lose their sensitivity to auxins as maturity approaches. Gerhardt and Smith (1948) have reported that auxins applied to apricots, peaches, and pears after harvest had almost no detectable effect at all. This was established on a more quantitative basis by Southwick (1949) who demonstrated that post-climacteric apple fruits do not respond to auxins in terms of respiration or any of the other ripening phenomena measured.

In some rather startling work on the nature of the ripening process in avocado fruits, Millerd *et al* (1953) have brought forth good evidence that ripening of avocado proceeds as a function of the

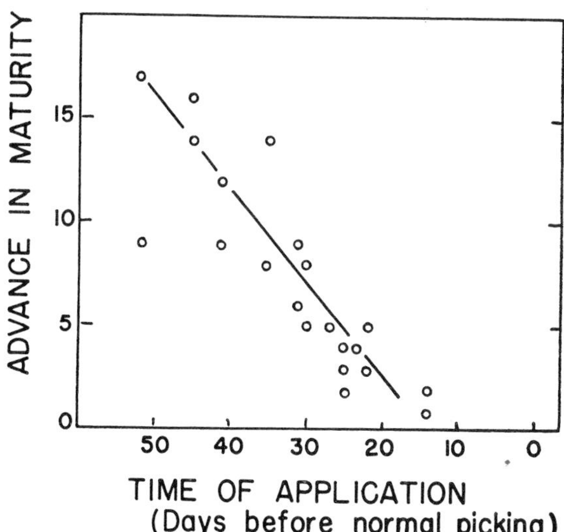

Fig. 123. The relative effectiveness of sprays of 2,4,5-trichlorophenoxyacetic acid (from 10 to 40 mg./l.) applied at various stages of development in hastening maturity of peaches (data of Weinberger, 1951).

availability of phosphate acceptors in the metabolic milieu. The climacteric rise in respiration rate is thought to be due to progressively increasing availability of phosphate acceptors in the fruit. Agents such as 2,4-dinitrophenol which uncouple oxidation from phosphorylation processes can stimulate respiration (and hence presumably the ripening process) only in the preclimacteric period, because only in that period do phosphate acceptors limit respiration. The relation of auxin effects upon respiration to phosphorylation phenomena were discussed in chapter V, where it was indicated that auxin effects involve the utilization of high-energy phosphate bonds—a process which would make phosphate acceptors available for further respiratory functions. In the light of these observations, it is not surprising that auxin effects upon ripening are smaller and smaller as the time of application approaches the time of ripening, for according to the evidence of Millerd *et al* phosphate acceptors limit respiration less and less as the climacteric approaches. Evidence for the same type of uncoupling action in the ripening of apples has been obtained by Pearson and Robertson (1952).

It has been reported that 2,4-D can induce ripening of stored bananas (Marth and Mitchell, 1949). This is probably not an effect of the auxin, but rather of the common impurity in 2,4-D preparations: 2,4-dichlorophenol. That the effects of this compound may be easily confused with effects of 2,4-D has been pointed out by Goldacre *et al,* 1953. This impurity is a strong uncoupling agent like 2,4-dinitrophenol, and would consequently be expected to increase the rate of ripening of green fruits.

It is interesting to note that ethylene can induce early ripening in harvested bananas but is ineffective on post-climacteric fruits (Hansen and Hartman, 1937).

STRENGTHENING FLOWERING STALKS

Auxins have been observed to strengthen pedicels or peduncles under the fruits of grape (Weaver and Williams, 1950) and lime (Erickson and Brannaman, 1950). It has been commonly observed that tomatoes show a thickening of the pedicel and enlargement of the sepals upon auxin application for parthenocarpic set.

As remarked in chapter XIV, the use of auxins to induce flowering in pineapple results in an unfavorable side effect in which the peduncle which supports the fruit becomes abnormally long and spindly. As a consequence the fruits often tip sideways from their own weight and much loss is incurred from sunburn to the sides of the fruits. A second application of auxin spray shortly after the naphthaleneacetic acid treatment to force flowering has been found to alleviate this situation.

AUXIN THERAPEUTICS

Inhibitory influences of auxins are not restricted to higher plants, but fungi, bacteria and virus organisms have been inhibited by auxins in a variety of instances. In a few cases these inhibitions are direct, but more generally the auxins seem to alter the constitution of higher plants in such a way as to discourage the growth of parasitic microorganisms.

An auxin inhibition of bacteria contaminating mold cultures has been reported by Stevenson and Mitchell (1945), and the possibility of controlling bacteria in *Penicillium* cultures was suggested.

Limasset *et al* (1948) reported that auxin could inhibit *X* and *Y* virus in tobacco. This was repeated using mosaic virus by Kutsky and Rawlins (1950). It is interesting to note that naphthaleneacetic acid and indolebutyric acid were effective against the virus, but several other auxins were without effect (Kutsky, 1952).

One of the most promising therapeutic uses of auxins is against fungal parasites. In studying apple canker, a disease caused by *Nectria galligerna,* Crowdy (1948) hoped that auxins might help to heal over the canker lesions. The application of indolebutyric acid produced rather startling therapeutic effects. This led him to measure the effects of the auxin upon growth of the organism in pure culture, but he found little toxicity there. The treatment of bean plants with a variety of phenoxyacetic acids led to the further discovery that the chocolate spot disease, caused by *Botrytis cineraea,* was effectively prevented by auxins and by anti-auxins, especially 2,4,6-trichlorophenoxyacetic acid and 2,4,6-trichlorophenoxyisobutyric acids (see chapter VII) (Crowdy and Wain, 1950, 1951). Applied to the roots, these materials move through the plant, probably in the transpiration stream, and act as systemic fungicides. The use of stronger auxins is complicated by excessive epinastic and distortive effects, whereas these compounds have much less formative effects on the host plant. Similar control of fusarium wilt (*Fusarium oxysporum* var. *cubense*) has been obtained with a variety of auxins (Davis and Dimond, 1953), even though the fungus is not particularly inhibited by the auxins (Hessayon, 1952). Davis and Dimond (1953) conclude that the metabolism of the plant is altered in such a way as to resist the pathogen.

The lack of correlation between auxin activity and systemic fungicidal action is puzzling. Some anti-auxins are effective against the chocolate spot of bean; phenyl acetic acid, which is a weak anti-auxin, is reported inactive against tobacco mosaic virus; and maleic hydrazide, which can act as an auxin antagonist, actually promotes growth of wheat rust lesions (Livingston, 1953). This latter effect may be more appropriately assigned to the alteration of carbohydrate content than to auxin antagonism.

The fungus, *Cladosporium herbarum,* which parasitizes plants by mycelial growth through cell walls, has been found to be stimulated in growth by auxins, apparently in part at least by stimulation of the exoenzyme pectin esterase produced by the pathogen (Waygood *et al,* 1954). Waygood (1954) has suggested that the resistance or susceptibility of plants to this pathogen may be related to their natural auxin contents.

Another therapeutic property of auxin is its ability greatly to enhance the action of antibiotics. Streptomycin has been used to prevent fire-blight, a bacterial disease of apple trees. The simultaneous application of indoleacetic acid with the antibiotic increased the disease protection up to 80 per cent (Goodman and Hemphill, 1954). The suggestion has been made by Iyengar and Starkey (1953) that there is a synergistic action between some antibiotics and auxin, though no data were given to support the proposal. Some evidence for such a synergism is given in chapter VII. The synergistic interaction appears to apply both to the growth effects and to the antibiotic effects.

Mention has been made in chapter XV of the effectiveness of auxins in controlling mold on nursery tree stock and on citrus fruits.

An interesting observation has been made by LaBaw and Desrosier (1954) that auxins can reduce the heat resistance of mold spores in canned products, which suggests an interesting possible use of auxins in food processing. The effect was not limited to auxins, but TIBA and some of the chlorinated benzoic acids which are not auxins have similar effects. These workers found that British Anti-Lewisite (1,2-dithiopropanol, a sulfhydryl protective agent) reversed the effects, suggesting a role of sulfhydryl substances in the spore survival system.

CONTROL OF APICAL DOMINANCE

Since the classic work of Thimann and Skoog (1934) which showed that auxins produced at the tip of the plant inhibit the growth of lateral buds, it has become more and more evident that the auxin system controls the branching habit of all higher plants. Thus plants with an abundant supply of natural auxin maintain a strong apical dominance and, conversely, plants with a relatively low auxin supply develop a more branched habit (Delisle, 1937).

There are several cases in agriculture where a reduction of apical dominance is desirable. In these cases the apical bud is often mechanically broken off to force branching. This cultural practice is spoken of as *pinching*.

That antagonists of auxins could bring about the same loss of apical dominance and the same degree of branching as pinching has been demonstrated by Beach and Leopold (1953). Their data in figure 124 demonstrate that maleic hydrazide in concentrations of 600 or 1000 mg./1. resulted in as much branching of chrysanthemums as did pinching. No loss in quality of the flower was encountered. In a similar manner ethylene and TIBA (2,3,5-triiodobenzoic acid) have been found to encourage basal shoots of roses (Asen and Hamner, 1953).

In the commercial production of tobacco the flowering tips are removed from the plants some time before harvest, because the flowers adversely affect the leaf quality. When the tips are removed, apical

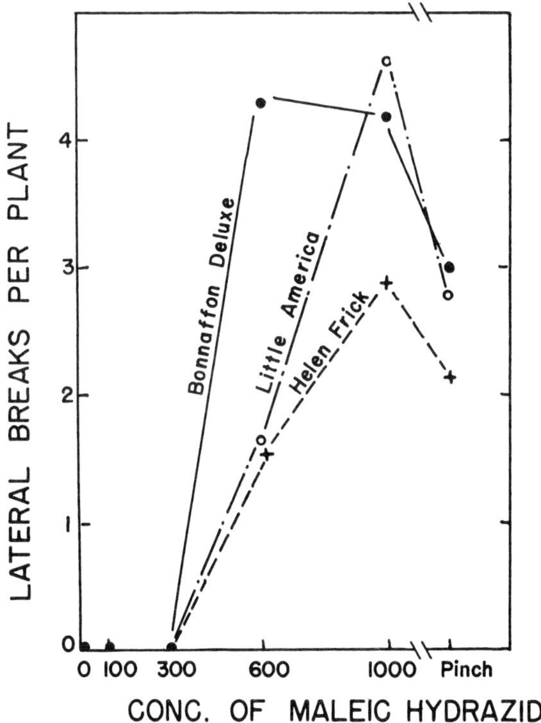

Fig. 124. The removal of apical dominance in three varieties of chrysanthemum by foliar applications of maleic hydrazide as compared with pinching (manual removal of the apical bud). Concentrations of maleic hydrazide expressed in mg./1. (Beach and Leopold, 1953).

dominance is also removed and lateral shoots commence growth. This undesirable second growth has been controlled with auxins and with oils applied to the severed tip. More recently, maleic hydrazide has been found to prevent the growth of lateral suckers (Naylor and Davis, 1950; Grant, 1953). The effect is not a modification of apical dominance but rather a direct inhibition of growth. The maleic hydrazide treatment has the advantage of being an overall plant spray, whereas the auxin or oil treatments must be placed carefully on each severed stem tip.

An undesirable side effect from the use of auxins in forcing pineapples to flower is the increased apical dominance which occurs in the plants. This is expressed as a reduction in the number of slips and suckers developing on the peduncle and stem of the forced plant. Because slips and suckers are the planting material for the pineapple crop, the loss of such lateral bud development can become a severe economic liability. Clark and Kerns (1943) reported that naphthaleneacetic acid which had been sprayed on young fruits to increase fruit size had a remarkable effect in increasing the number of slips and suckers as shown in figure 125. The more detailed researches of Whang (1948) have indicated that chlorophenoxyacetic acid applied approximately five days after flower forcing with naphthaleneacetic acid results in consistent gains in the number of slips and suckers obtained.

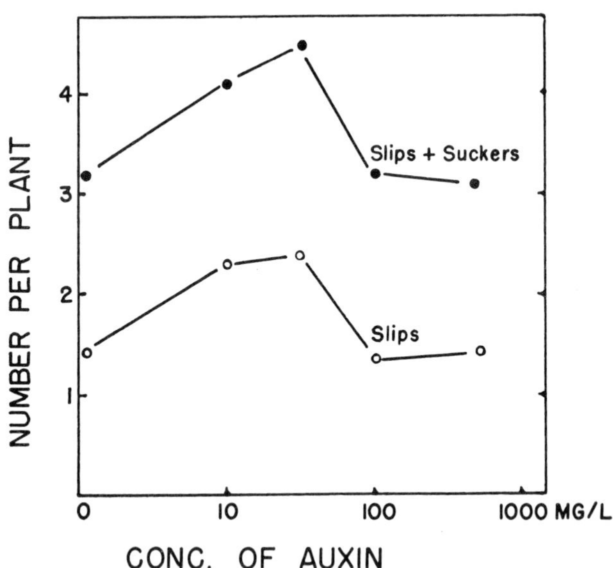

Fig. 125. The effects of naphthaleneacetic acid in increasing numbers of lateral buds (slips and suckers) in the pineapple plant (Clark and Kerns, 1943).

The means by which these auxin applications to pineapple can bring about a decrease in apical dominance is obscure.

OTHER USES

It is interesting to note that the application of auxins to flowers or fruits may cause either an abortion of the ovule (Swanson *et al,* 1949) or, contrariwise, an improvement of fertilization (Wester and Marth, 1949). Some attempts have been made to utilize the beneficial effects of auxin on fertilization in plant breeding procedures (Wester and Marth, 1949), but the effects have not been consistent enough to achieve widespread use.

The influence of auxins in retarding abscission have been utilized in the Christmas greens industry to prevent the abscission of leaves and fruits of holly (Milbrath and Hartman, 1942). They also are sometimes incorporated into insect sprays for orange trees to prevent the leaf abscission which may follow (Stewart and Ebeling, 1946). Again, when young fruits are frosted the retarded auxin transport apparently makes the fruits prone to abscise, a situation which can be prevented by auxin spray (Crane, 1954). An auxin antagonist such as maleic hydrazide can be incorporated into a defoliation spray for cotton and further encourage abscission (Hall *et al,* 1953).

The property of auxins in producing epinastic curling of leaves has been utilized by Franklin (1948) to facilitate the bolting of lettuce. It seems that in head lettuce of some varieties the flowering scape is unable to push its way through the leaves and consequently in lettuce breeding work each head must be slashed with a knife to permit emergence of the flowers. Auxins sprayed on the lettuce in some instances produced an improved bolting, presumably because epinastic curling of the leaves permited the scape to come through.

A use of auxin in altering the crotch angle of trees has been reported by Verner (1938).

Lastly, 2,4-D has been found to be effective in killing back ragweed plants sufficiently to prevent pollen release in the autumn (Smith *et al,* 1946). With the affliction of hay fever so widespread, it is curious that this technique has not become more commonly used. Beginning in 1948 Canadian areas used as summer retreats by hay-fever sufferers have fought back the encroachment of ragweed by 2,4-D sprays particularly along roadsides.

CHAPTER XVIII

Potentials of Auxins and Auxin Research

With the continued development of the auxin field it has become more and more evident that the concept of the *growth* hormone in plants must be expanded to a concept of the hormonal control of growth, development and metabolism. The streams of flow of the growth hormone from each of the plant extremities (figure 1) control not only the growth characteristics of the plant, but they also control the differentiation of tissues and organs of various sorts, they play a multitude of intimate roles in the reproductive functions of flower initiation, pollination, embryo development, *et cetera,* and they determine to a large extent the morphological constitution of the plant as an organism. The growth hormone, then, appears to be a major influence in determining the characteristics and development of the plant as an organism. In applying auxins to plants, the myriad of growth hormone actions is being altered artificially, and because of the immense number of natural functions of the growth hormone in plants, auxin applications can have an immense number of different uses.

THE QUANTITATIVE ASPECT OF AUXIN EFFECTS

In looking back over the many and heterogeneous effects of auxin on growth and development of plants, it is strikingly evident that different quantities of auxin can produce entirely different or even opposite effects. Thus growth can be promoted or inhibited by auxin. Tropisms can be positive or negative depending upon sensitivity to auxin. Abscission and flowering can be accelerated or retarded depending on the location of the auxin and other factors. At the cellular level either differentiation or dedifferentiation can be induced by auxin.

Each phenomenon in growth and development which is affected by auxins has its own concentration optimum, so that a given auxin concentration may promote one phenomenon and inhibit another. A particularly clear case of this is found in the effects of auxin concentrations on growth of different organs. As shown in figure 43, the optimal auxin concentration for growth of stems is higher than that for buds, which is in turn higher than that for roots. Consequently a given auxin application may promote stem growth and inhibit the growth of the other two types of organs.

The quantitative effects of auxins are further complicated by the interactions of auxin with other plant constituents. In the discussion of differentiation it was shown that the effect of a given amount of auxin might produce quite opposite effects depending upon the presence or absence of other growth materials. Thus Skoog and Tsui (1948) found that the addition of auxin to tobacco stem sections inhibited bud formation, but in the presence of adenine the auxin inhibition disappeared. Leopold and Guernsey (1953) demonstrated that auxins applied to pea seeds inhibited flowering, but that the additional application of carbohydrates reversed the inhibition. These latter workers also found that a given auxin application could have quite opposite effects on flowering, depending upon the subsequent temperature experience, probably because of the effects of temperature in altering the plant constituents.

Still a further complication in the quantitative responses to auxin is found in the form and nature of the auxins indigenous to the plant. It is well known that auxins may exist in either free or bound forms in the plant, and there are probably several bound forms of auxin yet to be discovered. In discussing responses of plants to different quantities of auxin it is difficult to determine whether one should speak in terms of free auxin, bound auxin, or both.

Different degrees of sensitivity are found not only between different tissues and organs but also between different ages of the same tissue or organ. For example, a tissue which is weakly differentiated is much more sensitive to auxin than a mature, well-differentiated tissue.

The multiplicity of these complicating factors points up the necessity for a strong background in auxin physiology by the research worker. Even with such a background it is difficult enough to interpret variations in effects and to be intelligently alert for the subtle differences that may be brought about by a given treatment. Without a sound understanding of auxin physiology the research worker is certainly at a disadvantage in knowing what to look for and what potentialities and limitations auxin treatments may have.

Perhaps one of the most remarkable things about research on

auxin today is that so much is known about the gross effects of auxins and so little is known concerning the mechanism underlying these actions. Surely a knowledge of the means by which auxins act at the metabolic level will have immense implications in the intelligent application of auxins in the technology as we know it today. Further it seems very likely that a knowledge of the mechanism of auxin action will open up new possibilities for auxin applications which have remained undiscovered to date. All these considerations make it particularly remarkable that more attention has not been given toward improving our fundamental understanding of the mechanism of auxin action.

WHAT CAN AUXINS DO FOR AGRICULTURE?

Examination of the uses of auxins in agriculture indicates th auxins present the agriculturist with three types of tools.

The first tool is the ability of auxins to overcome certain *limitations* of growth and development imposed by brief insufficiencies of the environment. The most obvious examples of this type of usefulness of auxin are in the control of fruit-set and of fruit drop. When weather conditions are unfit for normal pollination and setting in the tomato, the application of auxins can initiate the growth phase which would normally take place at the time. Likewise if weather conditions at the end of the summer are such as to encourage premature drop of apple fruits, the application of auxins can retain fruits on the trees until harvest.

The second tool which auxins supply is a control of the *type* of growth which will take place. The simplest example of this type of usefulness is in the rooting of cuttings where the capacity to grow is inherent in the cutting, but this capacity needs to be directed toward the development of roots to attain the goal of successful propagation.

The third tool which auxins present is the property of facilitating the mechanization of agriculture. This is perhaps the most important tool of all in that it is the basis for the greatest use of auxin, the herbicidal use, and it makes possible the most widespread economic gains. The thinning of flowers and fruits is another instance where an auxin spray is substituted for manual labor. The chemical control of flower initiation in pineapple is another good example of auxins facilitating mechanization—in this case the mechanization of harvesting.

While these three tools may be very useful under certain circumstances, it is quite clear that two major reservations should be kept in mind concerning their usefulness. In the first place the agricultural uses of auxins are liable to create new agricultural problems of their own. A striking instance of this is the side effects resulting from the forcing of flowering in the pineapple by naphthaleneacetic acid. The spectacular results which are obtained in this type of application are not without limitations, for, as has been pointed out in previous sections, the auxin sprays may produce such undesirable effects as the production of a peduncle too long and thin to support the fruit, and the accentuation of apical dominance in the peduncle and stem results in a reduced production of slips for planting material. Another side effect is the production of smaller fruits in the pineapple, for as van Overbeek (1946) has shown, the size of the fruit is a function of the size of the plant at the time of floral initiation, and obviously the forcing of plants before the time they would naturally initiate flowers results in fruit production by smaller plants and hence smaller fruits. Another instance of uses of auxins creating new problems is found in the many reports by herbicide workers that auxin applications which will effectively kill the weeds may also have detrimental effects upon the crop plant. For each use of auxin in agriculture there appears to be at least one detrimental side effect and the actual usefulness of the method depends on the net gain between the beneficial effects and the detrimental effects.

The second reservation that should be kept in mind concerning auxin use is that auxins will never replace good agricultural practice. It is perfectly clear that weak plants are most susceptible to auxin damage, and consequently the lower the quality of the crop at the time auxin is applied, the greater the potential for undesirable side effects. This points up the even greater need for good agricultural practices when auxins are going to be employed.

THE PROSPECT FOR THE FUTURE

It is undeniably true that the trend of research in auxin physiology is more and more toward technology and less and less toward fundamental research. One need not be reminded that the early studies in auxin physiology were all carried out by fundamental research workers until the first commercial application of auxins became evident—that of rooting. From that time on, technological research has taken over a greater and greater share of the research on auxins.

It is rather startling to find in the report of the Committee for Professional Status and Training of the American Association of Plant Physiologists (Bonner *et al,* 1950), that 81 per cent of the plant physiologists in the United States are in the applied fields. Furthermore, of the 19 per cent listed as not being in technological work, a large percentage is in experiment station and industrial positions where some practical research is undoubtedly demanded of them. With the current trend toward increased amounts of financial support for practical research in plant physiology, technological studies are spreading from the agricultural schools into the fundamental science departments, and one cannot help but notice that a considerable number of technological studies reported in the plant physiological literature are coming now from botany departments and biological science departments.

The diversion of biological researchers away from fundamental science will inevitably lead to reduced productivity in terms of technological progress. It may deserve repeating here that essentially every major advance in science and technology has arisen from the fundamental sciences. The entire field of auxin physiology itself arose from studies by fundamental research men on such non-technological problems as the reasons why plants turn toward light. It may be pertinent to note that the most rapidly developing sciences today are those most careful to maintain sufficient funds for the fundamental studies which underlie them.

It seems certain that for continued progress in the technological science of auxin physiology, an adequate research program of fundamental auxin problems must be maintained. If every auxin physiologist and technologist carried on at least one research problem of a fundamental nature this would have the doubly beneficial effect of keeping him aware of fundamental problems and permitting a more rapid evolution of the fundamental science itself.

The trend away from fundamental research and the potentially adverse effect that this trend may bring about has been eloquently pointed out by van Overbeek (1951):

> "The outlook for the remote future seems less bright. Here no specific reference is made to plant hormones but to new applications of plant physiological research in general. These applications, so new that one cannot imagine them at present, depend invariably upon results obtained in fundamental research, that type of research which is undertaken with the sole aim of extending the horizons of our intellect. One could liken the relation between applied and fundamental research to the relation between logging operations and reforestation. The forests planted today will yield forest products tomorrow."

Bibliography

ÅBERG, B. 1950. On auxin antagonists and synergists in root growth. Physiol. Plantarum., 3:447–461.

——— 1953. Studies on plant growth regulators. VIII. On optically active plant growth regulators. Ann. Royal Agric. Coll. Sweden, 20:241–295.

ADDICOTT, F. T. 1943. Pollen germination and tube growth as influenced by pure growth substances. Plant Physiol., 18:270–279.

——— AND R. S. LYNCH 1951. Acceleration and retardation of abscission by indoleacetic acid. Science, 114:688–689.

AKAMINE, E. K. 1951. Persistence of 2,4-D toxicity in Hawaiian soils. Bot. Gaz., 112:312–319.

ALBAUM, H. G., S. KAISER AND H. A. NESTLER 1937. The relation of hydrogen ion concentration to the penetration of indoleacetic acid into *Nitella* cells. Amer. Jour. Bot., 24:513–518.

ALEX, J. F., R. T. COUPLAND, J. L. BOLTON AND W. J. WHITE 1950. Effect of methoxone on alfalfa seed fields. Proc. N. C. Weed Contr. Conf., 7:115.

ANDERSEN, S. AND J. HERMANSEN 1950. Effect of hormone derivatives on cultivated plants. II. Spraying of cereals with 2,4-D and 4K2M at different dates. K. Vet.-og Landbohjskole, Arsskr., 1950:141–203.

ANDREAE, W. A. 1952. Effect of scopoletin on indoleacetic acid metabolism. Nature, 170:83.

——— AND S. R. ANDREAE 1953. Studies on indoleacetic acid metabolism. I. The effect of methyl umbelliferone, maleic hydrazide, and 2,4-D on indoleacetic acid oxidation. Canadian Jour. Bot., 31:426–437.

ARAKERI, H. R. AND R. S. DUNHAM 1950. Environmental factors relating to pre-emergence treatments of corn with 2,4-D. Univ. Minn. Tech. Bull. 190.

ARLE, H. F., O. A. LEONARD AND V. C. HARRIS 1948. Inactivation of 2,4-D on sweet potato slips with activated carbon. Science, 107:247–248.

ASEN, S. AND C. L. HAMNER 1953. Effect of growth-regulating compounds on development of basal shoots of greenhouse roses. Bot. Gaz., 115:86–89.

ASHBY, W. C. 1951. Effects of growth regulating substances and aldehydes on growth of roots. Bot. Gaz., 112:237–250.

AUCHTER, E. C. AND J. W. ROBERTS, 1935. Spraying apples for the prevention of fruit-set. Proc. Amer. Soc. Hort. Sci., 32:208–212.

AUDUS, L. J. 1949. The biological detoxication of 2,4-D in soil. Plant and Soil, 2:31–35.

——— 1950. Biological detoxication of 2,4-D in soils: isolation of an effective organism. Nature, 166:356.

——— 1951. The biological detoxication of hormone herbicides in soil. Plant and Soil, 3:170–192.

——— 1952. Fate of sodium 2,4-dichlorophenoxy ethyl sulphate in soil. Nature, 170:886.

——— 1953. *Plant Growth Substances*. Leonard Hill Ltd., London.

——— AND R. THRESH 1953. A method of plant growth substance assay for use in paper partition chromatography. Physiol. Plantarum., 6:451–465.

AVERY, G. S. JR. 1935. Distribution of phytohormone in leaf of *Nicotiana,* and its relation to polarized growth. Bull. Torrey Bot. Club, 62:313–330.

——— J. BERGER AND B. SHALUCHA 1941. The total extraction of free auxin and auxin precursor from plant tissue. Amer. Jour. Bot., 28:596–607.

——— P. R. BURKHOLDER AND H. B. CREIGHTON 1937. Production and distribution of growth hormone in shoots of *Aesculus* and *Malus* and its probable role in stimulating cambial activity. *Ibid.,* 24:51–58.

——— P. R. BURKHOLDER AND H. B. CREIGHTON 1937. Growth hormone in terminal shoots of *Nicotiana* in relation to light. *Ibid.,* 24:666–673.

——— AND E. B. JOHNSON 1947. *Hormones and Horticulture.* The McGraw-Hill Company, New York.

BALANSARD, J. AND F. PELLISSIER 1942. Action de l'hétéroauxin sur le boutrage foliare de quelques Begoniacées. Compt. Rend. Sec. Biol., 136:305–308.

BANDURSKI, R. S. 1946. Spectrophotometric method for determination of 2,4-D. Bot. Gaz., 108:446–449.

BARLOW, H. W. B. 1952. The importance of abscission in fruit production. Proc. XIII Internat. Hort. Congress, 1:145–152.

BARTON, L. V. 1940. Some effects of treatment of non-dormant seeds with certain growth substances. Contr. Boyce Thompson Inst., 11:181–206.

BATJER, L. P. 1942. Temperature in relation to preharvest drop sprays on apples. Proc. Amer. Soc. Hort. Sci., 40:45–48.

——— AND P. C. MARTH 1945. New materials for delaying fruit abscission of apples. Science, 101:363–364.

——— AND A. H. THOMPSON 1948. The transmission of effect of naphthalene-acetic acid on apple drop as determined by localized applications. Proc. Amer. Soc. Hort. Sci., 51:77–80.

——— AND A. H. THOMPSON 1948. Three years' results with chemical thinning of apples in the Northwest. *Ibid.,* 52:164–172.

——— A. H. THOMPSON AND F. GERHARDT 1948. A comparison of naphthalene-acetic acid and 2,4-D sprays for controlling preharvest drop of Bartlett pears. *Ibid.,* 51:71–74.

——— AND M. UOTA 1951. Effect of 2,4,5-TP on fruit-set of pears and apples. *Ibid.,* 58:33–36.

BEACH, R. G. AND A. C. LEOPOLD 1953. The use of maleic hydrazide to break apical dominance of chrysanthemum. Proc. Amer. Soc. Hort. Sci., 61:543–547.

BEAL, J. M. 1938. Histological responses of Lilium to indoleacetic acid. Bot. Gaz., 99:881–911.

——— 1945. Histological reactions of beans to phenoxy compounds. *Ibid.,* 107:200–217.

——— 1946. Reactions of decapitated beans to certain phenoxy compounds. *Ibid.,* 108:166–186.

——— 1951. Histological responses to growth substances. In Skoog (Ed.), *Plant Growth Substances.* Univ. of Wis. Press, Madison.

BEIN, M., R. SIGNER AND W. H. SCHOPFER 1947. Influence of penicillin on root formation of Zea mays: incidence of β-indoleacetic acid (heteroauxin) in commercial penicillin. Experientia, 3:291–292.

BENNETT, J. P. AND F. SKOOG 1938. On the relation of growth-promoting substances to the rest period in fruit trees. Plant Physiol., 13:219–225.

Bennet-Clark, T. A. and N. P. Kefford 1953. Chromatography of the growth substances in plant extracts. Nature, 171:645–647.

——— M. S. Tambiah and N. P. Kefford 1952. Estimation of plant growth substances by partition chromatography. *Ibid.,* 169:452–453.

Bentley, J. A. 1950. Growth-regulating effect of certain organic compounds. Nature, 65:449.

——— and A. S. Bickle 1952. Studies on plant growth hormones II. Jour. Exptl. Bot., 3:406–423.

——— and S. Housley 1952. Studies on plant growth hormones I. *Ibid.,* 3:393–405.

Berger, J. and G. S. Avery, Jr. 1943. Action of synthetic auxins on dehydrogenases of the *Avena* coleoptile. Amer. Jour. Bot., 30:297–302.

——— and G. S. Avery, Jr. 1944. Isolation of an auxin precursor and an auxin (IAA) from maize. *Ibid.,* 31:199–203.

——— and G. S. Avery, Jr. 1944. Chemical and physiological properties of maize auxin precursor. *Ibid.,* 31:203–208.

Berry, H. K., H. E. Sutton, L. Cain and J. S. Berry 1951. Development of paper chromatography for use in the study of metabolic patterns. Univ. Texas Bull., 5109:22–55.

Biale, J. B. and F. F. Halma 1937. The use of heteroauxin in rooting of subtropicals. Proc. Amer. Soc. Hort. Sci., 35:443–447.

Biebl, R. 1953. Resistenz pflanzlicher Plasmen gegen 2,4-D. Protoplasma, 42:193–208.

Blaauw, A. H. 1918. Licht and Wachstum III. Mededel. Landbouwhoogesch. Wageningen., 15:89–204.

Blackman, G. E. 1945. A comparison of plant growth substances with other selective herbicides. Nature, 155:500–501.

——— 1950. Principles of selective toxicity and action of selective herbicides. Sci. Progress., 152:637–651.

——— 1950. Selective toxicity and the development of selective weedkillers. Jour. Roy. Soc. Arts, 98:500–517.

——— M. A. Holly and K. Holly 1949. Control of hoary pepperwort. Agriculture, 56:6–11.

——— K. Holly and H. A. Roberts 1949. The comparative toxicity of phytocidal substances. Soc. Expt. Biol. Symp., 3:283–317.

Blank, F. and H. E. Deuel 1943. (cited by Meinl and von Guttenberg, 1952) Vjschr. Naturforsch. Ges. Zurich 87.

Block, R. J., R. Lestrange and G. Zweig 1952. *Paper Chromatography—A Laboratory Manual.* Academic Press, Inc., New York.

Boas, T. and F. Merkenschlager 1925. Reizverlust, hervogerufen durch Eosin. Ber. Deutsch. bot. Ges., 43:381–390.

Bonner, J. 1933. The action of the plant growth hormone. Jour. Gen. Physiol., 17:63–76.

——— 1933. Studies on the growth hormone of plants. IV. On the mechanism of the action. Proc. Natl. Acad. Sci., 19:717–719.

——— 1934. The relation of hydrogen ions to the growth rate of the *Avena* coleoptile. Protoplasma, 21:406–423.

——— 1936. The growth and respiration of *Avena* coleoptile. Jour. Gen. Physiol., 20:1–11.

——— 1949. Limiting factors and growth inhibitors in the growth of the *Avena* coleoptile. Amer. Jour. Bot., 36:323–332.

——— 1949. Relations of respiration and growth in the *Avena* coleoptile. *Ibid.,* 36:429–436.

——— 1949. Further experiments on flowering in *Xanthium*. Bot. Gaz., 110:625–627.

——— 1950. The role of toxic substances in the interactions of higher plants. Bot. Rev., 16:51–65.

——— 1950. Arsenate as a selective inhibitor of growth substance action. Plant Physiol., 25:181–184.

——— Chairman, Committee for Professional Status and Training. 1950. The status of plant physiology in the United States: the number, interests and rate of training of plant physiologists. Plant Physiol., 25:529–538.

——— 1951. Analysis of the responses of plants to length of day. (Abstract) Science, 113:145.

——— 1953. The hormonal control of plant growth. *The Harvey Lectures,* Series 48. Academic Press Inc., New York.

——— AND R. S. BANDURSKI 1952. Studies of the physiology, pharmacology and biochemistry of auxins. Ann. Rev. Plant Physiol., 3:59–86.

——— R. S. BANDURSKI AND A. MILLERD 1953. Linkage of respiration to auxin-induced water uptake. Physiol. Plantarum., 6:511–522.

——— AND H. BONNER 1948. The B vitamins as plant hormones. Vitamins and Hormones, 6:225–270.

——— AND J. THURLOW 1949. Inhibition of photoperiodic induction in *Xanthium* by applied auxin. Bot. Gaz., 110:613–624.

BORGSTRÖM, G. 1939. Anthogenesis in etiolated pea seedlings. Bot. Notiser, 1939: 830–838.

——— 1939. *The Transverse Reactions of Plants.* C. W. K. Gleerup, Lund, Sweden.

BORTHWICK, H. A. AND M. W. PARKER 1941. Influence of localized low temperature on photoperiodic induction. Bot. Gaz., 102:792–800.

BOSE, J. C. 1907. *Comparative Electrophysiology.* Longmans, Green and Co., London.

BOUILLENNE, R. AND F. W. WENT 1933. Recherches experimentales sur la néoformation des racines dans les plantules et les boutures des plantes supérieures. Ann. Jard. Bot. Buitenzorg, 43:25–202.

BOYSEN-JENSEN, P. 1913. Über die Leitung des phototropischen Reizis in der *Avena* Koleoptile. Ber. Deutsch. bot. Ges., 31:559–566.

——— 1936. *Growth Hormones in Plants.* McGraw-Hill Book Co., Inc., New York.

——— 1936. Über die Verteilung des Wuchstoffes in Keimstengeln und Wurzeln während phototropischen und geotropischen Krümmung. K. Danske Videnskab. Selakab, Biol. Meddel., 13:1–31.

——— 1936. Über ein Mikromethode zur quantitativen Bestimmung der Wuchsstoffe der A Gruppe. Planta, 26:584–594.

——— AND N. NIELSEN 1926. Studien über die hormonalen Beziehungen zwischen Spitze und Basis der *Avena* Koleoptile. *Ibid.,* 1:321–331.

BRANDES, E. W. AND J. VAN OVERBEEK 1949. Auxin relations in hot-water-treated sugarcane stems. Jour. Agric. Res., 77:223–238.

BRANDON, D. 1939. Seasonal variations of starch content in the genus *Rosa* and their relation to propagation by stem cuttings. Jour. Pomol. Hort. Sci., 47:147–148.

BRAUNER, L. 1927. Untersuchungen über das geoelektrische Phänomen. Jahrb. wiss. Bot., 66:381–428.

——— 1952. Über pH Veränderungen bei der Photolyse des Heteroauxins. Naturwiss., 39:282–284.

——— 1953. Untersuchungen über die Photolyse des Heteroauxins I. Zeitschr. Bot., 41:291–341.

——— AND M. BRAUNER 1954. Untersuchungen über die Photolyse des Heteroauxins II. Zeitschr. Bot., 42:83–124.

BRIAN, R. C. AND E. K. RIDEAL 1952. On the action of plant growth regulators. Biochim. et Biophys. Acta., 9:1–18.

BROWN, J. B., H. B. HENBEST AND E. R. H. JONES 1950. Studies on compounds related to auxin *a* and auxin *b*. Part III. Jour. Chem. Soc., 1950:3634–3638.

BROWN, J. W. 1946. Effect of 2,4-D on the water relations, accumulation and distribution of solid matter, and the respiration of bean plants. Bot. Gaz., 107: 332–343.

——— AND J. W. MITCHELL 1948. Inactivation of 2,4-D in soil as affected by soil moisture, temperature, manure and autoclaving. Bot. Gaz., 109:314–323.

——— AND R. L. WIENTRAUB 1950. A leaf repression method for evaluation of formative activity of plant growth regulator substances. Bot. Gaz., 111:448–456.

——— AND R. L. WIENTRAUB 1952. Influence of temperature on formative response of bean seedlings to 2,4-D. *Ibid.,* 113:479–482.

BRYAN, W. H. AND E. H. NEWCOMB 1954. Stimulation of pectin methylesterase activity of cultured tobacco pith by indoleacetic acid. Physiol. Plantarum, 7:290–297.

BRYANT, L. R. AND L. W. RASMUSSEN 1951. Use of 2,4-D in orchard bindweed control. Proc. Amer. Soc. Hort. Sci., 58:131–135.

BUCHHOLTZ, K. P. 1948. Pre-emergence treatments with 2,4-D and other herbicides to control weeds in field crops other than corn. N. C. Weed Control Conf. Res. Rep., 5:IV Summary.

——— 1952. Control of weeds in canning peas with MCP. Proc. N. C. Weed Control Conf., 9:75–77.

BURG, F. W., T. J. ARCENEAUX AND I. S. NELSON 1946. Preliminary notes on the effect of water hardness on the herbicidal action of 2,4-D compounds. Sugar Bull., 24:175–176.

BURKHOLDER, C. L. AND M. MCCOWN 1941. Effect of scoring and of naphthylacetic acid and amide spray upon fruit-set and of the spray upon preharvest fruit drop. Proc. Amer. Soc. Hort. Sci., 38:117–120.

BURMA, D. P. 1953. Partition mechanism of paper chromatography: adsorption of chromatographed substances. Analyt. Chem., 25:549–553.

BURSTRÖM, H. 1950. Studies on growth and metabolism of roots. III. Adaptation against growth inhibition by aliphatic C_{12} and C_{11} acids. Physiol. Plantarum, 3:175–184.

——— 1950. Studies on growth and metabolism of roots. IV. Positive and negative auxin effects on cell elongation. Physiol. Plantarum, 3:277–292.

——— 1951. Studies on growth and metabolism of roots. V. Cell elongation and dry matter content. *Ibid.,* 4:199–208.

——— 1951. Studies on growth and metabolism of roots. VII. The action of α-phenoxy-propionic acids. *Ibid.,* 4:641–651.

——— 1953. Physiology of root growth. Ann. Rev. Plant Physiol., 4:237–252.

——— 1953. Studies on growth and metabolism of roots. IX. Cell elongation and water absorption. Physiol. Plantarum, 6:262–276.

——— 1953. Growth and water absorption of *Helianthus* tuber tissue. *Ibid.,* 6:685–691.

BURTON, D. F. 1947. Formative effects of certain chlorophenoxy compounds on bean leaves. Bot. Gaz., 109:183–194.

CAJLACHJAN, M. CH. 1936. New factors in support of the hormonal theory of plant development. Compt. Rend. (Doklady). Acad. Sci., 13:79–83.

——— 1936. On the mechanism of the photoperiodic reaction. *Ibid.,* 10:89–93.

——— 1938. Motion of blossom hormone in girdled and grafted plants. *Ibid.,* 18:607–612.

——— AND L. P. ZDANOVA 1938. Photoperiodism and creation of growth hormones. *Ibid.,* 19:107–111.

CAMPBELL, D. H. AND D. PRESSMAN 1944. A simplified lyophil apparatus. Science, 99:285–286.

CARLSON, M. C. 1929. Microchemical studies of rooting and non-rooting rose cuttings. Bot. Gaz., 87:64–80.

CARNS, H. R., J. HACSKAYLO AND J. L. EMBRY 1954. Relation of an indoleacetic acid inhibitor to cotton boll development (Abstract). A.I.B.S., Gainesville, Fla.

CHADWICK, L. C., R. R. MILLER AND D. ERSKINE 1951. Prevention of fruit formation on some ornamental trees. Proc. Amer. Soc. Hort. Sci., 58:308–312.

CHOLODNY, N. 1927. Wuchshormone und Tropismen bei den Pflanzen. Biol. Zentralbl., 47:604–626.

——— 1929. Über des Wachstum des vertikal und horizontal orientierten Stengels in Zusammenhand mit der Frage nach der hormonalen Natur der Tropism. Planta, 7:702–719.

——— 1934. Über die Bildung und Leitung des Wuchshormones bei den Wurzeln. *Ibid.,* 21:517–530.

——— 1936. On the theory of yarovisation. Compt. Rend. (Doklady) Acad. Sci., 3:8.

——— 1936. Hormonization of grains. *Ibid.,* 3:9.

CHRISTENSEN, E. 1954. Root production in plants following localized stem irradiation. Science, 119:127–128.

CHRISTIANSEN, G. S. AND K. V. THIMANN 1950. The metabolism of stem tissue during growth and its inhibition. I. Carbohydrates. Arch. Biochem. and Biophys., 26: 230–247.

CLAES, H. 1952. Wirkung von IAA und TIBA auf die Blutenbildung von *Hyoscyamus niger.* Zeit. für Naturforsch, 7b:50–55.

CLARK, B. E. AND WITTWER, S. H. 1949. Effect of certain growth regulators on seed stalk development in lettuce and celery. Plant Physiol., 24:555–576.

CLARK, H. E. AND KERNS, K. R. 1942. Control of flowering with phytohormones. Science, 95:536–537.

——— AND KERNS, K. R. 1943. Effects of growth-regulating substances on parthenocarpic fruit. Bot. Gaz., 104:639–644.

COLLINS, S. T. AND F. E. SMITH 1952. Preparation of optical isomers of α-(2,4-dichlorophenoxy) propionic acid and their growth-regulating activity. Jour. Sci. Food and Agric., 3:248–249.

COMMONER, B., S. FOGEL AND W. H. MULLER 1943. The mechanism of auxin action. The effect of auxin on water absorption by potato tuber tissue. Amer. Jour. Bot., 30:23–38.

——— AND D. MAZIA 1942. The mechanism of auxin action. Plant Physiol., 17: 682–685.

——— AND K. V. THIMANN 1941. On the relation between growth and respiration in the *Avena* coleoptile. Jour. Gen. Physiol., 24:279–296.

CONSDEN, R., H. GORDON AND A. J. P. MARTIN 1944. Quantitative analysis of proteins in a partition chromatographic method using paper. Biochem. Jour., 38:224–232.

COOPER, W. C. 1935. Hormones in relation to root formation on stem cuttings. Plant Physiol., 10:789–794.

——— 1936. Transport of root-forming hormone in woody cuttings. Plant Physiol., 11:779–793.

——— 1944. Vegetative propagation of *Derris* and *Lonchocarpus* with the aid of growth substances. Bot. Gaz., 106:1–12.

——— AND F. W. WENT 1938. Effect on root formation of re-treating cuttings with growth substance. Science, 87:390.

CORNS, W. G. 1950. Effects of 2,4-D on catalase, respiration and protein content of bean plants. Canadian Jour. Res., 28:393–405.

CRAFTS, A. S. 1948. A theory of herbicidal action. Science, 108:85–86.

CRANE, J. C. 1948. Fruit growth of four fig varieties as measured by diameter and fresh weight. Proc. Amer. Soc. Hort. Sci., 52:237–244.

——— 1952. Growth-regulator specificity in relation to ovary wall development in the fig. Science, 115:238–239.

——— 1953. Further responses of the apricot to 2,4,5-trichlorophenoxyacetic acid application. Proc. Amer. Soc. Hort. Sci., 61:163–174.

——— 1954. The effectiveness of 2,4,5-trichlorophenoxyacetic acid in reducing drop and promoting growth of frosted apricot fruit. Science, 119:383–385.

——— AND R. BLONDEAU 1949. Controlled growth of fig fruits by synthetic hormone application. Proc. Amer. Soc. Hort. Sci., 54:102–108.

——— AND R. M. BROOKS 1952. Growth of apricot fruits as influenced by 2,4,5-trichlorophenoxyacetic acid application. *Ibid.*, 59:218–224.

CROWDY, S. H. 1948. Treatment of apple canker lesions with plant growth substances. Nature, 161:320–321.

——— AND R. L. WAIN 1950. Aryloxyaliphatic acids as systemic fungicides. *Ibid.*, 165:937–938.

——— AND R. L. WAIN 1951. Studies on systemic fungicides. I. Fungicidal properties of the aryloxyalkylcarboxylic acids. Ann. Appl. Biol., 38:318–333.

CURTIS, O. F. 1918. Stimulation of root growth in cuttings by treatment with chemical compounds. Cornell Univ. Agric. Expt. Sta. Mem., 14:75–138.

CZAJA, A. TH. 1935. Wurzelwachstum, Wuchsstoff und die Theorie der Wuchsstoffwirkung. Ber. Deutsch. bot. Ges., 53:221–245.

DALLYN, S. AND O. SMITH 1952. Effect of growth substances on sprouting of carrots, turnips and onions. Bot. Gaz., 113:362–367.

DARWIN, C. 1881. *The Power of Movement in Plants.* The Appleton Co., New York.

DAVEY, A. E. AND C. O. HESSE 1942. Experiments with sprays in the control of preharvest drop of Bartlett pears in California. Proc. Amer. Soc. Hort. Sci., 40:49–53.

DAVIDSON, J. H. 1940. Temperature variation and the effectiveness of preharvest sprays on apples. State Hort. Soc. Mich., 70:109–112.

DAVIS, D. AND A. E. DIMOND 1953. Inducing disease resistance with plant growth regulators. Phytopath., 43:137–140.

DAY, B. E. 1952. The absorption and translocation of 2,4-D by bean plants. Plant Physiol., 27:143–152.

DAY, L. H. 1932. Is the increased rooting of wounded cuttings sometimes due to water absorption? Proc. Amer. Soc. Hort. Sci., 29:350–351.

DELISLE, A. L. 1937. The influence of auxin on secondary branching in two species of *Aster*. Amer. Jour. Bot., 24:159–166.

De Rose, H. R. and A. S. Newman 1947. Persistence of growth regulators in the soil. Soil Sci. Soc. Amer. Proc., 12:222–226.

Derscheid, L. A. 1952. Physiological and morphological responses of barley to 2,4-D. Plant Physiol., 27:121–134.

De Tar, J. E., W. H. Griggs and J. C. Crane 1950. Effect of growth regulators on set of Bartlett pears. Proc. Amer. Soc. Hort. Sci., 55:137–139.

Dhillon, A. S. and E. H. Lucas, 1950. Absorption, translocation and persistence of 2,4-D in plants. Bot. Gaz., 112:198–207.

Dijkman, M. J. 1933. A quantitative analysis of the geotropical curvature in dicotyledons. K. Akad. Wetenschap. Amsterdam. Proc. Sect. Sci., 36:749–758.

Dolk, H. E. 1929. Über die Wirkung der Schwerkraft auf Koleoptilen von *Avena sativa* II. K. Akad. Wetenschàp. Amsterdam. Proc. Sect. Sci., 32:1127–1140.

Dore, J. 1953. Seasonal variation in the regeneration of root-cuttings. Nature, 172: 1189.

Dostal, R. and M. Hosek 1937. Über den Einfluss von Heteroauxin auf die Morphogenese bei *Circaea.* Flora, 139:263.

Eames, A. J. 1950. Destruction of phloem in young bean plants after treatment with 2,4-D. Amer. Jour. Bot., 37:840–847.

——— 1951. Leaf ontogeny and treatments with 2,4-D. Amer. Jour. Bot., 38: 777–780.

Edgerton, L. J. and M. B. Hoffman 1951. Effectiveness of growth regulators in delaying the drop of McIntosh apple. Proc. Amer. Soc. Hort. Sci., 57:120–124.

——— and M. B. Hoffman 1952. The effect of thinning peaches with bloom and post-bloom sprays on the cold hardiness of fruit buds. *Ibid.,* 60:155–159.

——— and M. B. Hoffman 1953. The effect of some growth substances on leaf petiole abscission and preharvest fruit drop of several apple varieties. *Ibid.,* 62:159–166.

Elliott, B. B. 1952. Metabolic factors in floral initiation and growth. Ph.D. Dissertation, Purdue University, Lafayette, Indiana.

——— and A. C. Leopold 1953. An inhibitor of germination and of amylase activity in oat seeds. Physiol. Plantarum, 6:66–78.

Ellison, J. H. and O. Smith 1948. Effects of spraying a sprout inhibitor on potato plants. Proc. Amer. Soc. Hort. Sci., 51:397–400.

Emilsson, B. 1949. Studies on the rest period and dormant period in the potato tuber. Acta Agr. Suec., 3:189.

Ennis, W. B., R. E. Williamson and K. P. Dorschner 1952. Studies on spray retention by leaves of different plants. Weeds, 1:274–286.

Enzie, J. V. and G. W. Schneider 1941. Spraying for control of preharvest drop of apples in New Mexico. Proc. Amer. Soc. Hort. Sci., 38:99–103.

Erickson, L. C. 1951. Effects of 2,4-D on drop of navel oranges. Proc. Amer. Soc. Hort. Sci., 58:46–52.

——— and B. L. Brannaman 1950. Effects on fruit growth of a 2,4-D spray applied to lime trees. Proc. Amer. Soc. Hort. Sci., 56:79–82.

——— B. L. Brannaman and H. Z. Hield 1952. Response of Delicious and Rome Beauty apples to a preharvest spray of 2,4,5-TP in southern California. *Ibid.,* 60:160–164.

——— and P. DeBach 1953. Rooting lemon cuttings with fruits attached. Science, 117:102–103.

——— and S. Gault 1950. The duration and effect of 2,4-D toxicity to crops grown on calcareous soil under controlled irrigation conditions. Agron. Jour., 42:226–229.

Evenari, M. 1949. Germination inhibitors. Bot. Rev., 15:153–194.

Eyster, H. C. 1946. Effect of auxins on action of diastase in vitro. Plant Physiol., 21:68–74.

Faber, E. R. 1936. Wuchsstoffversuche an Keimwurzeln. Jahrb. wiss. Bot., 83: 439–469.

Fawcett, C. H., J. M. A. Ingram and R. L. Wain 1952. β-oxidation of ω-phenoxyalkylcarboxylic acids in the flax plant. Nature, 170:887.

Ferri, M. G. 1951. Fluorescence and photoinactivation of indoleacetic acid. Arch. Biochem. and Biophys., 31:127–131.

——— and L. V. de Camargo 1950. Influence of growth substances on movement of pulvini of bean plants. Acad. Brasil de Ciencias, 22:161–170.

Fertig, S. N. 1952. Preliminary report on weed control in small grains where legumes are seeded. N. E. Weed Control Conf., 6:235–244.

Fiedler, H. 1936. Entwicklungs—und reizphysiologische Untersuchungen an Kulturen isolierter Würzelspitzen. Zeitschr. Bot., 30:385–436.

Fillmore, R. H. 1950. Control of plant development with maleic hydrazide. Arnoldia, 10:33–38.

Fitting, H. 1909. Die Beeinflussung der Orchideenbluten durch die Bestaubung und durch andere Umstande. Zeitschr. Bot., 1:1–86.

Floor, I. J. 1951. De vermeerdering van onderstammen voor fruitgewassen. Inst. Vered. Touinbou. Wageningen, 25:1–14.

Fogg, G. E. 1947. Quantitative studies on the wetting of leaves by water. Proc. Roy. Soc., 134:503–522.

Foster, J. R. 1952. Comparison of present methods of application. Proc. N. C. Weed Control Conf., 9:36–38.

Foster, R. J., D. H. McRae and J. Bonner 1952. Auxin-induced growth inhibition a natural consequence of two-point attachment. Proc. Natl. Acad. Sci., 38:1014–1022.

Franklin, D. F. 1948. Hormone sprays to facilitate bolting of lettuce. Proc. Amer. Soc. Hort. Sci., 51:453–456.

Freed, V. H. 1948. Qualitative reaction for 2,4-D. Science, 107:98–99.

Freiberg, S. R. and H. E. Clark 1952. Effects of 2,4-dichlorophenoxyacetic acid upon the nitrogen metabolism and water relations of soybean plants grown at different nitrogen levels. Bot. Gaz., 113:321–333.

French, R. C. and H. Beevers 1953. Respiratory and growth responses induced by growth regulators and allied compounds. Amer. Jour. Bot., 40:660–666.

Fults, J. and M. Johnson 1950. A cumulative fluorescent chemical found in certain plants treated with 2,4-D identified as scopoletin (Abstract). Western Weed Control Conf., Denver. (Cited in van Overbeek *et al,* 1951).

Funke, H. and H. Söding 1948. Über das Wuchsstoff-Hemmstoffsystem der Hafer-Koleoptile und der Kartoffelknolle. Planta, 36:341–370.

Gall, H. J. F. 1948. Effects of 2,4-D on starch digestion and reducing activity in bean tissue cultures. Bot. Gaz., 110:319–323.

Gallup, A. H. and F. G. Gustafson 1952. Absorption and translocation of radioactive 2,4-dichloro-5-iodophenoxyacetic acid by green plants. Plant Physiol., 27:603–612.

Galston, A. W. 1947. Effect of 2,3,5-triiodobenzoic acid on growth and flowering of soybeans. Amer. Jour. Bot., 34:356–360.

——— 1949. Riboflavin sensitized photo-oxidation of indoleacetic acid and related compounds. Proc. Natl. Acad. Sci., 35:10–17.

——— 1950. Phototropism II. Bot. Rev., 16:361–378.

——— AND R. S. BAKER 1949. Studies on the physiology of light action. II. The photodynamic action of riboflavin. Amer. Jour. Bot., 36:773–780.

——— AND R. S. BAKER 1951. Studies on the physiology of light action. III. Light activation of a flavoprotein enzyme by reversal of a naturally occurring inhibition. *Ibid.,* 38:190–195.

——— AND R. S. BAKER 1951. Studies on the physiology of light action. IV. Light enhancement of auxin-induced growth in green peas. Plant Physiol., 26:311–317.

——— AND R. S. BAKER 1953. Studies on the physiology of light action. V. Photoinductive alteration of auxin metabolism. Amer. Jour. Bot., 40:512–516.

——— J. BONNER AND R. S. BAKER 1953. Flavoprotein and peroxidase as components of the indoleacetic acid oxidase system of peas. Arch. Biochem. and Biophys., 49:456–470.

——— AND L. Y. DALBERG 1954. The adaptive formation and physiological significance of indoleacetic acid oxidase. Amer. Jour. Bot., 41:373–380.

——— AND M. E. HAND 1949. Studies on the physiology of light action I. Auxin and the light inhibition of growth. *Ibid.,* 36:85–94.

GANE, R. 1935. The formation of ethylene by plant tissues and its significance in the ripening of fruit. Jour. Pomol. Hort. Sci., 13:351.

GARDNER, F. E., P. C. MARTH AND L. P. BATJER 1939. Spraying with plant growth substances to prevent apple fruit dropping. Science, 90:208–209.

——— P. C. MARTH AND L. P. BATJER 1940. Spraying with plant growth substances for control of the preharvest drop of apples. Proc. Amer. Soc. Hort. Sci., 37:415–428.

GAUCH, H. G. AND W. M. DUGGAR, JR. 1953. The role of boron in the translocation of sucrose. Plant Physiol., 28:457–466.

GAUTHERET, R. J. 1952. Récherches sur l'action de l'hydrazide maleique et de l'acide indole-acétique sur les cultures de tissus de Topinambour. Compt. Rend. Acad. Sci., 234:2218–2221.

GAWADI, A. G. AND G. S. AVERY JR. 1950. Leaf abscission and the so-called abscission layer. Amer. Jour. Bot., 37:172–180.

GEIGER-HUBER, M. AND H. HUBER 1945. Über die Ursache des gegensatzlichen geotropischen Verhaltens von Spross und Wurzel. Experientia, 1:26–28.

GERHARDT, F. AND D. F. ALLMENDINGER 1945. The influence of α-naphthaleneacetic acid spray on the maturity and storage physiology of apples, pears, and sweet cherries. Proc. Amer. Soc. Hort. Sci., 46:118.

——— AND E. SMITH 1948. The storage and ripening response of western-grown fruits to post-harvest treatment with growth regulators. *Ibid.,* 52:159–163.

GOLDACRE, P. L. 1951. Hydrogen peroxide in the enzymic oxidation of heteroauxin. Australian Jour. Sci., 4:293–302.

——— A. W. GALSTON AND R. L. WEINTRAUB 1953. The effect of substituted phenols on the activity of the indoleacetic acid oxidase of peas. Arch. Biochem. and Biophys., 43:358–373.

GOODMAN, R. N. AND D. D. HEMPHILL 1954. The effects of indoleacetic acid on the plant disease inhibiting properties of antibiotics. Science, 119:347–348.

GOODSPEED, T. H., J. M. MCGEE AND R. W. HODGESON 1918. Note on the effects of illuminating gas and its constituents in causing abscission of flowers. Univ. Calif. Publ. Bot., 5:439–450.

GOODWIN, R. H. 1937. The role of auxin in leaf development in *Solidago* sp. Amer. Jour. Bot., 24:43–50.

GORDON, S. A. 1946. Auxin-protein complexes of the wheat grain. Amer. Jour. Bot., 33:160–169.

——— 1953. Physiology of Hormone Action. In W. E. Loomis (Ed.) *Growth and Differentiation.* The Iowa State College Press, Ames.

——— AND F. S. NIEVA 1949. Biosynthesis of auxin in the vegetative pineapple. I. and II. Arch. Biochem. and Biophys., 20:356–385.

——— AND R. P. WEBER 1951. Colorimetric estimation of indoleacetic acid. Plant Physiol., 26:192–195.

GORTER, C. J. 1932. Groeistofproblemen bej Wortels. Diss. Utrecht, 1932.

GORTNER, W. A. 1952. Water of crystallization of naphthaleneacetic acid and its salts. Science, 115:122–123.

GOSSARD, A. C. 1941. Rooting pecan stem tissue by layering. Proc. Amer. Soc. Hort. Sci., 38:213–214.

GRACE, N. H. 1939. Vegetative propagation of conifers. I. Rooting of cuttings taken from the upper and lower regions of a Norway spruce tree. Canadian Jour. Res., 17C:178–180.

GRANT, K. T. 1953. Sucker control in tobacco with maleic hydrazide. The Lighter, 23:15–16.

GRIGGS, W. H., B. T. IWAKIRI AND J. E. DE TAR 1951. Effect of 2,4,5-TP on fruit-set and characteristic of pear. Proc. Amer. Soc. Hort. Sci., 58:37–45.

GUNCKEL, J. E. AND K. V. THIMANN 1949. Studies of development in long shoots and short shoots of *Ginkgo biloba* L. III. Auxin production of short shoots. Amer. Jour. Bot., 36:145–151.

GUSTAFSON, F. G. 1936. Inducement of fruit development by growth-promoting chemicals. Proc. Natl. Acad. Sci., 22:628–636.

——— 1939. The cause of natural parthenocarpy. Amer. Jour. Bot., 26:135–138.

——— 1939. Auxin distribution in fruits and its significance in fruit development. *Ibid.,* 26:189–194.

——— 1941. Extraction of growth hormones from plants. *Ibid.,* 28:947–951.

——— 1941. Lack of inhibition of lateral buds by the growth promoting substance phenyl acetic acid. Plant Physiol., 16:203–206.

GUTHRIE, J. D. 1933. Change in glutathione content of potato tubers treated with chemicals that break the rest period. Contr. Boyce Thompson Inst., 5:331–340.

——— 1939. Control of bud growth in potatoes with growth regulating substances. *Ibid.,* 11:29–53.

——— 1940. Role of glutathione in breaking rest period of buds by ethylene chlorohydrin. *Ibid.,* 11:261–270.

HAAGEN-SMIT, A. J. 1951. The history and nature of plant growth hormones. In F. Skoog (Ed.), *Plant Growth Substances,* Univ. of Wisc. Press, Madison.

——— W. B. DANDLIKER, S. H. WITTWER AND A. E. MURNEEK 1946. Isolation of indoleacetic acid from immature corn kernels. Amer. Jour. Bot., 33:118–119.

——— W. D. LEECH AND W. R. BERGREN 1942. The estimation, isolation and identification of auxins in plant materials. *Ibid.,* 29:500–505.

HACKETT, D. P. 1951. The osmotic change during the auxin-induced water uptake by potato tissue. Plant Physiol., 27:279–284.

——— AND K. V. THIMANN 1952. The effect of auxin on growth and respiration of artichoke tissue. Proc. Natl. Acad. Sci., 38:770–775.

HALL, W. C., G. B. FRUCHELUT AND H. C. LANE 1953. Chemical defoliation and regrowth inhibition in cotton. Tex. Ag. Mech. Coll. Syst. Bull. 759, 1953.

HAMNER, C. L. AND H. M. SELL 1950. Selective inhibitory action of methyl umbelliferone (Abstract). A.I.B.S., Columbus.

HAMNER, K. C. AND E. J. KRAUS 1937. Histological reactions of bean plants to growth-promoting substances. Bot. Gaz., 98:735–807.

HANCOCK, C. R. AND H. W. B. BARLOW 1953. Assay of growth substances by a modified straight growth method. Ann. Rep. E. Malling Res. Sta. for 1952, pp. 88–94.

HAND, D. B. 1939. Molecular weight and association of the enzyme urease. Jour. Amer. Chem. Soc., 61:3180–3183.

HANKS, R. W. 1946. Removal of 2,4-D from six soils by leaching. Bot. Gaz., 108: 186–191.

HANSEN, B. 1951. Impurities in methoxone and their influence on plants. Physiol. Plantarum, 4:667–676.

HANSEN, E. AND H. HARTMAN 1937. Effect of ethylene and metabolic gases upon respiration and ripening of pears before and after cold storage. Plant Physiol., 12:441–454.

HARTMANN, H. T. 1952. Spray thinning of olives with naphthaleneacetic acid. Proc. Amer. Soc. Hort. Sci., 59:187–195.

HAUSER, E. W. AND D. W. YOUNG 1952. Penetration and translocation of 2,4-D compounds. Proc. N. C. Weed Control Conf., 9:27–31.

HAWKER, L. E. 1932. Experiments on the perception of gravity by roots. New Phytol., 31:321–328.

HAY, J. R. AND K. V. THIMANN 1954. Translocation of high concentrations of 2,4-D and 2,4,5-T (Abstract). A.I.B.S., Gainesville, Fla.

HEIDT, K. 1931. Über das Verhalten von Explantaten der Wurzelspitze in nahrstoffreien Kulturen. Arch. Exp. Zellforsch., 11:693–724.

HEINICKE, A. J. 1917. Factors influencing the abscission of flowers and partially developed fruits of the apple. Cornell Agr. Expt. Sta. Bull. 393.

HEMBERG, T. 1947. Studies of auxins and growth-inhibiting substances in the potato tuber and their significance with regard to its rest period. Acta Hort. Bergiani, 14:133–220.

——— 1949. Significance of growth inhibiting substances and auxins for rest period of potato. Physiol. Plantarum, 2:24–36.

——— 1949. Growth inhibiting substances in buds of *Fraxinus*. *Ibid.,* 2:37–44.

——— 1950. Effect of glutathione on growth inhibiting substances in resting potato tubers. *Ibid.,* 3:17–21.

——— 1951. Rooting experiments with hypocotyles of *Phaseolus vulgaris*. *Ibid.,* 4:358–369.

——— 1952. Significance of acid growth inhibiting substances for rest period of potato. *Ibid.,* 5:115–129.

——— 1954. Studies on the occurrence of free and bound auxins and of growth inhibiting substances in the potato tuber. Physiol. Plantarum 7:312–322.

HEMPHILL, D. D. 1949. Importance of time of application of hormone sprays to tomato. Proc. Amer. Soc. Hort. Sci., 54:261–264.

HENDERSON, J. H. M. AND J. BONNER 1952. Auxin metabolism in normal and crown-gall tissue of sunflower. Amer. Jour. Bot., 39:444–451.

HERNANDEZ, T. P. AND G. F. WARREN 1950. Some factors affecting the rate of inactivation and leaching of 2,4-D in different soils. Proc. Amer. Soc. Hort. Sci., 56:287–293.

HESSAYON, D. G. 1952. Effect of auxins on mycelial growth of *Fusarium oxysporum* var. *cubense*. Nature, 169:803–804.

HESSE, C. O. AND A. E. DAVEY 1942. Experiments with sprays in the control of fruit drop of apricot and peach. Proc. Amer. Soc. Hort. Sci., 40:55–62.

HEYN, A. N. J. 1932. Récherches sur les relations de la plasticité des membranes cellulaires et la croissance des végétaux. Compt. Rend. Acad. Sci., 194:1848–1850.

HIBBARD, A. D. AND A. E. MURNEEK 1950. Thinning peaches with hormone sprays. Proc. Amer. Soc. Hort. Sci., 56:65–69.

HILL, G. D. AND C. J. WILLARD 1952. Herbicides and adjuvants on Canada thistle. Proc. N. C. Weed Control Conf., 9:24–25.

HITCHCOCK, A. E., 1935. Tobacco as a test plant for comparing the effectiveness of preparations containing growth substances. Contrib. Boyce Thompson Inst., 7:349–364.

——— AND P. W. ZIMMERMAN 1930. Rooting of greenwood cuttings as influenced by the age of tissue. Proc. Amer. Soc. Hort. Sci., 27:136–138.

——— AND P. W. ZIMMERMAN 1935. Absorption and movement of synthetic growth substances from soil as indicated by responses of aerial parts. Contr. Boyce Thompson Inst., 7:447–476.

——— AND P. W. ZIMMERMAN 1939. Comparative activity of root-inducing substances and methods of treating cuttings. *Ibid.,* 10:461–480.

——— AND P. W. ZIMMERMAN 1940. Effects obtained with mixtures of root-inducing and other substances. *Ibid.,* 11:143–160.

——— AND P. W. ZIMMERMAN 1942. Root-inducing activity of phenoxy compounds in relation to their structure. *Ibid.,* 12:497–507.

——— AND P. W. ZIMMERMAN 1943. Summer sprays with naphthaleneacetic acid retard opening of buds on fruit trees. Proc. Amer. Soc. Hort. Sci., 42:141–145.

HOFFMAN, M. B. AND L. J. EDGERTON 1952. Comparison of NAA, 2,4,5-TP and 2,4,5-T for controlling harvest drop of McIntosh apples. Proc. Amer. Soc. Hort. Sci., 59:225–230.

——— L. J. EDGERTON AND A. VAN DOREN 1942. Some results in controlling the preharvest drop of apples. *Ibid.,* 40:35–38.

HOFFMANN, O. L. 1953. Inhibition of auxin effects by 2,4,6-Trichlorophenoxyacetic acid. Plant Physiol., 28:622–628.

——— AND A. E. SMITH 1949. A new group of plant growth regulators. Science, 109:588.

——— AND E. P. SYLWESTER 1950. Physiological effects of maleic hydrazide. Proc. N. C. Weed Control Conf., 7:104–106.

——— AND E. P. SYLWESTER 1953. Comments on quack grass control with maleic hydrazide. Weeds, 2:66–67.

HOLLEY, R. W., F. P. BOYLE, H. K. DURFEE AND A. D. HOLLEY 1951. Study of the auxins in cabbage using counter-current distribution. Arch. Biochem. and Biophys., 32:192–199.

HOWLETT, F. S. 1939. The modification of flower structure by environment in varieties of *Lycopersicum esculentum.* Jour. Agric. Res., 58:79–117.

——— 1949. Tomato fruit-set and development with particular reference to premature softening following synthetic hormone treatment. Proc. Amer. Soc. Hort. Sci., 53:323–336.

——— 1950. Use of hormones in vegetable crop production. Proc. Ohio Veg. and Potato Growers Assn., 35:34–50.

——— AND P. E. MARTH 1946. Aerosol applications of growth substances to the greenhouse tomato. Proc. Amer. Soc. Hort. Sci., 48:458–474.

INGESTAD, T. 1953. Kinetic aspects on the growth-regulating effect of some phenoxy acids. Physiol. Plantarum, 6:796–803.

IYENGAR, M. R. S. AND R. L. STARKEY 1953. Synergism and antagonism of auxin by antibiotics. Science, 118:357–358.

JENSEN, H. L. AND H. I. PETERSEN 1952. Detoxication of hormone herbicides by soil bacteria. Nature, 170:39–40.

JERCHEL, D. AND R. MÜLLER 1951. Papierchromatographie der β-Indolylessigsäure. Naturwiss., 38:561–562.

JOHNSON, E. L. 1936. Susceptibility of 70 species to x-rays. Plant Physiol., 11:319–342.

JONES, E. R. H., H. B. HENBEST, G. F. SMITH AND J. A. BENTLEY 1952. 3-Indolylacetonitrile: a naturally occurring plant growth hormone. Nature, 169:485.

JORGENSON, C. J. AND C. L. HAMNER 1948. Weed control in soils with 2,4-D and related compounds, and their residual effects under varying environmental conditions. Bot. Gaz., 109:324–333.

KATUNSKIJ, V. M. 1936. On the causes of pre- and post-floral movements of peduncles and scapes. Compt. Rend. (Doklady) Acad. Sci., 12:343–346.

KAWALKI, W. 1894. Untersuchungen über die Diffusionsfahigkeit einiger electrolyte in alkohol. Ann. Phys. und Chemie, 52:166–190.

KELLY, S. 1949. The effect of temperature on the susceptibility of plants to 2,4-D. Plant Physiol., 24:534–536.

——— AND G. S. AVERY JR. 1949. The effect of 2,4-dichlorophenoxyacetic acid and other physiologically active substances on respiration. Amer. Jour. Bot., 36:421–426.

KENT, M. AND W. A. GORTNER 1951. Effect of pre-illumination on response of split pea stems to growth substances. Bot. Gaz., 112:307–311.

KING, G. S. 1946. 2,4-D herbicides for water hyacinths (abstract). Amer. Jour. Bot., 33:837.

KING, L. J., J. A. LAMBRECHT AND T. P. FINN 1950. Herbicidal properties of sodium 2,4-dichlorophenoxyethyl sulfate. Contrib. Boyce Thompson Inst., 16:191–208.

KLEIN, W. H. 1951. Factors in flower initiation. Ph.D. Dissertation, Purdue University, Lafayette, Indiana.

——— AND A. C. LEOPOLD 1953. Effect of maleic hydrazide on flower initiation. Plant Physiol., 28:293–298.

KLINGMAN, G. C. AND G. H. AHLGREN 1951. Effects of 2,4-D on dry weight, reducing sugars, total sugars, polysaccharides, nitrogen and allyl sulfide in wild garlic. Bot. Gaz., 113:119–134.

KNIGHT, R. C. 1926. The propagation of fruit tree stocks by stem cuttings. I. Observations on the factors governing the rooting of hard-wood cuttings. Jour. Pomol. and Hort. Sci., 5:248–266.

KOEPFLI, J. B., K. V. THIMANN AND F. W. WENT 1938. Phytohormones: structure and physiological activity. Jour. Biol. Chem., 122:763–780.

KÖGL, F. 1933. On plant hormones (auxin A and auxin B). Rep. British Assoc., 600–609.

——— AND O. A. DE BRUIN 1950. Synthèses dans le domaine des auxines II. Soc. Chim. Néerl., 69:729–752.

——— AND A. J. HAAGEN-SMIT 1931. Über die chemie des Wuchsstoffs. K. Akad. Wetenschap. Amsterdam. Proc. Sect. Sci., 34:1411–1416.

——— A. J. HAAGEN-SMIT AND H. ERXLEBEN 1934. Über ein neues auxin (hetero-auxin) aus hain. XI Mitteilung. Zeitschr. Physiol. Chem., 228:90–103.

——— AND D. G. F. R. KOSTERMANS 1934. Hetero-auxin als Stoffweckselprodukt niederer pflanzlicher Organismen. Isolierung aus hefe. XIII Mitteilung. *Ibid.*, 228:113–121.

——— AND D. G. F. R. KOSTERMANS 1935. Über die konstitutionsspezifität des hetero-auxins. XVI Mitteilung. *Ibid.*, 235:201–216.

——— AND B. VERKAAIK 1944. Über die antipoden der α-(β-Indolyl) propionsäure und ihre verschieden starke physiologische Wirksamkeit. *Ibid.*, 280:167–176.

KRAMER, M. AND F. W. WENT 1949. The nature of the auxin in tomato stem tips. Plant Physiol., 24:207–221.

KRAUS, E. J. AND H. R. KRAYBILL 1918. Vegetation and reproduction with special reference to the tomato. Oregon Sta. Bull., 149:1–90.

——— AND J. W. MITCHELL 1947. Growth-regulating substances as herbicides. Bot. Gaz., 108:301–350.

KRAUSS, B., J. FO, H. E. CLARK AND G. T. NIGHTINGALE 1948. Use of BNA sprays to delay ripening, improve pineapple yields and fruit shape. Pineapple Research Inst. Special Report, 10:1–14.

KRIES, O. H. 1946. Persistence of 2,4-D in soil in relation to water, organic matter and lime. Bot. Gaz., 108:510–525.

KRUYT, W. 1954. A study in connection with the problem of hormonization of seeds. Ph.D. Thesis. University of Utrecht.

KULESCHA, Z. 1948. Use of trypsin for extraction of plant-growth substances from plant tissues. Compt. Rend. Soc. Biol., 142:931–933.

KUTSKY, R. 1952. Effects of indolebutyric acid and other compounds on virus concentration in plant tissue cultures. Science, 115:19–20.

——— AND T. E. RAWLINS 1950. Inhibition of virus multiplication by naphthaleneacetic acid in tobacco tissue. Jour. Bact., 60:763–766.

KVAMME, O. J., C. O. CLAGETT AND W. B. TREUMANN 1949. Kinetics of the action of the sodium salt of 2,4-dichlorophenoxyacetic acid on the germ lipase of wheat. Arch. Biochem. and Biophys., 24:321–328.

LABAW, G. D. AND N. W. DESROSIER 1954. The effect of synthetic plant auxins on the heat resistance of bacterial spores. Food Res., 19:98–105.

LAIBACH, F. 1933. Versuche mit Wuchsstoffpaste. Ber. Deutsch. bot. Ges., 51:386–392.

——— 1934. Zum Wuchsstoffproblem. Der Züchter, 6:49–53.

——— AND O. FISCHNICH 1935. Künstliche Wurzelneubildung mittels Wuchsstoffpaste. Ber. Deutsch. bot. Ges., 53:528–539.

——— AND O. FISCHNICH 1936. Über Blattbewegungen unter dem Einfluss von künstlich zugeführtem Wuchsstoff. Biol. Zentralbl., 56:62–68.

——— AND F. J. KRIBBEN 1950. Über die β-Indolylessigsäure für die Blutenbildung. Ber. Deutsch. bot. Ges., 63:119–120.

LANG, A. 1952. Physiology of flowering. Ann. Rev. Plant Physiol., 3:265–307.

LANGSTON, R. G. 1954. The reproductive physiology of plants with special reference to peppermint. Ph.D. Dissertation. Purdue University, Lafayette, Indiana.

LARSEN, P. 1940. Über Hemmung des Streckungswachstums durch natürlich vorkommende, ätherlösliche Stoffe. Planta, 30:160–167.

——— 1944. 3-Indole acetaldehyde as a growth hormone in higher plants. Dansk Bot. Ark., 11:1–132.

——— 1947. *Avena* curvatures produced by mixtures of growth promoting and growth retarding substances. Amer. Jour. Bot., 34:349–356.

——— 1949. Conversion of indole acetaldehyde to indoleacetic acid in excised coleoptiles and in coleoptile juice. *Ibid.,* 36:32–41.

——— 1951. Formation, occurrence and inactivation of growth substances. Ann. Rev. Plant Physiol., 2:169–198.

——— 1951. Enzymatic conversion of indole acetaldehyde and naphthalene acetaldehyde to auxins. Plant Physiol., 26:697–707.

LA RUE, C. D. 1936. Effect of auxin on abscission of petioles. Proc. Natl. Acad. Sci., 22:254–259.

LEAPER, J. M. AND J. R. BISHOP 1950. Relation of halogen position to physiological properties in the mono- di- and trichlorophenoxyacetic acids. Bot. Gaz., 112:250–258.

Lee, O. C. and L. F. Bewick 1947. Results of uniform experiment. III. The relative susceptibility to 2,4-D of annual and winter annuals at different stages of growth. Proc. N. C. Weed Contr. Conf., 4:210.

Le Fanu, B. 1936. Auxin and correlative inhibition. New Phytol., 35:205–220.

Lek, H. A. A. van der 1934. Over den invloed der knoppen op de wortelvorming der stekken. (With summary: On the influence of the buds on root-development in cuttings). Mededel. Landbouwhoogesch. Wageningen., 38:1–95.

Leopold, A. C. 1949. Physiological effects of flower forcing in pineapple (Abstract). A.A.A.S., New York.

——— 1949. The control of tillering in grasses by auxin. Amer. Jour. Bot., 36:437–440.

——— and F. S. Guernsey 1952. A role for malic acid in tomato fruit-set. Arch. Biochem. and Biophys., 41:64–73.

——— and F. S. Guernsey 1953. Flower initiation in Alaska pea. I. Evidence as to the role of auxin. Amer. Jour. Bot., 40:46–50.

——— and F. S. Guernsey 1953. Modification of floral initiation with auxins and temperatures. Amer. Jour. Bot., 40:603–607.

——— and F. S. Guernsey 1953. Auxin polarity in the Coleus plant. Bot. Gaz., 115:147–154.

——— and F. S. Guernsey 1953. The effect of nitrogen upon fruit abnormalities in tomato. Proc. Amer. Soc. Hort. Sci., 61:333–338.

——— and F. S. Guernsey 1953. A theory of auxin action involving coenzyme A. Proc. Natl. Acad. Sci., 39:1105–1111.

——— and F. S. Guernsey 1953. Interaction of auxin and temperatures in floral initiation. Science, 118:215–216.

——— and F. S. Guernsey 1954. Flower initiation in the Alaska pea. II. Chemical vernalization. Amer. Jour. Bot., 41:181–185.

——— and F. S. Guernsey 1954. Coenzyme A and auxin-induced growth (in press).

——— F. S. Guernsey and K. I. Fawcett 1953. Report of Director, Agr. Expt. Sta. (in press).

——— and W. H. Klein 1952. Maleic hydrazide as an anti-auxin. Physiol. Plantarum., 5:91–99.

——— and F. I. Scott 1952. Physiological factors in tomato fruit-set. Amer. Jour. Bot., 39:310–317.

——— F. I. Scott, W. H. Klein and E. Ramstad 1952. Chelidonic acid and its effect on plant growth. Physiol. Plantarum., 5:85–90.

——— and K. V. Thimann 1949. The effect of auxin on flower initiation. Amer. Jour. Bot., 36:342–347.

LeTourneau, D. and N. Krog 1952. Use of chromotropic acid for quantitative determination of 2,4-D. Plant Physiol., 27:822–827.

Levitt, J. 1947. The thermodynamics of active (non-osmotic) water absorption. Plant Physiol., 22:514–525.

——— 1948. The role of active water absorption in auxin-induced water uptake by aerated potato discs. Plant Physiol., 23:505–515.

Lewcock, H. K. 1937. Acetylene to induce flowering in pineapple. Queensland Agr. Jour., 48:532–543.

Limasset, P., F. Levieil and M. Sechet 1948. Influence of phytohormone on the development of viruses X and Y in tobacco. Compt. Rend. Acad. Sci., 227:643–645.

LINDNER, R. C. 1939. Effects of indoleacetic acid and naphthaleneacetic acid on development of buds and roots in horseradish. Bot. Gaz., 100:500–527.

LINEWEAVER, H. AND D. BURK 1934. The determination of enzyme dissociation constants. Jour Amer. Chem. Soc., 56:658–666.

LINSER, H. 1951. Versuche zur chromatographischen Trennung pflanzlicher Wuchsstoffe. Planta, 39:377–401.

LIPMANN, F. 1953. On chemistry and function of coenzyme A. Bact. Rev., 17:1–16.

LIVERMAN, J. L. AND J. BONNER 1953. The interaction of auxin and light in the growth responses of plants. Proc. Natl. Acad. Sci., 39:905–916.

——— AND A. LANG 1953. Flowering of long-day plants as a result of auxin treatment (Abstract). A.I.B.S. Madison, Wisconsin.

LIVINGSTON, G. A. 1950. In vitro tests of abscission agents. Plant Physiol., 25:711–721.

LIVINGSTON, J. E. 1953. The control of leaf and stem rusts of wheat with chemotherapeutants. Phytopath., 43:496–499.

LOOMIS, W. E. 1949. Basic research in weed control. Proc. N. C. Weed Contr. Conf., 6:101–103.

LOUSTALOT, A. J., M. P. MORRIS, J. GARCIA AND C. PAGAN 1953. 2,4-D affects phosphorus metabolism. Science, 118:627–628.

——— AND T. J. MUZIK 1953. Effect of 2,4-D on apparent photosynthesis and developmental morphology of velvet bean. Bot. Gaz., 115:56–66.

LU, C. S. AND R. M. ROBERTS 1952. Effect of temperature on setting of Delicious apples. Proc. Amer. Soc. Hort. Sci., 59:177–183.

LUCAS, E. H., I. M. FELBER, C. L. HAMNER AND H. M. SELL 1948. The effect of buffers on the growth inhibiting properties of sodium 2,4-D. Mich. Agr. Expt. Sta. Quart. Bull., 30:289–297.

——— AND C. L. HAMNER 1947. Inactivation of 2,4-D by absorption on charcoal. Science, 105:340.

LUCKWILL, L. C. 1948. A method for the quantitative estimation of growth substances based on the response of tomato ovaries to known amounts of 2-naphthoxy-acetic acid. Jour. Hort. Sci., 24:19–31.

——— 1948. Hormone content of the seed in relation to endosperm development and fruit drop in the apple. *Ibid.,* 24:32–44.

——— 1952. Application of paper chromatography to the separation and identification of auxins and growth-inhibitors. Nature, 169:375–376.

——— 1953. Studies of fruit development in relation to plant hormones. I, Hormone production by the developing apple seed in relation to fruit drop. Jour. Hort. Sci., 28:14–24.

——— 1953. Studies of fruit development in relation to plant hormones. II The effect of naphthalene acetic acid on fruit-set and fruit development in apples. *Ibid.,* 28:25–40.

LUND, E. J. 1947. *Bioelectric Fields and Growth.* University of Texas Press, Austin.

LUNDEGÅRDH, H. 1947. Mineral nutrition of plants. Ann. Rev. Biochem., 16:503–528.

——— 1949. Influence of auxin anions on growth of wheat roots. Arkiv. Bot., 1:289–293.

LYNEN, F., L. WESSELY, O. WIELAND AND L. RUEFF 1952. Zur β-oxydation der Fettsäuren. Angew. Chem., 64:687.

MACDANIELS, L. H. 1936. Anatomical aspects of apple flower and fruit abscission. Proc. Amer. Soc. Hort. Sci., 34:122–219.

——— AND M. B. HOFFMAN 1941. Apple blossom removal with caustic sprays. *Ibid.,* 38:86–88.

MCCARTNEY, J. S. 1948. A study of the effects of naphthaleneacetic acid on prolongation of rest in the latham raspberry. Proc. Amer. Soc. Hort. Sci., 52:271–275.

MCCOWN, M. 1943. Anatomical and chemical aspects of abscission of fruits of apple. Bot. Gaz., 105:212–220.

MCIRATH, W. J. AND D. R. ERGLE 1953. Further evidence of the persistence of the 2,4-D stimulus in cotton. Plant Physiol., 28:693–702.

MCLANE, S. R., E. W. DEAN, J. W. BROWN, C. R. CONNELL, W. H. HOWARD AND C. E. MINARIK 1953. Halogenated phenyl alkyl ethers as plant growth regulators. Weeds, 2:288–291.

MCNEW, G. L. AND O. L. HOFFMAN 1948. The growth regulant, herbicidal and physical properties of chemicals related to 2,4-D. Res. Report N. C. Weed Contr. Conf., 5:8.

MCRAE, D. H. AND J. BONNER 1952. Diortho substituted phenoxyacetic acids as anti-auxins. Plant Physiol., 27:834–838.

——— AND J. BONNER 1953. Chemical structure and anti-auxin activity. Physiol. Plantarum., 6:485–510.

MANN, L. K. AND P. A. MINGES 1949. Experiments on setting fruit with growth-regulating substances. Hilgardia, 19:309–337.

MARQUARDT, R. P. AND E. N. LUCE 1951. Determination of small amounts of 2,4-D in milk. Analyt. Chem., 23:1485–1486.

MARTH, P. C. 1942. Effects of growth regulators on development of roses during common storage. Bot. Gaz., 104:26–49.

——— AND F. F. DAVIS 1945. Relation of temperature to selective herbicidal effects of 2,4-D. Bot. Gaz., 106:463–472.

——— AND C. L. HAMNER 1943. Vegetative propagation of *Taraxacum kok-saghyz* with aid of growth substances. *Ibid.,* 105:35–48.

——— L. HAVIS AND V. E. PRINCE 1950. Effects of growth regulators on development and ripening of peaches. Proc. Amer. Soc. Hort. Sci., 55:152–158.

——— AND J. W. MITCHELL 1949. Apparent antagonistic effects of growth regulators. Bot. Gaz., 110:514–518.

MATELL, M. 1953. Stereochemical studies on plant growth regulators. VII. Optically active α-(2-methyl-4-chlorophenoxy)-propionic acid and α-(2,4-dichlorophenoxy)-n-butyric acid and their steric relations. Arkiv. Kemi., 6:365–373.

MAXON, M. A., B. S. PICKETT AND H. W. RICKEY 1940. Effects of Hormodin A, a growth substance, on the rooting of cuttings. Iowa Agr. Expt. Sta. Res. Bul., 280:931–973.

MAYER, A. M. AND M. EVANARI 1951. The influence of two germination inhibitors (coumarin and 2,4-D) on germination in conjunction with thiourea and cysteine. Bull. Res. Council Israel, 1:125–129.

——— AND M. EVANARI 1952. Relation between structure of coumarin derivatives and activity as germination inhibitors. Jour. Exptl. Bot., 3:246–252.

MEINL, G. AND H. VON GUTTENBERG 1952. Über den Einfluss von Wirkstoffen auf die Permeabilität des Protoplasmas. III & IV. Planta, 41:167–189.

MEVIUS, W. 1927. Kalziumion und Wurzelwachstum. Jahrb. wiss. Bot., 66:183–253.

MICHAELIS, L. AND M. L. MENTEN 1913. Die Kinetik der Invertinwirkung. Biochem. Zeitschr., 49:333–369.

MICHEL, B. E. 1951. Effects of indoleacetic acid upon growth and respiration of kidney bean. Bot. Gaz., 112:418–436.

MICHENER, D. H. 1938. Action of ethylene on plant growth. Amer. Jour. Bot., 25:711–720.

——— 1942. Dormancy and apical dominance in potato tubers. *Ibid.*, 29:558–562.

MILBRATH, J. A. AND H. HARTMAN 1942. Cause and control of defoliation in holly. Oregon Agric. Expt. Sta. Bull., 413:1–11.

MILLER, C. 1953. Reversible inhibition of cell division and enlargement in plant tissues by 2,6-diaminopurine. Proc. Soc. Expt. Biol. and Med., 83:561–565.

MILLER, H. J. 1952. Plant hormone activity of substituted benzoic acids and related compounds. Weeds, 1:185–188.

MILLER, J. H. AND R. S. DUNHAM 1950. Influence of volume of herbicide upon legumes in oats. N. C. Weed Contr. Conf. Res. Rept., 7:111.

MILLER, L. P. 1933. Effects of sulphur compounds in breaking dormancy of potato tubers and inducing changes in enzyme activities of treated tubers. Contr. Boyce Thompson Inst., 5:29–81.

MILLERD, A. 1951. Respiratory oxidation and energy transfer by plant systems. Ph.D. Dissertation. California Institute of Technology, Pasadena (Cited by Bonner and Bandurski, 1952).

——— J. BONNER AND J. B. BIALE 1953. The climacteric rise in fruit respiration as controlled by phosphorylative coupling. Plant Physiol., 28:521–531.

MINARIK, C. E., D. READY, A. G. NORMAN, H. E. THOMPSON AND J. F. OWINGO 1951. New growth regulating compounds. II Substituted benzoic acids. Bot. Gaz., 113:135–142.

MITCHELL, J. W. AND J. W. BROWN 1945. Effect of 2,4-D on the readily available carbohydrate constituents in annual morning glory. Bot. Gaz., 107:120–129.

——— AND B. C. BRUNSTETTER 1939. Colorimetric methods for the quantitative estimation of indole(3)acetic acid. *Ibid.*, 100:802–816.

——— W. M. DUGGAR AND H. G. GAUCH 1953. Increased translocation of plant growth modifying substances due to application of boron. Science, 118:354–355.

——— AND C. L. HAMNER 1944. Polyethylene glycols as carriers for growth regulating substances. *Ibid.*, 105:474–483.

——— AND P. C. MARTH 1946. Germination of seeds in soil containing 2,4-D. *Ibid.*, 107:408–416.

——— D. P. SKAGGS AND W. P. ANDERSON 1951. Plant growth-stimulating hormones in immature bean seeds. Science, 114:159–161.

MOEWUS, F. 1949. Der Kressewurzeltest, ein neuer quantitativer Wuchsstofftest. Biol. Zentralbl., 68:118–140.

——— AND L. MOEWUS 1952. Sensitivity of cress roots to indoleacetic acid. Nature, 170:372.

——— L. MOEWUS AND H. SKWARRA 1952. Nachwies von zwei Wuchsstoffen in Samen der Kresse. Planta, 40:254–264.

MOORE, E. L. AND W. O. THOMAS 1952. Some effects of shading and para-chlorophenoxyacetic acid on fruitfulness of tomatoes. Proc. Amer. Soc. Hort. Sci., 60:289–294.

MOORE, R. H. 1950. Effects of maleic hydrazide on plants. Science, 112:52–53.

MOSKOV, B. S. 1936. Die photoperiodische Reaktion der Blätter und die Möglichkeit einer Ausnützung derselben bei Pfropfungen. Bull. Appl. Bot. Gen. and Pl. Breed. Ser. A., 17:25–30.

——— 1939. Transfer of photoperiodic reaction from leaves to growing points. Compt. Rend. (Doklady) Acad. Sci., 24:489–491.

——— AND I. E. KOSCHEZHENKO 1939. The rooting of woody cuttings as dependent upon photoperiodic conditions. *Ibid.*, 24:392–395.

MUIR, R. M. 1942. Growth hormones as related to the setting and development of fruit in *Nicotiana tabacum*. Amer. Jour. Bot., 29:716–720.

——— 1947. The relationship of growth hormones and fruit development. Proc. Natl. Acad. Sci., 33:303–312.

——— 1951. The growth hormone mechanism in fruit development. In Skoog (Ed.): *Plant Growth Substances*. Univ. of Wis. Press, Madison.

——— C. H. HANSCH AND A. H. GALLUP 1949. Growth regulation by organic compounds. Plant Physiol., 24:359–366.

MULLISON, W. R. 1951. The relative herbicidal effectiveness of several derivatives of 2,4-D and 2,4,5-T. Plant Physiol., 26:773–777.

——— AND R. W. HUMMER 1949. Some effects of vapor of 2,4-D derivatives on seeds. Bot. Gaz., 111:77–85.

——— AND E. MULLISON 1948. Effects of growth regulators on fruit set, yield, and blossom-end rot of tomatoes grown under high temperatures. *Ibid.,* 109:501–506.

MURNEEK, A. E. 1940. Reduction and delay of fruit abscission by spraying with growth substances. Proc. Amer. Soc. Hort. Sci., 37:432–434.

——— 1943. Caustic sprays to modify alternate fruit production. *Ibid.,* 42:177–181.

——— 1950. Relative value of hormone sprays for apple thinning. *Ibid.,* 55:127–136.

——— 1952. Plant growth regulators during fertilization and post-fertilization periods. *Ibid.,* 59:207–217.

——— AND F. G. TEUBNER 1953. The dual action of naphthaleneacetic acid in thinning of apples. *Ibid.,* 61:149–154.

——— S. H. WITTWER AND D. D. HEMPHILL 1944. Supplementary hormone sprays for greenhouse-grown tomatoes. *Ibid.,* 45:371–381.

MUZIK, T. J., A. J. LOUSTALOT AND H. J. CRUSADO 1951. Movement of 2,4-D in soil. Agron. Jour., 43:149–150.

MYERS, R. M. 1940. Effect of growth substances on the abscission layer in leaves of Coleus. Bot. Gaz., 102:323–338.

NANCE, J. F. 1949. Inhibition of salt accumulation in excised wheat roots by 2,4-dichlorophenoxyacetic acid. Science, 109:174–176.

NAYLOR, A. W. 1950. Effects of maleic hydrazide on flowering of tobacco, maize and cocklebur. Proc. Natl. Acad. Sci., 36:230–232.

——— AND E. A. DAVIS 1950. Maleic hydrazide as a plant growth inhibitor. Bot. Gaz., 112:112–126.

——— AND B. N. RAPPAPORT 1950. Studies on the growth factor requirements of pea roots. Physiol. Plantarum., 3:315–333.

NEELY, W. B., C. D. BALL, C. L. HAMNER AND H. M. SELL 1950. Effect of 2,4-D on invertase, phosphorylase and pectin methoxylase activity in bean plants. Plant Physiol., 25:525–528.

NEFF, M. S. AND E. N. O'ROURKE 1951. Factors affecting initiation of roots in transplanted tung trees. Proc. Amer. Soc. Hort. Sci., 57:186–190.

NEWCOMB, E. H. 1951. Effect of auxin on ascorbic oxidase activity in tobacco pith cells. Proc. Soc. Exptl. Biol. and Med., 76:504–509.

NEWMAN, A. S. AND J. R. THOMAS 1949. Decomposition of 2,4-D in soil and liquid media. Soil Sci. Soc. Amer. Proc., 14:160–164.

NIEDERGANG, E. AND F. SKOOG 1952. A reinterpretation of effects of TIBA on growth in terms of its effect on polarity and auxin transport (Abstract). A.I.B.S., Ithaca, N. Y.

NIELSEN, N. 1930. Untersuchungen über einen neuen wachstumsregulierenden Stoff: Rhizopin. Jahrb. wiss. Bot., 73:125–191.

NITSCH, J. P. 1950. Growth and morphogenesis of the strawberry as related to auxin. Amer. Jour. Bot., 37:211–215.

——— 1952. Plant hormones in the development of fruits. Quart. Rev. Biol., 27:33–57.

NORTHEN, H. T. 1942. Relation of dissociation of cellular protein by auxin to growth. Bot. Gaz., 103:668–683.

NUTMAN, P. S., H. G. THORNTON AND J. H. QUASTEL 1945. Inhibition of plant growth by 2,4-D and other plant growth substances. Nature, 155:498–500.

OBSIL, K. 1939. Zur Frage der Blühhormone. Planta, 29:468–476.

ODLAND, M. L. AND N. S. CHAN 1950. Effect of hormones on fruit-set of tomatoes at low temperatures. Proc. Amer. Soc. Hort. Sci., 55:328–334.

OFFORD, H. R. AND V. D. MOSS 1948. Comparison of toxicity of 2,4-D and 2,4,5-T to Ribes. Res. Report N. C. Weed Contr. Conf., 5:31.

OGLE, E. 1953. Persistence and fate of herbicides applied to soil. Ph.D. Dissertation. Purdue University, Lafayette, Indiana.

OLSON, P. J., S. ZALIK, N. J. BREAKEY AND D. A. BROWN 1951. Sensitivity of wheat and barley at different stages of growth to treatment with 2,4-D. Agron. Jour., 43:77–83.

O'ROURKE, F. L. 1942. Influence of blossom buds on rooting of blueberry. Proc. Amer. Soc. Hort. Sci., 40:332–334.

OSBORNE, D. J. 1952. A synergistic interaction between indolylacetonitrile and indoleacetic acid. Nature, 170:210.

——— AND R. L. WAIN 1950. Studies on plant growth-regulating substances. II. Synthetic compounds inducing morphogenic responses in the tomato plant. Jour. Hort. Sci., 26:60–74.

——— AND R. L. WAIN 1951. Studies on plant growth regulating substances. III. Production of parthenocarpic pomaceous fruits. *Ibid.*, 26:317–327.

OSTROM, C. E. 1945. Effects of growth regulators on development of tree seedlings. Bot. Gaz., 107:139–183.

OVERHOLSER, E. L., F. L. OVERLEY AND D. F. ALLMENDINGER 1943. Three-year study of preharvest sprays in Washington. Proc. Amer. Soc. Hort. Sci., 42:211–219.

PAÁL, A. 1919. Über phototropische Reizleitung. Jahrb. wiss. Bot., 58:406–458.

PACHECO, H. 1951. Caractérisation de l'acide indol-acétique dans un jus de pomme de terre par chromatographie de partage sur papier. Bull. Soc. Chim. Biol., 33:1915–1918.

PALSER, B. A. 1942. Histological responses of *Vicia faba* to indoleacetic acid. Bot. Gaz., 104:243–263.

PATERSON, D. R., S. H. WITTWER, L. E. WELLER AND H. M. SELL 1952. Effect of preharvest foliar sprays of maleic hydrazide on storage of potatoes. Plant Physiol., 27:135–142.

PEARSE, H. L. 1943. The effect of nutrition and phytohormones on the rooting of vine cuttings. Ann. Botany (N.S.), 7:123–132.

——— 1946. Rooting of vine and plum cuttings as affected by nutrition of the parent plant and by treatment with phytohormones. Union S. Africa Dept. Agr. Sci. Bull. 249.

PEARSON, J. A. AND R. N. ROBERTSON 1952. The climacteric rise in respiration of fruit. Australian Jour. Sci., 15:99–100.

PENFOUND, W. T. AND V. MINYARD 1947. Relation of light intensity to the effect of 2,4-dichlorophenoxyacetic acid on water hyacinth and kidney bean plants. Bot. Gaz., 109:231–234.

PENTZER, W. T. 1941. Studies on the shatter of grapes with special reference to the use of solutions of naphthaleneacetic acid to prevent it. Proc. Amer. Soc. Hort. Sci., 38:397–399.

PILET, P. E. 1951. Contribution a l'Étude des hormones de croissance (Auxins) dans la racine de *Lens culinaris*. Mem. Soc. Vaud. Sci. Nat., 10:137–244.

PRICE, C., W. S. STEWART AND L. C. ERICKSON 1950. Effects of growth regulators on bolting of sugar beets. Proc. Amer. Soc. Sugar Beet Technol., 1950:130–136.

PRIDHAM, A. M. S. 1942. Factors in the rooting of cuttings. Proc. Amer. Soc. Hort. Sci., 40:579–582.

——— 1947. Effect of 2,4-D on bean progeny seedlings. Science, 105:412.

PURVIS, O. N. 1940. Vernalization of fragments of embryo tissue. Nature, 145:462.

——— AND F. G. GREGORY 1945. Devernalization by high temperature. *Ibid.,* 155:113.

RANDHAWA, G. S. AND R. C. THOMPSON 1948. Effect of hormone sprays on yield of snap beans. Proc. Amer. Soc. Hort. Sci., 52:449–452.

RASMUSSEN, L. W. 1947. The physiological action of 2,4-D on dandelion, *Taraxacum officinale*. Plant Physiol., 22:344–391.

READY, D. AND V. Q. GRANT 1947. Rapid sensitive method for determining 2,4-D in aqueous solution. Bot. Gaz., 109:39–44.

REDEMANN, C. T., S. H. WITTWER AND H. M. SELL 1950. Precautions in the use of lanolin as an assay diluent for plant growth substances. Plant Physiol., 25:356–358.

——— S. H. WITTWER AND H. M. SELL 1951. Fruit-setting factor from ethanol extracts of immature corn kernels. Arch. Biochem. and Biophys., 32:80–84.

——— S. H. WITTWER AND H. M. SELL 1951. Characterization of indoleacetic acid and its esters. Jour. Amer. Chem. Soc., 73:2957.

REHM, S. 1952. Male sterile plants by chemical treatment. Nature, 170:38.

REINDERS, D. E. 1942. Intake of water by parenchymatic tissue. Rec. Trav. bot. Néerl., 39:1–140.

REINERT, J. 1952. Über die Bedeutung von Carotin und Riboflavin für die Lichtreizaufnahme bei Pflanzen. Naturwiss., 39:47–48.

——— 1953. Über die Wirkung von Riboflavin und Carotin beim Phototropisms von Avenakoleoptilen. Zeit. Bot., 41:103–122.

REINHOLD, L. 1954. The uptake of indoleacetic acid by pea epicotyl segments and carrot disks. New Phytol., 53:217–239.

RHODES, A. AND R. B. ASHWORTH 1952. Mode of action of growth regulators in plants. Nature, 169:76.

——— W. G. TEMPLEMAN AND M. N. THRUSTON 1950. Effect of the plant growth regulator 2-methyl-4-chloro phenoxyacetic acid on mineral and nitrogen contents of plants. Ann. Botany, NS14:181–198.

RICE, E. L. 1948. Absorption and translocation of ammonium 2,4-dichlorophenoxyacetic acid by bean plants. Bot. Gaz., 109:301–314.

——— 1950. Effects of various growth regulators on flowering in several crop plants. *Ibid.,* 112:207–213.

——— AND L. M. ROHRBAUGH 1953. Effect of kerosene on movement of 2,4-D and some derivatives through destarched bean leaves in darkness. *Ibid.,* 115:76–81.

ROBBINS, W. W., A. S. CRAFTS AND R. N. RAYNOR 1952. *Weed Control.* The McGraw-Hill Co., New York.

ROBERTS, H. A. AND G. E. BLACKMAN 1950. Studies in selective weed control. III. The control of annual weeds in leguminous crops with 2,4-dinitro-6-secondary-butyl-phenol. Jour. Agri. Sci., 40:263–274.

ROBERTS, R. H. AND B. E. STRUCKMEYER 1943. The efficiency of harvest sprays after a freeze. Proc. Amer. Soc. Hort. Sci., 42:198.

——— AND B. E. STRUCKMEYER 1944. Use of sprays to set greenhouse tomatoes. Proc. Amer. Soc. Hort. Sci., 44:417–427.

ROBERTSON-CUNINGHAME, R. C. AND G. E. BLACKMAN 1952. Effects of preliminary treatment on subsequent resistance of *Lemna* to 2,4-D. Nature, 170:459.

RODGERS, E. G. 1952. Brittleness and other responses of corn to 2,4-D. Plant Physiol. 27:153–172.

RODRIGUEZ, A. B. 1932. Smoke and ethylene in fruiting of pineapple. Jour. Dept. Agr. Puerto Rico, 26:5–18.

ROHRBAUGH, L. M. AND E. L. RICE 1949. Effect of application of sugar on the translocation of sodium 2,4-D by bean plants in the dark. Bot. Gaz., 111:85–89.

——— AND E. L. RICE 1954. Relation of phosphorus nutrition to absorption and translocation of 2,4-D in tomato plants (Abstract). A.I.B.S., Gainesville, Fla.

SACHS, J. 1880. Stoff und Form der Pflanzenorgane I. Arb. Bot. Inst. Würzburg, 2:452–488.

SAMPSON, H. C. 1918. Chemical changes accompanying abscission in Coleus. Bot. Gaz., 66:32–53.

SCHEUERMANN, R. 1951. Der Einfluss wasserlöslicher Vitamine auf die Wirksamkeit von Heteroauxin in Wachstumsprozess der höheren Pflanzen. Planta, 40:265–300.

SCHNEIDER, C. L. 1938. The interdependence of auxin and sugar for growth. Amer. Jour. Bot., 25:258–270.

SCHOENE, D. L. AND O. L. HOFFMANN 1949. Maleic hydrazide, a unique growth regulant. Science, 109:588–590.

SCHRANK, A. R. 1951. Electrical polarity and auxins. In Skoog (Ed.): *Plant Growth Substances.* Univ. of Wis. Press, Madison.

SELL, H. M., R. W. LUECKE, B. M. TAYLOR AND C. L. HAMNER 1949. Changes in chemical composition of the stems of red kidney bean plants treated with 2,4-dichlorophenoxyacetic acid. Plant Physiol., 24:295–299.

SEN, S. P. AND A. C. LEOPOLD 1954. Paper chromatography of plant growth regulators and allied compounds. Physiol. Plantarum, 7:98–108.

SEQUEIRA, L. AND T. A. STEEVES 1954. Auxin inactivation and its relation to leaf drop caused by the fungus *Omphalia flavida.* Plant Physiol., 29:11–16.

SERR, E. F. AND H. I. FORDE 1952. Sprays for control of preharvest drop of Peerless almonds. Proc. Amer. Soc. Hort. Sci., 60:193–196.

SEUBERT, E. 1925. Über Wachstumsregulatoren in der Koleoptile von *Avena.* Zeitschr. Bot., 17:49–88.

SHAW, W. C. AND C. V. WILLARD 1949. The effect of 2,4-D on small grains (Abstract). Amer. Soc. Agronomy, Milwaukee.

SHEPARD, P. H. 1939. Spraying apples for the prevention of fruit-set. Mo. Ft. Expt. Sta. Circ. 28.

SHIGEURA, G. 1948. Report of Director, Hawaii Agr. Expt. Sta., p. 138.

SHOJI, K., F. T. ADDICOTT AND W. A. SWETS 1951. Auxin in relation to leaf blade abscission. Plant Physiol., 26:189–191.

SHOWACRE, J. L. AND H. G. DUBUY 1947. The relation of water availability and auxin in the growth of *Avena* coleoptiles, and its meaning for a theory of tropisms. Amer. Jour. Bot., 34:175–181.

Siegel, S. M. and A. W. Galston 1953. Experimental coupling of indoleacetic acid to pea root protein. Proc. Natl. Acad. Sci., 39:1111–1118.

——— and A. W. Galston 1954. Peroxide genesis in plant tissues and its relation to auxin destruction and growth (Abstract). A.I.B.S., Gainesville, Fla.

——— and R. L. Weintraub 1952. Inactivation of indoleacetic acid by peroxides. Physiol. Plantarum, 5:241–247.

Silberger, J. and F. Skoog 1953. Changes induced by indoleacetic acid in nucleic acid contents of tobacco pith tissue. Science, 118:443–444.

Simons, H. M. and L. E. Scott 1952. Attempts to inhibit sprouting of sweet potato with growth regulators. Proc. Amer. Soc. Hort. Sci., 59:426–432.

Singletary, C. C. 1950. Hormone effects on tomato fruit-set and development. Ph.D. Dissertation, Purdue University.

Sircar, S. M. and T. M. Das 1951. Growth hormones of rice grains germinated at different temperatures. Nature, 168:382.

——— and B. N. De 1948. Studies in the physiology of rice. IV. Effect of photoperiodic induction on nitrogen metabolism of winter paddy. Proc. Natl. Inst. Sci. India, 14:263–270.

Skoog, F. 1934. The effect of X-rays on growth substance and plant growth. Science, 79:256.

——— 1935. Effect of X-irradiation on auxin and plant growth. Jour. Cell. and Comp. Physiol., 7:227–270.

——— 1939. Experiments on bud inhibition with indoleacetic acid. Amer. Jour. Bot., 26:702–707.

——— 1940. Relationships between zinc and auxin in the growth of higher plants. *Ibid.*, 27:939–951.

——— 1944. Growth and organ formation in tobacco tissue cultures. *Ibid.*, 31:19–24.

——— (Ed.) 1951. *Plant Growth Substances.* Univ. of Wis. Press, Madison.

——— and B. J. Robinson 1950. A direct relationship between indoleacetic acid effects on growth and reducing sugar in tobacco tissue. Proc. Soc. Exptl. Biol. and Med., 74:565–568.

——— C. L. Schneider and P. Malan 1942. Interactions of auxins in growth and inhibition. Amer. Jour. Bot., 29:568–576.

——— and K. V. Thimann 1940. Enzymatic liberation of auxin from plant tissues. Science, 92:64.

——— and C. Tsui 1948. Chemical control of growth and bud formation in tobacco stem and callus. Amer. Jour. Bot., 35:782–787.

Slade, R. E., W. G. Templeman and W. A. Sexton 1945. Plant growth substances as selective weed-killers. Nature, 155:497–498.

Smith, E. P. 1926. Acidity of the medium and root production in Coleus. Nature, 117:339–340.

Smith, F. G. 1951. Respiratory changes in relation to toxicity. In Skoog (Ed.): *Plant Growth Substances.* Univ. of Wis. Press, Madison.

——— C. L. Hamner and R. F. Carlson 1946. Control of ragweed pollen production with 2,4-D. Science, 103:473–474.

Smith, H. H. 1946. Quantitative aspects of aqueous spray applications of 2,4-D for herbicidal purposes. Bot. Gaz., 107:544–551.

Smith, M. S., R. L. Wain and T. Wightman 1952. Antagonistic action of certain stereoisomers on the plant growth-regulating activity of their enantiomorphs. Nature, 169:883.

SMITH, O. 1935. Pollination and life-history studies of the tomato. Cornell Univ. Memoir 184.

——— M. A. BAEZA AND J. H. ELLISON 1947. Response of potato plants to growth regulators. Bot. Gaz., 108:421–431.

SMOCK, R. M., L. J. EDGERTON AND M. B. HOFFMAN 1951. Effects of maleic hydrazide on softening and respiration of apples. Proc. Amer. Soc. Hort. Sci., 58:69–72.

——— AND C. R. CROSS 1947. Effect of some hormone materials on respiration and softening of apples. *Ibid.,* 49:67–77.

SNOW, R. 1929. The young leaf as the inhibiting organ. New Phytol., 28:345–358.

——— 1936. Upward effects of auxin in coleoptiles and stems. New Phytol., 35:292–304.

SÖDING, H. 1923. Werden von der Spitze der Haferkoleoptile Wuchshormone gebildet? Ber. Deutsch. bot. Ges., 41:396–400.

——— 1952. *Die Wuchsstofflehre.* Georg Thieme Verlag, Stuttgart.

SOUTHWICK, F. W. 1946. Effect of growth regulators on softening, respiration and soluble solids of peaches and apples. Proc. Amer. Soc. Hort. Sci., 47:84–90.

——— 1949. Further studies on the influence of methyl alpha naphthaleneacetate on ripening of apples and peaches. *Ibid.,* 53:169–173.

——— J. E. DEMORANVILLE AND J. F. ANDERSON 1953. The influence of some growth regulators on preharvest drop, color and maturity of apples. *Ibid.,* 61:155–162.

——— AND W. D. WEEKS 1950. Some attempts to thin apples with naphthaleneacetic acid type materials after calyx. *Ibid.,* 56:70–75.

——— AND W. D. WEEKS 1952. The influence of chemical thinning treatments on yield and flowering of apples. *Ibid.,* 60:165–172.

SOUTHWICK, L. 1939. Relation of seeds to preharvest McIntosh drop. Proc. Amer. Soc. Hort. Sci., 36:410–412.

——— 1940. Spur nitrogen and preharvest McIntosh drop. *Ibid.,* 37:435–436.

——— AND J. K. SHAW 1941. Effect of hormone sprays on harvest drop of apples (Abstract). *Ibid.,* 38:121–122.

STANIFORTH, D. W. 1952. Effect of 2,4-D on meristematic tissues of corn. Plant Physiol., 27:803–811.

——— AND W. E. LOOMIS 1948. Surface tension and synergism in 2,4-D sprays. Res. Report N. C. Weed Control Conf., 5:11.

STEEVES, F. A., G. MOREL AND R. H. WETMORE 1953. A technique for preventing inactivation at the cut surface in auxin diffusion studies. Amer. Jour. Bot. 40:534–538.

STEINBERG, R. A. 1949. A possible explanation of symptom formation in tobacco with frenching and mineral deficiencies. Science, 110:714–715.

STERLING, C. 1951. Origin of buds in tobacco stem segments cultured in vitro. Amer. Jour. Bot., 38:761–767.

STEVENSON, E. C. AND J. W. MITCHELL 1945. Bacteriostatic and bactericidal properties of 2,4-D. Science, 101:642–644.

STEWARD, F. C., P. R. STOUT AND C. PRESTON 1940. The balance sheet of metabolites for potato discs showing the effect of salts and dissolved oxygen on metabolism at 23° C. Plant Physiol., 15:409–447.

STEWART, W. S. 1949. Effects of 2,4-D and 2,4,5-T on citrus fruit storage. Proc. Amer. Soc. Hort. Sci., 54:109–117.

——— AND W. EBELING 1946. Preliminary results with 2,4-D as a spray-oil amendment. Bot. Gaz., 108:286–294.

——— C. Gammon and H. Z. Hield 1952. Deposit of 2,4-D and kill of wild grape by helicopter spray. Amer. Jour. Bot., 39:1–5.

——— and C. L. Hamner 1942. Treatment of seeds with synthetic growth substances. Bot. Gaz., 104:338–347.

——— and H. Z. Hield 1950. Effects of 2,4-D and 2,4,5-T on fruit production of lemon trees. Proc. Amer. Soc. Hort. Sci., 55:163–171.

——— H. Z. Hield and B. L. Brannaman 1952. Effects of 2,4-D on fruit-drop and quality of Valencia oranges. Hilgardia, 21:301–329.

——— and L. J. Klotz 1947. Some effects of 2,4-D on fruit drop and morphology of oranges. Bot. Gaz., 109:150–162.

——— L. J. Klotz and H. Z. Hield 1951. Effects of 2,4-D on fruit-drop and quality of navel oranges. Hilgardia, 21:161–193.

——— J. E. Palmer and H. Z. Hield 1952. Use of 2,4-D and 2,4,5-T to increase storage life of lemons. Proc. Amer. Soc. Hort. Sci., 59:327–334.

——— and E. R. Parker 1948. Trials of 2,4-D on grapefruit. Citrus Leaves, 28:6–7.

——— and N. W. Stuart 1942. The distribution of auxins in bulbs of Lilium. Amer. Jour. Bot., 29:529-532.

Stier, H. L. and H. G. duBuy 1938. Influence of phytohormones on flower and fruit product of tomato. Proc. Amer. Soc. Hort. Sci., 36:723–731.

Stoutemyer, V. T. 1938. Talc as a carrier of substances inducing rooting in cuttings. Proc. Amer. Soc. Hort. Sci., 36:817–822.

——— 1941. A comparison of rooting induced by acid and amide growth substances. *Ibid.*, 39:253–258.

——— and A. W. Close 1946. Rooting cuttings and germinating seeds under fluorescent and cold cathode lighting. *Ibid.*, 48:309–325.

——— and F. L. O'Rourke 1945. Rooting of cuttings from plants sprayed with growth regulating substances. *Ibid.*, 46:407–411.

Stowe, B. B. and K. V. Thimann 1954. The paper chromatography of indole compounds and some indole-containing auxins of plant tissues. Arch. Biochem. and Biophys., (in press).

Struckmeyer, B. E. 1951. Comparative effects of growth substances on stem anatomy. In Skoog (Ed.): *Plant Growth Substances.* Univ. of Wis. Press, Madison.

——— and R. H. Roberts 1950. Possible explanation of how naphthaleneacetic acid thins apples. Proc. Amer. Soc. Hort. Sci., 56:76–78.

Sumner, J. B. and K. Myrbäck 1950. *The Enzymes: Chemistry and Mechanism of Action.* Volume I, Part I. Academic Press Inc., New York.

Swanson, C. P. 1946. A simple bio-assay method for the determination of low concentrations of 2,4-dichlorophenoxyacetic acid in aqueous solutions. Bot. Gaz., 107:507–509.

——— G. LaVelle and S. H. Goodgal 1949. Ovule abortion in *Tradescantia* as affected by aqueous solutions of 2,4-D. Amer. Jour. Bot., 36:170–175.

Synerholm, M. E. and P. W. Zimmerman 1947. Preparation of a series of 2,4-dichlorophenoxyaliphatic acids. Contr. Boyce Thompson Inst., 14:369–382.

Tafuro, A. J. and E. Marshall 1952. Effect of different applications of varying rates of MCP to irrigated and non-irrigated alfalfa seedlings. N. E. Weed Contr. Conf., 6:259–264.

Tang, Y. W. and J. Bonner 1947. The enzymatic inactivation of indoleacetic acid. I. Arch. Biochem. and Biophys., 13:11–25.

TANG, P. S. AND S. W. LOO 1940. Tests on after effects of auxin seed treatment. Amer. Jour. Bot., 27:385–386.

TAYLOR, D. L. 1947. Effects of 2,4-dichlorophenoxyacetic acid on gas exchange of wheat and mustard seedlings. Bot. Gaz., 109:162–176.

TERPSTRA, W. 1953. Extraction and identification of growth substances. Doctoral Dissertation, University of Utrecht, Netherlands.

TEUBNER, F. G. 1953. Identification of the auxin present in apple endosperm. Science, 118:418.

THIMANN, K. V. 1934. Studies on the growth hormone of plants VI. The distribution of the growth substance in plant tissues. Jour. Gen. Physiol., 18:23–34.

——— 1935. On the plant growth hormone produced by *Rhizopus suinus.* Jour. Biol. Chem., 109:279–291.

——— 1935. On an analysis of activity of two growth-promoting substances on plant tissues. Proc. Kon. Acad. Wet. Amsterdam, 38:896–912.

——— 1936. Auxins and the growth of roots. Amer. Jour. Bot., 23:561–569.

——— 1936. On the physiology of the formation of nodules on legume roots. Proc. Natl. Acad. Sci., 22:511–514.

——— 1937. On the nature of inhibitions caused by auxins. Amer. Jour. Bot., 24:407–412.

——— 1948. Plant growth hormones. *The Hormones: Physiology, Chemistry and Applications.* Academic Press, Inc., New York.

——— 1951. The synthetic auxins: relation between structure and activity. In Skoog (Ed.): *Plant Growth Substances.* Univ. of Wis. Press, Madison.

——— 1952. The role of ortho substitutions in the synthetic auxins. Plant Physiol., 27:392–404.

——— (Ed.) 1952. *The Action of Hormones in Plants and Invertebrates.* Academic Press Inc., New York.

——— AND J. BEHNKE-ROGERS 1950. The use of auxins in the rooting of woody cuttings. Maria Moors Cabot Foundation, Publication No. 1, Petersham, Mass.

——— AND W. D. BONNER 1948. The action of triiodobenzoic acid on growth. Plant Physiol., 23:158–161.

——— AND W. D. BONNER 1949. Inhibition of plant growth by protoanemonin and coumarin and its prevention by BAL. Proc. Natl. Acad. Sci., 35:272–276.

——— AND A. L. DELISLE 1942. Notes on the rooting of some conifers from cuttings. Jour. Arnold Arboretum, 23:103–109.

——— AND J. B. KOEPFLI 1935. Identity of the growth-promoting and root-forming substances of plants. Nature, 135:101.

——— AND R. H. LANE 1938. After-effects of treatment of seed with auxin. Amer. Jour. Bot., 25:535–543.

——— AND E. F. POUTASSE 1941. Factors affecting root formation of *Phaseolus vulgaris.* Plant Physiol., 16:585–598.

——— AND C. L. SCHNEIDER 1938. The role of salts, hydrogen ion concentration and agar in the response of the *Avena* coleoptile to auxins. Amer. Jour. Bot., 25:270–280.

——— AND C. L. SCHNEIDER 1938. Differential growth in plant tissues. Amer. Jour. Bot., 25:627–641.

——— AND C. L. SCHNEIDER 1939. The relative activities of different auxins. Amer. Jour. Bot., 26:328–333.

——— AND F. SKOOG 1933. Studies on the growth hormone in plants. Proc. Natl. Acad. Sci., 19:714–716.

——— AND F. SKOOG 1934. Inhibition of bud development and other functions of growth substance in *Vicia Faba*. Proc. Roy. Soc. Ser. B., Biol. Sci. London, 114:317–339.

——— AND F. SKOOG 1940. The extraction of auxin from plant tissues. Amer. Jour. Bot., 27:951–960.

——— F. SKOOG AND A. BYER 1942. The extraction of auxin from plant tissues. II. Amer. Jour. Bot., 29:598–606.

——— AND F. W. WENT 1934. On the chemical nature of the root forming hormone. K. Akad. Wetenschap. Amsterdam. Proc. Sect. Sci., 37:456–459.

THOMAS, R. M. AND J. E. PRIER 1952. An improved lyophilizer. Science, 116:96.

THOMPSON, A. H. 1951. The effect of 2,4,5-TP sprays in delaying the preharvest drop of several apple varieties. Proc. Amer. Soc. Hort. Sci., 58:57–64.

THOMPSON, H. E., C. P. SWANSON AND A. G. NORMAN 1946. New growth-regulating compounds. I Summary of activities of some compounds by three tests. Bot. Gaz., 107:476–507.

THOMPSON, R. C. AND W. F. KOZAR 1939. Stimulation of germination of dormant lettuce seed by sulphur compounds. Plant Physiol., 14:567–573.

TORREY, J. G. 1950. The induction of lateral roots by indoleacetic acid and root decapitation. Amer. Jour. Bot., 37:257–264.

TRAUB, H. P., W. C. COOPER AND P. C. REECE 1939. Inducing flowering in pineapple. Proc. Amer. Soc. Hort. Sci., 37:521–525.

TSUI, C. 1948. The role of zinc in auxin synthesis in the tomato plant. Amer. Jour. Bot., 35:172–178.

TUKEY, H. B. AND R. F. CARLSON 1945. Breaking the dormancy of peach seed by treatment with thiourea. Plant Physiol., 20:505–516.

——— AND C. L. HAMNER 1945. Retardation of pre-harvest drop of apples through aerosol application of growth-regulating substances. Proc. Amer. Soc. Hort. Sci., 46:102–108.

TULLIS, E. C. AND W. C. DAVIS 1950. Persistence of 2,4-D in plant tissue. Science, 111:90.

VAN DER WEIJ, H. G. 1932. Der Mechanismus der Wuchsstofftransportes. Rec. Trav. Bot. Neerland., 29:381–496.

——— 1933. Über Wuchsstoff bei Eleagnus. K. Akad. Wetenschap. Amsterdam. Proc. Sect. Sci., 36:760–761.

VAN OVERBEEK, J. 1932. An analysis of phototropism in dicotyledons. K. Akad. Wetenschap. Amsterdam. Proc. Sect. Sci., 35:1325–1335.

——— 1933. Wuchsstoff, Lichtwachstumsreaktion und Phototropismus bei *Raphanus*. Rec. Trav. Bot. Neerland., 30:537–626.

——— 1935. The growth hormone and dwarf type of growth in corn. Proc. Natl. Acad. Sci., 21:292–299.

——— 1936. Growth substance curvatures of *Avena* in light and dark. Jour. Gen. Physiol., 20:283–309.

——— 1938. Auxin production in seedlings of dwarf maize. Plant Physiol., 13: 587–598.

——— 1940. Auxin in marine algae. *Ibid.,* 15:291–299.

——— 1944. Auxin, water uptake and osmotic pressure in potato tissue. Amer. Jour. Bot., 31:265–269.

——— 1946. Control of flower formation and fruit size in pineapple. Bot. Gaz., 108:64–73.

——— 1951. Use of growth substances in tropical agriculture. In Skoog (Ed.): *Plant Growth Substances.* Univ. of Wis. Press, Madison.

——— 1952. Agricultural application of growth regulators and their physiological basis. Ann. Rev. Plant Physiol., 3:87–108.

——— Chairman, Committee of American Society of Plant Physiologists. 1954. Nomenclature of chemical plant regulators. Plant Physiol., 29:307–308.

——— R. Blondeau and V. Horne 1951. Transcinnamic acid as an anti-auxin. Amer. Jour. Bot., 38:589–595.

——— R. Blondeau and V. Horne 1951. Difference in activity between 2,4-D and other auxins. Plant Physiol., 26:687–696.

——— and J. Bonner 1938. Auxin in isolated roots growing *in vitro*. Proc. Natl. Acad. Sci., 24:260–264.

——— and H. J. Cruzado 1948. Flower formation in the pineapple plant by geotropic stimulation. Amer. Jour. Bot., 35:410–412.

——— and H. J. Cruzado 1948. Note on flower formation in the pineapple induced by low night temperatures. Plant Physiol., 23:282–285.

——— S. A. Gordon and L. E. Gregory 1946. An analysis of the function of the leaf in the process of root formation in cuttings. Amer. Jour. Bot., 33:100–107.

——— D. Olivo and E. M. S. de Vásquez 1945. Rapid extraction method for free auxin and its application in geotropic reactions of bean and sugarcane. Bot. Gaz., 106:440–451.

——— M. A. Tio, L. E. Gregory, and E. S. de Vásquez 1943. Puerto Rico Univ. Ann. Rept., Inst. Trop. Agr., 79–103.

——— E. S. de Vásquez and S. A. Gordon 1947. Free and bound auxin in the vegetative pineapple plant. Amer. Jour. Bot., 34:266–270.

——— and I. Velez 1946. Use of 2,4-D as a selective herbicide in the tropics. Science, 103:472–473.

——— and F. W. Went 1937. Mechanism and quantitative application of the pea test. Bot. Gaz., 99:22–41.

Van Raalte, M. H. 1950. Root formation by the petioles of *Ageratum Houstonianum* as a test for auxin activity in tropical countries. Ann. Bogorienses, 1: 13–26.

——— 1951. Interaction of indole and hemi-auxins with indoleacetic acid in root formation. I and II. Kon. Neder. Akad. Wetens. Proc., C54:21–29, 117–125.

Veldstra, H. 1944. Researches on plant growth substances. IV. The relation between structure and activity. Enzymologia, 11:97–137.

——— 1953. The relation of chemical structure to biological activity in growth substances. Ann. Rev. Plant Physiol., 4:151–198.

Verkaaik, B. 1942. De auxine van een lichtgevaelige schimmel en onderzoekingen over antipoden van een synthetische groeistof. Doctoral Dissertation, University of Utrecht, Netherlands.

Verner, L. 1938. Effect of a growth substance on crotch angles in apple trees. Proc. Amer. Soc. Hort. Sci., 36:415–422.

Vernon, L. P. and S. Aronoff 1952. Metabolism of soybean leaves. IV. Translocation. Arch. Biochem. and Biophys., 36:383–398.

Vlitos, A. J. 1952. The influence of environment on the activity of Crag Herbicide No. 1. Proc. NE Weed Control Conf., 1952:57–62.

Von Denffer, D., M. Behrens and A. Fischer 1952. Papierelektrophoretische Trennung von Indolderivation aus Pflanzenextrakten. Naturwiss., 39:258–259.

——— M. Behrens and A. Fischer 1952. Papierchromatographischer und papierelektrophoretischer Nachweis des β-Indolacetonitrils und des β-Indolaldehyds in Extrakten aus Kohlpflanzen. Naturwiss., 39:550–551.

——— and A. Fischer 1952. Papierchromatographischer Nachweis des β-Indol-aldehyds in photolytisch zersetzter IES-Lösung. Naturwiss., 39:549–550.

Von Guttenberg, H. 1942. Über die Bildung und Aktivierung des Wuchsstoffes in den höheren Pflanzen. Naturwiss., 30:109–112.

——— and E. Lehle-Joerges 1947. Über das Vorkommen von Auxin und Hetero-auxin in Ruhenden und Kermenden Samen. Planta, 35:281–296.

Vyvyan, M. C. 1946. Experiments with growth substance sprays for reduction of pre-harvest drop of fruit. Jour. Pomol. and Hort. Sci., 22:11–37.

Wagenknecht, A. C. and R. H. Burris 1950. Indoleacetic acid inactivating enzymes from bean roots and pea seedlings. Arch. Biochem. and Biophys., 25:30–53.

Wain, R. L. 1949. Chemical aspects of plant growth-regulating activity. Ann. Appl. Biol., 36:558–562.

——— 1951. Plant growth-regulating and systematic fungicidal activity: the aryl-oxyalylcarboxylic acids. Jour. Sci. Food and Agric., 2:101–106.

Wald, G. and H. G. duBuy 1936. Pigments of the oat coleoptile. Science, 84:247.

Warmke, H. E. and G. L. Warmke 1950. Role of auxin in differentiation of root and shoot of *Taraxacum* and *Cichorium*. Amer. Jour. Bot., 37:272–280.

Warner, G. C. and F. W. Went 1939. Rooting of cuttings with indoleacetic acid and vitamin B_1. Plant Culture Pub. Co. Pasadena, California (cited by Avery and Johnson, 1947).

Warren, G. F. and J. E. Larsen 1952. Herbicidal mixtures for weed control in vegetable crops. Proc. N. C. Weed Contr. Conf., 9:72.

Watson, D. P. 1948. An anatomical study of the modification of bean leaves as a result of treatment with 2,4-D. Amer. Jour. Bot., 35:543–555.

Way, R. D. and T. E. Maki 1946. Effects of prestorage treatment of hardwood and pine seedlings with naphthaleneacetic acid. Bot. Gaz., 108:219–232.

Waygood, E. R. 1954. An hypothesis to explain certain aspects of the physiology of plant resistance to specific fungal pathogens (Abstract). A.I.B.S., Gainesville, Fla.

——— J. Mosie, and L. Kapica 1954. The effect of plant growth regulating substances on the production of pectin esterase by *Cladosporium herbarum* (Abstract). A.I.B.S., Gainesville, Fla.

Weaver, R. J. 1947. Reaction of certain plant growth regulators with ion exchangers. Bot. Gaz., 109:72–84.

——— 1948. Activated carbon in contratoxification of plant growth-regulators. Bot. Gaz., 110:300–312.

——— and H. R. DeRose 1946. Absorption and translocation of 2,4-D. *Ibid.,* 107:509–521.

——— C. E. Minarik and F. T. Boyd 1946. Influence of rainfall on effectiveness of 2,4-D sprayed for herbicidal purposes. *Ibid.,* 107:540–544.

——— C. P. Swanson, W. B. Ennis and F. T. Boyd 1946. Effect of plant growth regulators in relation to stages of development of certain plants. *Ibid.,* 107: 563–568.

——— and W. O. Williams 1950. Response of flowers of Black Corinth and fruit of Thompson Seedless grapes to applications of plant growth regulators. *Ibid.,* 111:477–485.

——— and W. O. Williams 1951. Response of grapes to plant growth regulators. *Ibid.,* 113:75–85.

Weber, R. P. and S. A. Gordon 1953. Enzymatic radiosensitivity in auxin biosynthesis (Abstract). A.I.B.S. Madison, Wis.

Webster, W. W. Jr. and A. R. Schrank 1953. Electrical induction of lateral transport of 3-indoleacetic acid in the *Avena* coleoptile. Arch. Biochem. and Biophys., 47:107–118.

WEINBERGER, J. H. 1951. Effect of 2,4,5-T on ripening of peaches. Proc. Amer. Soc. Hort. Sci., 57:115–119.

WEINTRAUB, R. L. AND J. W. BROWN 1950. Translocation of exogenous growth-regulators in the bean seedling. Plant Physiol., 25:140–149.

——— J. W. BROWN, J. C. NICKERSON AND K. N. TAYLOR 1952. Molecular structure and activity of growth regulators. I Abscission inducing activity. Bot. Gaz., 113:348–362.

——— J. W. BROWN, J. A. THORNE AND J. N. YEATMAN, 1951. A method for measurement of cell-elongation promoting activity of plant growth regulators. Amer. Jour. Bot., 38:435–440.

WELLER, L. E., S. H. WITTWER AND H. M. SELL 1954. The detection of indoleacetic acid in cauliflower heads. Jour. Amer. Chem. Soc. 76:629–630.

WENT, F. W. 1928. Wuchsstoff und Wachstum. Rec. Trav. Bot. Neerland., 25:1–116.

——— 1932. Eine botanische Polaritätstheorie. Jahrb. wiss. Bot., 76:528–557.

——— 1934. A test method for rhizocaline, the root-forming substance. K. Akad. Wetenschap. Amsterdam. Proc. Sect. Sci., 37:445–455.

——— 1934. On the pea test method for auxin, the plant growth hormone. K. Akad. Wetenschap. Amsterdam. Proc. Sect. Sci., 37:547–555.

——— 1935. Hormones involved in root formation. Proc. 6th Int. Bot. Cong., 2:267–269.

——— 1936. Allgemeine Betrachtungen über das Auxin-Problem. Biol. Zentralbl., 56:449–463.

——— 1939. Further analysis of the pea test for auxin. Bull. Torrey Bot. Club, 66:391–410.

——— 1941. The polarity of auxin transport in inverted Tagetes cuttings. Bot. Gaz., 103:386–390.

——— 1944. Plant growth under controlled conditions. III. Correlation between various physiological processes and growth in the tomato. Amer. Jour. Bot., 31: 597–618.

——— 1945. Plant growth under controlled conditions. V. Relation between age, light, variety and thermoperiodicity of tomatoes. *Ibid.,* 32:469–479.

——— 1949. Phytohormones: structure and activity. II. Arch. Biochem. and Biophys., 20:131–136.

——— J. BONNER AND G. C. WARNER 1938. Aneurin and the rooting of cuttings. Science, 87:170.

——— AND K. V. THIMANN 1937. *Phytohormones.* The Macmillan Co., New York.

WESTER, R. E. AND MARTH, P. C. 1949. Some effects of a growth regulator mixture in controlled cross-pollination of lima beans. Proc. Amer. Soc. Hort. Sci., 43: 315–318.

WETMORE, R. H. AND G. MOREL 1949. Polyphenol oxidase as a problem in organ culture and auxin diffusion studies of horsetails and ferns (Abstract). Amer. Jour. Bot., 36:830.

WHANG, W. Y. 1948. Para-chlorophenoxyacetic acid to increase slip production. Pineapple Res. Inst. Seminar, May 7.

WILDE, M. H. 1951. Anatomical modifications of bean roots following treatment with 2,4-D. Amer. Jour. Bot., 38:79–91.

WILDMAN, S. G. AND J. BONNER 1948. Observations on the chemical nature and formation of auxin in the *Avena* coleoptile. Amer. Jour. Bot., 35:740–746.

——— J. Campbell and J. Bonner 1948. The proteins of green leaves. II. Auxin, adenine, pentose and phosphorus content of spinach fraction I (Abstract). Amer. Jour. Bot., 35:813–814.

——— M. G. Ferri and J. Bonner 1947. The enzymatic conversion of trytophan to auxin by spinach leaves. Arch. Biochem. and Biophys., 13:131–144.

——— and S. A. Gordon 1942. The release of auxin from isolated leaf proteins of spinach by enzymes. Proc. Natl. Acad. Sci., 28:217–228.

——— and R. M. Muir 1949. Observation on the mechanism of auxin formation in plant tissues. Plant Physiol., 24:84–92.

Willard, C. J. 1947. Discussion on corn. Proc. N. C. Weed Contr. Conf., 4:26.

Winklepleck, R. L. 1937. Delaying blossom date of peaches. Hoosier Hort., 21: 152–154.

Withrow, A. P. and R. B. Withrow 1943. Translocation of the floral stimulus in Xanthium. Bot. Gaz., 104:409–416.

Withrow, R. B. and F. S. Howlett 1946. New carriers for plant growth regulators. Plant Physiol., 21:131–139.

Wittwer, S. H. 1943. Growth hormone production during sexual reproduction of higher plants. Univ. of Mo. Agric. Exper. Sta. Res. Bull. #371, 1–58.

——— L. L. Coulter and R. L. Carolus 1947. A chemical control of seedstalk development in celery. Science, 106:590.

——— and C. M. Hansen 1951. The reduction of storage losses in sugar beets by pre-harvest foliage sprays of maleic hydrazide. Agron. Jour., 43:340–341.

——— H. Jackson and D. P. Watson 1954. Control of seedstalk development in celery by maleic hydrazide. Amer. Jour. Bot., 41:435–439.

——— and A. E. Murneek 1949. Further investigations on value of "hormone" sprays and dusts for snap beans. Proc. Amer. Soc. Hort. Sci., 47:285–293.

——— and R. C. Sharma 1950. Control of storage sprouting in onions by pre-harvest foliage sprays of maleic hydrazide. Science, 112:597.

——— R. C. Sharma, L. E. Weller and H. M. Sell 1950. The effect of pre-harvest foliage sprays of certain growth regulators on sprout inhibition and storage quality of carrots and onions. Plant Physiol., 25:539–549.

——— H. Stallworth and M. J. Howell 1948. Value of a "hormone" spray for overcoming delayed fruit-set for outdoor tomatoes. Proc. Amer. Soc. Hort. Sci., 51:371–380.

Wolf, D. E., G. Vermillion, A. Wallace and G. H. Ahlgren 1950. Effect of 2,4-D on carbohydrate and nutrient content and kill of soybeans. Bot. Gaz., 112:188–197.

Wood, J. W. and T. D. Fontaine 1952. Synthetic plant growth-regulators. III. 2,4-D derivatives of amino acids. Jour. Organ. Chem., 17:891–896.

Woodford, E. K. 1950. Experimental techniques for evaluation of herbicides. N.A.A.S. Quarterly Review, 9:1–10.

Wort, D. J. 1949. The response of buckwheat to treatment with 2,4-dichlorophenoxyacetic acid. Amer. Jour. Bot., 36:673–676.

——— and L. M. Cowie 1953. Effect of 2,4-D on enzyme activities in wheat. Plant Physiol., 28:135–139.

Yamaki, T. 1948. Growth of *Avena* coleoptiles in relation to growth substances and pH. Misc. Rept. Res. Inst. Nat. Resour., 11:37–40.

——— and K. Nakamura 1952. Formation of indoleacetic acid in maize embryo. Sci. Papers Coll. Gen. Educ. Univ. Tokyo, 2:81–98.

Yasuda, S. 1934. Parthenocarpy caused by the stimulus of pollination in some plants of *Solanaceae*. Agric. and Hort., 9:647–656. (English summary, p. 656.)

YOUNG, D. W. AND C. E. FISHER 1950. Toxicity and translocation of herbicides in Mesquite. Proc. N. C. Weed Control Conf., 7:95–99.

ZALIK, S., G. A. HOBBS AND A. C. LEOPOLD 1951. Parthenocarpy in tomatoes induced by para-chlorophenoxyacetic acid applied to several loci. Proc. Amer. Soc. Hort. Sci., 58:201–207.

ZIELINSKI, Q. B. AND R. GARREN 1952. Effects of beta-naphthoxyacetic acid on fruit size in the Marshall strawberry. Bot. Gaz., 114:134–139.

——— P. C. MARTH AND V. E. PRINCE 1951. Effects of 2,4,5-T on maturation of prunes. Proc. Amer. Soc. Hort. Sci., 58:65–68.

ZIMMERMAN, P. W. 1951. Formative effects of growth substances on stem anatomy. In Skoog (Ed.): *Plant Growth Substances*. Univ. of Wisc. Press, Madison.

——— W. CROCKER AND A. E. HITCHCOCK 1933. Initiation and stimulation of roots from exposure of plants to carbon monoxide gas. Contr. Boyce Thompson Inst., 5:1–17.

——— AND A. E. HITCHCOCK 1937. The combined effect of light and gravity on the response of plants to growth substances. *Ibid.,* 9:455–461.

——— AND A. E. HITCHCOCK 1939. Experiments with vapors and solutions of growth substances. *Ibid.,* 10:481–508.

——— AND A. E. HITCHCOCK 1942. Substituted phenoxy and benzoic acid growth substances and the relation of structure to physiological activity. *Ibid.,* 12:321–343.

——— AND A. E. HITCHCOCK 1942. Flowering habit and correlation of organs modified by triiodobenzoic acid. *Ibid.,* 12:491–496.

——— AND A. E. HITCHCOCK 1951. Growth regulating effects of chlorosubstituted derivatives of benzoic acid. *Ibid.,* 16:209–213.

——— AND F. WILCOXON 1935. Several chemical growth substances which cause initiation of roots and other responses in plants. *Ibid.,* 7:209–229.

——— A. E. HITCHCOCK AND F. WILCOXON 1939. Responses of plants to growth substances applied as solutions and as vapors. *Ibid.,* 10:363–376.

ZIMMERMAN, W. A. 1936. Untersuchungen über die raumliche und zeitliche Verteilung des Wuchsstoffes bei Bäumen. Zeitschr. Bot., 30:209–232.

ZUKEL, J. W. 1952. Literature summary on maleic hydrazide. U. S. Rubber Co. MHIS, 6:1–28.

——— 1954. Literature summary on maleic hydrazide. U. S. Rubber Co. MHIS, 6B:1–21.

ZUSSMAN, H. W. 1949. Factors involved in sequestering 2,4-D. Agr. Chemicals, 4:27–29.

APPENDIX

Auxins and other growth regulators commonly recommended for agricultural applications

Use	Plant Type or Species	Growth Regulator	Concentration or Rate of Application
Rooting	herbaceous plants	Sodium or ammonium salts of indolebutyric acid, naphthaleneacetic acid, or both	500–2,000 ppm in talc
	woody dicots	Same	800–12,000 ppm in talc
	conifers	Same	8,000–12,000 ppm in talc
Parthenocarpy	tomato	*p*-chlorophenoxyacetic acid, or β-naphthoxyacetic acid	25–50 mg./l.
	fig	benzothiazole-2-oxyacetic acid	100 mg./l.
Fruit thinning	apple	naphthaleneacetic acid	5–50 mg./l.
		naphthaleneacetamide	10–100 mg./l.
	peach	naphthaleneacetic acid	40–60 mg./l.
	olive	Same	100–125 mg./l.
Preharvest drop control	apple	naphthaleneacetic acid or 2,4,5-trichlorophenoxypropionic acid	5–50 mg./l.
	apricot	naphthaleneacetic acid	10 mg./l.
		2,4,5-trichlorophenoxyacetic acid	50–100 mg./l.
	pear	naphthaleneacetic acid or 2,4-D	2.5 mg./l.
	orange	2,4-D isopropyl ester	8–10 mg./l.
	lemon	diethanolamine salt of 2,4,5-trichlorophenoxyacetate	5–8 mg./l.
Flower induction	pineapple	sodium naphthaleneacetate	25–30 mg./l.
		2,4-D	5–10 mg./l.
Prolonging dormancy	potato	methyl naphthaleneacetate	1 g./bushel
		Same	10–150 mg./l. (foliar)
		maleic hydrazide	500–2,500 mg./l. (foliar)
	carrots	methyl naphthaleneacetate	1 g./bushel
	onions	maleic hydrazide	50–2,500 mg./l. (foliar)
Herbicides	herbaceous dicots	Sodium, ammonium or alkanolamine salts of 2,4-D, 2,4,5-trichlorophenoxyacetate or 2-methyl-4-chlorophenoxyacetate	$\frac{1}{8}$–2 lbs./acre
	woody dicots	Same (esters)	2,000–25,000 mg./l.
	soil applications	Same (salts)	$\frac{1}{8}$–4 lbs./acre

Index